Assuming the Risk

ASSUMING THE RISK

The Mavericks, the Lawyers, and the Whistle-Blowers Who Beat Big Tobacco

Michael Orey

Little, Brown and Company

Boston   New York   London

First Edition

Library of Congress Cataloging-in-Publication Data
Orey, Michael.
    Assuming the risk : the mavericks, the lawyers, and the whistle-blowers
who beat big tobacco / by Michael Orey. — 1st ed.
        p.   cm.
    ISBN 0-316-66489-8 (hardcover)
    1. Horton, Nathan Henry, d. 1987 — Trials, litigation, etc.
2. American Tobacco Company — Trials, litigation, etc.   3. Products
liability — Tobacco — Mississippi — Holmes County.   I. Title.
KF228.H666074   1999
346.7303'8 — dc21   99-20616

10 9 8 7 6 5 4 3 2 1

MV-NY

Book design by Barbara Werden

Printed in the United States of America

To Sharon

Contents

Assuming the Risk

Prologue

Nathan Henry Horton had been right to fear the darkness, right to worry that it would be nighttime when death would come. Shortly after midnight, on January 27, 1987, he lay in a hospital bed in Jackson, Mississippi, choking and gasping for breath. A tumor filled the entire upper lobe of his left lung and pressed downward, crushing the lobe below. The cancer had also invaded the bronchus, the airway branching off the windpipe, and it was here that the illness took its final, deadly turn. Malignant cells steadily infiltrated a blood vessel until, finally, it hemorrhaged. Blood welled up in the left upper lobe bronchus, and then poured out into the inverted-tree-shaped structure of the bronchial tree, flooding the left lower lobe and streaming across to the right lung as well.

No amount of coughing could clear the flow as Horton made his last, desperate attempts to draw in air. There was simply nowhere for the air to go. Awfully, mercifully, in the early morning blackness, Horton died, drowned in his own blood.

* * *

It had started with a sore shoulder. In the summer of 1985, Horton, a carpenter and contractor in Holmes County, an hour north of Jackson in central Mississippi, began to feel pain in his left arm above the elbow. At work building houses, he noticed the arm also tired quickly. His eldest son, Nathan Jr., then a pharmacy student at the University of Mississippi, thought the problem might be muscle fatigue, and he suggested that his father drink more water. But the pain persisted and even began keeping Horton up at night, so in early August he went to a local clinic, where a doctor found he had high blood pressure and prescribed medication to lower it.

Still, the soreness continued, and Horton, who hated needles and avoided going to the dentist, didn't tolerate pain well. So he went back to the clinic a week later, and this time the doctor prescribed Motrin, thinking he might be suffering from bursitis. When Horton returned in mid-September, with pain not only in his arm but in his neck and left side as well, the doctor referred him to an orthopedist. But the private physician visits were getting expensive, so Horton, who had served in the Navy, went to the Veterans Administration hospital in Jackson, where a doctor continued the treatment for bursitis.

When the pain did not ebb, more extensive tests were done. A series of chest X-rays during the fall of 1985 revealed that Horton had emphysema. Debilitating in other ways, emphysema was unlikely to be the cause of his arm pain. And in other respects, his X-rays were unremarkable. A bronchoscopy — in which a lighted tube is inserted into the bronchi to allow visual examination — did not reveal any tumor, nor did bronchial washings, which collected samples of cells from inside Horton's lungs.

Then, during a follow-up X-ray at the VA in January 1986, doctors noted an enlarging mass in Horton's left lung, and they recommended a needle biopsy to remove a small sample of tissue for analysis. The procedure terrified Horton. The doctors might call the device that they would insert into his lung a needle, but Horton described it as a "rod." When he found out there was no way to anesthetize him, he nearly refused. "If I had to do it over again, I wouldn't do it," he said later. "Can you imagine somebody just pushing something in you and you sitting and watching 'em? And they didn't have no way of deadening me, or anything. And they just give me two pipes to hold, and I held long as I could onto 'em. And that's the only painkiller that I had."

Things would get much worse. The diagnosis was cancer, and, as for so many cancer patients, the treatment would induce far more suffering than the initial stages of the disease. Horton was not a candidate for surgery; his cancer was too far along for that. Instead, he had radiation therapy, though doctors told him there was no hope of a cure. The best they could do was to try to shrink the tumor, delay its deadly march. They gave him five years to live, overestimating by four.

To Horton, the radiation treatments felt like jolts of electricity shooting through his body. A friend who visited him at the hospital recalled him pressing the nurse call bell for more pain medication, only to be told he had to wait two hours between doses. When he finally did get the medicine, his throat was so raw — a result of radiation exposure — that he couldn't swallow the capsules, so he unscrewed them and tried just washing the powder down. At home between rounds of treatment, Horton was weak and wasted. Five feet eleven inches tall and about 170 pounds when his illness was diagnosed, he quickly dropped 40 pounds, and lay at home curled up and skeletal. His throat hurt so much he could barely eat, and the pain medication burned his stomach.

Doctors gave Horton prescriptions to treat symptoms, and more prescriptions to treat side effects. Periodically he needed blood transfusions, and he held tight to his wife Ella's hand while a nurse poked and prodded to get a needle into his ever-more-difficult-to-find veins. Yet it was a losing battle. The cancer cells multiplied inside him exponentially, and as 1986 progressed, his condition steadily deteriorated. Breathing became difficult. Already both his lungs were riddled with emphysematous bullae, air sacs that are overexpanded and destroyed, so when he breathed in, the oxygen entering them passed uselessly into a void, instead of into the blood. As the tumor grew, that too reduced breathing capacity. Toward the end of the year, he couldn't walk fifty feet without resting, and seldom ventured outside his house.

And there were other problems. Healthy lungs cleanse themselves by secreting mucin, which is then whisked up the throat along with any inhaled particulate matter. Horton had long ago lost that battle: an autopsy would show that the interior of his lungs was black with carbon. For Horton, in fact, mucin was doing more harm than good. With the tumor obstructing drainage, the fluid poured into his chest cavity, setting the stage for pneumonia.

The mild ache that had first caused Horton to seek medical attention had become a consuming pain, difficult even to describe. "It's hard to — it's — it's hard to explain the — the pain," Horton said haltingly in December 1986, a few weeks before his death. "I don't just know how to put it. It ain't like a pain where somebody hits you or something like that, but it's — it's a sickening pain where you can't sleep half the time with it." Toward the end of the year, he also began coughing up blood.

The doctors had told him it would end that way, that he would choke to death on his own blood. Years later, his wife Ella Mae Horton would wonder why they told him, because from the moment the blood started coming up, he lived with the fear that each day would be his last. That's when nighttime became so frightful. Darkness would descend like a cloak of death, transforming sleep from an act of repose into one of surrender. So Horton tried not to sleep. "His nights were long," Ella recalled. "He would lay there and just stare up and tears be running down his eyes. So many nights I would just catch his hand and hold his hand. . . . He was in pain so much if I would hold — try to hug him he would say it hurt. So most time we just laid there and held hands."

By the beginning of 1987 the tumor had destroyed his left lung. Part of the gray-white mass had also spread into his chest cavity, where it pressed against blood vessels running to his heart. Then the bleeding began. Horton was rushed to the intensive care unit of Jackson's University Medical Center. Doctors performed a tracheotomy, cutting a hole in his throat and inserting a breathing tube into his right lung. But there was no saving him. Horton knew that. "I'm going to leave. I'm going to heaven and I want you to meet me there," he told Ella just hours before he died.

He was fifty years old.

Part 1

A Toe in Tobacco

1

By Mississippi standards, colonization came late to Holmes County. While the French and Spanish were staking claims along the coast in the 1700s, the north-central part of the state was largely uninhabited. According to an account written by J. Daniel Edwards, a local Holmes County historian, various Indian tribes that had lived in the area had abandoned it by about 1720, leaving it essentially unpopulated for a hundred years. The land was still considered Indian territory, though, until the Treaty of Doaks Stand in 1820 and the Treaty of Dancing Rabbit Creek ten years later brought the region under U.S. control.

The best way to get a sense of Holmes County today is to enter it from the north, taking Route 49E out of Greenwood in neighboring LeFlore County. This takes you along the eastern flank of the Mississippi Delta, flat and cultivated as far as the eye can see, a carpet of shimmering green in the summer, bursting fluffy white, as though topped by warm-weather snow, when the cotton bolls open in the fall. Cotton is still king in this area — gins and seed presses dot the landscape — but the cost of growing it, its need for vast quantities of herbicides and pesticides in particular, has made it less clearly the crop of choice. Soybeans, wheat, rice, and corn also grow in the rich Delta soil.

For all their fecundity, these fields convey a sense of desolation. The region, whose desperate need for laborers to plant and weed and pick cotton made it reliant on slaves and then sharecroppers, now seems almost devoid of people. Occasionally a pickup truck cuts across the horizon or a crop-dusting plane buzzes low over the fields. Even at harvesttime, activity is isolated: giant machines make their mechanized march across the land, picking four rows of cotton at a time. But few prosper from the land's bounty: With a per capita income of $9,500, Holmes County is one of the poorest counties in Mississippi, which, with a statewide per capita income of about $17,000, is the poorest state in the nation.

Route 12 heads east out of the town of Tchula (pronounced CHOO-luh), and the two-lane highway cuts across level land for about a mile. Then the road rears sharply up, and suddenly you have left the Delta and are in the rolling terrain that Mississippians call "the Hills." Pitching up and down now, the road progresses steadily to higher ground. There are still cotton fields here, but they intermix with stretches of uncultivated land, much of it woods. Entire groves of trees in many places are completely draped in kudzu, giving the appearance of some topiary project gone horribly awry. Giant human- and animal-like forms seem to be struggling to burst forth from the smothering green shroud. A joke in the South has it that if a cow stands too long in one spot, it will end up covered by the weed. Relentless in its growth, kudzu crawls across fields and into the gullies and ravines that crisscross the land.

As Route 12 enters Lexington, it curves down past a sign made of wrought iron that reads IS JESUS CHRIST LORD OF LEXINGTON, the question mark either missing or never intended. From here it's a straight shot into the town square, where the redbrick facade and clock tower cupola of the courthouse loom up like a cutout from a folk art painting. Lexington, population 2,200, is the county seat; all over Mississippi, similar town squares with courthouses at their center serve as the civic heart of their county. In Oxford, home to William Faulkner, a historical marker on the courthouse quotes this passage from his *Requiem for a Nun:*

But above all, the courthouse: the center, the focus, the hub; sitting looming in the center of the county's circumference like a single cloud in its ring of horizon, laying its vast shadow to the uttermost rim of the horizon; musing, brooding, symbolic and ponderable, tall as cloud, solid as rock, dominating all: protector of the weak, judicate and curb of the passions and lusts, repository and guardian of the aspirations and the hopes . . .

Ellipsis and all, the plaque ends there, the maker perhaps out of bronze or out of breath.

On the lawn outside the Lexington courthouse is something else that can be found in town squares throughout Mississippi: an obelisk-style monument to the Civil War. The product of a Confederate memorial movement active in the South from the 1870s until World War I, the monuments tend to express a certain view of the conflict. THE MEN WERE RIGHT WHO WORE THE GRAY AND RIGHT CAN NEVER DIE, declares the one in Lexington, dedicated by the United Daughters of the Confederacy in 1908. On the ground next to the obelisk is a polished granite stone laid in 1976, on the bicentennial of the American Revolution. The stone is partly overgrown with grass, and you have to stand on it if you want to read the testaments to the Civil War.

Chartered in 1836, Lexington developed slowly prior to that war. But as the county seat, it became a magnet for banking and business. Several wagon and carriage manufacturers established operations in town, proximate as it was to forests of the choice hardwoods such as hickory, walnut, oak, and ironwood favored by that trade. Nearby springs gave rise to steam grist and lumber mills, and in 1859 local residents raised $500,000 for the construction of a cotton mill. As the local newspaper noted, that meant that "merchants may buy supplies of cotton fabric at home rather than from the unscrupulous Yankees."

By the turn of the century, Lexington had emerged as the economic and political center of Holmes County. In 1908, Samuel Cohen, a Lithuanian immigrant, opened a dry goods store on the square, and he was joined by other Jewish merchants who had originally come to the region as peddlers. Cohen's Department Store serves customers to this day, run by Philip Cohen, Samuel's grandson. But when the younger Cohen steps out of his shop and surveys the town square today, he sees none of the vitality that drew his grandfather there. As has happened in small towns everywhere, customers have fled to the Wal-Marts and other national chains in the outlying strip malls. The square looks and feels tired now, even taking into account the languor induced by the often-steamy climate. The movie theater has long been shuttered, and the Ben Franklin five-and-dime finally gave up in the early 1990s. Amid empty storefronts, the shops that remain seem to be struggling to hang on. Almost every building could use a coat of paint.

Nevertheless, the square is not devoid of activity. There's still some shopping that can be done, and the courthouse — which also houses the tax assessor's office and a meeting room for the county supervisors — remains an unavoidable destination for many. A steady stream of traffic flows around the square, which serves as a junction for the main north–south and east–west routes in the county. Occasionally trucks rumble by, piled high with timber or hauling giant sections of prefabricated homes made at a plant just east of town. On certain Tuesdays, on the north steps of the courthouse, banks auction off property they have foreclosed on.

And for a brief few weeks in 1988, Lexington and its courthouse became the arena of a legal struggle pitting a poor black man and his family against a giant American corporation. While Lexington quickly faded from public view, the battle that was launched there raged on in Mississippi for nearly ten years, and would reverberate around the nation before it came to its dramatic end.

2

There are four funeral homes in Lexington, Mississippi. Three serve a black clientele, one a white, a ratio that mirrors the racial composition of Holmes County's population of 21,000. The three black funeral parlors, including the one where Nathan Horton's body was readied for burial, are clustered on the south side of the town square, on what local residents call Beale Street. On maps, though, it is called Yazoo Street, presumably because it runs south to Yazoo County. Yazoo is a local Indian word that means "death" or "waters of the dead."

The funeral service was held in a large brick church on Yazoo Street. It was a sunny day, unusually warm for the end of January, even for Mississippi. After the pastor delivered the eulogy, friends of Horton rose and made brief remarks. Warren Booker, who coached Horton as a high school football player, recalled his prowess on the gridiron. A man who built houses with Horton also spoke. Then, from amid the sea of black faces that filled the church, a white man came forward and took the pulpit.

Few in attendance needed an introduction to Don Barrett, a prominent lawyer in Holmes County. Barrett, about to turn forty-two, appeared youthful. With curly blond hair and a pink, cherubic face, he looked something like the Gerber baby grown up. Barrett not only looked white, he was white in ways that led some mourners to mutter about why he would appear at a black man's funeral. What he said, particularly toward the end of his remarks, made them wonder even more.

Barrett speaks in soft Southern tones, and at times his speech sounds mushy, as though he has cotton stuffed between his cheek and gums. Solemnly, he addressed the crowd:

> This is a double honor for me today. It is an honor to be asked to sit with the family of my friend Nathan Horton. It is also an honor to be allowed to speak from the pulpit of St. Paul's Church of God in Christ, the home church of this great denomination which has swept this country and which has saved literally hundreds of thousands of souls for Jesus Christ. This pulpit is a holy place and I am humbled by this honor.

> I want to speak to you about two Nathan Hortons. The Nathan Horton that was and the Nathan Horton that is now.

> Nathan Horton was a loving husband and father. He loved and cared for and was devoted to his wife and all of his children. I think the fact that the family listed all of Nathan's stepchildren as his children on the funeral program was a beautiful gesture that shows the love in his family.

> Nathan Horton was a loving friend to many people in this county. Nathan was a hardworking home builder. A contractor. And he did beautiful work.

> He provided jobs for dozens of people over the last sixteen years in Holmes County. Nathan told me once that he often took jobs when he knew he couldn't make money, just so Holmes County people could have work.

> Back in the early 1970s Holmes County desperately needed a medical clinic to provide services to the poor, but there was no money to pay for the labor to build it. So Nathan and two other people, who may be here today, donated their skill and labor and built it. As a result, hundreds of poor Holmes County people got medical care for years because of him.

That's the Nathan Horton that was. I was proud to be his friend.

Let me tell you now about the Nathan Horton that is. Nathan and I visited and became close friends over the past few months. We talked about fishing in the spring.

We talked about religion, how it is not good enough to be good, to do good works, to just know there is a God. We talked about how it was necessary to trust in Jesus and give your life to him in order to get salvation.

We talked about the last day of his life. I was with him for over two hours and he said, "Don, hold my hand." And he asked me to pray for him, and I did. I prayed for him and with him. And I can tell you that I know without any doubt that Nathan Horton is in heaven right now with God Almighty and with his savior Jesus Christ.

And where he is there is no more pain, and no more tears, because his savior has taken those away.

One final thing: Nathan Horton was a national leader in the fight for justice for the three hundred and fifty thousand people killed each year by the tobacco companies. One black man every fifteen minutes dies from smoking disease.

The American Tobacco Company may have thought its troubles were over when Nathan died. I have a message for them: Their troubles are just beginning, because Nathan's family have picked up that banner that says Justice and they are marching with it, and Fred Clark [a fellow attorney] and I are proud to be marching with them.

I say this to the American Tobacco Company: We're coming at you, we're not gonna stop, you can run but you can't hide.

I ask you to pray for us continually in this fight. The tobacco company has power and wealth, but they don't have the power like this group praying. Please help us. Thank you.

Barrett's closing remarks were odd for a memorial service, and would be a matter of contention in weeks to come. But they indicated how it was that Barrett's and Horton's lives had come to intertwine. In his last year on earth, Horton had sought to avenge his impending premature demise by suing the makers of the cigarettes he felt caused his cancer, and Barrett became his lawyer. In the last few months of his life, Horton became deeply religious and proclaimed himself "born again." In this experience, too, Barrett was at Horton's side as a spiritual companion.

For anyone who had known Don Barrett for any length of time, the spectacle of him sharing spiritual intimacies at a black man's bedside, of him speaking at that man's funeral, and of him crying, as he did, at the man's grave was one to behold. And they would know that only a tremendous transformation could have brought that about.

In his eulogy, Barrett spoke of "two Nathan Hortons." One could easily speak of two Don Barretts as well.

There's a picture on the wall of Don Barrett's office titled "Southern Steel." It depicts a scene from a battle fought in Okolona, Mississippi, in 1864, in which Confederate General Nathan Bedford Forrest, shown with eyes flashing and sword raised high, is charging into a group of Union cavalrymen. He is vastly outnumbered, almost encircled by Union troops, but it is the men in blue who are shown cringing and pulling back, clearly frightened by the Southerner's audacity and fury. Barrett, an avid student of the Civil War since college, can offer an almost blow-by-blow account of the battle, in which Forrest and a small contingent routed far larger forces, chasing them back to Memphis. He doesn't mention that Forrest is believed to have ordered the massacre of roughly three hundred captured black Union soldiers, or that after the war, he was the first Imperial Wizard of the Ku Klux Klan.

"I admire it because it's taking on something impossible and being successful at it," Barrett once explained as his reason for having the picture on his wall. But there's more to it than that. The Civil War and its legacy have served to shape Barrett's view of the world. As a young man his passionate attachment to the old order led him to acts of intransigence and defiance. And even as his more extreme positions have moderated and evolved over the years, a part of him continues to take personally the war and the subsequent indignities inflicted on the South; a part of him will always revel in the triumph, however fleeting, of the horseman in "Southern Steel."

For a starting point on the conflict, Barrett can turn to his own family's chronicle. "Our family lived on Barrett Plantation, named Newstead, in Hinds County, five miles West of Jackson," wrote Cornelia Barrett Ligon, sister of Don Barrett's great-grandfather, in an essay titled "Memories of the War Between the States." "We owned many slaves," she continued. "The plantation we lived on was ten miles long and ten miles across."

That plantation suffered repeated raids by Federal troops as they tightened the noose around Vicksburg, about thirty miles to the west. "One would have to witness a raid before a just conception could be formed," Cornelia wrote:

> Such destruction, such ruin, houses burning in every direction, done by an army of thousands of men, and done so quickly; they even drew all the water out of the wells and cisterns and cut the ponds and drained them. . . . The Yankees carried off large quantities of our silverware and jewelry, also elegant silk dresses and expensive lace shawls, and everything they found in women's wearing apparel. During a raid the awful confusion can better be described thus: every room, every hall, every gallery, outhouses and all the yard were filled with Union soldiers at the same time. They robbed and looted and left things bare and desolate.

Although told through the eyes of a girl — Cornelia was eleven when the war started — the account vividly depicts the battles waged around the plantation, where wounded and dying men from both sides sought sanctuary. General Ulysses Grant himself briefly bivouacked at the Barrett home, according to Cornelia's account. Walking through a battlefield with her mother, she noted, "Some of the dead were scarcely covered, with an arm or leg exposed, and some with head uncovered. The weather was warm and the bones and skulls and teeth were exposed. It was a gruesome sight!"

Throughout the war, Cornelia's older brother Thomas — Don Barrett's great-grandfather — made periodic visits to his home, even as he fought with the Mississippi College Rifles. But in early July 1863, at the age of sixteen, he was captured when Vicksburg finally fell to Grant's forces. During the siege of Vicksburg, the publisher of the local newspaper, the *Daily Citizen*, ran out of printing stock, and resorted to publishing his single-sheet bulletin on the back of wallpaper. His final edition, published July 2, boasted of General Robert E. Lee "striking terror to the hearts of all Yankeedom." At the same time, it described Southerners resorting to mule and cat meat for food. On July 4 the final edition was reprinted, identical save for a notice in the lower right corner that read:

> Two days brings about great changes. The banner of the Union floats over Vicksburg. . . . No more will [this paper] eulogize the luxury of mule meat and fricasseed kitten — urge Southern warriors to such diet nevermore. This is the last wall paper *Citizen*, and is, excepting this note, from the types as we "yankee printers" found them. Copies will be valuable in years to come as a curiosity.

Young Thomas Barrett, it so happens, did keep a copy, and it stands today, sandwiched in Plexiglas, in Don Barrett's office, the stenciled print of nineteenth-century wallpaper fully visible on the back.

It was Thomas Barrett's son, William Oliver Barrett, who first settled in Holmes County. No one knows what drew him there, but after taking a business course in New Orleans, he arrived by train in Lexington in the 1890s and set up a clothing store on the town square. He prospered, boosting sales with gimmicks such as offering a free pocket watch to everyone who bought a suit. He also diversified, founding a wholesale grocery company, which he ultimately sold to the owner of the Sunflower grocery chain. William Barrett's only mistake in the grocery business may have been selling the Coca-Cola bottling franchise, which he ran for a time out of the back of his store. But he had plenty of other business to tend to. In 1929 William helped found the First National Bank of Holmes County, on whose board of directors his son Pat (Don's father) and grandson Pat Jr. sit today. William Barrett also owned an interest in Omega Plantation, in the western part of the county, where sharecroppers grew cotton on about 1,500 acres.

Pat Barrett, who was born in 1909 and was one of William's six children, recalls that each summer the entire family would decamp to the Gulf Coast near Biloxi for a vacation. Some would join William Barrett in his monstrous Cadillac, which would wend its way down sand and dirt roads, taking two days with an overnight stop to reach the shore (it takes about five hours today). Pat Sr.'s mother Rachel would take the youngest children and travel down by train. They would be joined by the family cook and William's majordomo, a black man named Doctor Hodges.

William Barrett's diversified entrepreneurship had left his family well off, with entrenched land and business interests in Holmes County and the neighboring region. Added to that, the decades-old exclusionary practices of Jim Crow left the Barretts and white families like them akin to feudal lords, dominant both economically and politically, even where blacks outnumbered whites 3 to 1.

William Barrett died in 1952, just a few years before the winds of change began to buffet the South. It can hardly be surprising that many whites reacted to the assault on the established order, which began with the U.S. Supreme Court's 1954 school desegregation decision, *Brown v. Board of Education,* with resistance. In Mississippi this took many forms, one of which was the creation, in communities throughout the state, of local, all-white Citizens' Councils — an "uptown Ku Klux Klan," in the words of one distinguished editor at the time. Pat Barrett Sr., who had set up a law practice on the town square in 1933, was a member of Lexington's Citizens' Council. He was also the prosecuting attorney for Holmes County, from 1937 to 1970.

Economic pressure was one tool wielded by the Citizens' Council against those deemed sympathetic to integration and other measures aimed at assuring equality among the races. A principal object of such pressure in Holmes County was Hazel Brannon Smith, publisher of the *Lexington Advertiser.* Smith, a dyed-in-the-wool Southerner who hailed from Alabama and modeled the house she built in Lexington after Tara, from the movie version of *Gone with the Wind,* was actually a proponent of segregation, but she was willing to expose and speak out against overt acts of racial violence. And while not advocating school integration, she did counsel support for the rule of law. She also condemned the climate of fear that segregationists were creating in the state. That was enough for the Citizens' Council to organize a boycott of her paper by both advertisers and subscribers, and when that failed to drive her out of business,

Citizens' Council members helped organize a rival newspaper, the Holmes County *Herald*, in 1958.

Of course, it was the *Lexington Advertiser* that was out of step with prevailing white opinion at the time in Mississippi. It was one of a handful of papers in the state that took a more progressive view of integration. Both of the major Jackson newspapers were staunch advocates of preserving the status quo. And while many white Southerners had grumbled about efforts of the federal government to broaden civil rights for blacks, Ross Barnett in Mississippi and George Wallace in Alabama rode into the governors' offices of their states advocating a far more militant form of Southern opposition. Many Citizens' Councils came to employ more than just rhetoric and social and economic pressure. Often lurking behind their attacks on those who opposed them was a not very subtle threat of violence.

Such thinking has a way of rubbing off on those of impressionable age. On November 10, 1960, the *Advertiser* ran a picture of a flaming cross and the following personal account by Hazel Brannon Smith:

> The flaming eight-foot cross, pictured above, was placed on the lawn about 100 feet from my home Monday night, October 31, after 9:15 p.m.
>
> The ones who placed the cross there put the torch to it and then set off firecrackers to attract attention to their deed.
>
> The culprits ran when my guests and I stepped out of the house — but they couldn't run fast enough — and I took the tag off their Chevrolet station wagon as they fled to the woods to hide.
>
> A short while later the same station wagon was parked behind the home of Pat Barrett, Lexington lawyer and prosecuting attorney for Holmes County.
>
> The vehicle had not been difficult to trace — since the name "Don Barrett" was written in soap across the back window.
>
> It turned out that Mr. [Pat] Barrett was the owner of the car.

Don Barrett acknowledged his role in the incident in a 1997 interview and professed shame for it. "We didn't appreciate the significance of what we were doing," he said, noting he was just fifteen at the time.

Three years after the cross-burning, young Don Barrett himself significantly amplified on the sentiment the act symbolized when he was interviewed by a reporter for the *New York Times Magazine*. In the fall of 1963 the *Times* had sent Margaret Long, an Atlanta-based writer, to assess the mood on campus at the University of Mississippi one year after the entry of the first black student, James Meredith, had been met with violent protests. Her article, "A Southern Teen-Ager Speaks His Mind," ended up being entirely about Don Barrett, who had just enrolled as a freshman. Charming and articulate, Barrett essentially offered himself up as a spokesman for unapologetic Southern white militancy. "I feel, as do most of the white population of the South, that the Negro is inherently unequal," Barrett told Long, going on to say that it took the white man to teach blacks how to speak, wear clothes, and generally act civilized. In places where they haven't been so uplifted, he said, "they're still eating each other." Barrett went on at length about his belief in the inferiority of blacks, all by way of justifying his opposition to anything that would upset the established Southern order, from school integration to increased voting rights for blacks.

"We are determined to keep our way of life," Barrett said, adding that he would even take up arms to do so. "People say Nigras are catching up — that's wonderful — but that's no justification for social change in 1963 for what might happen in 500 or 1,000 years," he said.

Of course, Mississippi and other Southern states were in the midst of a torrent of change that over the next ten or fifteen years would largely upend Barrett's cherished social order. Federal court decisions and civil rights legislation, most notably the Voting Rights Act of 1965, steadily altered the legal and political landscape, even if they did not change attitudes. Whites in Holmes County shifted from a posture of open defiance to a more defensive siege mentality. By 1967, for example, they had formed private "academies," preferring to pay tuition than to send their children to be educated in public schools with blacks.

For much of this period Barrett was a student, getting his undergraduate degree from Ole Miss in 1967, and then staying on to attend law school. After getting his J.D. in 1969, he returned to Lexington, joining his father and older brother Pat Jr. in law practice. The Barretts were engaged in what is commonly referred to as a country practice, taking pretty much anything local citizens brought across the threshold, from wills and divorces to matters connected with property and business transactions to routine litigation. In 1971, Pat Barrett Sr. became counsel to the Holmes County Board of Supervisors, the governing body for the county, and over the years the Barrett office has also represented the city of Lexington and other towns in the county. Beginning in the seventies, these entities became defendants in civil rights cases claiming voting rights violations, inadequate provision of municipal services, and employment discrimination, and it was the Barrett family that defended them.

No longer a teenager, Don Barrett, as a young lawyer in his father's firm, began to use the weapons of the law in his battle to preserve the status quo. To Charles Victor McTeer, a Baltimore-born black attorney who moved to Mississippi to do civil rights work in 1972, Don Barrett was the enemy, someone who "represented as much the standard-bearer of racism in this state as anyone." Looking back on the period, McTeer said: "You have to picture what the Delta was like in the civil rights days. It wasn't the heartland of cordiality. There were clear lines that were drawn, and Don was on one side of that line and I was on the other."

But Don Barrett has been able to cross that line. Today McTeer works on cases with Barrett, lunches at his house, and calls him "a dear friend." Johnny Walls, another black civil rights lawyer active in the Delta who has known Barrett over the years, says, "He is now a very likable guy."

The factors that have produced this transformation are complex. In part, there was simply an acknowledgment by Barrett of the new reality that had emerged in the South. "There was a way of doing things, a strong order," Barrett explained, and then "there was a revolution and our side lost." The revolution was the civil rights movement, and, in the wake of it, Barrett noted, "we thought all these dire things, and we were all going to have to move away or something, it'd just be unbelievable here in the South. You know, we were proved wrong. Time proved that we were wrong, and any of us with any sense said, 'Gee, we were wrong.' . . . This county is eighty percent black. I'm around black people all the time,

I live in a black sea. If you can't get along with blacks, you gotta get out of here."

And Barrett was not about to leave the land he cherished. So, beginning early in the eighties, he began to adapt. In 1980, Frederick Clark, a black attorney fresh out of the University of Mississippi law school and working in a legal services office in Lexington, got a note from Barrett. Clark, then twenty-six, had just won a 9–0 reversal from the Mississippi Supreme Court on a case he had originally lost at the trial level on behalf of some landowners who were fighting to keep the state from taking their property to build a recreational dam. Barrett congratulated Clark on his victory, and invited him to drop by for a visit.

Clark, who was raised on a farm in Ackerman, Mississippi, about an hour east of Holmes County, had quickly learned of the Barrett family's reputation on matters of race when he arrived in Holmes County. So he was intrigued when, in a series of conversations, Don Barrett suggested that they might collaborate on cases when Clark entered private practice, which he did in late 1980, setting up shop in Greenwood, in neighboring LeFlore County. Purely from the standpoint of maintaining a successful law practice, Barrett had reason to want to ally himself with an African-American lawyer in the courtroom: With their heavy black-majority populations, Holmes and other counties were regularly seating predominantly black juries. Yet as wary as he was of Barrett's background and motives, Clark came to find him amiable and sincere. That assessment was shared by Walls, who worked opposite Barrett in a personal-injury case involving an exploding butane tank. "I really think, based on personal observation, that his change is on a human level, not just for the purpose of earning a buck," Walls says.

Which is not to say that Barrett became a fully reconstructed Southerner. He denies, for example, that the Civil War was fought primarily over slavery. And he has been active in helping to restore gravesites of Confederate soldiers. In 1983, Barrett became the state director of the Farmers Home Administration (FmHA), a division of the U.S. Department of Agriculture that makes crop loans and finances construction of low-income housing in depressed rural areas. Asked to account for expenditures — much of it on housing — Barrett fired off a blistering three-page response that displays not only his mastery of impassioned rhetoric, but also his permanent outrage at the indignities perpetrated on the South. The October 1984 letter to the Farmers Home Administration head in Washington began:

> You have asked me how I could have engineered, in good con-science, the spending of $335 million for FmHA housing funds this year in Mississippi, when no other state got a third that much.
>
> Ron Caldwell, my FmHA counterpart in Wisconsin, complained to me that "the North pays the taxes and the South spends the money," and he wants to know why.
>
> Let me tell the both of you.
>
> In 1984 the South is at the bottom of the economic ladder. We are climbing up, but we are still at the bottom. Why are we there? Do you think that Southerners — Mississippians — are stupid, or lazy, or trifling? Do we have some defect of intellect, of character, of soul, which has doomed us to second class citizenship?
>
> Don't kid yourself.
>
> In 1861 the South was prosperous and happy. Civilization flour-ished here as nowhere else on this continent. Then we were invaded and overwhelmed by the Northern Union with its limitless supplies of men and armaments.
>
> The devastation, death and destruction heaped upon us is elsewhere unknown in the history of warfare. People nowadays can't conceive of the scope of the devastation. Genghis Khan, Attila the Hun, and Joe Stalin were pikers compared to Grant, Sherman, Beast Butler, and Sheridan.
>
> The South in 1865 resembled the landscape of the moon. Pillaged farms, burned out homes, rubble and ashes where cities had stood, torn-up railways, bankrupt financial institutions: the Yankees left noth-ing. . . .
>
> What happened to the people of the South?
>
> Let's look at the men. In Mississippi in 1861 there were some 70,000 white men between the ages of 18 and 45. Yet 78,000 Mississippians enlisted in the army of the Confederacy. Of that 78,000 fully one-fourth were killed at Shiloh, Vicksburg, Chickamauga,

Manassas, Cold Harbor, and a thousand little places you never heard of. Killed always doing the same thing: defending their families, their little farms, their homes, against the Northern invaders.

Tens of thousands more were disabled for life. . . . In 1866 one half of the entire budget of the State of Mississippi was for the purchase of artificial limbs.

Many thinking people believe that our women suffered even more grievously than their men. Aside from the physical suffering, insult, and deprivation, aside from the personal loss of fathers, husbands, sons, and brothers, the Southern women suffered the worst hurt of all — the crucifixion of soul that came from sacrifices made in vain. . . .

However, the foregoing is not the point of this essay. The war lasted four years. Left alone, we could have overcome that. The oppression that followed lasted until World War II. I'm not just talking about the military occupation and misrule of Reconstruction. Those crimes are well-known to any school boy and need not be catalogued here.

Let me state the case clearly. The Northern leadership determined that the prostrate South should be kept in economic vassalage, and instituted an effective plan which did just that.

Barrett then detailed decades of economic oppression of the South following the war. He closed his letter with the following:

You see then what a blessing the FmHA housing program has been to the South. You see why we clearly need such help. Having been kept in an economic hole for nearly a century, we need the boost that FmHA was designed to give.

In light of this historical perspective, Mr. Shuman, I'm quite sure you see that the $335 million we obtained for Mississippi is quite justified. We look on it down here as a token payment on a long overdue debt.

Don't you agree?

Barrett's tenure as state director for the Farmers Home Administration was marred by a federal investigation in the mid-1980s of certain FmHA investments in Mississippi, including funds that had gone to a

Mississippi construction company set up by Barrett's then brother-in-law, a car dealer from Texas. Barrett was never charged with any wrong-doing, but for a period the matter caused him a good deal of worry. "It was a bad time, it was an embarrassing time," he said years later. "I shouldn't have done that," he said, referring to the transaction with his brother-in-law. Unfortunately for Barrett, the investigation was under way while he was on a short list of nominees for a federal judgeship. Of course, his race record also presented a hurdle, but Barrett was aggressively trying to put concerns on that score to rest. Hazel Brannon Smith, to whom Barrett had helped deliver the burning cross, was convinced enough of his changed attitudes that she wrote a letter on his behalf. "Don is one of many of our young people who have been able to adjust to the changing times in which we live," she wrote to Senator Thad Cochran. "I am satisfied that as he grows older his horizons will continue to widen." In the end, though, the nomination went to a black lawyer in the state.

During the tribulations of this period, Barrett underwent a spiritual renewal that furthered and deepened the transformation of his views on a range of issues, including race. "I grew up in the Methodist church," Barrett recounts. "If anybody had asked me when I was a young adult, was I a Christian, [I would have said] of course I'm a Christian. You know, I go to church every Sunday." But that, Barrett came to conclude, is "not what being a Christian really is" and he became "born again." That means, he explains, "that you make an intellectual decision that you are a sinner, that you are beyond salvation for anything you can do yourself, that you accept the fact that Jesus Christ was the son of God and died and was crucified for your sins personally, and that you accept that gift and repent of your sins and say you are going to lead a new life."

In some ways that new life was readily apparent to others. Barrett stopped going to the office on Sundays, for example, and seemed to rededicate himself to his family — his wife and one-time high school sweetheart Nancy and their three children. But there were inner changes as well, deeply personal ones that Barrett will talk about only if pressed. "As I have become a Christian and I have started reading the Bible," Barrett says, "I was struck by both the Old and New Testament, how God through the prophets, and then God through his Son — the main teaching is compassion for people who are not as fortunate as you are. And you cannot make that fit with any sort of racial animus. I mean, we are all brothers, we are all children of the same God. . . . You've got to love people, and you've got to love them unconditionally. That's what God does to us."

The "new" Don Barrett, the one who finally acceded to the political and social changes that had swept across the land, and who adopted a repentant and embracing religiousness, did not fully replace the "old" Don Barrett, the unregenerate Southerner who clings to idealized visions of antebellum Dixie and who goes teary-eyed recounting Confederate heroics. One's heritage and upbringing — and the attitudes that go with it — are not so easily discarded, a longtime colleague of Barrett's has suggested. But Barrett did renounce his more extreme views, and he emerged in the mid-eighties dedicated to new ways.

3

During his stint at the Farmers Home Administration, Barrett had turned his law practice over to his brother Pat. When he returned to practice in mid-1985, Don Barrett had a chance to start with a clean slate. He decided to focus on two areas: environmental contamination and personal injury. Barrett's return to lawyering proved to be a boon to Fred Clark. Just as it may have been advantageous for Barrett to forge links with black trial lawyers, there were also compelling business reasons for a young black trial lawyer like Clark to avail himself of the resources and reputation of the Barrett firm, and they collaborated on a number of cases. In one case, for example, Clark represented the family of a man who had been electrocuted while working for a tree-trimming company. Teaming up with Barrett, he won a $640,000 settlement, the biggest ever in Holmes County at the time.

In general, Holmes County was earning a reputation as a place where corporate defendants didn't want to be sued. "Holmes County and Don Barrett — you combine those two and you just assume that a jury's gonna give him whatever he's asking," says one local attorney for a large out-of-state corporation. In the early eighties, Barrett had filed suit against South Central Bell Telephone on behalf of an elderly black woman who had her phone service cut off. Nancy Epps lived alone in a rural area and depended greatly on her phone, and was so distressed when it was cut off that she needed medical attention, the suit claimed. Before the lawsuit, Epps had turned to Barrett to help her get the service restored. When Barrett had called to do this, one of the phone company representatives told him: "You know how those people are," apparently referring to blacks. When it became clear during the litigation that Barrett would have to take the witness stand to recount this remark, he turned the case over to James Upshaw, a seasoned white lawyer from nearby Greenwood, since an attorney in a trial may not also appear as a witness. Largely on the strength of that remark, Upshaw got a jury to award Epps $75,000 in compensatory and $3 million in punitive damages. Although the Supreme Court ultimately threw out the punitive portion of the award, it was a signal of juror sentiment in the community.

Prosecutors, meanwhile, found Holmes County to be a place where it was almost impossible to get a criminal defendant convicted. Indeed, three area judges recall that during one two-and-a-half-year period in the eighties, prosecutors were not able to obtain a single guilty verdict in cases they tried there. It seems likely that this was driven by the same factor that led to large damage awards in civil cases: blacks' disaffection with a social and economic system — and all the institutions representing it, from corporations to law enforcement agencies — that had persecuted them and left them trodden down for generations. In civil and criminal cases alike, an opportunity to render a verdict became an opportunity for revenge.

In early 1986, Fred Clark came to talk to Don Barrett about Nathan Horton. Clark's wife Margaret was a Holmes County native, and through her family he had gotten to know Horton casually, and even fished with him on occasion. When doctors told Horton that cigarette smoking was responsible for his cancer, he decided to talk to Clark about filing a lawsuit. Two other cigarette lawsuits had been in the news in late 1985 and early 1986 and may have caught Horton's attention. One had been filed by Melvin Belli, the flamboyant, self-promoting San Francisco plaintiff's lawyer who had acquired the moniker "the King of Torts." In Louisiana in 1958 Belli had tried the first tobacco liability case to reach a jury.

Twenty-seven years later, he was still at it, and still unsuccessful: In December 1985, in the Galbraith case, a Santa Barbara, California, jury rendered a verdict for the defendant, R. J. Reynolds. Another lawsuit, the Cipollone case in New Jersey, was still in the pretrial phase, but had also drawn some media attention.

A suit against a tobacco company, Clark knew, would require experience and resources beyond what he alone could offer, so he took the idea to Barrett. For Barrett, tobacco litigation represented exactly the kind of major personal-injury work that he hoped would become the core of his practice. He and Clark briefly discussed what it would mean to go up against the formidable resources of a tobacco company. They were aware — but undaunted — that in thirty years of litigation no cigarette company had ever paid a penny in damages to a plaintiff in a health-related liability suit. But the landscape had changed greatly over three decades. Product-liability law had evolved in ways that significantly favored a consumer suing a manufacturer for injuries caused by a defective product. The scientific evidence to prove that cigarettes were disease-causing — and therefore defective — had gone from scant to conclusive. Starting in 1964, the Surgeon General of the United States had issued a series of reports chronicling tobacco's legacy of disease and death, and a flock of medical experts were available to testify on the subject. And Barrett and Clark had something else: They had Nathan Horton, a black man, terminally ill, who would seek justice before what would almost certainly be a predominantly black jury in his native Holmes County.

On May 12, 1986, *Nathan Henry Horton v. The American Tobacco Company* was filed in Holmes County Circuit Court. Purely for the purpose of keeping the case in Holmes County, the suit named a second defendant as well: New Deal Tobacco and Candy Company, the local distributor of Pall Mall cigarettes, Horton's brand. Bringing a Mississippi company into the suit assured that Pall Mall's manufacturer, American Tobacco, could not "remove" (transfer) the case to federal court in Jackson, a step that required that none of the defendants be from the state. For all intents and purposes, though, American was the sole defendant, a fact underscored by the tobacco giant's underwriting of New Deal's legal costs and covering the distributor against any damage award.

The Horton case was the first cigarette liability suit ever filed in

Mississippi, and from the day it was filed Don Barrett would act as Nathan Horton's lead counsel, with Fred Clark in a supporting role. The case was assigned to Judge Gray Evans.

Prior to the lawsuit, Barrett and Horton had dealings with each other on one occasion. In the late seventies, Barrett had hired Horton to build an addition to the "duck camp" — a hunting lodge — owned by Barrett, his brother, and some friends on the grounds of Random Shot Plantation. The 2,400 acres of Delta land was in neighboring Humphreys (pronounced without the *H*) County. William Barrett had bought the plantation from the widow of his longtime friend Archibald Pepper in about 1942. Legend has it that Pepper's father, Captain Daniel Gilbert Pepper, had laid claim to the property after taking a boat up the Yazoo River and saying, "I'll take a random shot and stop here."

Horton also came from a landed family, but their circumstances could not have been more different than the Barretts'. Nathan Horton was born in July 1936, delivered by a midwife on his family's farm in northeastern Holmes County's Bowling Green community. The Horton family had been in the area for at least as long as the Barretts. Horton's paternal grandfather, Wadis, farmed in an area called Shady Grove, just outside Lexington, and his paternal grandmother's family farmed in the area as well. But while the Barretts traced their family tree back to the time of Cromwell, Horton's roots prior to this century are lost in obscurity.

That his family had owned land for generations was not unusual. Blacks have historically owned a great deal of the land in Holmes County, according to LaVerne Lindsay, a longtime employee of the state's agricultural extension service and an amateur historian of black history in the area. But these holdings have not translated into wealth. For one thing, the clay and sandy loess soil of the Hills does not match the productivity of the Delta, which, even without fertilizer, can yield two or three times more cotton per acre than fertilized land elsewhere. Also, in contrast to the sprawling plantations in the Delta, the black farms in the Hills have tended to be small, family-run, subsistence operations.

Nathan Horton's father, known simply as T.C. Horton, raised a little bit of everything. He kept cows and pigs, and planted corn, cotton, peanuts, sweet potatoes, watermelons, and sugarcane. T.C. also ran a molasses mill on his property. One of the same mules used to plow the fields would be hitched up to the grinding wheel of the mill and then walked in slow circles around and around. As juice was squeezed from the cane, it dripped into a large metal pan that had a fire burning underneath. After the liquid boiled down to an amber-brown syrup, T.C. scooped it up in one-gallon pails.

Nathan Horton, along with his two sisters and brother, helped work the farm. Although the family owned a tractor, much of the plowing was done with mules, and weeding and picking were also done by hand. For all the toil, Horton's childhood was stable and secure. He went to the nearby Greenborough Baptist Church on Sundays, and attended school through the twelfth grade. He also discovered the pleasures of tobacco. T.C. kept cans of Prince Albert tobacco in the house and rolled his own cigarettes. Nathan liked the smell, and at some point as a child he started sneaking some for himself, fluffing up the remaining tobacco in the can to make it look as though none had been removed. He became a regular smoker as a high school student. By then, he was able to earn pocket change by doing odd jobs, and on weekends, when he could get into town, he would buy one or two packs of cigarettes and try to make them last the week. The brand he favored was Pall Mall, because it was the only long cigarette that wasn't filtered, which he thought made it a good value. "You got all cigarette for your money," he later explained. Sometimes he would smoke a series of cigarettes down so far that the ember would nearly burn his fingers. He would then dump the tobacco out of the remaining nubs and roll a new cigarette.

Nathan Horton was careful not to smoke around his parents, knowing he would incur the wrath of his mother in particular. Smoking was also forbidden at school, but teachers occasionally caught him puffing in the bathroom, and it once earned him a two-day suspension. Horton took carpentry courses at the vocational high school he attended and also excelled at football, playing guard and tackle. Warren Booker, who taught shop and coached the football team, regularly admonished the young athletes not to smoke. Horton had trouble taking this warning to heart, however, since he couldn't help noticing that Booker himself smoked Lucky Strikes.

In 1955 Horton joined the Navy, where he had ready access to dis-count-price cigarettes at the commissary. He continued to buy unfiltered Pall Malls, the brand he would stick with for the rest of his life. In short order he became a two-pack-a-day smoker. During a leave from the ser-vice in 1956, Horton returned to Lexington and married the first of his four wives. A preacher performed the ceremony at a house on Cemetery Street.

After leaving the Navy with an honorable discharge in the fall of 1957, Horton led an itinerant existence for about a dozen years, moving from town to town, job to job, and wife to wife. Then, in 1970, he moved back to Holmes County and settled down, working as a construction super-visor for home builders. In 1977 he launched his own contracting busi-ness, which he ran until the pain in his left side forced him to quit in August 1985.

These broad outlines of Horton's life history were familiar to Don Barrett and Fred Clark when they filed suit on his behalf in May 1986. They would learn much more. For while they intended their lawsuit to be about a *product* — Pall Mall cigarettes — and its propensity to cause ill-ness, American Tobacco Company's lawyers knew that nothing served them better in the courtroom than to make the case be about the *plaintiff*, with his weaknesses laid bare for all to see. So they would devote their tremendous resources to digging up every unflattering fact they could about Nathan Henry Horton. They would not be disappointed.

The American Tobacco Company presented any litigation opponent with a formidable foe. It was part of American Brands, a corporate enterprise that had a market value of nearly $6 billion. In 1986 American Tobacco itself generated revenues of $1.1 billion and operating profit of $430 mil-lion. Still, as big and profitable as it was, in 1986 the American Tobacco Company was a business in decline, its market share hovering around 7 percent. That had not always been so. At the beginning of the twentieth century, American Tobacco for all intents and purposes *was* the cigarette industry.

The company had risen out of the devastation of the Civil War, a rags-to-riches tale that might have strained the credulity of even Horatio Alger.

In 1865, Washington Duke, a forty-five-year-old Confederate soldier who had been captured and imprisoned in the waning days of the conflict, was released and allowed to return home. Having only 50 cents, which he had obtained from a Northern soldier in exchange for a five-dollar Confederate bill, he walked the 137 miles. The farm he returned to in Durham, North Carolina, had been looted by Federal troops; about all they'd left behind was a pair of blind mules, some flour, and a batch of cured tobacco leaf. Duke found a ready market for the tobacco, and decided to make it his business. He was not alone. Other growers in the Durham area quickly capitalized on the surging demand for the mild, golden Bright tobacco grown in the region.

Through the Civil War, most Americans either chewed their tobacco or smoked it in a pipe. The cigarette began to come into vogue only in the latter decades of the nineteenth century, and it was the ability of James Buchanan Duke, Washington's eldest son, to seize on that trend and exploit it that catapulted W. Duke Sons & Company into its position as the nation's leading cigarette maker by the end of the 1880s. But a 40 percent market share wasn't enough for young Buck Duke, who, in keeping with other industrial titans of the times, preferred combination over competition. In April 1889 Duke and the heads of the four other major cigarette makers met at a hotel on lower Fifth Avenue in New York City and agreed to unite their operations. Duke emerged as president of the newly named American Tobacco Company.

By 1904 American Tobacco was a sprawling colossus that made 88 percent of the nation's cigarettes and dominated the market for other tobacco products as well. But the American public was no longer tolerant of the giant corporate monopolies born in the days of the robber barons, and Teddy Roosevelt and his trustbusters set out to dismantle them. The American Tobacco Company was on their hit list, and in 1911 the U.S. Supreme Court upheld the government's view that the company should be broken up. Of the new corporate entities carved out of the old behemoth, one kept the American Tobacco name as well as a 37 percent share of the U.S. cigarette market. Other spin-offs included companies that would remain well-known names in the cigarette business through the end of the twentieth century: R. J. Reynolds, Lorillard, Liggett & Myers, and British-American Tobacco.

American Tobacco's flagship brand in the new century was Lucky Strike, which for decades battled Reynolds's Camel for market leadership. American also sold Pall Mall, a brand it had acquired in 1907, which was named for a fashionable London street where eighteenth-century dandies had played a precursor of croquet called pall-mall. In 1939 the company launched a reformulated and redesigned version of Pall Mall, wonderfully described by Richard Kluger in his encyclopedic history of the tobacco industry, *Ashes to Ashes:*

> The chief distinction of Pall Mall was that it had been lengthened into a "king" size, a fact explicitly illustrated in all the 1939–40 ads by a little boxed diagram comparing it with standard-brand lengths and implying that you enjoyed more puffs for the same money. Then there was the gorgeous red pack with the gracefully elongated white letters of the name . . . and beneath it, in case you hadn't got the message of its snob appeal, was the slogan "Wherever Particular People Congregate." For good measure, the crest bore *two* Latin mottoes, vying hard for the honor of being the more preposterously inappropriate: *"In hoc signo vinces"* ("Under this sign you triumph"), the divine message reported by the Roman emperor Constantine after dreaming he saw a Christian cross in the sky and later adopted as the banner and motto of the Crusaders; and *"Ad astra per aspera"* ("To the stars through adversity"), the state motto of Kansas.

As king-size cigarettes, Pall Malls were 85 millimeters long instead of 70 (about $3\frac{1}{3}$ inches instead of $2\frac{3}{4}$). Advertisements not only emphasized the fact that consumers could enjoy a longer smoke, they also made statements that verged on health claims. "Pall Mall's modern design brings you an entirely new kind of smoking pleasure," trumpeted a typical 1941 ad. "For this streamlined cigarette is deliberately designed to give you a much smoother, less irritating smoke. You see, tobacco is its own natural filter. In Pall Mall the smoke is measurably filtered — filtered over a 20% longer route of Pall Mall's traditionally fine tobaccos."

Of course, as Kluger pointed out, the ads omitted to state "that unless the smoker stubbed out the Pall Mall when he normally quenched his standard-length brand, he would absorb more, not fewer, irritants." And thrifty smokers like Nathan Horton bought Pall Malls not because they offered a "filtered" smoke, but because they contained extra tobacco, which they smoked to the 84th millimeter.

The task of bringing the new Pall Mall to market was assigned to Paul Hahn. As a young lawyer in 1931, Hahn had left Chadbourne Stanchfield & Levy, the New York firm that took care of the bulk of American Tobacco's legal work, and joined the client to handle a variety of business duties, including advertising and public relations. He rose quickly through the ranks, and in 1950 became president of American Tobacco. Under Hahn's stewardship, Pall Mall became a huge success, reigning as the number-one-selling U.S. cigarette for a six-year period in the late fifties and early sixties. The fortunes of the company as a whole, however, took a downward turn on Hahn's watch. Ironically, because of America's dedication to Pall Mall as a cigarette that supposedly filtered itself, the company virtually ignored the public's surging demand for filtered cigarettes in the second half of the 1950s. Competitors, meanwhile, rushed filtered brands to market. By the mid-1960s, American Tobacco had slid to the number-two position in the U.S. cigarette market, and it continued to decline precipitously thereafter.

Consumers flocked to filtered cigarettes largely in response to the first widespread publicity about scientific reports linking smoking with cancer. In 1952 a British medical journal reported a study of London hospital patients that demonstrated a strong statistical link between smoking and cancer. And in 1953 researchers at New York's Sloan-Kettering Institute induced the growth of malignant tumors in mice by painting their backs with a distillate of cigarette smoke. These studies generated media attention and some degree of public alarm — enough so that the tobacco industry felt compelled to respond. Spearheading that response was Paul Hahn. Late in 1953, Hahn sent telegrams to the presidents of other major tobacco companies, inviting them to New York to develop a strategy to deal with the negative press. Three weeks after the meeting of the executives at the Plaza Hotel on December 15, the companies took out full-page advertisements in newspapers around the country to address the public.

Headlined "A Frank Statement to Cigarette Smokers," the text challenged the reports that had raised health concerns:

We feel it is in the public interest to call attention to the fact that eminent doctors and research scientists have publicly questioned the claimed significance of these [mouse painting] experiments.

Distinguished authorities point out:

1. That medical research of recent years indicates many possible causes of lung cancer.

2. That there is no agreement among the authorities regarding what the cause is.

3. That there is no proof that cigarette smoking is one of the causes.

4. That statistics purporting to link cigarette smoking with the disease could apply with equal force to any one of many other aspects of modern life. Indeed, the validity of the statistics themselves is questioned by numerous scientists.

"For more than 300 years," the statement continued defensively, "tobacco has given solace, relaxation, and enjoyment to mankind. At one time or another during those years critics have held it responsible for practically every disease of the human body. One by one those charges have been abandoned for lack of evidence."

Still, the statement said it was "a matter of deep concern" that suspicions had been raised about links between smoking and disease. "We accept an interest in people's health as a basic responsibility, paramount to every other consideration in our business." To that end, the industry announced the creation of the Tobacco Industry Research Committee to investigate "all phases of tobacco use and health."

But two developments would make the industry's commitment to public health devilishly tricky to manage. One was the filing in 1954 of product-liability suits against cigarette makers, alleging the product had caused disease — the first of hundreds of such suits the industry would face in years to come. The second development was on the health front: The trickle of information linking cigarettes to disease quickly became a torrent. That Paul Hahn, who instigated the industry campaign to deal with the health scare, was an attorney was fitting. For in the face of this twin onslaught from the law and from medical science, attorneys would come to play critical roles in the affairs of the cigarette companies, sometimes in quite surprising ways.

4

On April 15, 1918, the Supreme Court of Mississippi issued the following decision in *Bryson Pillars v. R. J. Reynolds Tobacco Company:*

> The appellant [plaintiff] sued . . . R. J. Reynolds Tobacco Company, manufacturer of "Brown Mule Chewing Tobacco," for damages resulting to the appellant from chewing a piece of Brown Mule tobacco in which was concealed a decomposed human toe. . . . It seems that appellant consumed one plug of his purchase, which measured up to representations, that it was tobacco unmixed with human flesh, but when appellant tackled the second plug it made him sick, but, not suspecting the tobacco, he tried another chew, and still another, until he bit into some foreign substance, which crumbled like dry bread, and caused him to foam at the mouth, while he was getting "sicker and sicker." Finally, his teeth struck something hard; he could not bite through it. After an examination he discovered a human toe, with flesh and nail intact. We refrain from detailing further harrowing and nauseating details. The appellant consulted a

physician, who testified that appellant exhibited all of the characteristics of ptomaine poison. The physician examined the toe and identified it as a human toe in a state of putrefaction, and said, in effect, that his condition was caused by the poison generated by the rotten toe. At the close of the evidence for the plaintiff the trial judge, at the request of the defendants, entered a verdict for the defendants, and from a judgement responsive to this instruction, an appeal is prosecuted to this court.

Generally speaking, the rule is that the manufacturer is not liable to the ultimate consumer for damages resulting from defects and impurities of the manufactured article. This rule is generally based upon the theory that there is no contractual relation existing between the ultimate consumer and the manufacturer. From time to time, the courts have made exceptions to the rule. The manufacturers of food, beverages, drugs, condiments, and confections have been held liable to ultimate consumers for damages resulting from the negligent preparation of their products. The contention of the defendants here is that the limit has been reached by the courts, and that the facts of this case do not warrant an exception in favor of the plaintiff, and this view was adopted by the learned trial court. The exceptions already made were for the protection of the health of the people, and to insure scrupulous care in the preparation of those articles of commerce so as to reduce to a minimum all danger to those using them.

If poisons are concealed in food, or in beverages, or in confections or in drugs, death or the impairment of health will be the probable consequence. We know that chewing tobacco is taken into the mouth, that a certain proportion will be absorbed by the mucous membrane of the mouth, and that some, at least, of the juice or pulp will and does find its way into the alimentary canal, there to be digested and ultimately to become a part of the blood. Tobacco may be relatively harmless, but decaying flesh, we are advised, develops poisonous ptomaines, which are certainly dangerous and often fatal. Anything taken into the mouth there to be masticated should be free of those elements which may endanger the life or health of the user. No one would be so bold as to contend that the manufacturer would be free from liability if it should appear that he purposely mixed human flesh with chewing tobacco, or chewing gum. If the manufacturer would be liable for intentionally feeding putrid human flesh to any and all consumers of chewing tobacco, does it not logically follow that he would be liable for negligently bringing about the same result? It seems to us that this question must be answered in the affirmative. . . .

We can imagine no reason why, with ordinary care, human toes could not be left out of chewing tobacco, and if toes are found in chewing tobacco, it seems to us that somebody has been very careless.

We will reverse the judgment of the lower court.

This was the common law at work, in all its folksy, flexible majesty. Under the common-law system, adopted from the British at this nation's birth, court decisions in individual cases — and the opinions explaining those decisions — give rise to a body of rules governing all manner of human affairs. While a chief aim of the courts is to assure certainty and predictability in the application of law, leading to a tendency to adhere to rules handed down in previous cases, the beauty and power of the common law lies in its adaptability. The facts of each case brought before a court are unique and, at times, may call for modification or even wholesale rejection of long-established principles. Changes in social philosophy may similarly lead to such reconsideration and adaptation. The common law often develops differently in different states, and similar facts may not produce similar results.

After considering the horrifying facts of poor Mr. Pillars's case, the Mississippi Supreme Court had to decide whether the law afforded him a remedy. As the court noted, manufacturers were not generally held liable to the "ultimate consumer" for defects in their products. That was another inheritance from the British. Along with adopting the common-law system, courts in many states also adopted rules set forth in particular English decisions, not surprising given the several-hundred-year head start the mother country had in developing such case law. One of those rulings came in an 1842 case known as *Winterbottom v. Wright*. In that case, the defendant was a craftsman who had been hired by the postmaster to keep a fleet of mail coaches in good repair. A coach driver was injured as a result of poor maintenance and sued, but the court held that the defendant was not liable because the contract was between the defendant and the postmaster, not between the defendant and the driver. In legal terms, the driver and the defendant were not "in privity": no privity, no liability. The case was subsequently read broadly to mean that recourse for defective goods is available only between the original contracting parties.

That law may have made some sense in an era when goods were produced in limited numbers and sold locally, often passing directly from a manufacturer to a buyer. But in the wake of the Industrial Revolution, with the development of mass production, the ability to market products over great distances, and the advent of the middleman, the privity requirement began to yield harsh results. Just a decade after the decision in *Winterbottom,* courts in the United States began to recognize exceptions under which a manufacturer might be found liable to a third party, such as an end consumer. Those exceptions included goods that were considered "imminently" or "inherently" dangerous.

In the early years of the twentieth century, courts made further exceptions to the privity rule when the product involved was a food, beverage, or drug. Coca-Cola, believed to be a health tonic, fell into both of the latter categories at that time and, as the subject of a steady stream of lawsuits, became a vehicle for the development of exceptions to the privity doctrine. A 1915 opinion by the Supreme Court of Tennessee described one such case against Coca-Cola Bottling Works:

> Mrs. Lou Boyd was a lady in delicate health who was in the habit of occasionally drinking coca cola [*sic*] as a tonic and for its invigorating effects. Her husband bought for her a sealed bottle of this beverage from a dealer in Nashville. He carried the bottle home and poured a portion of its contents into a glass. His wife drank the liquid poured out, and immediately became intensely nauseated and suffered seriously from its effects.
>
> Mr. Boyd examined the bottle and found therein a cigar stub about two inches long which had apparently been in the liquid for some time.

Citing the modern trend in case law, the Tennessee court rejected the defense that there was no contract between the bottler and the plaintiff. "It is to be presumed that the contents of sealed packages put on the market to be used as a food or beverage are fit to be so used," the court wrote.

But when it came to tobacco, Tennessee would chart a course different from that of neighboring Mississippi. Just four months after its decision in the Coke case, the Tennessee Supreme Court issued another opinion in a suit against Liggett & Myers Tobacco Company brought by a J. J. Cannon. Again, it recounted the facts:

> Cannon purchased of a retail dealer in the city of Memphis a five-cent plug of Star Navy chewing tobacco. . . . Cannon bit a "chew" from the plug, and within a few minutes his mouth began to smart. Examining the remnant of the plug, he found impressed and imbedded under its top wrapper or leaf cover a large black bug, which he had just bitten into. He took the partly masticated quid from his mouth, and found "a black something mashed up in it" — a part of the bug he had chewed. Cannon's face was soon in a swollen condition; he became dizzy, and sent for a physician to alleviate his pain.

In this case, the court ruled, privity barred the door to any plaintiff's recovery. It would not make the exception to privity that it had made for Coca-Cola:

> We think it manifest that tobacco is not a foodstuff. It does not tend to build bodily tissue, and as to the average adult its tendency is widely thought to retard the building up of fatty tissue. In respect of its use by the young, it cannot be doubted that it tends to stunt normal development and even growth in stature. The desire or appetite for food is natural and common to all of the human race, while the desire for tobacco must be created. . . . This court has held that tobacco in one form, the cigarette, is not a legitimate article of commerce, because possessed of no virtue, being bad inherently.

Consumers in the late twentieth century are likely to consider the result reached by the Mississippi Supreme Court in the Pillars case more just. And it hardly took a great leap of jurisprudence to reach it. The court's broadening of manufacturers' liability so that it included products that are masticated as well as ingested was typical of most developments in the common law in that it was incremental. Occasionally, though, the law does move in giant steps, and nowhere has this been more true over the last hundred years than in the area of product liability.

The first case resulting in a radical departure from established doctrine involved Donald MacPherson, a New Yorker who was thrown from his car after a defective wooden wheel on the car suddenly crumbled. At first glance, the opinion handed down by New York Court of Appeals Justice Benjamin Cardozo in 1916 looked like one more effort to create an exception to the privity requirement. But it did more than that: it set the requirement on a path to oblivion. Cardozo, a towering figure on the New York court and later the U.S. Supreme Court, crafted an exception that all but swallowed up the rule:

> If the nature of a thing is such that it is reasonably certain to place life and limb in peril when negligently made, it is then a thing of danger. If to the element of danger there is added knowledge that the thing will be used by persons other than the purchaser [e.g., it is sold through a dealer or retailer], and used without new tests, then, irrespective of contract, the manufacturer of this thing of danger is under a duty to make it carefully.

Cardozo's decision, steadily followed in one state after another, removed the privity barrier in suits concerning all manner of products. But it was still predicated on the consumer being able to show that the product defect was the *fault* of the manufacturer — that there had been some *negligence* in designing or making the item. In subsequent years, other courts would dispense with even this requirement as they developed the doctrine of *strict liability*.

Coca-Cola once again figured in the law's forward march. Gladys Escola, a waitress in California, was placing bottles of Coke in a restaurant refrigerator when one exploded, inflicting a five-inch-long gash on her hand. Although it was clear such a thing should not have happened, Escola's lawyers told the court that they were unable to point to any specific act of negligence. That should no longer matter, said California Supreme Court Justice Roger Traynor. His opinion supporting the court's 1944 ruling for Escola became a manifesto for strict liability, with no pretense of treating the theory as a natural extension of earlier rulings. "Even when there is no negligence," Traynor wrote, "public policy demands that responsibility be fixed wherever it will most effectively reduce the hazards to life and health inherent in defective products that reach the market." He then enumerated the reasons for fixing that responsibility on the manufacturer, who, he noted, is in the best position to anticipate and guard against hazards, and who can purchase insurance to compensate those harmed and spread this cost in the marketplace as part of the price of the product.

Traynor's opinion set forth the tenets of what became known as *strict liability in tort* — an area of law under which a duty may arise to compensate an injured party without any regard to a contractual relationship. A separate line of cases achieved much the same result — strict liability — by hewing more closely to the language of contracts and laws governing the sale of goods. Rulings in these cases held that an "implied warranty" of safety accompanied consumer products into the marketplace and, in essence, traveled with the product to anyone who used it. If the product proved unsafe and caused injury, a manufacturer could be held liable for breach of this warranty.

As product-liability law transformed itself in one state after another, Mississippi plaintiffs continued to perish in the swamp of privity. Despite its "step forward for the health and life of the public" when it came to chewing tobacco, the Mississippi Supreme Court declined to dispense with the requirement for most other products. For example, when a part on a lumber truck broke, plunging the vehicle into a ditch and killing its driver, the court in 1928 refused to allow the driver's family to recover from Ford Motor Company, because he had no contractual relationship with the company. It was not until 1966 that the court overruled its decision in the Ford case, abandoning the privity requirement and adopting strict liability in tort as the law of the state.

5

Nathan Horton's complaint against American Tobacco asserted claims for strict liability in tort and for breach of warranty, both express and implied. It sought compensatory damages of $1.5 million for such things as Horton's medical expenses, his diminished earning capacity, and his pain and suffering. It also sought $10 million in punitive damages for American's "intentional and grossly negligent conduct" and its "conscious and reckless disregard and indifference to the rights, welfare, health and safety of the American public and Plaintiff." (The total amount sought was later upped to $17 million.)

For all its hotly worded accusations and multimillion-dollar demands, the six-page document created no particular alarm when, a short time after its May 1986 filing, it landed a thousand miles away, at Park Avenue and Forty-sixth Street in New York City, on the desk of Paul Randour. Randour was senior vice president and general counsel of American Brands, the corporate parent of American Tobacco, and cigarette liability lawsuits had become almost a routine item of business for the company. Because of its dominant market share for much of the century, American Tobacco was a defendant in the vast majority of suits that had been filed. Indeed, American Brands' 10-K for 1986 (the annual report filed with the Securities and Exchange Commission, which included information through March 1987) cited the Horton case as just one of 80 pending suits filed against American Tobacco by individual smokers. The company had also been brought in as a defendant in 133 asbestos lawsuits, in which asbestos manufacturers pointed to American and other tobacco companies and said it was cigarettes, not asbestos exposure, that caused the claimants' illnesses.

Yet the tone of the section of the 10-K describing legal proceedings was sanguine. As to the past, it noted: "At March 25, 1987 [American Tobacco] had disposed of 123 actions and the industry 198, all without recovery by the plaintiffs." Of the 11 cases brought by individual smokers that had made it to trial, the report boasted, "each resulted in a judgment for the defendant or defendants."

As to the future, the 10-K noted:

> It has been reported that certain groups of attorneys are interested in promoting product liability suits against tobacco manufacturers. [American Tobacco Company's] counsel, Chadbourne & Parke, have advised that, in their opinion . . . [the company] has meritorious defenses to the above mentioned actions and threatened actions. The actions will be vigorously defended on the merits.

Chadbourne & Parke was the modern name of the firm that had represented American Tobacco since the 1920s. It was a close-knit relationship. Firm founder Thomas Chadbourne counted Percival Hill, American's president from 1912 to 1925, as a card-playing buddy. Chadbourne lawyer Paul Hahn had moved to the tobacco company and rose to become its president. And in 1986, just before the Horton suit was filed, Chadbourne corporate lawyer Paul Randour became American's general counsel. He immediately forwarded the complaint to his old firm.

Litigation partner Janet Brown, one of only a handful of women in the upper echelons of a major law firm in 1986, had been Chadbourne's chief tobacco lawyer for years. But she was approaching the end of her career. While she continued to make major strategic decisions in tobacco cases overseen by the firm, a younger partner, Thomas Bezanson, was stepping into the role as lead lawyer in the area. Tall, lanky, and pale, Bezanson was just forty when the Horton suit was filed. He had moved from the position of associate attorney to partner at Chadbourne in six years, faster than anyone in the firm's history. In the 1970s Bezanson had helped defend American in a price-fixing suit brought against cigarette makers by tobacco growers; the suit was ultimately dropped after a court refused to approve the case as a class action. Bezanson's focus shifted with his client's legal problems. In the eighties, that meant product liability.

The first wave of the legal assault on the tobacco industry — cases brought in the 1950s and 1960s — had died out without a single success for plaintiffs. A variety of factors combined to defeat claimants: unfavorable rulings; uncompromising and exhaustive defense tactics that often left plaintiffs financially unable to proceed; and, in the few cases that did make it to trial, juries unsympathetic to the plight of someone who chose to smoke. But by the early 1980s, plaintiffs' lawyers, emboldened by developments in product-liability law, were once again setting their sights on cigarette makers, and the so-called second wave of tobacco litigation began.

Chadbourne was ready — even to the point of lining up local counsel in states where lawsuits had *not* been filed. In Mississippi, Chadbourne retained Jackson attorney Richard Edmonson, a choice dictated in part by the fact that many other of the more substantial defense firms in the state were already working for the asbestos industry — a conflict, since that industry was pointing the finger at tobacco in its own liability cases. Edmonson agreed to stand by in the event his services were needed. "I never thought a suit would be filed, quite frankly," he recalled years later. But in May 1986, he was called to duty.

"Do you contend that plaintiff was negligent in either starting to smoke cigarettes or in continuing to smoke cigarettes?" "Is cigarette smoking hazardous to the health of smokers?" "Can prolonged smoking of cigarettes cause lung cancer?" Don Barrett addressed these and a series of other questions to American Tobacco in a set of interrogatories that he served on the company along with the complaint. It was the opening salvo of discovery, the process in litigation during which each side can compel the other — through such means as interrogatories, depositions, and document requests — to provide information about the case. In this instance, Barrett's "contention interrogatories" sought to force American Tobacco to declare its positions on key issues in the case.

Discovery is the protracted, often tedious, in-the-trenches side of litigation. Requests for information from one side often produce lengthy objections from the other and a claim that some or all of the information sought need not be provided. This in turn leads to motions before the court to compel turnover of the information, as the lawyers, bickering like children, call on the judge to intervene. The process can lead to delay and enormous expense, turning a lawsuit into a war of attrition. Barrett, like most plaintiffs' lawyers, could not afford to fight such a war for long. American Tobacco Company could, and its lawyers would move frequently to delay the trial, which Judge Gray Evans had scheduled to begin in March 1987.

Evans was fifty-seven at the time the Horton case was filed. He has a big, lumbering frame, large ears, a large nose, and floppy hands. Relatively new to the bench — he was appointed as a judge in 1982 after practicing law in Greenwood for twenty-three years — he got the case from the assigning judge. "He said this will be a long, drawn-out affair," Evans recalled. "I said 'yeah' without having any idea that it would turn out to be what it turned out to be, which was a big headache and a mess and lots of disagreements."

American's response to Barrett's first set of interrogatories was typical. It began by asserting a series of "general objections" that applied to nearly all of Barrett's questions. The interrogatories sought information that was privileged, already known to him, or publicly available, the objections stated. Additionally, the questions sought information that was irrelevant, were "so vague and ambiguous that they are not subject to reasoned interpretation," were "unduly burdensome or oppressive in that the burden of obtaining the information purportedly called for substantially outweighs any probative value the information may have," and so on. Individual questions then drew their own particular objections. Both sides made repeated trips to the Holmes County courthouse to get discovery disputes resolved. "The number of motions I heard and the time I took to hear them was monumental," Judge Evans said years later.

Over time, American did answer many of Barrett's queries. As to whether smoking caused cancer, the company offered a response that was almost identical to the position taken in the "Frank Statement to Cigarette Smokers" thirty-two years earlier: "There is a scientific controversy regarding the relationship, if any, between cigarette smoking and health." On the question of whether it had been negligent of Horton to smoke, the response was even more equivocal: After calling the question "premature," the company noted that "whether any person's actions constitute negligence depends on what that person did, the circumstances under which he did it, his knowledge at the time and a host of other factors."

It seemed odd for a manufacturer to be suggesting that a consumer who had used its product as intended could somehow be negligent for doing so. American's lawyers were treading gingerly, though inelegantly, as they tried to decide what sort of "affirmative defense" they would employ in the case. After hedging their first response, they subsequently replied that Horton had been "contributorily negligent" in smoking. That meant that if the jury found American Tobacco liable for Horton's illness, that liability should be offset by the degree to which the jury felt Horton also bore responsibility, because of his decision to smoke. But that was a risky position, because under Mississippi law even if the jury found Horton 99 percent responsible and American just 1 percent, it could still assess millions in damages. So American ultimately dropped its claim of contributory negligence in favor of saying that Horton had "assumed the risk" of smoking. Under the law, if a jury found that he had assumed the risk, he would not be able to recover anything from American.

All in all, the company was laying the groundwork for a defense of its product that would straddle two inconsistent positions. Its lawyers and executives would deny that there was any proof that cigarettes caused cancer. At the same time, they maintained that anyone like Horton who chose to smoke assumed the risk of getting such a disease. "It was," Richard Edmonson acknowledged years after the case ended, "certainly an awkward argument to make." There was, he said, "a balance you really couldn't make in there — it really didn't make any sense." As local counsel, Edmonson and lawyers at his firm handled much of the day-to-day work on the case, though the Chadbourne lawyers were also busy and controlled the overall strategy in the case.

American's legal team embarked on its own discovery on a scale that would dwarf the plaintiffs' efforts. Starting with a simple set of interrogatories about Horton's life history and a request for his medical records, Chadbourne dispatched private investigators to places Horton had lived to interview everyone they could find who had known him. Then the depositions began. From mid-1986 to late 1987 American's lawyers took more than 130 depositions, questioning members of Horton's family, friends, coworkers, and doctors about nearly every aspect of his life.

A principal objective of American's lawyers was to catalog substances Horton had been exposed to in his life that might serve as alternative causes of his cancer. This led to a series of questions about Horton's diet. Although Richard Edmonson conducted the bulk of the depositions, portions of the questions, including those on diet, had been scripted by Chadbourne, based on its experience in numerous other tobacco suits. It would prove to be a disappointing line of inquiry for the defense team.

"What would you normally cook for Nathan?" Edmonson asked Danette Horton in a deposition taken at Barrett's offices in Lexington in November 1986.

"He liked greens and mashed potatoes and peas and bread," replied Danette, Horton's first wife, who was married to him from 1956 to 1960.

"What kind of meat?" Edmonson continued, pushing toward less healthy fare.

"He liked chicken."

"Fried chicken?"

"Yes."

"Did he like fried foods?"

"Well, sort of. He would eat roast fish and salads." . . .

"What about diet drinks? Did he ever have diet drinks?"

"Not that I know of."

"What about charcoal steaks?"

"No."

Edmonson tried again with Horton's second wife, "Cheryl" (a pseudonym), whose stormy two-year marriage to Horton ended in 1962. "Did Nathan do any of the cooking himself?" Edmonson asked.

"Some eggs or something when he thought I was going to poison him," she said.

"When he thought you were going to poison him?" Edmonson repeated.

"You know how it is," she explained, "when you kind of argue or something, then, you know, if I had cooked something, sometimes he wouldn't eat it."

Edmonson moved on. "Do you know if there were any kind of foods that Nathan could not eat or would not eat?" he asked.

"No, not really. He likes beans and greens the best, you know . . . My kids and I like hamburgers and pork chops and fried chicken. He didn't really care for french fries and stuff like that. Mostly boiled food."

By the time Horton's third wife, Gloria Turner, appeared for questioning, Edmonson had shortened the food inquiry to a few quick questions. "What kind of foods did [Horton] eat?" he asked.

"He liked boiled foods," Turner said. Boiling was just not a helpful answer when it came to carcinogenesis.

"Most anything he would eat would be boiled?" Edmonson continued.

"Yes."

"What about fried foods? Did he eat any fried foods?"

"Well, if he did, he ate it with someone else, because I didn't know how to do it."

But in a deposition of Horton's older sister, Ruth Mae Smith, Edmonson appeared to have hit pay dirt. Smith recalled that Horton liked "soul food."

"I appreciate soul food," Edmonson said. "That means a lot of fried food?"

"No, it doesn't have to," Smith replied, dashing Edmonson's hopes. "Soul food consists of sweet potatoes, butter beans, any type of green, mustards, black-eyed peas, crowder peas and stuff like that. That is what I call soul food. It doesn't have to be a lot of fried food."

"When you cook soul food, don't you normally, for example, butter beans or your peas, you put in a piece of ham hock or something like that?" Edmonson persisted.

"They are good like that, but he never liked his food too rich, I recall that. He never did like a lot of grease and lots of richness in his food."

There was, of course, far more than food to ask about, and the defendants had much better luck when they asked about Horton's exposure to substances in the workplace. After leaving the Navy, Horton had settled in Waterloo, Iowa, and for four years, from 1958 to 1961, Horton did chipping and grinding work at the John Deere tractor company there. Tractor motor cylinder blocks, fiery red out of their molds, moved down a line past Horton and his colleagues, who used chipping hammers and air grinders to remove sand and hardened bits of iron that had seeped out where the mold halves had joined. It was hot and dirty work. In addition to the particles that would fly off the cylinder blocks, dirt, blown by large fans, swirled around the room, covering everyone who worked there in a layer of grit. By the middle of the day, said Isiah Frizell, one of Horton's coworkers, in his deposition, you couldn't tell if a man was black or white unless you pulled the goggles off his face. While they did wear eye protection, Frizell and Horton both said they did not wear masks, and they were constantly spitting brownish-black crud out of their mouths and blowing it out their noses.

As they pursued every aspect of Horton's dietary, work, and health history, American's lawyers learned about other aspects of Horton's life as well. Horton, it turned out, had had run-ins with the law. He spent time in jail in Waterloo in connection with an alleged theft of beer from a convenience store, and while that incident does not appear to have led to a conviction, it did lead to his being fired from John Deere. Then, in 1963, he was convicted of armed robbery in Illinois, and served two years at the state penitentiary in Joliet.

The depositions also delved deeply into Horton's personal life, which, in the sixties in particular, was dissolute and punctuated by violence. Even before his first marriage had ended, Horton had met Gloria Turner, who was fifteen, in a park in Des Moines and gotten her pregnant. At the same time, he had taken up with Cheryl in Waterloo, and each of them bore him a daughter in September 1960. Horton married Cheryl in October 1960, and had another daughter with her a year later. Cheryl, it became clear during depositions, had been a prostitute, and she and Horton turned their house in Waterloo into a full-service den of iniquity: gambling, prostitutes, drinks, and drugs were available, a friend of Horton's testified.

Appearing for her deposition in tight-fitting clothes and sporting fake diamond-implanted fingernails, Cheryl testified that she and Horton fought all the time. At times he struck her, but she would fight back. In January 1962 she hit Horton with a skillet and broke two of his fingers. Some of the fights were over his gambling. He loved to play cards and dice, which he did at the back of nightclubs and in private homes in Waterloo. He did not play for small stakes, and sometimes lost his entire paycheck from John Deere in one evening, leaving Cheryl wondering how she could buy food for herself and her two baby daughters.

In 1967, Horton, divorced from Cheryl, married Gloria Turner, who had given birth to one of his daughters seven years earlier. Their relationship was also tumultuous. In 1968 she stabbed him in the shoulder with a butcher knife. After roughly a year of separation, she lived with him briefly in Dallas, where he had moved. Edmonson found this difficult to piece together during Gloria's deposition.

"Did you resume living with him that three-week period of time before or after you stabbed him?" he asked Gloria, trying to clarify the chronology.

"Well, I started living with him after I stabbed him, in Dallas," she replied.

"Okay. I'm sorry. I thought you had said you stabbed him in Des Moines."

"I did. I did stab him in Des Moines."

"And you lived with him three weeks in Des Moines?"

"That was before I stabbed him."

"Okay. That's what I was getting at."

"Okay."

Horton's brief marriage to Gloria produced no additional children. To the four children he did have — one with his first wife, two with Cheryl, and one with Gloria — Horton was neither a father nor a provider, leaving them and their mothers to support themselves. Danette, his first wife, turned to welfare to help raise Nathan Jr. And after years of meager payments, Cheryl sued Horton to collect more child support, but it didn't do much good: during the time their two daughters were growing up, he paid her a total of $1,435.

Horton met Ella, who would become his fourth and last wife, in 1970, when he was sent by her landlord to do some repairs in her apartment building in Waterloo. Horton had told the landlord he would fix a ceiling for free if the landlord would introduce him to Ella. The two hit it off, and moved back to Mississippi, which was also Ella's birthplace. In his native Holmes County, Horton settled into a stable, industrious existence. But some things didn't change. He continued to gamble, arriving at the end of a workday at the Et Cetera club or Dot's place on Beale Street in Lexington, and playing cards far into the night. He also persisted in his promiscuous ways.

In a deposition of Florestine Meeks, Horton's thirty-four-year-old niece who worked with him in his contracting business, one of American's lawyers, Clinton Guenther, asked her about Horton's extramarital dalliances. "Can I say something?" Meeks interjected after a series of questions about a woman named Ruby.

"Sure," said Guenther.

"You're just asking too much private business about a man outside of life," Meeks protested.

"Well, this is why I'm asking that, because I want to find out how close he and Ruby were. I'm not trying to find out private things about Nathan's life or Ruby's life."

"You asking them," Meeks said.

"I'm trying to find out because Nathan has sued the American Tobacco Company for seventeen million dollars. That ought to give me a right to ask some questions," Guenther responded.

It was, at times, hard to divine a connection between the questions American's lawyers asked about the intimate details of Horton's life and a lawsuit concerning the health effects of smoking. It is true that once Horton died and his family members sought damages on their own behalf, the suit did put the nature and quality of his family relationships at issue. A child could not claim that Horton's passing had resulted in lost support, for example, if Horton in reality had provided little or no support. American was also entitled to try to establish that all of Horton's offspring had been identified to preclude future claimants from emerging once the suit was over. But at times, the questioning degenerated into pure pruri-ence, as it did with Meeks.

Continuing his questioning about Ruby, Guenther asked, "Well, now, I know you said that she pulled up her dress and showed Nathan her underclothes. Was it nice underwear? Was it expensive underwear?"

Meeks could stand up for herself. Later in the deposition, after return-ing from a break, Guenther asked, "What have you and [Fred] Clark been discussing on the breaks?"

"That is personal," Meeks said.

"Hasn't been anything about the deposition?" Guenther pressed her.

"Whatever we talked about is really our business what we was talking about," Meeks shot back. "We could have been getting it on. Now, you don't know that."

6

Florestine Meeks was deposed in Lexington. Many of the other depositions took place out of state, in places Horton had lived, from St. Louis to Waterloo to Dallas. This was an expensive undertaking, what with the cost of travel, hotels, court reporters, and so forth, but that didn't stop the defendants from sending three or four lawyers to each deposition, while Horton was represented by one, usually Fred Clark. American Tobacco was not only underwriting the costs of its codefendant New Deal on these expeditions. Judge Evans had ordered the cigarette maker to pay Clark's expenses for the out-of-town discovery as well.

During the road show, Clark recalls, there was a fair amount of camaraderie among the lawyers, especially those from Mississippi. One of his fellow Mississippians was James Upshaw, the white lawyer from Greenwood who had teamed up with Barrett to win the enormous verdict for the elderly black woman against the telephone company. Now Upshaw was on the opposite side, representing American's codefendant New Deal. An ample-sized man with graying hair and a beard, Upshaw looks somewhat like Colonel Sanders, the Kentucky

Fried Chicken icon. Like Clark, Upshaw also remembers enjoying himself during discovery, though his idea of fun was a bit antiquated, to say the least. In Iowa, he recalls, he liked to provoke reaction from the locals by introducing Clark as his valet, Buckwheat, a reference to the black character in the 1950s television show *The Little Rascals*. At a restaurant in Cedar Falls, Upshaw pointed to Clark and asked the hostess, "Do you mind if I bring my slave in with me?" He then explained, deadpan, that they were from Mississippi, where he would never dream of asking such a question, but he wondered if it would be acceptable in Iowa.

Clark endured these indignities without protest, and years later discusses them without animus. Clark sees Upshaw, born in 1931, as a relic of another era who has made only limited strides toward adopting a more enlightened attitude on race. "He thinks he's liberal, thinks he's recognized that things have changed in Mississippi," Clark says. "In reality, he's insensitive to what people find offensive." Upshaw, though, says people have become too touchy. He fondly recalls his days in the Navy, when, he says, nobody minded being called a dago or a mick. "These days," he says, "we've grown very sensitive about everything in this country. I don't know why."

Upshaw impressed his colleagues with his capacity to drink prodigious amounts of alcohol at the end of a day of work and then show absolutely no effect the following morning. "I've never had a hangover in my life," Upshaw boasts. He and Chadbourne's Tom Bezanson seemed particularly to enjoy each other's company, but when the Chadbourne lawyers were absent, Upshaw occasionally referred to them as "hebes," a reference to Jewish lawyers at the firm.

William Bradner Jr., a Chadbourne senior litigator now retired from the firm, recalls Upshaw boasting about his antics with Clark. "Upshaw is an unreconstructed redneck," Bradner says. "I wouldn't put him on a case in Long Island for all the money in the world." But for a case in central Mississippi, Janet Brown, the Chadbourne attorney overseeing the firm's tobacco work, thought Upshaw was just right.

Richard Edmonson, the Jackson attorney Chadbourne had engaged for the case, "was a gentleman, and gentlemen weren't going to win down there," Bradner explains. "You had to get somebody who would yell and whoop and holler." Jim Upshaw, who along with his coarseness had a commanding — and at times bullying — presence, fit the bill. He was "a gut fighter," in Bradner's words. Edmonson had also been more pessimistic than Upshaw about the defendants' chances of winning a trial in Holmes County, and Chadbourne wanted somebody with a more positive outlook. So in December 1986, with the case in the middle of discovery, Brown engineered a switch, bringing Upshaw on as the lead Mississippi counsel for American Tobacco and a new lawyer, Calvin King, in for New Deal. Although Edmonson continued to work for American, he was pushed, unhappily, to the periphery.

Horton's legal team also changed. As the case progressed, Don Barrett felt the need for more horsepower, and he found it through a kind of plaintiffs' lawyer dating service run by Richard Daynard, a professor and anti-tobacco activist at Boston's Northeastern University School of Law. In 1985 Daynard had begun hosting seminars for plaintiffs' attorneys involved in cigarette litigation. The idea was to promote the pooling of resources and sharing of information, a small step aimed at counterbalancing the massive forces and coordinated tactics of the tobacco industry. Through one of these conferences, Barrett learned about Don Davis, a litigator from Austin, Texas, who had filed a number of smoking cases in that state. Davis was further up the learning curve on tobacco litigation than Barrett and had already lined up a number of prominent medical and scientific experts who could testify at trial. He also had something else he could contribute: money, thanks to a lucrative practice built on aviation accidents, medical malpractice, and other personal-injury work. Barrett persuaded Davis that Holmes County offered a better venue than Texas for a tobacco liability suit, and Davis put much of his other business aside and joined the Horton team.

Barrett's relationship with Davis was cordial but never close, and it would endure significant tensions as the litigation proceeded. From the moment he signed on, though, Davis's role on the case would be a prominent one. In December 1986, for example, Davis took a key deposition: that of Robert Heimann, who had retired as American's CEO in 1980.

The single most important person to give a deposition in the case, of course, was Nathan Horton himself. In a series of three sessions in July and December of 1986, both Barrett and lawyers for American led him through lengthy questioning. The sessions were videotaped, and for

Barrett, the most valuable thing to emerge from them was not what Horton said, but the picture of him saying it. Between the first session on July 9 and the last on December 4, Horton underwent a dramatic physical decline, his body progressively deteriorating under the onslaught of both the cancer and the treatment. Little evidence could be more powerful to a jury than this visual chronicle of Horton's demise. American's lawyers knew that and tried, without success, to get Judge Evans to prohibit the final deposition session on the grounds that it would be "inflammatory and unduly prejudicial."

But there was a payoff for the defense as well. Horton's claim that American had breached express warranties was based on the contention that advertisements for Pall Mall cigarettes stated the product was "wholesome" and free of health hazards. In Horton's deposition, however, he recalled that "they really never advertised Pall Malls that much, far as TV commercials." Then he said, "If they hadn't advertised Pall Mall at all, I — I would say I would've smoked them anyway." It was at this point that he explained he had started smoking Pall Malls simply because, as a long, unfiltered cigarette, they seemed a good value. "I don't think no commercial started me to smoking 'em," he said.

American pounced on these statements and used them as the basis for a motion to knock out the express-warranty claim in the case. "Discovery has revealed . . . that plaintiff never relied on American's advertising either in beginning or continuing to smoke," American's motion stated. There was little Horton's legal team could say in response. "The courts have recognized that advertisements influence people unconsciously or subliminally in their purchase and/or use of products," stated one particularly anemic line in their opposing papers. The judge ruled for American.

At the same time, American's lawyers gunned for the heart of Horton's complaint: strict liability in tort. The Mississippi Supreme Court had adopted strict liability in *State Stove Manufacturing Company v. Hodges,* a 1966 ruling involving an electric water heater that had exploded. In its decision, the court incorporated the language and theory of strict liability as it had been set forth in *The Restatement of Torts,* a multivolume synthesis and explication of tort law that judges around the country often turn to for an authoritative statement of common-law doctrine. Section 402A of the *Restatement* sets forth the rule on strict liability in tort as follows:

(1) One who sells any product in a defective condition unreasonably dangerous to the user or consumer or to his property is subject to liability for physical harm thereby caused to the ultimate user or consumer, or to his property . . .

(2) The rule stated in Subsection (1) applies although
    (a) the seller has exercised all possible care in the preparation and sale of his product, and
    (b) the user or consumer has not bought the product from or entered into any contractual relation with the seller.

It certainly seemed like language that would warm the cockles of any plaintiffs' lawyer's heart. In reality, it did just the opposite. When it was published in the early sixties — and quickly adopted in state after state thereafter — Section 402A became a death knell for cigarette liability suits, a major cause of their near disappearance for almost a decade and a half. The reason lay in a written comment that elaborated on the meaning of the term "unreasonably dangerous." Comment *i* explained:

The rule stated in this Section applies only where the defective condition of the product makes it unreasonably dangerous to the user or consumer. Many products cannot possibly be made entirely safe for all consumption, and any food or drug necessarily involves some risk of harm, if only from over consumption. Ordinary sugar is a deadly poison to diabetics, and castor oil found use under Mussolini as an instrument of torture. That is not what is meant by "unreasonably dangerous" in this Section. The article sold must be dangerous to an extent beyond that which would be contemplated by the ordinary consumer who purchases it, with the ordinary knowledge common to the community as to its characteristics. Good whiskey is not unreasonably dangerous merely because it will make some people drunk, and is especially dangerous to alcoholics; but bad whiskey, containing a dangerous amount of fusel oil, is unreasonably dangerous. Good tobacco is not unreasonably dangerous merely because the effects of smoking may be harmful; but tobacco containing something like marijuana may be unreasonably dangerous. Good butter is not unreasonably dangerous merely because, if such be the case, it deposits cholesterol in the arteries and leads to heart attacks; but bad butter, contaminated with poisonous fish oil, is unreasonably dangerous.

In other words, a plaintiff could not win damages for harm from smoking, because it is "ordinary and common knowledge" that "good tobacco" may cause disease.

The argument that people should not compensated for consuming something that they know may harm them might seem compelling. But this ignores the fact that cigarette makers went to great lengths to persuade the public that the medical case against smoking was not proven — even though the manufacturers possessed particular knowledge about its dangers. And in lumping tobacco together with other products, the authors of Comment *i* failed to make some critical distinctions: Whiskey makers would say that people should stop drinking before they are dangerously drunk; sugar refiners would say that diabetics should not consume sugar. Even butter can be distinguished: People don't die from eating sticks of it. Rather, butter, along with other high-fat foods, may collectively induce coronary artery disease, and to avoid that a person would not just stop eating butter, but would have to change his whole diet. Cigarettes are different: Used alone, as intended, with no known safe minimum dose, they cause illness and death. And of course, for many smokers they are addictive.

Be that as it may, under the *Restatement* view of the world, a plaintiff could recover only if she could show that the tobacco was tainted by something that shouldn't have been there. Obviously that requirement drove a stake through the heart of most cigarette liability cases, where the thrust of the complaint was that the product itself was defective. But tort law never rests, and by the early 1980s a new theory emerged that helped revive antitobacco lawyers' moribund ranks.

In some jurisdictions, courts developed what came to be known as a risk-utility analysis for product-liability claims. That meant that as part of determining whether a product was unreasonably dangerous, a jury could weigh the inherent risks of the product against the overall benefits the product conferred. A piece of farm equipment, for example, while dangerous, is also of great social utility; the danger, therefore, might be considered reasonable. A cigarette, presumably, would not fare so well in the balance.

The first count in Nathan Horton's complaint asserted a claim in strict liability based on the *Restatement* standard, which on its own seemed certain to fail if the court went along with the argument in Comment *i*. But the second count set forth the risk–utility theory. American Tobacco argued that risk–utility was not the law in Mississippi, that no court in the state had ever adopted the doctrine. Nonetheless, Judge Evans decided to break new ground, and announced that risk–utility would apply in the case. It was an important victory for Horton. While American's lawyers were not done arguing the issue, they also had other battles to fight.

Stripped of their packaging, different brands of cigarettes look pretty much the same. But when cigarettes are smoked, real distinctions among the different makes become clear — a given brand will have a characteristic taste. Manufacturers create this taste by blending different sorts of tobacco and by adding flavorings, such as licorice and chocolate. A range of other additives perform such functions as regulating the humidity, odor, and burn rate of the tobacco. Exactly what is added to cigarettes, however, is not a matter of public record.

Don Barrett wanted to know, and he specifically wanted to know what went into Nathan Horton's brand, Pall Mall. When Judge Evans granted Barrett's request and ordered American to turn over the list of ingredients, American's legal team went ballistic. They got permission from the judge to appeal the order immediately to the Mississippi Supreme Court. Imploring the high court to protect the company's trade secrets, American's brief stated: "Pall Mall's marketability rests upon its unique qualities. Its commercial success for over half a century has been maintained by keeping the secret of its manufacture from a highly competitive marketplace. It is impossible to calculate the value to American of this proprietary information."

The brief then documented the elaborate steps the company had taken to keep the Pall Mall recipe secret:

> Only twenty employees of American have access to the information and not all those employees have access to *all* the requested information. In other words, fewer than twenty people know all the ingredients. . . .
>
> As sworn to by an officer of American: (1) American maintains this information in a vault; (2) the twenty employees with access are covered by a multi-million-dollar bond; (3) each employee has strictly limited rights of access; (4) all access by these employees is recorded; and (5) American's contracts with "flavoring houses" prohibit disclosure of the identity of the particular component involved.

The Mississippi Supreme Court was not impressed. The company would have to turn over the list to Barrett.

Eight months after his complaint was filed, Horton died. On January 27, 1987 — the very day of his passing — his lawyers filed a motion with the court announcing they were converting the suit to a wrongful-death action, a claim brought by heirs seeking compensation for a family member's death. Two days later, a new complaint was filed, and two days after that, Barrett spoke at Horton's funeral. The crowd Barrett addressed did not consist only of mourners. Someone in the church had a concealed tape recorder and a recording of what was said found its way into the hands of American's lawyers.

Jim Upshaw had now taken the lead defense role, and he seized on Barrett's remarks as an opportunity to get the case moved out of Holmes County. Petitioning the court for a change of venue, Upshaw excoriated Barrett for using the solemn occasion of Horton's funeral to advance his litigation:

> As this Court well knows, Holmes County is a small community. There are only a few thousand potential jurors. The community is economically depressed, and social services are often lacking. The funeral oration seeks to exploit these characteristics by portraying Mr. Horton as a man to whom the people of Holmes County — particularly the

unskilled and the poor — owe a great debt for the jobs he supplied and the medical clinic he built.

In the rural counties of Mississippi, moreover, the local church holds a central position in the life and emotions of the community. This, too, was well known to Mr. Barrett when he chose to make an emotional appeal to a congregation made exceptionally receptive by the context of recent death. Many of those in the congregation were community leaders or opinion makers — an audience well able to carry Mr. Barrett's message throughout the County.

Years later Upshaw noted that he, too, had once spoken at a black man's funeral. But it was for his "yard man," Robert, who had been "like a member of the family." To this day Upshaw finds it hard to believe that Barrett had become so close to Nathan Horton. But even allowing that he had, it was what Barrett said at the funeral that galled him. "There's nothing wrong with getting up and saying he was a good friend and he was a great guy," Upshaw says (unable to resist adding that Horton "wasn't a good friend and he really wasn't a wonderful person"), but the remarks about the lawsuit "were a clear and unadulterated attempt to influence the jury."

Allegations and counterallegations of improper attempts to influence jurors would only escalate as the case progressed. In a filing opposing Upshaw's attempt to get the case moved out of Holmes County, Barrett claimed that his funeral remarks "would have remained only in the private memories of the Horton family and friends, if remembered at all, had not The American Tobacco Company engaged in the sleazy practice of paying an informer to eavesdrop at the funeral." In fact, Barrett charged, it was Upshaw who was guilty of trying to "prejudice the outcome of the case" by talking to reporters. Barrett then excerpted an article about the Horton case from the *Clarion-Ledger/Jackson Daily News* — the most widely distributed Sunday paper in the state — that quoted Upshaw:

> New Deal's attorney, James Upshaw of Greenwood, said last week that a victory by Horton would set a dangerous precedent for suits against hundreds of goods and beverage manufacturers. "What's next? Salt? Butter?" he asked.
>
> "Those are bad for you. If you eat too many corn flakes, drink too

much milk, that's bad for you. You get fat, and that's bad for your heart, right?" . . .

"Everybody knows smoking's bad for you. [A far stronger statement than he would ever make in the courtroom.] Until we get to be a regimented country, such as Russia, I think we should absolutely have the right to choose," Upshaw said.

Barrett, who wanted the case to stay in Holmes County, was quick to add in his legal filing that he didn't believe Upshaw

> was successful in his efforts to poison the well of jurors in Holmes County. Seven months will have passed between the remarks and trial. Moreover, we believe that Holmes Countians, like most Americans, tend to take what they read in newspapers with a big grain of salt. Finally, the court could take judicial notice that nobody takes Mr. Upshaw quite as seriously as does Mr. Upshaw.

Just two months earlier, in a letter to Judge Evans on a different subject, Barrett had noted, "Jim Upshaw is a friend of mine. He is more than that; he is a very close friend of mine. His friendship with me is so deep as to be beyond test or proving. I guess you could say, as my friend, he has tenure." But as the case progressed, the barbs traded by the two lawyers grew sharper, their suspicions of each other's tactics deeper. By the time the Horton litigation ended, the friendship was deeply chilled.

Judge Evans refused to change the location of the trial. He did, however, move the trial date, from March 1987 to August. The delay was bad news for Barrett. It meant the defense would be able to take more discovery, which meant more expense. The cost of fighting a cigarette maker was proving a tremendous burden to Barrett. In November 1987 he would report to the court that he and the other plaintiffs' lawyers had spent $160,000 on the case (in costs alone, not counting the value of attorney time). Bringing Don Davis in from Texas as cocounsel had helped keep the war chest from emptying out, but Barrett also engaged in less conventional fund-raising. He contacted Joseph Cherner, a one-time Wall Street bond trader who had taken his winnings from the world of finance and set up an antismoking organization, and asked him for a contribution.

Instead of a direct grant, Cherner put up funds in a different way: He placed a sum of money in escrow — years later he could not remember whether it was $10,000 or $100,000 — and said Barrett could have it if he won a trial. There was now a bounty on American Tobacco's scalp.

In July 1987 the defense got another postponement. Judge Evans set the trial for January 4, 1988. American's lawyers used this time to sharpen their attack on Horton's strict-liability claims. In addition to drafting their own brief on the issue, they supplied Judge Evans with a copy of a brief that had been filed in a New Jersey tobacco liability case by W. Page Keeton, explaining why a plaintiff should not be able to recover under Section 402A of *The Restatement of Torts*. Keeton was a luminary in the field of tort law, a longtime professor at the respected University of Texas School of Law, the editor of one of the most authoritative legal references on torts, and, to top it off, a member of the group of scholars that drafted the *Restatement* in the 1960s.

In an ill-considered move, Davis and Barrett attempted to discredit Keeton's brief by providing Judge Evans with transcribed excerpts from a speech Keeton had delivered on the subject of Section 402A, claiming that his remarks suggested that there were instances in which a plaintiff might recover in a cigarette suit. Unbeknownst to Davis and Barrett, though, Judge Evans was acquainted with Page Keeton. Keeton had been his torts professor during a year he'd spent at the University of Texas law school, and Keeton's younger brother had been Evans's fraternity brother that year. So Evans picked up the phone and called the esteemed professor. "I said, 'Will you help me with this,' " Evans recalls, "and he said, 'Of course I will.' " Keeton sent the judge a letter charging that the transcribed comments offered by Barrett and Davis were fragmentary, taken out of context, and were in no way inconsistent with the views he expressed in the New Jersey case. Cigarettes, Keeton wrote, "present inherent risks known to the ordinary consumer." Tort law, he continued, should not create liability for "the act of making such a product available to the consumer for the latter's knowing, personal choice." For Barrett and Davis, it was tantamount to having Thomas Jefferson write to say they were wrong in their interpretation of the Constitution.

Problems on other fronts were also keeping Barrett and his team busy. New Horton heirs kept popping up. During the summer of 1987, two women filed motions with the court, each claiming that her young son (one was six years old, the other three) was fathered by Horton, and asking that the child be permitted to join in the lawsuit. A separate proceeding found that the boys were indeed Horton's sons. A third woman also began the process of having the court declare Horton the father of her child, but she wanted to keep the fact secret from her husband, who thought the child was his. Told there was no way to assure the information wouldn't get out, she withdrew.

On a previous occasion when an out-of-wedlock child of Horton's had surfaced, the child's name had simply been added to the complaint. The two new claimants presented Barrett with a problem. Each was represented by his own counsel. That raised the prospect of two additional teams of lawyers joining the plaintiffs' side of the case. With his distrust of tobacco company legal tactics on the rise, Barrett worried that one of the new lawyers might actually be working in collusion with American and might somehow try to sabotage the case. (Upshaw scoffed when told of this.) At the very least, Barrett was concerned that having to coordinate trial preparation, and the trial itself, with these new lawyers would create a logistical and strategic nightmare. So he begged Judge Evans to deny the mothers' request to add their sons to the suit and instead allow him to represent the boys. Evans agreed.

American, in the meantime, had plugged a major gap in its trial team by hiring a black attorney. It had been clear from the outset that there might be racial undertones to a case brought on behalf of a black man against an out-of-state (and for all intents and purposes "white") corporate defendant that would be tried before a largely black jury. And from the moment of Barrett's funeral oration, it was clear that he planned to position race at the forefront of the lawsuit. "One black man every fifteen minutes dies from smoking disease," he had told the assembled mourners. Even without this kind of explicit playing of the race card, as it came to be known in the 1995 trial of O.J. Simpson, it would have made sense for American to field a black lawyer in a Holmes County courtroom. So Edward Blackmon, a tall, dapper trial lawyer from Canton, a town about thirty miles south of Lexington, joined the defense.

As the pretrial phase of the case inched forward, both sides solidified the positions they would take on critical issues in the case. After more than a year of hemming and hawing, American finally abandoned the claim that Horton had been negligent in choosing to smoke, and in July 1987 asserted that he had assumed the risk of smoking (denying, in the same answer, "that it has been scientifically established that cigarette smoking causes lung cancer"). Horton's lawyers had been equally indecisive in settling on a response to the interrogatory posed by American, "Do you contend that plaintiff is addicted to cigarettes manufactured by American?" A June 1987 answer opened with a wisecrack:

> Plaintiff has died since this interrogatory was propounded so certainly is not presently "addicted." However, he has described in detail in his depositions how difficult it was for him to quit smoking and he was certainly "addicted" in that respect. However, the term "addicted" is Defendant's term propounded in the question and is not a term Plaintiff would have used to describe his sustained, prolonged use of Defendant's product.

Two months later Barrett amended that response, stating simply yes, Horton was addicted. But the plaintiffs made little effort to gather evidence or testimony on the subject, and it would be almost absent as an issue at trial.

This might seem odd to anyone familiar with cigarette litigation in the mid-1990s, where addiction came to be regarded among plaintiffs' lawyers as a kind of magic bullet that might finally pierce the tobacco industry's armor. But in 1987, Barrett later explained, plaintiffs' lawyers feared that the use of the term *addiction* could backfire. The concern was that it conjured up images of heroin and cocaine addicts, and that smokers on the jury (not to mention Judge Evans, who was a smoker) might take offense at the comparison. The science of addiction, moreover, is complex and far from conclusive. A tobacco company defendant could, for example, point to government statistics showing that about half of all long-term smokers are able to quit. One of the biggest repositories of scientific information on nicotine addiction was the tobacco industry itself, but it wasn't until the mid-nineties that the extent of that knowledge came to be known.

7

Even as they prepared for trial, American's lawyers worked to get rid of the case or postpone it. Citing the prolonged chancery court hearings involving individuals claiming to be Horton's heirs, Jim Upshaw filed a motion — the company's third — seeking to have the trial delayed until the heirship proceedings had concluded. Judge Evans denied that motion, holding firm the January 4, 1988, trial date. But in a separate decision, the judge handed American a tremendous victory: On September 1, 1987, he struck Horton's claim for strict liability and, in a reversal of his previous ruling, axed the risk-utility claim, as well.

Seven months earlier, the judge had effectively eliminated the express-warranty claim because Horton had stated that advertising had no bearing on his decision to smoke Pall Malls. Now he had gotten rid of the strict-liability tort claims. As for implied warranty — which he had yet to rule on — the judge made clear that to support such a cause of action, Horton's lawyers would have to show that Pall Mall cigarettes contained something beyond just tobacco, that an additive to, or adulteration of, the product was responsible for Horton's illness.

Barrett was devastated. This was supposed to have been a case about how smoking tobacco causes cancer, about how tobacco — which made up more than 90 percent of a cigarette's ingredients, and which was the substance that doctors and scientists the world over had implicated for its propensity to cause disease — had killed Nathan Horton. In a few single-page orders, Judge Gray had transformed the litigation. Now, if they got to trial at all, they would have to focus on some other substance in the cigarette. In short, Barrett seemed relegated to the position of Bryson Pillars in 1918: To win, he would have to find a toe in the tobacco.

And Barrett worried whether he had enough such evidence to get to trial. While the judge had ordered American to turn over a list of the additives in Pall Mall, there was no great body of scientific data linking these substances to specific disease, as there was for tobacco. Finding experts and reports to document these links would be costly, time-consuming, and possibly fruitless. If Barrett wasn't able to buttress this aspect of his case, he feared, the judge might not even let a jury hear the matter; he might end the whole lawsuit by entering a judgment for the defense. This was certainly not shaping up into the kind of case Don Davis had expected when Barrett lured him to Mississippi.

Judge Evans scheduled a hearing on the implied-warranty claim for the middle of September 1987. About a week before the hearing, Barrett's phone rang. A nervous-sounding man at the other end, who identified himself as "Jim Smith," told Barrett, "The Lord just told me to call you." The man, who had read newspaper accounts of the Horton case, and who had tracked Barrett down by calling the Lexington police department, said he had worked at American Tobacco's cigarette plant in Reidsville, North Carolina, and had seen a chemical sprayed on the tobacco. The chemical, the man said, came from containers marked with a skull and crossbones, and appeared to be highly dangerous to people. Barrett was aware that American sometimes sprayed portions of its factory with an insecticide called 2,2-dichlorovinyl dimethyl phosphate, or DDVP. During a deposition, a company official had even discussed the use of DDVP, but had claimed that it was never sprayed directly on tobacco. "Mr. Smith" was claiming otherwise.

Barrett got the jittery "Smith" to agree to a meeting at the Raleigh-Durham airport the next day. But when Barrett arrived, nobody approached him. "I was just sick to my stomach," Barrett recalls. The terminal was nearly empty, and Barrett had about lost hope when he noticed an older man standing in a corner, shielded by a potted plant. "I walked over and said, 'You're Jim Smith, aren't you?' " Barrett remembers, "and he looked at me with his pained look and said 'Yeah.' He said, 'I lost my nerve, I was fixin' to go home.' "

Actually, Barrett knew the man's real name, having persuaded him during his phone call to leave his telephone number. Barrett had then called a reverse-directory service and was told that the number belonged to a Fred Strader. At the airport Strader told Barrett that he was too afraid to go public with his information himself, but that a former coworker of his would be willing to talk. Strader took Barrett to meet Walter Dickerson, then fifty-nine, who had worked as a maintenance man at American Tobacco's plant in Reidsville for thirty-two years until retiring in 1979. When Barrett met him, he was at the Annie Penn Memorial Hospital in Reidsville, being treated for lung cancer. With a notary public accompanying him, Barrett sat at Dickerson's bedside and wrote out by hand an affidavit based on what Dickerson told him:

> I have personal knowledge that during third shift tobacco was regularly sprayed with chemicals at night. We were told that we were spraying to get rid of the bugs on the tobacco. . . . This chemical was sprayed on all tobacco used to make cigarettes in the plant. The tobacco which had been sprayed was not washed or otherwise cleaned to get the spray off after the spraying. The tobacco with the residue from the spray on it was made into cigarettes.

Although Dickerson didn't remember the name of the chemical, it was clear he was talking about DDVP, and he did offer some compelling testimony about its toxicity. He said workers who handled the product got monthly blood tests to monitor their exposure, and that a company official had told him it could damage his nervous system. "Where some of the chemical dripped on metal railings or concrete floors it would eat them up," Dickerson said. "I saw where it happened."

A few weeks later, still in his hospital bed, Dickerson gave a videotaped deposition. In addition to describing the spraying of DDVP, he also

mentioned, under questioning by Barrett, that the beetles and beetle lar-
vae killed by the spray remained in the tobacco that was made into cigarettes. Barrett also got Dickerson to describe seeing rats in tobacco
warehouses and how he once found a mouse tail in a cigarette at the plant.
(The machine the cigarette came from was disassembled, and the rest of
the mouse was found and removed.) A few months after his deposition,
Dickerson was dead.

Adopting a more high-tech approach, Don Davis, too, undertook a
crash effort to identify impurities. He enlisted the services of William
Longo, a Ph.D. in materials science and engineering in Gainesville,
Florida, who specialized in using an electron microscope to find and analyze inorganic fibers. Davis asked Longo to see whether any asbestos was
present in Pall Mall cigarettes. Longo sent his secretary to a 7-Eleven
store to buy a pack. He then took the paper and tobacco from a single cigarette and placed it in a small glass beaker, which in turn was placed in a
chamber for low-temperature plasma ashing: Longo removed air from the
chamber and pumped in pure oxygen. He then induced a radio frequency
around the chamber that caused the oxygen to become highly reactive —
glowing pink, like a neon light. The oxygen in this state caused the tobacco
to oxidize, forming a gaslike substance that was removed from the system.
What was left was a fine powder, or ash, made up of the inorganic product that was present in the cigarette. But when he examined the residue
under an electron microscope, at a magnification of 20,000 times, all
Longo could report was that he had found two "asbestos-like" fibers in
the sample Pall Mall.

It wasn't much — Davis asked Longo to do additional testing — but
for the time being, combined with Dickerson's statements about DDVP,
it was enough to persuade Judge Evans to keep Horton's implied-
warranty claim alive. Satisfied that the case was on a proper legal footing,
the judge let Barrett and Davis know that their case could proceed. "I'm
going to let you try your case," he told them at court hearings. Thus, even
with the requirement that the plaintiffs prove some contamination to
the tobacco, the judge was also going to let them present the same evidence they would have if the case had been about the dangers of tobacco
alone. The judge was attempting to steer a compromise course. Product-
liability law was rapidly evolving, and Judge Evans didn't think the

Mississippi Supreme Court had clearly stated what Mississippi law should be in that area. So once the Horton team came up with some evidence of contamination "that was strong enough to survive a motion," the judge later recalled, "then I thought I ought to let [them continue]. I knew the [state] Supreme Court was going to get a whack at it. . . . If the law is not clear and it is an important case — something that a lot rides on and a lot of future things ride on — the Supreme Court ought to be the one that decides it, not a trial judge."

With their near-death-of-lawsuit experience behind them, and the case moving into its final pretrial phase in the fall of 1987, Barrett and Davis gained renewed hope. Once they got to trial, they figured, they had an excellent chance of persuading a jury that there was something wrong with a product that had killed millions of people, including Nathan Horton, and that the maker of that product should be held responsible.

During the last few months of 1987, much of the legal maneuvering was devoted to determining which of the evidence gathered during discovery would be admitted at trial. A critical battleground involved the information American had gathered about Horton's character. As part of their assumption-of-risk defense, American's lawyers planned to paint Horton as a risk-taker in many aspects of his life. The idea was that this would buttress the contention that his choice to take up smoking was, like other activities in his life, made with an awareness that there *might* be adverse consequences. Combined with the rhetoric of "personal choice" and a flag-waving paean to freedom and the American way, the nobody-made-him-smoke defense had proved a winner for the tobacco industry in every case that had gone to trial.

But there was also a more cynical side to the assumption-of-risk defense. It offered a window through which a cigarette maker could — if permitted by the judge — parade before the jury many of the more unsavory aspects of the plaintiff's life and character. Jim Upshaw was relentless in his effort to try to present evidence of Horton's turbulent life, particularly his run-ins with the law. In a hearing on December 30, 1987, before Judge Evans, Upshaw even tried to portray Horton's bad behavior as heroic, his risk-taking transgressions as acts of independence that ought to be admired, not condemned:

> One of the things that we are intending to show in this case, as I say, was his lifestyle and . . . the fact that he was his "own man" and that no one told him what to do or the risk of any endeavor never deterred him, including the risk of smoking and the possibility of the . . . health hazards associated with it. He was not deterred by felony statutes or society's prohibition against violence. We need to show that — what type of man he was. He did what he wanted to do; he knew there were laws; he did it anyway.
>
> They put behavior and convictions in issue, may it please the Court, the plaintiffs did, by saying that he had no choice. . . . It is germane to our defense of this lawsuit. Who was Nathan Horton? What kind of guy was Nathan Horton? Was he cast from milk toast or was he on the other side of the spectrum, a super independent, strong-willed, determined, self-determining man who knew risk and voluntarily and knowingly exposed himself to the perils of those risks. . . .
>
> Nathan Horton was an extraordinary man. He was not the average ordinary guy you see walking out on the street. . . . He testified himself that when he knew something might not ought to be done . . . he said I'll sometimes go home and think about it overnight and make my mind up and do it come hell or high water, no matter what anybody else tells me to do. We've got to show what type of man Nathan Horton was and how can we show that, Judge, except over a period of time, from the time he was in the Navy and out and his lifestyle with the women he lived with . . . the gambling, the other offenses that he committed, the carrying concealed weapons, the violence that he visited upon others, the smoking pot, the several things that he did.

On another occasion Upshaw argued that it would be necessary for American to refer to the time Horton spent in the Illinois state penitentiary, because Horton had testified that he had cut back on smoking while in prison. This testimony, Upshaw argued, would help rebut the plaintiffs' addiction claims — even though addiction would barely figure in the plaintiffs' case. Another reason to mention Horton's time in prison was that he was exposed to paint fumes and insulation there, Upshaw argued. "American must have the opportunity to explore this evidence for its bearing on the possible origins of Mr. Horton's lung problems," Upshaw contended.

Judge Evans was not persuaded. While he wouldn't keep out all evidence of Horton's character and behavior, he issued a ruling on the spot barring the defendants from introducing evidence of Horton's criminal history and of his violent encounters with his ex-wives and others. It was December 30 — just five days before the scheduled start of the trial — and the judge was using the day to decide more than a dozen evidentiary motions of varying degrees of importance. Aware that their efforts to delve into the most intimate aspects of Horton's life might be used against them, American's lawyers asked that the plaintiffs be precluded from telling the jury about the discovery American conducted in this area. "If we were not going to be able to put [the evidence] on," Upshaw later explained, "then we didn't want the jury to be mad at us for conducting what we thought was legitimate discovery." The judge granted this request.

A series of motions filed by American's counsel sought to exclude virtually every form of scientific data linking smoking to disease. Surgeon Generals' reports, epidemiological studies and statistical theories, anecdotal and demographic data, and animal studies should all be kept out, the lawyers argued, because they failed to prove causation in an individual case, reached no conclusions about Pall Mall cigarettes in particular, might lead to impermissible speculation on causation by the jury, and — because the case hinged on tobacco additives — "reported no findings and reached no conclusions concerning . . . certain non-tobacco substances which the plaintiffs have belatedly alleged to be causal agents present in Pall Mall cigarettes."

If these motions were granted, Horton's case would be eviscerated. And the judge had told Barrett and Davis that he wasn't going to do that to them. "I'm going to let you try your case," he had told them. So these motions were all denied.

Part of the plaintiffs' case, of course, would be the videotaped deposition of Walter Dickerson. There was a problem, however: Dickerson, who was white, had used what years later, in the O.J. Simpson case, became known as "the N-word" in referring to another worker at American Tobacco's plant, and Barrett wanted the word deleted, "since the word 'nigger' is highly and unfairly prejudicial." The judge agreed.

Then there was the Nazi army problem. Months earlier, Horton's and American's lawyers had exchanged the names and qualifications of the expert witnesses they planned to call at trial. One of the plaintiffs' experts, a University of Arkansas pharmacology professor named Karl Heinz Ginzel, indicated on his résumé that he had received his high school diploma in Vienna, Austria, in 1939 and his M.D. there in 1948. Noticing this gap, Upshaw learned during Ginzel's deposition that he had served in the German army. Barrett wanted the judge to bar American from mentioning this, but Upshaw wanted the jury to hear it.

"Does this have anything whatsoever to do with Dr. Ginzel's qualifications as an expert?" the judge asked during his marathon evidentiary hearing.

"We're not trying to show he was a Nazi, or anything like that, Judge," Upshaw argued,

> but we think it's important. . . . Dr. Ginzel didn't seem to be ashamed at all that he served in the German army, and frankly, apparently he served in a unit that was wiped out. He's one of the few that survived his unit, apparently, on the Russian front or whatever. As a matter of fact, I don't have anything against even a Nazi that's fighting a Russian, but anyway, I don't see that that speaks too badly for Dr. Ginzel, but it is a part of who Dr. Ginzel is.

Judge Evans cut him off — about the only way to get Upshaw to stop talking. The defendants "shall not attempt to put information regarding Dr. Ginzel's military service with the German army from 1939 through 1942 in evidence," he ruled.

With these rulings, Judge Evans set the stage for trial. After liberal discovery, each side knew what the other had in the way of evidence. And the judge's rulings put each side on notice about what kind of evidence would be admitted. A trial, after all, was meant to be an open and orderly presentation of facts, not a forum for surprise attacks. Despite this advance preparation, the Horton case would contain more surprises than anyone could have predicted.

8

Christmas 1987 did not offer much of a holiday to those involved in the Horton case, coming, as it did, just as the final pretrial motions, briefs, and hearings were reaching a crescendo. New Year's similarly gave little reprieve. Tom Bezanson, who along with a coterie of other Chadbourne lawyers and support staff had moved to Mississippi as final preparations for the trial got under way, called his wife from Jim Upshaw's office on New Year's Eve.

For the tiny town of Lexington, Mississippi, the dawning of 1988 brought with it an aura of excitement and anticipation. A Holmes County man and his Holmes County lawyer had roped a major national corporation and hauled it to trial before a Holmes County judge. Now they would ask a Holmes County jury for $17 million. It was a vast sum anywhere. In rural Mississippi it was unfathomable.

An event a day or two before the trial opened made it clear that it would be anything but an ordinary proceeding: Copies of the 1963 *New York Times Magazine* article in which Don Barrett had made disparaging remarks about blacks mysteriously appeared in various places around the county. To this day, no one has taken credit for the effort to remind area residents of Barrett's segregationist past.

Even without incidents like this, it was obvious that Lexington was about to earn its fifteen minutes of fame. Journalists from newspapers around the country descended on the town. TV vans were parked near the courthouse, while their reporters roamed the square. It was only thanks to a motion by Jim Upshaw, granted by Judge Evans, that their cameras were barred from the courtroom.

Why all this attention when roughly 114 other tobacco liability suits were pending around the country? Because the Horton case had actually made it to trial, and, for all the delays, had done so quickly, given the general pace of civil litigation. Another closely watched suit, the Rose Cipollone case in New Jersey, had been filed in 1983 — three years before *Horton* — but would not come to trial until February 1988. Only a handful of those 114 other cases would ever get to trial; the vast majority would drop away owing to neglect, lack of financial resources, or tobacco industry victories in the pretrial phase.

The particulars of the Horton case also piqued the media's interest. For starters, there was the novelty of a suit brought on behalf of a black cancer victim going before a black jury in a poor rural county; that alone did not bode well for American. Then there was Mississippi law to consider. In Mississippi state court, a plaintiff could win by persuading just nine of the twelve jurors, rather than all twelve as required in federal court. Mississippi was also the first state to enact what was known as a *pure comparative fault* law. In many other states a jury that weighs the fault of each party could not find for a plaintiff if it found him more than 50 percent responsible for his injuries. In Mississippi, though, a jury could find the plaintiff 99 percent responsible, but, based on the defendant's 1 percent fault, could still award major damages.

American's lawyers argued strenuously to keep comparative fault out of the case; they had dropped it as a defense, they pointed out, in favor of assumption of risk. So it was the plaintiffs who were asking that the jury be allowed to apply the doctrine, on the bet that jurors would hold Horton at least partly responsible for smoking. The judge agreed to let the plaintiffs argue comparative fault, subject to a final ruling on the issue at the end of the trial, before instructing the jury. Morton Mintz, a veteran

Washington Post reporter who had covered tobacco for a number of years and was attending the Horton trial, saw that as a critical victory for the plaintiffs. "How can [the jury] find the company zero percent at fault?" he asked at the time.

Journalists were not the only out-of-towners attending the Horton trial en masse. Stock analysts at Wall Street investment firms were also monitoring the trial closely. A win or loss for American would affect prices for all tobacco company stocks, since investors looked to the result in a single trial as an indicator of future trends. Although the tobacco industry was hugely profitable, the mere *specter* of a litigation calamity exerted a depressive effect on tobacco stock prices. A loss for American would magnify that downward pressure by inspiring other plaintiffs' lawyers around the country to take on the industry. A win would not remove the litigation cloud, but would likely lift stock prices as investors determined the ramparts remained secure.

Salomon Brothers, one of Wall Street's largest trading houses, sent Joseph Longinotti to observe the trial. At thirty-four, Longinotti was a latecomer to the securities industry. A one-time lawyer for the Internal Revenue Service, the native New Yorker had decided on a career change and entered a training program to become a stock trader at Salomon in the fall of 1987. His timing was not propitious, since on October 19 of that year the market suffered one of its biggest single-day drops in history, and jobs all over Wall Street suddenly evaporated. Although Longinotti continued with the training program, he was told that it was not likely there would be a position for him at the end. But he did have a law degree, and when he returned from his New Year's holiday on January 4, 1988, a Monday, Salomon asked him if he could get to Mississippi — fast — to monitor *Horton*. Why not? Longinotti decided.

That same day, court convened in Lexington to tend to the first order of business for the trial: picking a jury. It was chilly outside, much colder than usual for that part of the country, but the heating system in the old courthouse overcompensated, so it was hot and stuffy as ninety potential jurors assembled for the selection process.

"Ladies and gentlemen," Judge Evans greeted them,

you have been summoned here to hear one case. I am sure most of you by this time know what that case is. . . . It is a great and very important job that you have been asked to do. You are asked to do this almost without any compensation. . . . Unfortunately, the legislature of the State of Mississippi has not seen fit to raise the juror's pay to that which is reasonable, and I will announce to you now that for your services you will get fifteen dollars a day, so you see it is a civic duty that you do rather than something for which you receive just compensation; and in a democracy, all people have to give something to get something back to make it all work.

To be qualified for jury service in Holmes County, the judge explained, they had to be at least twenty-one years old, able to read and write, and either a property owner or a registered voter. More quaintly, he told them: "You must have never been convicted of an infamous crime or the unlawful sale of intoxicating liquor within the past five years. You must neither be a habitual drunkard nor a common gambler. Any of you who are disqualified for any of these reasons, we will take that up at this time."

Seven members of the jury pool indicated they could not read or write, and the judge dismissed them. A number of others left when the judge said that anyone sixty-five or older had the option of claiming an exemption. The judge also released those who claimed hardship: a woman who had to give her disabled husband insulin shots, for example, and a self-employed cosmetologist who said she couldn't afford to close her shop for the projected four- to six-week duration of the trial.

No one knew more about the individuals in the jury pool than American's lawyers. Ninety days before the start of the trial, the names of the prospective jurors were released to both sides, and American hired local citizens to help them gather every bit of information they could on members of the pool. With Jim Upshaw and Edward Blackmon overseeing their efforts, these "jury consultants" tried to scope out prospective jurors' smoking habits, health history, employment, education, involvement in previous litigation, ties to Nathan Horton or Don Barrett, church attendance, and anything else that might be helpful in evaluating whether they would be likely to be sympathetic to the tobacco company.

So by the time jury selection began, there was little Upshaw didn't already know about the individuals in the room. Indeed, he took it upon himself to volunteer some information. Approaching the bench and signaling Barrett to join him, Upshaw said: "We have information that we have got an eighty-seven-year-old and an eighty-three-year-old and a seventy-eight-year-old [prospective] juror. They are going to have a hell of a time sitting here for a month to six weeks."

"Well, probably we'll just handle that quietly," Judge Evans replied.

"We also have . . . information that you've got three N.C.M.s [people who had been adjudicated non compos mentis — mentally incompetent] on the jury [panel]." The judge promised to look into that, too.

Even as Upshaw maneuvered to get his client the best possible jury, he continued to look for ways to delay the case. An opportunity presented itself in the form of a segment on the CBS News show *60 Minutes* titled "Tobacco on Trial" that had aired the previous night, January 3, 1988. During a mid-morning break in jury selection, Upshaw moved to have the trial delayed "until such time as we can be sure that the inflammatory and highly unfair and prejudicial damage that has been caused by the program has lessened by the passage of time." The segment, reported by Mike Wallace, had led with the Horton case, then cut to some cigarette suits in New Jersey, and then returned to *Horton*, specifically to videotaped images of a wasted Nathan Horton in his last deposition. It was understandable that Upshaw was upset. The tone of the piece was relentlessly antitobacco, and it highlighted the aggressive and prying tactics used by industry lawyers in investigating a plaintiff's life. The piece "amounts to nothing less than an outright character assassination, not only of the industry, but of our company and of the attorneys," Upshaw indignantly told Judge Evans. "It makes it appear that the tobacco company and its lawyers have set out to inappropriately dredge up irrelevant information from the past about a man, Mr. Horton, who was weak and down."

Upshaw saw an opportunity to do more than just ask for a delay. He argued:

Now that the jury has been primed and preconditioned by Mr.
Wallace, *60 Minutes*, CBS, to think that the defendants have conducted

an extensive discovery investigation in an effort to beat the plaintiff into submission [by] questions about illegitimate children, venereal diseases and failed businesses [mentioned by Wallace as questions asked of Horton], fairness demands that we be allowed to introduce evidence of Mr. Horton's prior convictions for armed robbery and burglary and his physical violence visited upon his wives and other people.

This in a trial that was supposed to be about whether a company should be held responsible for its product causing a man's illness and death. Upshaw's disingenuousness knew no bounds. "We must be allowed to show Mr. Horton the way he was," he implored, "not only for the relevance to his risk-taking, but also to his credibility, which has been heightened and highlighted and brought to the forefront by the *60 Minutes* program."

Barrett could not get a word in edgewise, but he didn't need to. The judge overruled Upshaw's motion.

It was not even lunchtime on the first day of the trial, and already it was clear that Upshaw would be a domineering presence in the courtroom. He let nothing go; his style was to harass and bully his opposition — and sometimes the judge — into submission, aided in the process by a booming voice and large physique. Even when he didn't prevail, his tactics were often effective, rattling witnesses, disrupting opposing counsel's rhythm, and, when the jury was present, getting his point across to them anyway.

Judge Evans had barely resumed questioning prospective jurors, and was in the midst of asking one about his contacts with the Horton family, when Upshaw cut in.

UPSHAW: I suggest Mr. Barrett quit signaling to him, your honor.

BARRETT: I beg your pardon?

UPSHAW: I'm looking right at you, Don.

BARRETT: Well —

UPSHAW: I object to that, may it please the court.

JUDGE EVANS: Let the record show don't anybody signal or anything.

BARRETT: I'm certainly not signaling anybody about anything.
JUDGE EVANS: I understand, Mr. Barrett. I was not aware of
anything that took place.

After the judge's initial filtering of the jury pool, reducing the number of prospective jurors to thirty-seven, it was the lawyers' turn to ask
questions, in a process known as voir dire (pronounced vwah-DEER in
most of the United States, but vor-DYRE in the South). Barrett was not
ten sentences into his voir dire when Upshaw made the first of what would
be a series of increasingly agitated objections. The purpose of voir dire is
to allow attorneys on each side to quiz prospective jurors to ascertain attitudes, biases, or proclivities that might shape their views of the case. It is
meant to be an aid in the selection of the jurors — as well as the alternates — who will actually hear the case. But Upshaw objected that
Barrett's voir dire sounded more like an opening argument, and he was
right. To an extent, that is something trial lawyers do all the time, but
Barrett was less subtle than most.

At one point he said: "If you sit on this case, you will see that our evidence is going to establish, and you'll be surprised to learn, that Pall Mall
cigarettes are not what you think they are. Our evidence is going to show
that a Pall Mall cigarette is not what it looks like. It's not good pure tobacco
in a white paper, pure wrapping." Later, he hit the issue of causation:
"Did Pall Mall cause or contribute to Nathan's cancer or his emphysema
is a critically important point. That's — we have the burden of proving
that. Exactly how cigarettes cause cancer is a different question and we do
not have that burden of proof." By way of explanation, he noted, "Two
hundred years ago nobody really understood the biological mechanism of
the miracle of birth, but that don't mean that people didn't know how to
make babies."

Occasionally Barrett asked the prospective jurors a question, such as
"Are you willing to listen to our evidence . . . before you make up your
mind in this case?" or "Can each of you accept that preponderance of the
evidence, the burden [of proof] that we have?" but it was largely a cha-
rade, and Upshaw knew that:

UPSHAW: May it please the court, we object again. He's misstating the law again.

BARRETT: I am certainly not misstating the law.

UPSHAW: Well, the court knows you are.

JUDGE EVANS: Well, step up and let's talk about it.

UPSHAW: He's commenting on the weight of the evidence and every-thing else. . . . Furthermore, he's asking jurors to promise him things.

BARRETT: I've heard him do it for thirty years, Judge.

UPSHAW: I know it, but I've been wrong when I did it every time, too.

When Barrett finished, Upshaw moved for a mistrial, which the judge denied.

During his own voir dire, Upshaw did ask questions that seemed cal-culated to help in the selection of jurors. For one thing, they required actual answers. He wanted to know, for example, how many of the prospective jurors knew somebody who smoked and got lung cancer, and how many would elect to sit in the no-smoking section of an airplane or restaurant. But that was hardly the extent of it. Upshaw, too, used the opportunity to preview key arguments, posing them as questions:

Do all of you agree that if [a] person, an American citizen who does make that choice [to smoke] . . . that he should be responsible for the consequences of his act or for his personal choice? Do you believe in personal accountability or responsibility, you know, like we Baptists believe that everyone when you get up, they open the Good Book on you, you are going to be accountable for what you've done?

The court reporter indicated that "all jurors responded affirmatively" and Upshaw continued:

Is there anyone here that does not understand, and I know you do understand this, but that cigarettes are a legal product? You don't have to go buy them under a bridge or under a culvert like you do marijuana or heroin or crack or something. They are a legal product sold in every state in the United States. Do all of you understand that?

All jurors responded affirmatively.

Do any of you believe that it has been absolutely proven and that there's no doubt about it in the scientific community that smoking causes lung cancer? . . . Or do all of you understand that there's still a raging controversy about what causes lung cancer?

All jurors responded affirmatively.

In addition to getting points across about the substance of his case, Upshaw used voir dire to advance another purpose as well: to establish a personal connection between his client and the prospective jurors. "We are the American Tobacco Company out of Oak Grove, Virginia, and Reidsville, North Carolina," he told them, naming the two small Southern towns where American had its research and development facility and its plant — not Stamford, Connecticut, site of the executive offices. And he expressed concern for the jurors' personal comfort, letting them know that if, because of a bladder problem or some other reason, they needed to go to the bathroom frequently, they could tell the judge. "Frankly, I have to do that myself quite frequently," he said. "When you get up to my age you begin to have a little prostate problem and whatever, you have to do things like that, so I don't mind confessing that." On other occasions during the trial, Upshaw made personal references to his own life. "We are human beings, too" seemed to be the message he wanted to convey.

The questioning and speechifying continued after the lunch break, as the lawyers steadily winnowed the candidates. In the late afternoon, Upshaw reported that one of the remaining women had a bottle of whiskey in her purse. "She will be drunk by tomorrow," he said. Judge Evans thought she seemed drunk already, and dismissed her after confirming with the sheriff that she was a "habitual drunkard."

By the end of the day, the jury had been selected. There were no surprises. Eleven of the twelve jurors were black, as were all four alternates. Nine of the jurors were women. Three smoked. None had more than a high school education.

After the jurors were sworn to an oath by the court clerk, the judge said, "Thank y'all very much. You are released for the day."

They returned to work the next morning at 8:30. It was still wintry cold outside; inside, it was insufferably hot. The courtroom was on the second floor, up a steep flight of stairs. It was the largest space in the courthouse, but had once been even larger. Alterations in 1976 added jury rooms and other offices along the east and west sides of the courtroom, which meant it no longer had any windows. Still, it was an ample space, and the renovations had not eliminated the original pressed metal ceiling or a decorative wooden spindlework screen mounted on the wall over the judge's bench. As lawyers and spectators faced the bench, jurors sat to their right, in heavy wooden chairs.

Don Barrett's opening statement, not surprisingly, echoed much of his voir dire, though with even more advocacy, as the law, in this setting, gave him some leeway to do. At the outset, he announced that his side conceded that Horton had been "to some extent negligent" for smoking. "So we accept our share of the responsibility and we will ask the jury at the end of this trial to reduce the actual damages of whatever you award . . . by the percentage that you think Nathan Horton bears responsibility." Upshaw had already objected to the plaintiffs' bringing comparative fault into the case and, at least temporarily, had lost, so he sat quietly as Barrett continued:

> We are going to prove to you what Nathan Horton had no way of knowing. A Pall Mall cigarette is an adulterated, contaminated bunch of junk. We are going to prove to you that the American Tobacco Company has, for many, many years, knowingly dumped into its Pall Mall cigarettes all kinds of chemicals, pesticides, and poisonous additives.

This case, Barrett argued, was no different from any other product-liability suit:

> If somebody gets sick from drinking a Coca-Cola that's got a mouse in it, Coca-Cola has to pay for the damages. . . . Every industry does

that in the United States, and it's the American law and the American way of just basic, basic justice that a company should pay fair compensation for an injury caused by its product.

A mouse in a Coke bottle, a toe in a package of tobacco: Barrett was going to make sure this case looked like it was about impurities, even though many of the witnesses would not limit their testimony to that subject. They would talk about the harm *cigarettes* caused, the compounds in cigarette smoke that caused disease, and tobacco would be what was really on trial.

Barrett split the opening statement with Fred Clark. Clark's role in the trial would be minimal, but, as the sole black lawyer on the Horton team, his presence was critical. Clark had the role of introducing the jurors to Nathan Horton, summarizing his life history. That required some delicacy and some preemptive disclosure. "We would not for one minute stand here and tell you that Nathan Horton led a perfect life or that he was a perfect man," Clark told the jurors. "Like most of us, Nathan Horton fell short of the grace of God. . . . Nathan drank a little, he gambled a little, and he ran around some, but he was still a good man." Then Clark added, "We anticipate that the tobacco company in this case will try to defend this lawsuit by personally attacking Nathan Henry Horton now that he is no longer here to defend himself."

When Clark was done, Upshaw moved for a mistrial. He was furious not only about Clark's claim that American would be attacking Horton, but about numerous aspects of Barrett's statement. "He repeatedly argued his case, instead of making an opening statement," Upshaw complained (something lawyers do so frequently, in fact, that their initial summary of the case is often called an "opening argument").

"The motion will be overruled," Judge Evans decreed.

"Our proof is going to show that Mr. Horton made a personal choice to smoke," Upshaw told the jury in his opening statement. "Now the proof will show that Mr. Horton clearly knew all of the risks or the risk associated with smoking cigarettes, even before he started scratching Prince Albert out of his daddy's can at the age of about thirteen or fourteen. Most of you on the jury probably did the same thing. I did the same thing." Under the doctrine of assumption of risk, he told them, that meant that "he alone should be held responsible for the results of his decision, of his free, personal, knowing, and voluntary decision."

And precisely what risk was it that he so knowingly assumed as a young teenager around 1950? Upshaw told the jury that experts for the defense would testify that cancer "is a poorly understood disease and there are many things about cancer we do not know. . . . If there are not many things about it that we don't know, then why are we spending so many billions of dollars a year on research attempting to determine the root causes of cancer?" Research institutions everywhere, he said, were "attempting to prove the causes of cancer; and our proof will show they haven't done it yet."

If Upshaw had his way, this would be a trial about a person, not a product. "Who was Nathan Henry Horton?" he asked the jury.

Who was he? Mr. Clark told you who he was. Well, now I am going to tell you a few things that our proof is going to show who he was. . . . Number one, what will pervade our proof and the plaintiffs' proof, it will permeate it throughout this lawsuit, it will be like a white thread running through a red blanket, it will be very clear, is that Nathan Henry Horton was a strong-willed, determined, strong-minded man, and you will learn throughout this lawsuit that no one told Mr. Horton what to do or what not to do. . . .

He was a strong man. Frankly, most of us admire that type of person. We also, most of us, our proof is going to show, believe that that type of person is responsible for his decisions; but our proof is going to show that when a decision was to be made to smoke, he made it. To quit or not quit, he made it. . . . No one, absolutely no one, including the two or three wives that he had, the girlfriends over the years that he had, the children that he had, no one, his doctors or anyone . . . told him what to be, where to live, where to work, what to do or what not to do. Nathan Horton was what we call his own man, and was in fact a man among men. He was not a pansy waist [sic] little weak guy that the plaintiffs would have you believe that couldn't do what he wanted to do.

As he had in pretrial motions, Upshaw pursued the dual tack of building Horton up so he could tear him down. Horton, he told the jurors, was the best football player on the team. He joined the Navy at a time when most blacks joined the Army. He worked in Holmes County as a self-employed contractor. "Throughout his life, he did lots of things that involved risks because he did things his own way," Upshaw said.

> For example, he did enjoy gambling. Mr. Clark told you that. He enjoyed it; he did it. . . . Frankly, and not that this has anything what-soever, and we're not trying to character assassinate him, but he occa-sionally wanted to smoke a marijuana cigarette, but we're not saying marijuana had anything whatsoever to do with his problems. But . . . the fact that he wanted to smoke a joint or whatever you wanted to call it, a marijuana cigarette, every now and then, he did it. He did whatever he wanted to do. . . . On occasion he even risked his marriages by doing exactly what he wanted to do. As a matter of fact, two or three of his marriages ended up in divorce. He did exactly what he wanted to do and it just didn't work out. There is nothing wrong with that. I've been divorced. What I'm saying is — and frankly, the reason I am, because I personally chose to do something I wanted to do and my wife divorced me. I mean I'm not bad-mouthing Nathan Henry Horton for doing exactly what he wanted to do. He was a strong-willed man, but he did what he wanted to do.

Finally, Upshaw tried to defuse the Horton team's efforts to introduce comparative negligence into the case:

> Our proof is that no one, no one, including the Horton family, has the right to blame Nathan Henry Horton for the choices that he freely made in his lifetime, and he didn't blame himself. . . . You are not going to hear us saying he was negligent. There is no balance to be struck, there is no blame to lay on Mr. Horton. He did what he wanted to do. . . . He, as all of us, our position is, is responsible for the choices he made.

At times even the participants in the trial seemed to forget that there was a second defendant in the case: the New Deal Tobacco and Candy Company. During one conference in the judge's chambers, as Upshaw,

Barrett, Don Davis, and Judge Evans were hashing out a matter relating to a witness, New Deal's attorney, Calvin King, interjected a comment. It was greeted with a round of ribbing:

> UPSHAW: Calvin, did you ask Don [if] you could speak?
>
> JUDGE EVANS: We forgot Mr. King here. Mr. King, you can pipe in anytime you want to. You represent a party here. . . .
>
> KING: Yes sir.
>
> BARRETT: Calvin reminds [me] of what [someone] said about Hubert Humphrey, that he is a modest man and [has] much to be modest about.

Of course, King — with his client's legal expenses entirely under-written by American — had set the stage for his near invisibility with his opening statement. He told the jury: "I have nothing whatsoever on behalf of New Deal that I can add to what Mr. Upshaw has said except this: New Deal adopts one hundred percent, totally, the defenses of the American Tobacco Company, both in letter and spirit, and that is nobody made him do it."

That ended the first day of the trial.

9

Joseph Longinotti, the trial observer for Salomon Brothers, made it to Lexington in time for the opening statements. Indeed, he had gotten to the courthouse early on the morning the statements began, and held the door open in a chilly rain for Don Barrett, who was lugging a box of files from his office. Introducing himself, Longinotti got a perplexing response. "Longinotti," Barrett said. "That's a good ol' Southern name." A few days later Longinotti met Barrett's father, Pat Sr. And the elder Barrett also remarked on his good ol' Southern name. At this point, Longinotti felt compelled to ask about the nature of the joke. It was no joke at all. Pat Sr. explained that the family of Louis Longinotti had been prominent bankers and merchants for decades in the neighboring town of Durant. Louis's widow, it turned out, was still alive, and when Joe Longinotti went to visit her he learned that a branch of his family had come to Mississippi decades earlier via New Orleans.

Even with a relative in Holmes County, Longinotti found the transition from the streets of New York to the Lexington town square jolting. But over time, he became friendly with a number of locals, who welcomed him into their homes for meals. The Barretts even gave him a desk and phone in the basement of their law office, which proved a lifesaver for Longinotti. He and others had come equipped with cellular phones, only to find that cellular service had not reached rural Mississippi in early 1988. The courthouse had no pay phones, and a lone, somewhat erratic pay phone stood outside in the square. That was not good enough for those who needed to feed their employers reports of breaking developments at the trial.

For their first witness, the Horton team announced that they would play the videotaped deposition of Walter Dickerson. Before the tape was played, though, Jim Upshaw made a motion. Barrett had erased the word *nigger* from Dickerson's testimony. It would be better, Upshaw argued, to keep the word in and then bleep it, so it was clear that the man had said something that the court had ruled out. Plainly Upshaw thought that if he could call attention to the deletion with an audible signal, jurors might take notice and figure out what had been said; otherwise it might slip past them. The judge denied Upshaw's request.

Watching on a TV monitor, jurors saw Dickerson, pale as his hospital bed linen, talk about the "poison" sprayed on the tobacco and the worms that were left behind. Dickerson blamed his exposure to the DDVP for his partial loss of sight in one eye. On cross-examination — also on the videotape — Upshaw suggested that Dickerson's failure to collect for his eye injury in a worker's compensation hearing had embittered him toward American Tobacco and was the reason for his testimony.

The Horton team's next witness was Preston Leake, American Tobacco's director of research and development and chairman of the company's quality assurance committee. Leake was actually present in the courtroom — American had designated him to be the company's in-person corporate representative, a way of humanizing the company and of demonstrating that it took the case seriously. He was in attendance every day of the trial, but the Horton lawyers elected to show the jury video-taped excerpts from two depositions. In the first, taken in May 1987, Leake said American did use DDVP in tobacco storage areas to control cigarette beetles, but said the insecticide "probably does not" get on the tobacco.

Seven months later, following Dickerson's surprise appearance and testimony, Barrett had deposed Leake again. Armed with new company documents on DDVP, requested following Dickerson's deposition, Barrett asked Leake once again about the exposure of tobacco to the pesticide. Leake acknowledged that in the 1970s the company had looked into the possibility that DDVP residue might be getting onto Pall Mall Gold, Pall Mall Filter Kings, and Carlton cigarettes — all filtered brands — that were stored in an "overhead-style conveyor and reservoir," referred to by its acronym, OSCAR. But then Barrett made the fatal error of asking one question too many. Was there anything different, he wanted to know, about the exposure of these filtered brands to DDVP and the exposure of unfiltered Pall Mall regulars — Horton's brand. "Yeah," Leake replied, "Pall Mall regular were never stored in an OSCAR."

Altogether, the DDVP testimony produced a weak and ineffectual opening for the Horton team. Don Davis finally moved off the subject and asked Leake, "Is there any ingredient or material in Pall Malls which causes or contributes to cause lung cancer?" Leake replied, "I don't believe there is anything in the smoke from Pall Mall cigarettes, fresh, whole smoke, that the smoker would normally receive in smoking a cigarette which would cause an adverse effect." The phrase "fresh, whole smoke" proved to be something of a mantra for American's witnesses denying the ill effects of smoking, as though saying it that way somehow made it so.

The plaintiffs' job, of course, was to prove that this was not so, and finally, with the calling of their first live witness, they set about in earnest to make the medical and scientific case against smoking. Karl Heinz Ginzel took the stand on the morning of the third day of trial. The sixty-six-year-old, German-accented pharmacology professor from the University of Arkansas had done extensive research on lung toxicology, with a focus on the effects of smoke particulate matter on lung tissue. He was appearing — without charge to the Horton team — as an expert witness on the subject.

Under questioning by Don Davis, Ginzel offered the jury a primer on smoking and health. In 1915, he noted, Americans consumed about 14 billion cigarettes. After World War I, that number began a steep and steady increase, reaching 600 billion a year by the 1980s. Paralleling that rise, but lagging by about twenty years, was an increase in annual deaths from lung cancer, the delay resulting from the fact that it takes about two decades of exposure to cigarette carcinogens for healthy cells to become cancerous.

With Davis presenting him study after study, Ginzel explained that the more a person smokes, the greater his chances are of getting cancer. And people who start in their teens, he said, are especially at risk: Not only will they end up smoking more cigarettes over their lifetime than someone who starts at a later age, they are in many cases still growing, and growing tissue is particularly vulnerable to carcinogens.

Davis next moved into an exploration of what it was in cigarettes that caused cancer. The World Health Organization, Ginzel noted, had classified tobacco smoke itself as a human carcinogen. But tobacco smoke is made up of roughly four thousand chemicals, and Ginzel ticked off a scary-sounding list of multisyllabic mutagens that pass into smokers' lungs. The American Conference of Industrial and Hygienic Scientists, Ginzel said, had declared that humans should have no exposure by any route — respiratory, oral, or cutaneous — to two carcinogens, 4-aminobiphenyl and 2-naphthylamine, and yet they are both contained in cigarette smoke. Benzene, vinyl chloride, arsenic, and chromium — all human carcinogens, all in cigarette smoke, Ginzel testified. Nicotine, Ginzel said, presented a dual threat to smokers: In addition to hooking them on cigarettes, it also got transformed into nitrosamines, which Ginzel described as "very effective, very potent carcinogens."

Nicotine, Ginzel pointed out, is a "strong poison" and was once used as an agricultural pesticide. Indeed, the U.S. Occupational Safety and Health Administration had set workplace exposure limits of 80 parts per billion. But the smoke of one cigarette contains anywhere from 430,000 to 1,080,000 parts per billion. Similarly, cigarette smoke contains between 24,900 and 57,300 parts per million of carbon monoxide, while the OSHA limit is 50. All told, Ginzel said, the concentration of particles in cigarette smoke is up to 10,000 times greater than that found in the air around a freeway at rush hour.

"Dr. Ginzel," Davis asked, "why can cigarette smoke have concentrations in excess of what is allowed by OSHA for regulating exposures in the workplace?"

"Because OSHA does not regulate cigarettes," Ginzel explained.

"Are cigarettes under the Food and Drug Administration?" Davis asked.

"Cigarettes are excepted from regulation by the Food and Drug Administration," Ginzel said.

> Further, nicotine is a drug of dependence but is not listed under the Controlled Substances Act, which controls all other drugs of dependence. Nicotine is excepted from [the federal Toxic Substances Control Act]. Nicotine is not regulated by OSHA, not regulated by the [Environmental Protection Agency], it is not regulated by the Consumer Product Safety Commission.

"Is there any agency of the government that you're aware of that regulates the amounts of exposures or concentrations in cigarettes?" Davis queried.

"No, none."

"Do you know of any agency in the United States that regulates what companies put into their tobacco?"

"No, I am not aware of that."

Ginzel had just explained one of the most astounding facts about the cigarette: Despite being a product that was absorbed directly into the bloodstream, that altered people's moods, that created dependency in many of its users, and that had cut a swath of illness and death through the populace, it was utterly unregulated by any government agency charged with protecting the health and safety of American citizens.

Davis closed out his questioning of Ginzel by walking through some calculations: Figuring 10 puffs per Pall Mall cigarette times 40 cigarettes (two packs) a day times 30 years of smoking (it was actually 35, but it's easier to multiply by 30), Davis noted that Horton received 4,380,000 "doses of carcinogen into the lungs."

"Doctor," he asked, "from a medical standpoint do you have an opinion, based on a reasonable medical probability, as to whether or not that amount of doses of carcinogens from Pall Mall cigarettes will cause carcinogenic lung cancer?"

"It is definitely my opinion that this is sufficient to produce cancer," Ginzel said.

Ed Blackmon cross-examined Ginzel, but accomplished little. He established that Ginzel had once been a smoker himself and had quit without medical intervention. Ginzel, however, noted that he'd had an intervention of a different sort. "My daughter destroyed my cigarettes and I was very thankful to her when she was a child," he said.

Blackmon, unwittingly heading down a blind alley, asked Ginzel if he used fertilizers in his garden. Ginzel said he used only horse manure and Blackmon asked, "What do you find in horse fertilizer, Doctor? . . . Tell me the chemical makeup of horse manure."

"I couldn't tell you the chemical makeup, I'm sure," Ginzel said.

Blackmon pressed on: "It would depend on what the horse ate, wouldn't it? Huh? Wouldn't it? Am I right, Doctor?"

"I'm sure it would," Ginzel replied, clearly confused by the direction of the questioning.

"Let's just suppose," Blackmon persisted, "that your horse wandered off in somebody's field, garden, where they put out some fertilizer containing nitrosamines, and all those other things you've mentioned . . ."

"Yeah," said Ginzel, finally catching Blackmon's drift. "*Nitrosamines* are not in horse manure, are not in fertilizers. *Nitrates* are in fertilizers."

"Nitrates, Doctor. You know I am a layman on this, Doctor, and you correct me." Nitrates had nothing whatsoever to do with the case, and Blackmon moved on.

On several occasions during the trial, Judge Evans had to caution jurors to stay alert. For the press, though, the trial was of interest simply because it was happening at all, and, of course, because the end offered a potential bombshell: a verdict against a cigarette maker.

The tenor of the press coverage prior to and during the trial was decidedly pro-plaintiff, a situation fed partly by the sympathies of the reporters, and partly by the fact that it was the Horton lawyers and their allies who provided the quote-hungry throng with a steady stream of commentary. For example, Richard Daynard, the antitobacco activist from Northeastern University law school, flew into town for a few days to observe the trial, and afterward offered reporters his analysis of events. By contrast, the American team maintained a strict no–comment policy. As much as possible, Jim Upshaw explained later, he wanted the jury to regard this as "just another trial," while his opponents "were trying to make it a national media event."

But even the Horton lawyers had to agree that with the trial barely begun, the press was out of control. Every time there was a break in the proceedings, photographers rushed into the courtroom, shoving cameras, boom microphones, and bright lights in participants' faces. Once they inadvertently pulled the cord on the court reporter's stenography equipment. On another occasion Don Davis had trouble getting to a bench conference because he was surrounded by reporters. During a break in Ginzel's testimony, Davis and Barrett joined Upshaw in asking the judge for some relief from the unruliness. Upshaw pleaded: "I don't mind them reporting that this big, important, nationally important trial is going on here . . . let them take our pictures going to and coming from [the courtroom], let them get their recorders out in the hall, let them interview each other like they do every afternoon, I don't care, just leave us alone in the courtroom." The judge admonished the media to do just that.

For the rest of the week, though, nobody would have to worry about the press. A winter storm blew into the region, canceling court sessions on Thursday and Friday. Temperatures in Holmes County plummeted into the twenties. Snow and freezing rain fell, making travel treacherous. By Monday, the weather had moderated, and the trial resumed.

For the citizens of Holmes County, the proceedings were the hottest ticket in town, and the courtroom was packed with area residents taking in the show. One day Joe Longinotti, the observer for Salomon Brothers, leaned over to a farmer-looking type next to him and pointed to two attractive young women in the audience. "Who are they?" he wanted to know. "They're Hookers," the man replied. Not surprisingly, Longinotti was taken aback. But he soon learned that the Hookers had been a prominent family in Holmes County for generations. Indeed, there were other Hookers in the crowd. As the trial had been getting under way, Bootsy Hooker, a cotton farmer from north of town, had come into Lexington and been buttonholed by a stock analyst, who asked if he knew any paralegals who could take notes on the trial. Why, sure, Bootsy replied; he immediately called his wife Pam and told her to put on nice clothes and come into town. Pam, who had not a whit of paralegal experience, soon ended up reporting on trial developments for two or three members of the Wall Street crowd.

10

The Horton team's plan to use race as an issue became manifest with the calling of LaSalle Doheny Leffall Jr. to the stand. The fifty-seven-year-old chairman of surgery at Howard University Medical Center in Washington, D.C., had an impressive résumé. After graduating first in his class from Howard's medical school in 1957, Leffall had gone on to a fellowship at New York's renowned Memorial Sloan-Kettering Cancer Center and had then served as chief of a general surgery section in a U.S. Army field hospital in Germany. Returning to Howard as an assistant professor in surgery in 1962, Leffall rose through the ranks to the top of the department, serving along the way as a visiting professor at eighty-three other medical schools, including those at Yale, Harvard, Columbia, and Johns Hopkins. He had served as president of the American Cancer Society, was a consultant in surgical oncology to the National Cancer Institute and to the Walter Reed Army Medical Center, and had treated President Ronald Reagan for colon cancer.

Even with all his administrative and consulting duties, Leffall still found time to do hands-on medicine.

Responding to one of Don Davis's questions, Leffall described his daily routine:

Well, I just happen to be a morning person so I tend to get up early, around three-thirty or a quarter to four, and get to the hospital about four-thirty and do paperwork until six, and then I start seeing my patients on rounds from six until seven, seven-thirty, and have some breakfast and go to the operating room, and usually . . . I would be in my surgical conference there and then operating until noon, and in the afternoon have different conferences, meeting students, meeting the dean, meeting different people in the department.

Lawyers in any case would be thrilled to have an expert witness with Leffall's qualifications and experience. He also happened to be black. For the Horton team, though, happenstance had nothing to do with it; for them, it was one of Leffall's most important credentials, a fact that quickly became evident during Davis's questioning. After having the doctor list a number of awards he had received for his medical work, Davis made sure to ask, "Have you ever received any awards from the NAACP?"

"Yes," Leffall replied, "I've been quite active in our community in the Washington area and I received that Humanitarian Award." Davis also asked, "Tell us just briefly, have you personally conducted any studies to determine the lung cancer incidence in black Americans?" He had co-authored one, published in 1973.

"Your Honor," Davis said at the conclusion of his questions on Leffall's qualifications, "I offer Dr. Leffall as an expert in the field of surgical oncology among black Americans and ask the court to rule that he is qualified to give opinions to the jury's assistance."

"He will be received as an expert," Judge Evans ruled, a decision he had to make for anyone proffered by either side to give expert, or "opinion," testimony. But then Jim Upshaw cut in: "I was unaware that he was only being offered as an expert in the field of surgical oncology in *black* Americans. I thought he was just in the field of surgical oncology."

"I think I should have just said surgical oncology," Davis said.

"Well, we will receive him either way, or both ways," Judge Evans said. Which is exactly how Davis planned to use him. Plaintiffs' Exhibit No. 25

was the 1973 report Leffall had coauthored, titled "Alarming Increase of the Cancer of the Lung Mortality in the U.S. Black Population (1950–1967)." The report showed that cancers of the esophagus, pancreas, prostate, womb, and cervix were all more prevalent among black Americans than among whites. So was cancer of the lung.

"Dr. Leffall, of all the cancers that you've studied, which one has increased the most rapidly among black men?" Davis asked.

"It's been lung cancer," Leffall replied.

"Doctor, in your opinion, what is the cause of this significant increase in lung cancer in black Americans?" Davis wanted to know.

"Well, looking at all of the facts and all of the data, we think it's, without any question, related to cigarette smoking — the smoking of cigarettes."

Davis then had Leffall present a variety of statistics on smoking among blacks. A 1985 report, for example, showed that 41 percent of black men and 32 percent of black women smoked, versus 32 percent and 28 percent of white men and women, respectively. Another study compared the age-adjusted death rates from lung cancer for blacks and whites (per 100,000 people). In 1969, it was 63 for black males, 55 for white; by 1989 it was 94 for black males, 69 for white.

Why this race data was relevant evidence for the jury is not clear. It made no more sense than using similar data in a suit against an automobile manufacturer to show that more blacks than whites were killed in a certain kind of vehicle. The plaintiffs weren't claiming that blacks were more susceptible than whites to cigarette smoke. As Leffall himself testified, the higher incidence of lung cancer among blacks could be explained by higher smoking rates among blacks. There could be only one purpose: to arouse the passions of a predominantly black jury, to make a kind of political appeal to them to avenge the death of Nathan Horton in the name of racial justice. Strangely, though, the defense never objected to this kind of evidence.

Davis did have some questions for Leffall that weren't related to race. He asked Leffall whether he knew "of a single professional or medical association that has concluded that smoking does not cause lung cancer." Leffall was aware of none. Davis also asked Leffall what he thought about

Upshaw's claim in his opening statement that there was a "raging controversy" about whether smoking causes lung cancer.

"There is no controversy," Leffall replied.

Closing his questioning of Leffall with a flourish, Davis asked, "Is lung cancer a pleasant death?"

"It's a horrible death," said Leffall.

"Is it very painful?"

"It's a horrible death," Lefall repeated.

"We pass the witness," Davis concluded.

One measure of how strong the defense thinks a plaintiff's witness has been is how long the defense's cross-examination of that witness is. Upshaw's cross-examination of Leffall lasted twice as long as Davis's direct. Much of it consisted of a tedious rehash of Leffall's testimony on smoking and cancer rates among blacks, as Upshaw tried, without success, to persuade Leffall that the data seemed to indicate that something other than smoking was responsible.

Upshaw also worked to rehabilitate his assertion that the causes of lung cancer are a matter of "controversy." Isn't it true, he asked, "that cancer induction is a very complex process and we have a long way to go before we totally or fully understand [it]?"

Leffall replied, "You don't have to fully understand something when you have data that incontrovertibly shows there is a causation from one thing to the other, and based on all the facts that we know, in everything that I have heard and seen and witnessed as a practicing surgeon, as a surgical oncologist, cigarette smoking causes cancer."

Why, Upshaw wanted to know, had Leffall answered the identical question in his deposition with a simple "yes"?

"Well, this is a different forum, and I think I have to try to explain it more fully," Leffall explained. This was a witness who was not going to be pushed around.

Upshaw tried a different tack: "Dr. Leffall, it has been recently reported that radon is responsible for approximately one-fifth of all the lung cancer deaths. Have you read those statistics?"

"I have heard some people talk about that, that radon may be related." . . .

"And a lot of people really believe it's really significant because of lung cancer, and some people don't particularly believe it's that strong. Is that correct sir?"

"That is correct."

"So that would be what we would call a legitimate scientific controversy among scientists and physicians nowadays, wouldn't it?"

Here, too, Leffall fought Upshaw to at least a draw. Yes, he acknowledged, some people were looking into whether such things as radon, and wood dust, and a whole host of other things might cause lung cancer, but what was unknown or uncertain didn't change what was known: that 85 or 90 percent of lung cancers are caused by cigarette smoking.

But the acknowledgment that 10 to 15 percent of lung cancers are caused by something else gave Upshaw an opening. He got Leffall to agree that as a carpenter, Horton was exposed to wood dust, and as a chipper and grinder at John Deere, he was almost certainly exposed to silica (coming off the stone or sand grinding belt), another suspected lung carcinogen.

If Upshaw was making headway, it was slow and labored. He would ask Leffall to agree with flat-out assertions, and Leffall constantly felt the need to explain and qualify his responses. Finally, even Judge Evans couldn't take it. "Let's see if we can't have some agreement here a little sooner than we're getting at it," he said. "We are going over this and over it and over it three or four or five times."

Upshaw used the end of his cross-examination to establish two interrelated points. One was that, whatever statistical associations might exist linking smoking to lung cancer, that data "does not prove the cause of lung cancer in Nathan Henry Horton." (Although Leffall really had to agree with this point, he resisted, saying it "proves it as much as it can be proved.") Second, Upshaw raised questions about what kind of lung cancer Horton had. Horton's lawyers maintained that he had adenocarcinoma, a form widely associated with cigarette smoking. But under questioning by Upshaw, Leffall agreed that in certain respects Horton's tumor differed from typical adenocarcinomas. For one thing, it was found in the upper lobe of his left lung and his mediastinum (part of the chest cavity), while most adenocarcinomas originate on the periphery of the lung. Also, Horton's tumor was extremely fast-growing; adenocarcinomas are typically slow-growing.

For all his expertise in oncology, Leffall was not really the right person to answer questions relating to the typing of Horton's cancer — though that didn't stop Upshaw from using him to make his points. Typing a cancer is really a pathologist's job, and the Horton team had a series of pathologists lined up to testify. One of them, Billy Ray Ballard, took the stand after Leffall.

Ballard had been present as an observer at Horton's autopsy and, using photos and blowups of color slides, he led jurors on a graphic tour of the havoc wrought in Horton's lungs by both cancer and emphysema. They saw his sliced-open lung, filled by the deadly gray-white mass; they saw his distended, fluid-filled bronchus; they saw the emphysematous bullae — the overexpanded air sacs unable to deliver oxygen to the blood. Ballard gave a microscopic tour as well, showing jurors photographs of groups of cells taken from Horton's tumor. Many of the cells, Ballard said, had formed glands and secreted mucin — the substance that helps rid the lungs of particulate matter. "Any tumor that forms glands and produces mucin is defined as an adenocarcinoma," he explained.

On cross-examination, American's lawyers laid a trap. And it had nothing to do with pathology, but rather with exposing the other side's race-conscious approach to presenting their case. In response to a question from Ed Blackmon about how he'd been brought into the Horton case, Ballard said he had been asked by Robert O'Neal, his department head at the University of Mississippi Medical Center, because "he must have had some idea that I could render a judgment as to what this is all about."

Blackmon pounced, saying, "Now that you have brought that up, Dr. Ballard, we, in fact, you and I know the reason Dr. O'Neal brought you into the case."

Seeing where things were headed, Don Barrett immediately asked for a conference in the judge's chambers. Upshaw arrived with marked portions of O'Neal's deposition, which he read for the judge and assembled lawyers.

> My question was, "Why did you particularly suggest Dr. Ballard for this case?" . . . Dr. O'Neal's answer, and this is this man's boss [was], "Well, Dr. Ballard is very interested in cancer, and he's had this experience at Roswell Park in New York [a prominent cancer research

institution], and is just a good member of the department, and I think possibly that he's black, too. He might be more believable to some people because he's black."

O'Neal went on to say — and probably with the best of intentions, although it didn't necessarily sound that way — "Of course, Dr. Ballard is, in my mind, he's about as white as anybody I ever ran into. I don't even notice from day to day when I walk into the room. I forget that he's not white, I just forget it because we deal so much with each other. He's one of my closest associates."

Barrett objected to any of this being related to the jury. It involved, Barrett said, a private thought of O'Neal's that he had never communicated to the Horton team, and had nothing to do with why they had retained Ballard. But Judge Evans decided to let the matter play itself out. "I believe that Dr. Ballard can take care of himself, and you may get into it further," he said. "He's pretty sharp. He's taken care of himself so far. . . . I wished I lived a hundred years from now when we didn't get into race. It's an unfortunate situation."

"It's a fact of life," said Upshaw, and everyone returned to the courtroom. Years later Upshaw explained, "If I was on a jury and they ran a guy in there just because he was my race, I would feel they were being a little condescending toward me, and I wanted the jury to know that."

But Judge Evans was right: Ballard *could* take care of himself. Blackmon read O'Neal's statement that Ballard "might be more believable to some people because he's black," and asked Ballard if he agreed.

"Sure I agree with that, and I have no problems with that," Ballard responded. "You know, I live under no illusions whatsoever. I know if . . . the circumstances were different, probably another pathologist would have been chosen, and by the same token, if the circumstances were different, probably another lawyer would have been chosen."

Blackmon caught the barb. "Doctor," he retorted acerbically, "of course you may think of yourself in terms of race, but some of us don't when it comes to being professional and having ability."

"If we live under an illusion like that, sometimes we may at some point deceive ourselves," Ballard volleyed back.

"You agree with Dr. O'Neal, then?" Blackmon asked.

"Yeah, I agree with Dr. O'Neal," said Ballard.

It was going to be a long week. Ballard's testimony took most of Monday January 11. By the end of the day Friday, the Horton team would present another sixteen witnesses to the jury. But no week would be complete without a defense motion for a mistrial, and on Tuesday Upshaw dutifully made one. The protest this time had to do with photographs of Horton's cancer cells that Davis had used in his questioning of Ballard. The defense complained that they had not received advance copies of the photos, though they had received the microscope slides from which the photos were made. Judge Evans denied the motion.

In addition to Leffall, another star-caliber expert witness for the Horton side was Charles LeMaistre, the president of the University of Texas System Cancer Center, which was headquartered at the giant M. D. Anderson Hospital in Houston. As the chief administrator of the center, LeMaistre, age sixty-three, oversaw everything, from the institution's budget to patient care, from research activities to the cancer prevention program. Like Leffall, LeMaistre had served as the president of the American Cancer Society. And, although he was white, LeMaistre noted, at Davis's prompting, that he had served on a United Negro College Fund cancer research group and on the board of a black college in his hometown of Tuscaloosa, Alabama. His most important credential, though, dated back more than twenty years, when he was one of ten members of the advisory committee that prepared the landmark Surgeon General's report on smoking and health, issued in January 1964.

Led by Davis's questions, LeMaistre explained the committee's charge was to review existing evidence on smoking and health, not to do any new research. Only people who had not "exhibited bias" — publicly taken a position for or against the idea of a link between smoking and disease — were selected for the committee. Meeting regularly for a year and a half at the National Library of Medicine in Bethesda, Maryland, committee members pored over thousands of articles, reviewed autopsy and animal experiment data, and questioned scientists. Finally they produced their report. Among the principal conclusions, LeMaistre said, "was that there was a causal relationship between cigarette smoking and lung cancer." Since 1964, LeMaistre testified, adenocarcinoma had come to be regarded "as the most common form of lung cancer associated with cigarette smoking."

Upshaw's cross-examination got off to a cantankerous start.

UPSHAW: I timed you on direct examination Dr. LeMaistre, and you testified for fifty-five minutes. Does that sound approximately the correct length of time to you?

LeMAISTRE: Yes, sir.

UPSHAW: You started at 1:35 and you ended it at 2:30.

JUDGE EVANS: This may be interesting here, but I don't think it's necessary. Let's move on.

UPSHAW: I think this is interesting —

JUDGE EVANS: No, sir; no, sir. I won't permit that. You may proceed with your questioning. . . .

UPSHAW: Well, the only way I know how to do it is my way, Judge.

JUDGE EVANS: Well, you are unfortunately saddled with me, and you are going to do it my way or not at all.

Upshaw returned to questioning LeMaistre.

UPSHAW: Sir, I suggest to you that you have testified for forty-five minutes about what you have done, what the Surgeon General has done, what the Surgeon General's advisory committee has done, what other committees you served on have done, and it wasn't until the eight minutes before the end of your testimony that the name Nathan Henry Horton was even mentioned. Do you deny that that is what happened a moment ago?

LeMAISTRE: No, sir; if you say so, I will accept it.

UPSHAW: Because, as a matter of fact, you know relatively little, if nothing, about Mr. Horton other than what Mr. Davis has told you and the autopsy report that you have read. Is that correct, sir?

LeMAISTRE: That is basically correct, yes, sir.

UPSHAW: Now, I am going to talk to you a little bit about what the lawsuit is about, and it's about a human being named Nathan

Henry Horton, and not about all of your life experiences. Do you understand that?

LeMAISTRE: Yes, sir, I can understand you, Mr. Upshaw.

It was nasty in its execution, but Upshaw was carrying out one of the central objectives of the defense strategy: keeping the focus on the individual. Thus it was the defense that was the most ardent champion of the humanity of the claimant, the defense that constantly urged consideration of his *individual* physical and mental characteristics, as opposed to a compendium of impersonal group statistics offered by the plaintiffs.

"You can't use a Surgeon General's report to diagnose and treat cancer in a given individual case, can you, sir?" Upshaw half-asked, half-taunted LeMaistre. "As a matter of fact, the Surgeon General's reports [don't] deal with single individuals at all, do they, Doctor? They deal with mass populations, don't they? Large groups?" And: "This is a lawsuit by the family of an individual against my client, and it's not by the broad public against my client; is that correct, sir?"

Of course, when it was convenient to use statistics, the defense had no compunction about doing so. No sooner had Upshaw finished deriding the generality of the Surgeon General's reports than he showed LeMaistre a pamphlet published by the American Cancer Society in 1987 titled "Cancer Facts and Figures."

"It states on page twenty that there are an estimated forty million ex-smokers in the United States," Upshaw pointed out. "That's correct, isn't it, sir?"

"I believe the figure is closer to fifty million today," LeMaistre replied.

"All right," Upshaw said. "Do you have any reason to believe — and I assume that you don't, inasmuch as you never met him or didn't know him — whether or not Mr. Horton was any different than that forty or fifty million people that you just told me about that volunteered to quit smoking?"

When it came to making the point that Horton chose to smoke — and chose not to quit — the defense suddenly had no problem at all extrapolating from mass populations to a single individual.

Upshaw was right that LeMaistre knew little about Horton personally, and had never met him. LeMaistre had, however, recommended that a colleague of his at the University of Texas evaluate Horton to determine what substances Horton might have been exposed to during his life, other than cigarettes, that might have caused his cancer. Don Barrett and Don Davis needed their own evaluation of this to prepare for anything the defense might raise. So on December 30, 1987 — just four weeks before he died — Horton was bundled aboard a plane and flown to Houston to see Marcus Key, a physician and specialist in occupational diseases. In a session periodically interrupted by Horton's coughing spasms, Key compiled a history of Horton's occupational and environmental exposure, from the time he first worked on his father's farm to the onset of his cancer. Key summarized his findings in a report and, appearing as a witness at the trial, presented them to the jury.

Aware of Horton's work as a chipper and grinder for John Deere, Key noted that he had examined a 1985 chest X-ray and could find no evidence of silicosis. As for Horton's primary employment as a carpenter, Key wrote, "It should be noted that heavy exposure to wood dust among furniture makers had been associated with cancer of the para-nasal sinuses but not with lung cancer." In conclusion, he determined, "Except for the long history of cigarette smoking, there is nothing in Mr. Horton's occupational-environmental history that can be associated with lung cancer. As work histories go, Mr. Horton's is relatively innocuous."

But Key's contact with Horton had been brief — they met for less than two hours — and his report was cursory. On cross-examination, Upshaw was able to expose embarrassing gaps in Key's knowledge. In the section of his report discussing Horton's farm work, Key had written, "cotton poisons and pesticides used, but not by Mr. Horton." Was Key aware, Upshaw asked, "that Mr. Horton testified that he helped his father load pesticides on the truck for them to carry out into the fields?" Key was not. Key had also written that the section of the John Deere plant where Horton worked "was well ventilated," a statement at odds with descriptions offered by Horton and his coworkers in their depositions. Why hadn't he read any of the depositions? Upshaw asked. "In retrospect, maybe I should have," Key confessed.

Trial days could be long and tedious, and there was no bar or restaurant in Lexington for out-of-towners to go to afterward. But Bootsy and Pam Hooker saw to visitors' social needs. Bootsy, a five-foot-five, trimly fit ex-Marine, was gregarious and loquacious. Pam was quiet and warm. Together they threw open their house, nestled amid cotton fields and a forest of planted pine, and treated a parade of journalists and investment analysts to grilled steak and Southern cooking several times a week. They even took on a couple of houseguests. Bootsy, who had worked at a men's clothing store in Jackson in between stints farming cotton, still sold a line of dress shirts from his house, and took the opportunity to trot out his fabric swaths in case any of his company was interested. Joe Longinotti ordered two. Bootsy also took Longinotti deer hunting, though they came back empty-handed.

For the lawyers, the end of one trial day meant returning to their offices to prepare for the next. Upshaw's office in Greenwood was Command Central for American's team, and they had also rented a house in Lexington a few minutes' drive from the town square. One rumor during the trial had it that this outpost was under armed guard. That wasn't true, but even Robert Biggs, partner of demoted American defense attorney Richard Edmonson, recalls that "the Lex House," as it was called, seemed like it was operated by the CIA. There were paper shredders inside, you needed passes to get in, and the house backed onto a steep kudzu-covered ravine, making any kind of incursion from the rear highly improbable. Horton's legal team had it easier. They simply walked across the street to the Barrett law offices.

The stream of witnesses called by the plaintiffs for the remainder of the second week of trial offered a mixture of medical, scientific, and personal testimony. To drive home the overwhelming weight of evidence on the link between smoking and cancer, David Burns, an associate professor of medicine and a physician at the University of California at San Diego, took the stand. Burns had been extensively involved in preparing a half dozen of the most recent Surgeon General's reports, and he noted that each report had reiterated — and indeed strengthened — the statement in the original 1964 report that a causal link existed between smoking and lung cancer.

Doctors involved in the diagnosis and treatment of Nathan Horton's cancer also testified, and they chronicled the grim details of his decline. Offering a more personal view of Horton's suffering, Nathan Randall Horton — Horton's eldest son, born to his first wife — talked about his father's agony during the radiation treatments. Nathan Randall, a twenty-nine-year-old pharmacist, said he had urged his father to quit smoking long before he got ill, and Horton had tried a few times, but never succeeded.

"You bought your father a carton of cigarettes for Christmas, didn't you?" Ed Blackmon asked on cross.

"Yes, sir," Nathan Randall admitted.

I. H. Montgomery Jr. had been Horton's lifelong friend. They were the same age, had grown up on adjoining farms, had attended school and church together, and Montgomery had been the trainer for the high school football team. "Nathan was a tackle and a hard one. If he hit a man, he got up slow," Montgomery told the jury. In the early seventies, when Horton returned to Holmes County, the two men renewed their friendship and saw each other regularly. Under questioning by Barrett, Montgomery described visiting Horton in the hospital during his cancer treatments. Was he in pain? Barrett wanted to know.

"Very much so," Montgomery said. "He would grab the [call button] light and push it, and I heard the nurse say, you can't get any more now. You've got to wait the two hours. . . . She was referring to the painkiller."

On a separate subject, Barrett asked how Horton treated his stepchildren — the children of his fourth wife, Ella. "I've never seen a more caring man," Montgomery said, adding that Horton treated the stepchildren "just like they were his."

That gave the defense an opening to remind jurors about Horton's extramarital procreation and to cast doubt on how close a friendship he really had with Montgomery. "I don't know who he is" and "I don't know him" was all Montgomery could reply as Blackmon ticked off the list of Horton's offspring.

The defense used anyone who claimed to know Horton personally to make the point that Horton was independent and self-determined. These are positive attributes that few are likely to deny in describing someone they like, and as Blackmon demonstrated with Montgomery, if a witness showed any resistance, he could always be browbeaten into submission.

Referring to Horton's football-playing days, Blackmon asked, "Even at that early age, Mr. Horton showed traits of being a very independent and strong person, didn't he?"

"I feel a strong person," Montgomery replied. "I don't know how independent, because I would think a football team is a collective effort."

Blackmon persisted: "He did show leadership qualities at that time, didn't he?"

"I wouldn't say leadership qualities," Montgomery said. "I would say it was a team effort."

Did that mean Horton was a "follower," Blackmon wanted to know.

"No, I wouldn't say a follower or a leader," Montgomery explained. "He did, you know, like I said, he was a team member."

Blackmon moved on to other questions, but at the close of his cross-examination he came back to try, once again, to make his point.

"You said that Mr. Horton was not a leader and that he was not a follower. That leaves just one middle ground, am I correct, and that would be that he was an individualist?" he stated.

"Yes," Montgomery relented.

Another friend of Horton's, Clanton Beamon, got the same treatment. Beamon was the director of a nonprofit housing corporation that helped disadvantaged families in the Delta build their own homes. He had gotten to know Horton when Horton was hired in the 1970s as a construction supervisor for the corporation. "It took a leader to do that, didn't it?" Upshaw asked. "Was he a wimp, was he a weak guy?" Upshaw wanted to know. "Wasn't he a man among men?"

In the mid-seventies, a number of nonprofit housing corporations from around the country, including Beamon's, collaborated in making a film that explained their purpose and operation. A portion of the film showed Horton at work building houses, and Horton's lawyers wanted to show it to the jury. But Upshaw objected. Sending the jurors to lunch, Judge Evans stayed at the courthouse with the lawyers to review the film. "It will make a great humanitarian out of him," Upshaw protested.

"He was a humanitarian," Barrett said. "That is the point."

"We can say he was a great humanitarian, but we can't say he was a gangster," Upshaw grumbled. He suggested, facetiously, that perhaps they could find something "showing that he spent time in jail for burglary and armed robbery." The film, Upshaw complained, was trying to make a "folk hero" out of Horton, and even contained shots of folk singer Joan Baez.

"I don't think that is Joan Baez," said Barrett. "I think that is some Indian woman in New Mexico."

Judge Evans sustained Upshaw's objections, and the film was never shown.

In a separate hearing in the judge's chambers, the lawyers made preparations for showing the jury the videotaped deposition of Robert Heimann, American's CEO from 1973 to 1980. At the beginning of the deposition, Don Davis had asked Heimann about his educational background, and in particular about the subject of his doctoral thesis in sociology. Heimann, who had an unusual résumé for a tobacco executive, described it as "a multivariant statistical analysis to test one of the postulates of Karl Marx with respect to the formation of antagonistic capitalist and labor groups."

"You are referring to Karl Marx, the Communist?" Davis had followed up. Upshaw wanted that taken out. "They're trying to make it look like Mr. Heimann may be a Communist," he objected. "He's not a Communist. If he's nothing else, he's not a Communist."

"I have no problem with taking that out," Davis said. Davis didn't have to rely on a cheap gibe; Heimann's deposition contained far richer material. Short of having a tobacco company CEO admit outright that cigarettes cause cancer, the next best thing for plaintiffs was an unqualified *denial* of such a link. A denial was so at odds with the weight of both scientific and popular thinking on the subject that it couldn't help seeming ludicrous, mendacious, and insulting. Furthermore, it highlighted the hypocrisy of the assumption-of-risk defense. Heimann did not disappoint.

DAVIS: You are not, of course, a medical doctor, are you?

HEIMANN: No, no.

DAVIS: Do you think a medical doctor would be more qualified than you are to determine if cigarette smoking is hazardous to your health?

HEIMANN: Well, let me say without being boastful, that the real nub of this question is the proper use of statistics. That's how the whole megillah arose, and . . . most physicians have little or no knowledge of statistical nuances and would be easily taken in, misguided, by the improper use of statistics.

DAVIS: Do you think the Surgeon General of the United States is more qualified in his resources than you are to determine if cigarette smoking is hazardous to your health?

HEIMANN: Frankly, no.

And at another point:

DAVIS: As far as you're concerned, is the Surgeon General simply wrong in concluding that cigarette smoking causes lung cancer?

HEIMANN: I would use the term "misguided."

DAVIS: Okay, if he's misguided, then, I take it that your opinion is he's wrong?

HEIMANN: I was simply trying to be polite about it.

DAVIS: Okay, but not being polite about it, in your opinion, he's wrong?

HEIMANN: Dead wrong.

DAVIS: Congress is wrong in requiring these warnings [on cigarette packs], correct?

HEIMANN: We do not think they're justified.

DAVIS: So they're wrong?

HEIMANN: They're wrong.

Davis then ticked off a list of eleven public health agencies and organizations. "In your opinion are all these organizations wrong?" he asked. "Yes," said Heimann.

The substance of Heimann's remarks was arrogant enough, but the way he said them compounded the effect. It was not that he was rude; he answered each of Davis's questions patiently and politely. It wasn't even his somewhat patrician bearing. It was that he combined cocksureness with casualness in a way that evinced an utter lack of concern about the widely substantiated allegation that his company's principal product killed people. He either genuinely didn't believe that to be the case, or he simply didn't care.

It would have been a great way to end the week, but the timing didn't quite work out. On Friday, the Horton team called William Longo, the materials testing engineer Davis had retained to look for asbestos fibers in Pall Mall cigarettes. But in dull and highly technical testimony, all Longo could tell the jurors was that Pall Malls — and all other cigarettes he tested — contained some inorganic fibers. The significance of this was never explained, and Longo's testimony certainly put jurors' patience to the test, if it didn't put them to sleep. Already that week, during some detailed medical testimony, Judge Evans had interrupted to say, "I ask the jury to wake up a little bit."

The final witness of the week was Joseph DeFranza, a physician and researcher from the University of Massachusetts with a special interest in the role radiation plays in causing cancer in smokers. His testimony was also highly scientific, but at least he offered something that no other witness in the case would: a description of *how* cigarette smoke might cause cancer. For all the testimony that Horton's lawyers could marshal to explain that smoking does cause cancer, the precise mechanism of carcinogenesis was — and remains — poorly understood. It was not necessary to prove precisely how this occurred. As Don Barrett told jurors at the beginning of the trial, people knew what caused babies to be created without understanding the biological details. Still, having an explanation precluded American from pointing out that none had been offered.

DeFranza explained that a cell turns cancerous when its regulatory gene — the one that tells it to stop dividing — gets destroyed. Chemical carcinogens in cigarette smoke, he said, can damage genes by becoming attached to them. But radiation, he continued, can actually cut genes in half, and is therefore "much more effective in causing cancer because it actually destroys the gene." Radiation, DeFranza said, is part of tobacco smoke and, prompted by Davis's questions, he related in a quite conversational way how it got there.

"Everywhere in the world," he said,

> there is some uranium in the soil. It's not enough that you would want
> to mine it; it's not worth it. But it's in the soil everywhere. When some-
> thing is radioactive, it means that it gives off radiation, and when it

gives off radiation, it changes into something else. Uranium gives off radiation and eventually changes into another radioactive substance called radium. Radium gives off radiation and it changes into another radioactive element called polonium.

After a series of additional steps, he said, you end up with a nonradioactive substance: lead.

The radiation given off by the radium forms a radioactive gas called radon, which seeps out of the soil. DeFranza related what happens when this occurs in a tobacco field:

> These . . . radioactive substances all have static electricity . . . and, because of that, if there is any dust in the air, these things just stick to the dust. Now you have dust in the air which has these radioactive particles attached to them. So the radioactive dust floats around, and if it happens to come in contact with the tobacco leaf, it sticks there. Why . . . that happen[s] is that if you looked at the surface of the tobacco leaf with a microscope — you couldn't see it with a naked eye — you would see hairs like this [drawing on a blackboard]. They look like mushrooms. They are skinny and have a flat top and the top here is covered with a substance like sap or maple syrup. It is very sticky . . . and the dust particles become stuck to the hairs on the tobacco plant, and that's how the tobacco becomes radioactive.

When tobacco gets burned in a cigarette, DeFranza said, the radioactivity enters the smoke and then the smoker's lungs.

How was this any different from a person simply breathing radon from the air? Davis wanted to know. The difference, DeFranza said, had to do with solubility. Radioactive particles breathed through the air dissolve easily in lung fluid, enter the blood, and are eventually eliminated by the kidneys. But the radioactive particles that pass through burning cigarettes, DeFranza explained, "get changed, and what happens is that sap kind of gets melted and, as it cools, it solidifies, and the particles that are left, not only are they radioactive, but you can't dissolve them in anything." Researchers, he said, had tried to dissolve the particles in what's called a simulate lung fluid, which is a fluid made identical to what the fluid is inside the lungs, and they couldn't dissolve them, so they tried to boil them, and they still wouldn't dissolve, and they put them in acid, and they still couldn't get them to dissolve. So it's just like glass. You just can't get it dissolved . . . and if something can't be dissolved when it comes into the lung, it just stays there.

Not only did smokers have insoluble particles sitting in their lungs emitting radioactivity, the type of radiation emitted, DeFranza said, is known as alpha radiation, and depending which scientist you talked to, alpha radiation was anywhere from 8 to 100 times more dangerous than X-ray radiation. "When I say 'more dangerous,' I mean more effective at causing cancer," DeFranza said.

On cross-examination Ed Blackmon ticked off a list of other plants consumed by people and asked if they would also contain radiation. He stuck to a down-home menu to emphasize DeFranza's non-native status. How about turnip greens? he wanted to know. "Do you know what those are?" he asked. "You are from New Hampshire . . ."

"I don't know what they are," said DeFranza, provoking laughter in the courtroom.

"They are a favorite leafy plant," Blackmon explained. "Okay, what do you-all eat in New Hampshire?"

"Spinach," said DeFranza.

"Okay, if this trial was about spinach, instead of saying tobacco [contained radiation] you would say spinach, wouldn't you?" Blackmon asked.

Yes, DeFranza acknowledged, pointing out, however, that most plants don't have sticky hairs on them, and thus would pick up radiation through their roots.

"Let's use a sticky plant that we all know about," Blackmon continued. "How about okra? Ever heard of that?"

"I don't eat okra," DeFranza said, prompting more laughter. He said he would take Blackmon's word for the fact that okra had sticky hairs, but explained there was still a critical difference from tobacco: "You don't inhale okra, I assume."

"I don't know, Doctor, in New Hampshire they do it different than here," Blackmon parried, continuing the lighthearted exchange. But

DeFranza was loquacious, which made him hard for Blackmon to control, and without waiting for additional prompting, he launched into a lengthy discourse comparing tobacco to food. Radiation levels in tobacco, he said, measured 450 units, while wheat or meat or eggs measured between 1 and 3. "So tobacco," he said,

is a hundred times more radioactive than most foods. You mentioned greens. Greens would measure about sixty to ninety, so tobacco would be about four or five times more radioactive than any of the greens. As far as I know, there have been only two foods that have been measured that are more radioactive than . . . tobacco. One is reindeer meat, and that's because reindeer eat lichen. I don't eat lichen either, but they grow up in the Arctic, and the other is crab because the plankton in the ocean for some reason takes up this radioactivity, and the crabs eat the plankton and they become radioactive.

Again, he emphasized, that food is eaten, and most of the radioactivity passes harmlessly out of the body, while the radiation in tobacco smoke goes right into the lungs and stays there. "Does that answer your question?" DeFranza concluded.

"It answers more than my question," said Blackmon.

11

On weekends during the trial, Joe Longinotti, the Salomon Brothers observer, went home to New York. It gave him a chance to see friends, pick up a change of clothes, and eat something different. Not that he didn't appreciate Southern cooking — hefty and six feet four, he even asked Pam Hooker for her recipe for grits casserole. And having enjoyed so much hospitality from the Hookers and other people in Holmes County, Longinotti decided he would return the favor: One weekend he packed up two dozen bagels, along with lox and cream cheese and, returning to Lexington, set up a buffet just outside the courtroom. One bagel, however, was missing from the spread. The flight down had required a change of planes in Nashville, and on the New York to Nashville leg of the trip Longinotti, who traveled first class, found himself seated next to singer Dolly Parton. Parton was unhappy with the food on the flight, so Longinotti made her a bagel and cream cheese sandwich.

As the third week of trial got under way, Horton's lawyers prepared to call their final witnesses. But first, Lonnie Bailey, a lawyer in Jim Upshaw's firm, made a motion for a mistrial. He argued that the plaintiffs had violated one of Judge Evans's pretrial orders by questioning Joseph DeFranza about whether technology existed that could remove radioactive particles from cigarettes. Evans had excluded testimony on something known as the resin filter, because the plaintiffs had waited until the eve of trial to mention it. But in his brief testimony saying the technology did exist, DeFranza never mentioned the filter, and Evans denied the mistrial motion.

It was 9:00 A.M., and the lawyers were huddled in the judge's chambers, where Upshaw had another matter to raise. At five that morning, Upshaw said, he had been awakened by an anonymous phone call, and a male voice "gave me some of the most disturbing news about this lawsuit conceivable." The caller, Upshaw said, had told him that Jaquetta Griffin, one of the alternate jurors, repeatedly preached to other jurors during breaks that Horton's wife Ella had a substantial mortgage on her home, that the Hortons owed $35,000 in medical bills, and that the jury ought to award her something to cover these expenses. No evidence had yet been offered on Horton's medical bills, but Upshaw pointed out that the $35,000 figure "almost hits the medical on the nose."

Judge Evans was at a loss over what to do. He remembered flipping past a section headed "Misconduct of Jurors" in a trial handbook that was in his car, and he sent down for it. But after reviewing it, he told the lawyers that it offered no help. Prodded by Upshaw, Evans decided to question each of the jurors individually, with a court reporter — but none of the lawyers — present. Over the course of nearly an hour, he did just that, and in each case his questions about whether there had been any discussion about the outcome of the case, or what the Hortons might be entitled to, or whether there had been discussion of outstanding mortgage or medical bills, drew flat-out denials.

"I don't think there's anything else I can do," the judge then reported to the lawyers. "We will proceed." But Upshaw wasn't satisfied. "I want to move for a mistrial," he said, explaining that he felt the jury had been tainted by Jaquetta Griffin. At the very least, he said, Griffin should be removed as an alternate juror. The judge denied both requests. (In a 1997 interview, Griffin continued to deny that she had ever had any independent knowledge of the Hortons' expenses, and was unaware that she had been at the center of a misconduct motion.)

Early in the trial, the Horton team had presented the videotaped testimony of Preston Leake, American Tobacco Company's director of research and development. Most of that testimony dealt with whether the company's tobacco was contaminated with DDVP. Now Horton's lawyers decided they would call him to the stand for live questioning on other topics. Then they could close their case with the powerfully poignant testimony of Ella Horton, describing her husband's agonizing demise, and with the videotapes of Nathan Horton himself, visibly near death.

Upshaw, however, upended that plan. The decision to call Leake as a live witness, he protested, was a complete surprise and violated an agreement the lawyers had reached requiring advance notice of witnesses. Don Barrett responded, "Obviously, we don't want you to, you know, have him doctored up" — meaning American's lawyers might improperly script Leake's answers in advance — "or get him on an airplane and get him out of here where we couldn't get to him," a remark that made Upshaw even more agitated. The judge sided with Upshaw, and ordered that Barrett call Leake last.

So Ella Horton took the stand and, under questioning by Barrett, described her husband's final days. "Nathan's last year was painful every day," she said, relating the torture of his cancer treatments, the steady wasting away of his once robust body, and his growing fear of the nighttime and the finality it might bring. Of his last night in the emergency room, Ella said, "He knew his sickness. He knew what it was like. He knew he was going to die."

"Did Nathan Horton love you, Ella?" Barrett asked.

"Very much," she said.

"Did you love him?"

"A lot. I really did."

"Do you miss him?"

"I miss him very much."

The defense passed on the opportunity to cross-examine the witness.

If it wasn't Upshaw disrupting the Horton team's presentation of the end of their case, it was the weather. As the lawyers were getting ready to cue up the videotape of Nathan Horton's deposition, Judge Evans interrupted with an announcement: "Ladies and gentlemen, I have just sent the jury to a safe place. We have been warned that there is a tornado on the ground between here and Yazoo City. And for those of you who are not familiar with the geography, that's not very far away. It's heading in this direction. Therefore, I suggest you take some appropriate place to protect yourself. Court will be in recess until at least one o'clock."

The twister missed Lexington, and court resumed after lunch. Barrett began by playing the deposition taken in December 1986, less than eight weeks before Horton died. How was his medical condition compared with what it had been in July, when he was last deposed? Barrett began his questioning.

"To put it short: downhill," Horton said. During the previous deposition, he continued, he had felt "real well. I didn't have — didn't have too many problems then, and I thought every — well, I thought everything was in pretty good shape, but I found out different. Each day everything gets a little worse and a little worse. I have pain every day now."

For his lawyers, giving the jury the opportunity to see Horton and hear him talk about his life, his smoking, and his illness represented the culmination of their case, a kind of "Exhibit A" on the way tobacco could ravage a human life. But the videotape was a double-edged sword. For by bringing the focus back to the smoker — and away from the cigarette — the tape served American's strategy of making sure this was a case about a person, not a product. By showing portions of Horton's depositions that they had selected, American's lawyers were able to have Horton himself tell the jury that he liked to gamble, that he collected guns — including some that were "hot" — and that he had fathered a number of children out of wedlock, all activities that fit in with their profile of him as a risk-taker. And when it came to the risk at issue in the case, Horton acknowledged that, despite knowing from the time he was a child that smoking was bad for him, he never made a concerted effort to quit.

Was it okay for adults to smoke? he was asked.

"Well, let's put it this way," he said. "If you grown, you can, I would say, do what you want to do." The tobacco lawyers couldn't have said it better.

The Horton side's case dragged to an unspectacular end with the calling of Preston Leake to the stand. Don Davis led Leake through a lengthy description of the cigarette manufacturing process, notable only for Leake's description of the various flavorings added to Pall Mall cigarettes.

American's lawyers had battled tooth and nail prior to trial to prevent disclosure of the ingredients, but Leake said blithely, "Nothing secret about the materials. It's the quantities that we think are secret." The list included chocolate, cocoa, licorice, sugar syrups, maple sugar, vanilla, rum, and coumarin, an extract of the tonka bean that produces a vanilla-like flavor.

When Davis asked Leake whether American had ever tested the health effects of cigarette smoke on humans, Leake said the company relied on the Council for Tobacco Research (CTR), originally called the Tobacco Industry Research Committee, an organization launched by American Tobacco head Paul Hahn and other cigarette industry executives in 1954. On cross-examination, Upshaw was able to make much of American's support of the CTR. He had Leake explain that the CTR did no research of its own; instead, it had a Scientific Advisory Board composed of eminent doctors and scientists, whose job was to review applications and approve spending on research by other doctors and scientists around the country on the subject of smoking and health. Over and over again, Leake emphasized that members of the advisory board were "independent" and that the CTR put no restrictions of any kind on the research it funded. Reading from a CTR annual report, he noted: "The Council awards research grants to independent scientists who are assured complete scientific freedom in conducting their studies. Grantees alone are responsible for reporting or publishing their findings in the accepted scientific manner through medical and scientific journals and societies." To date, Leake noted, the CTR had given 592 scientists "in excess of one hundred million dollars."

On Thursday January 21, 1988, after nine days of testimony, Horton's lawyers rested their case. American's case would take just three days, and it began with Jim Upshaw calling Donald Gardner to the stand. Gardner, a toxicologist from Raleigh, North Carolina, who had once worked for the Environmental Protection Agency, had a simple message to convey to the jury: "We're exposed continuously to the sea of carcinogens all around us, but we aren't all dying of cancer," he said. Just because cigarette smoke contains carcinogens, he explained, doesn't mean it causes cancer. "The dose makes the poison" was his mantra. Everything can be toxic if you consume too much of it, he said, but at low concentrations many substances produce no effect on the body whatsoever. On a daily basis, he said, we are exposed to carcinogens "in our food, our air and water," but at levels the body can tolerate.

"Does that answer hold true for whole cigarette smoke?" Upshaw wanted to know.

"Absolutely," said Gardner, who added that he did not think the link between smoking and lung cancer had been proved.

As to testimony by plaintiffs' experts about radon in cigarette smoke, Gardner said he had done some calculations. A person would have to smoke 48,000 a day to get exposed to as much radon as the EPA allows in a twelve-by-eight-foot room, he said, adding, "I think that's quite impossible to do." DDVP, the insecticide about which the plaintiffs offered so much testimony, was an ingredient in the pest strips people hung in their homes to kill flies, Gardner noted. Assuming a worst-case scenario for contamination of cigarettes with DDVP, he said, a person would still have to smoke nearly 23,000 cigarettes in a day to equal the exposure one would get in a room with a pest strip.

Pharmacology professor Karl Heinz Ginzel, a plaintiffs' expert, had also testified about the use of maleic hydrazide, a sprout inhibitor, on tobacco plants. But, Gardner pointed out, the EPA allowed this product to be used on potatoes, and allowed up to 4,000 micrograms of maleic hydrazide residue in an ounce of potato chips. Again assuming a worst-case instance of tobacco exposure to maleic hydrazide, Gardner said, a smoker would have to puff through thirty-seven packs to get the same exposure as in an ounce of potato chips.

Gardner was followed on the stand by William Truly, a family medicine practitioner from nearby Madison County, who had reviewed Nathan Horton's medical records and told the jury it was impossible to conclude that smoking had led to his cancer. Truly's principal function on the stand seemed to be as a mouthpiece for American's canned position on cancer causation, which he delivered with very little prompting from his questioner, Ed Blackmon.

"Nathan Horton was an individual, and he was a unique individual," Truly said. "The Surgeon General and these other reports basically applied to large populations, and my interpretation as [to] what they mean is that people are at risk when they do certain kinds of things. If you get on [Interstate] Fifty-five you are at risk. If you sit in the courthouse and a tornado is coming, you're at risk." No expert, he said, could come to the courtroom and say what caused Horton's cancer. "Cancer is — is — there's a mystery about it," he said, waxing homiletical. "Whether it was his time to leave this earth, I don't know; or whether his name was on the roll, I don't know. Sometimes we don't wake up in the morning. Sometimes we face a tragic death. As we move from our mother's womb to our father's tomb, we don't know how and why we are going to die."

In addition to arguing that it was impossible to say what caused Horton's cancer, the defense called two experts to testify that the type of cancer Horton had was not adenocarcinoma, as the plaintiffs' experts had testified, but giant cell carcinoma, a very rare form of cancer not associated with smoking. Like Truly, these witnesses were African-American. The final expert called by the defense was Paul Jackson, a psychiatrist and the medical director of the chemical dependency unit at Mississippi's principal psychiatric hospital, known simply as the State Hospital.

Jackson testified that Horton "voluntarily chose to initiate smoking cigarettes and he voluntarily chose to continue smoking cigarettes." In essence, Jackson said, smokers really have to want to smoke, because it is an unnatural act.

> I don't know how many of you smoke, but starting smoking is a difficult process. . . . Learning how to inhale cigarettes is not a passive type of thing. It is something you have to adjust yourself to. . . . Eventually, you are able to . . . inhale the cigarette without coughing [but] your first . . . instinct, most natural instinct, when you inhale smoke . . . is to cough, to get rid of it. That takes a lot of energy.

Furthermore, he said, if Horton "had used even a portion of the energy that it took to learn how to smoke, he could have quit."

There was something comically perverse about this "defense" of smoking. But then, there also was something tragi-comic about Jackson himself. After graduating from medical school in Tennessee, he had entered a urology program at the University of Mississippi Medical

Center. But, he testified, he dropped out to get treated for alcoholism in 1983. "I wanted to continue in urology," he told the jury, "but [after four months of treatment] my confidence level was pretty low and I was not able — I was just not able to continue. The pressure was too much and I finally made the decision to leave about six months later and I went over to the Mississippi State Hospital, basically to recuperate." His personal experience with alcohol led him to shift his career interest toward treating chemical dependence. Each day, after tending to patients at the State Hospital, he tended to himself, driving to the Yana Club, a special place in the capital for people who are recovering from alcoholism or drug addiction. Jackson was also the medical director of the Harbor Houses, a chemical dependency facility that he visited in the evenings to check on patients.

Jackson likened Horton's fondness for cigarettes to his own predilection for coffee, which he documented in detail:

> When I get up in the morning, I routinely put on the pot of coffee, and I will drink two or three cups of coffee before I go to work. As a matter of fact, before I came here this morning, I had two or three cups of coffee. . . . I feel that coffee helps me to get going in the morning. . . . Well, I will drink coffee all morning. I will go from — I will be at Male Receiving — there is no coffee over there — and I will get my work done and I will go to the chemical dependency unit and get a cup of coffee, and I will sit down and review the charts. Then I will get several more cups of coffee before I go to lunch. . . . Okay, I will get several more cups of coffee before the end of the day at five. Then, I go to the Yana Club and drink another couple cups of coffee during that hour 'cause it is just an hour meeting, and after that I routinely go over to the Harbor Houses to admit anybody that is over there and I will have several more cups of coffee. Coffee has become part of my lifestyle.

One may wonder if, with this testimony, the defense proved too much. But it likely didn't matter. The plaintiffs had not made addiction an issue in the case, and the fact was they would have had a hard time doing so, since there was no evidence that Horton ever made a serious effort to quit. In fact, the evidence was to the contrary, and here Jackson testified quite effectively: Depositions and medical records, he pointed out, showed that over and over again in his life, Horton had been warned about the dangers of smoking, had been advised to quit, and had resolutely refused to do so. Jackson made particular reference to the deposition testimony of Evelyn Myles, and the defense called Myles to the stand to repeat what she had said.

In the early seventies Myles had worked with Horton building houses in the nearby town of Indianola. She had asthma and complained to Horton about his smoking and warned him of its dangers. "I told him just like it hurt me, it's going to hurt him," she testified. But, she said, he would "laugh it off" and say, "That's the only habit I've got, and I've got to die with something." For an assumption-of-risk defense, testimony didn't get any better than that.

On Tuesday January 26 the defense rested. "We had available to us a lot more extensive proof," Upshaw noted years later. But he felt American had put on an effective case, both through cross-examination of the plaintiffs' witnesses and through presentation of its own. If the company put on a long defense, Upshaw said, it would look like it had something to be defensive about. Another thought, he said, was "we can let the jury think they've been kept here four weeks by the plaintiffs, not by us."

The trial was almost over, but when the lawyers assembled in court the next day, Don Barrett had a surprise. Fred Strader, the jittery informant who had introduced Barrett to Walter Dickerson, was now ready to testify himself, and had flown into town the day before. Strader, Barrett said, would testify that "night after night for fourteen years" DDVP was sprayed directly on loose tobacco that was then made into Pall Mall cigarettes. He would also testify that American's factory was a "rat-infested, dirty plant" and that nothing was done to clean rat droppings and urine out of the tobacco. But Judge Evans would not allow it. The defense had not been given adequate notice of Strader's appearance, he ruled, and the issue had been well enough addressed at the beginning of the trial by Walter Dickerson's testimony.

The judge then brought up another matter from the beginning of the trial. He had ruled that Horton's lawyers could argue comparative fault to the jury — that jurors could, if they wanted, find that Horton and the American Tobacco Company each bore responsibility for his illness and death, and award damages based on American's share of the fault. But Evans had said he would revisit the issue at the end of the case, and now he announced his decision: Comparative fault would remain in the case, and he would instruct the jurors that they could apportion blame.

As *Washington Post* reporter Morton Mintz had asked at the start of trial, how could the jury find American zero percent at fault? Upshaw, naturally, had the same concern. He told the judge that the ruling was a "gross error" that would be overturned on appeal and result in having to try the case all over again. The defense team attempted an immediate appeal of the issue to the Mississippi Supreme Court, but the justices refused to intervene.

On Thursday January 28 — one year and one day after the death of Nathan Horton — the lawyers gave their closing arguments, which in good part consisted of ridiculing the evidence presented by the opposing side. In the middle of the day, the judge instructed the jury, dismissed the alternates, and sent the twelve jurors to deliberate. To reach a verdict, only nine of them had to agree.

Whatever decision the jury reached, it would reverberate around the nation. The most immediate impact would be on tobacco stock prices, and this made timing critical. With a moment's jump on the news, a large investor, such as a retirement or investment fund, might be able to unload tobacco stocks (in the event of a verdict against American, and a subsequent fall in share prices), or buy them (in the event of a defense victory, and a subsequent rise) *before* the market moved. Millions of dollars in profits or losses hung in the balance. That presented Salomon observer Joe Longinotti with a problem. Even though he had secured a phone at the Barrett law offices, precious minutes would elapse between the time he heard the jury verdict, left the courtroom, ran down the stairs, headed out of the courthouse, crossed the busy street, headed into the Barrett building, and rushed down yet more stairs to his desk. So when it was clear the case was going to the jury, Longinotti had Salomon send a secretary down from New York with a pair of walkie-talkies. The plan was that she would sit in the courtroom for the verdict and immediately relay the result to Longinotti, who, sitting by his borrowed phone, would promptly transmit word to New York. Rebecca Barfield, the tobacco analyst for First Boston Corporation, developed a similar plan. Pam Hooker brought a pair of her son's G.I. Joe walkie-talkies to the courthouse. When a verdict was announced, Pam was to run to a courthouse window and radio the result to Barfield, who would be standing at the lone pay phone in the town square.

By the end of the first day of deliberations, though, there was nothing to report. The jury worked into the evening, and then Judge Evans sent them to spend the night at a hotel in Greenwood to be sure they remained insulated from outsiders and news accounts. The next morning, however, the jurors reported to Evans that they were deadlocked. Yet at the same time, they told him that overnight the vote had switched from 7 to 5 in favor of one side to 7 to 5 in favor of the other. (The judge explicitly told them he did not want to know which side the votes were on.) He sent them back for additional deliberations, and then, just after noon, read them an additional charge to try to break the logjam. "In the course of your deliberations, do not hesitate to reexamine your own views and change your opinion if you are convinced it is erroneous," he told them. But he also said, "Do not surrender your honest convictions as to the weight or effect of the evidence solely because of the opinion of your fellow jurors or for the mere purpose of returning a verdict." He sent them back, once again, to deliberate.

Judge Evans was treading on dangerous ground, as Jim Upshaw repeatedly reminded him as the afternoon wore on. Any verdict was sure to be reversed on appeal if it appeared to be the product of pressure or coercion, and the longer the judge held jurors who said they were deadlocked, the greater the concern that some might change their votes solely to get it over with. So Upshaw kept harping on the coercion concern, hoping the judge would declare a mistrial. Don Davis, meanwhile, maintained that the "jury is doing what it is supposed to be doing" and that considering the length and complexity of the case, they should be allowed more time. "Give them one more night," he suggested to the judge. "What is one more day after all of this time and effort?"

Events, though, were conspiring against that. In the late afternoon, the bailiff was delivering coffee to the jurors when she learned that one was feeling ill. Two others had run out of prescription medications they were taking and needed refills. On top of that, the bailiff reported, the jurors were refusing to deliberate any longer and were sitting seven in one room, five in another, divided by their vote. Deciding to talk to them himself, Judge Evans confirmed the impasse. "I don't think it is going to change," one juror after another told him. At 4:50 in the afternoon, he announced a mistrial.

None of the participants could leave the courthouse without being waylaid by members of the press, hungry for the what–does–it–all–mean quotes and counterquotes they would build their reports on. A hung jury, of course, did not offer a definitive result, but in nearly everyone's eyes it amounted to a victory for American Tobacco and the tobacco industry. "Legal specialists said that if the plaintiffs couldn't win a clear victory in this case, there could be little hope of a verdict against a tobacco company" in any other tobacco liability cases that were pending, the *Wall Street Journal* reported. Such litigation, said Victor Schwartz, a Washington, D.C., specialist in product-liability law who represents corporations, was "a patient on life support."

Certainly Wall Street thought the industry had won. Shares of both Philip Morris and RJR Nabisco rose as news of the jury deadlock spread. Ironically, shares of American Tobacco's parent, American Brands, actually fell — but that was likely due to a takeover battle the company was locked in, not the Horton case.

Don Barrett, in his comments, retreated to metaphors of down-but-not-out: "Once you hit the bully in the bar, you don't give up the fight," he said; and "This particular wagon train didn't make it to California this particular time, but the wagon train will make it." Ed Blackmon told the assembled crowd on the courthouse lawn that the case represented a victory for freedom and freedom of choice. "I just felt this kind of wave of incredulity sweeping over me," recalled reporter Morton Mintz. "Here we are in Lexington, Mississippi, and here's a black lawyer defining freedom as whether you can choose to smoke or not."

Richard Daynard, the antitobacco crusader, tried, somewhat lamely, to put some positive spin on the result. "This is the very first time a tobacco case has gone to a jury and a verdict has not come back for the defendant," he said. That was too much for Jim Upshaw, who regarded Daynard as "an absolute raving zealot." As a colleague tried to pull him away, Upshaw shouted, "You're still batting a thousand, Daynard." Then he called him a "fruitcake." Daynard was visibly angry, and it looked like the two men might come to blows. "I almost decked him," Upshaw said later.

There was a raucous party at Upshaw's law offices that night. Amid the carousing, one guest was silent. The Upshaw firm, like many involved in personal-injury litigation, owned a life-size human skeleton, used for demonstrations in trials. Someone at the party had seen fit to sit it in a chair, crossing its legs. Wedged between two of its bony fingers was a cigarette.

Don Barrett, needless to say, did not party that evening. Nor did he immediately gather with his colleagues or family to commiserate. Instead, in the early darkness of a winter's eve, he slipped into the Methodist church, which sat empty but unlocked just off the town square. For two hours he knelt alone before the altar and prayed.

12

To Don Barrett, the Horton trial had not been just disappointing, it had been corrupt. Everyone was aware that American Tobacco had conducted extensive jury research for the trial, but Barrett suspected the effort had gone beyond information-gathering, and that attempts had been made to influence jurors' votes. Aided by his older brother and law partner Pat, Barrett went back to court less than a month after the declaration of a mistrial and asked Judge Evans to compel American to reveal the names of every local person the company had retained as a "jury consultant," along with how much each had been paid.

Some wild reports were circulating that some of these consultants had done more than just compile profiles of their fellow citizens. In an affidavit, the manager of a local convenience store said that one of her regular patrons told her during the trial that he was being paid fifty dollars an hour just to sit in the courtroom during the trial. When the trial was over, she claimed, he tried to pay for a cup of coffee with a hundred-dollar bill, which he peeled from a wad of hundreds. During the trial, Barrett had noticed that a number of prominent people from the community had attended the proceedings and sat on the defense side of the courtroom — behind the defense attorneys' table. Ed Blackmon acknowledged to reporters at the time that he had asked local residents to attend the trial as a "mirror jury" that he could question at the end of each day. "So what if I paid them?" he said. Barrett thought the purpose of the "mirror jury" was to show the real jury that there was local support for the tobacco company.

Three jurors reported in affidavits and in the press that they had been contacted during the trial by a local man, Norman Clark Jr., on a day the trial was postponed, and told that they didn't need to come to court. Upshaw acknowledged that Clark had been a paid jury consultant for American and had improperly contacted some jurors to spare them a trip to court, but denied that this conduct was illegal.

One juror, Luster Johnson, filed an affidavit saying that four of his fellow jurors had refused to deliberate and said from the outset that they were for the tobacco company. Ominously, Johnson continued, "I think somebody got to the jury because of the way [the four jurors] were acting by refusing to consider any evidence and the way they said that they didn't want to hear any evidence." He also noted that during the night the jury spent in the motel, the vote switched from 7 to 5 in favor of the Horton family to 7 to 5 in favor of American, and he suggested that this was suspicious. Joseph Cherner, the antismoking activist who had offered Barrett a bounty if he defeated American Tobacco, now put up a $5,000 reward for information leading to conviction on jury tampering in the case.

Separating truth from rumor, and shady but harmless activity from conduct that crossed over the line of legality, proved nearly impossible. Judge Evans refused to let the Barretts take the depositions of the eighteen people they named as suspected jury consultants, but he did schedule hearings on the misconduct allegations. The district attorney, meanwhile, started his own investigation, sending highway patrol officers to interview jurors in the case. Like the trial, the misconduct allegations attracted national media attention. "Snatching Defeat From Victory?" read a headline in a *National Law Journal* article that showcased the Barretts' allegations of tobacco company chicanery.

If mud was to be slung post-trial, American decided they would throw some back. Jim Upshaw filed a motion to have Don Barrett held in contempt, charging that prior to the trial he had requested the Holmes County sheriff not to serve jury summonses on white members of the jury pool, telling the sheriff that whites "are too conservative and will not give black people any money." This motion sent the sheriff himself scurrying to court to say that on two occasions Barrett had "laughingly and in a joking manner asked me not to find too many white people" and that "under no circumstances did it appear to me at either time that Don Barrett was in any way serious." The whole situation unraveled further as the Horton team sought to have Judge Evans disqualify himself from deciding anything about jury tampering, since the judge was a witness to events at the end of the jury deliberation. For its part, American filed notices to take the depositions of both Judge Evans and Don Barrett.

Things got ugly. Barrett hired a prominent lawyer from Greenville to represent him and his colleagues in their efforts to prove jury tampering. This lawyer got into such a heated argument with Upshaw at a hearing in April 1988 that Judge Evans had to bring a court deputy into his chambers in case the two men came to blows. The judge found the situation embarrassing. "I would hate for this exchange here this morning to have been made in the presence of the press," he told the lawyers after order had been restored. "I think it reflects badly on the bar and on our system of justice." Although he knew he couldn't hold secret hearings, he suggested that future proceedings be handled "discreetly" — they would be conducted in the judge's chambers or the court library, not the courtroom, and only those participating would be informed of the time and place.

In late May, Pat Barrett Jr. got a very unexpected phone call: Norman Clark Jr., the American Tobacco jury consultant, was on the line. A Holmes County native active in local politics, Clark, then forty-five, had worked in business for a number of years before setting up cotton and hog farming operations. He had attended Tougaloo College in Jackson, where he became friendly with fellow student Ed Blackmon, and then had gone on to study business at the University of Minnesota. He was bright, talkative, and something of an operator. Barrett hooked a recording device up to his phone.

After some initial conversation, Clark mentioned that he was having some regrets about working for the tobacco company in the Horton case.

"I would love to have seen Mrs. Horton get the money," he said. "Matter of fact, her husband built my hog farm."

"Really, Nathan did?" Pat Barrett replied.

"Yeah," said Clark, "he gave me the foundation, helped me with my blueprints, helped me with the concrete work and everything. We drank together, we partied together, and we chased women together."

Clark was annoyed that he had been publicly censured for contacting jurors and telling them not to come to court. He was only trying to be neighborly, he told Barrett. Then things got more interesting:

CLARK: It was improper what I did, but it wasn't against the law. But there was some other things that went on, Pat, like — you don't have to talk to a jury. If I wanted to change a juror's mind and his philosophy, I don't talk to him. I can talk to his mother, his brother, his sister, his next-door neighbor, all these folks got influence on him.

BARRETT: That is right.

CLARK: Hey, you get my point, now?

BARRETT: Yeah.

CLARK: Okay. Those are some of the things I wanted to discuss with Don, what happened.

BARRETT: Yeah, well, he, of course, is — knows our side of the case, you know, inside and out, and he's, he's real understanding and he'd be, I'm sure [he] would listen to you long as you wanted to talk to him about anything. One other thing — I'm gonna change the subject just a little bit, and you know, you don't say nothin'.

CLARK: Am I on tape?

BARRETT: Naw, not on this end.

CLARK: Go ahead.

BARRETT: What I'm talking about is uh, in my opinion and the people I've talked to, I would bet everything I could borrow from now on that — and not you, I don't think you'd do it — but somebody, somebody on behalf of the tobacco company actually communicated with some of those people that were on the jury during the trial and got something to 'em or to some of the kinfolks or something, I think. So, in other words, some tobacco money got to a couple of 'em, and that is a separate thing from what you're talking about of being friendly to them and that kind of thing.

CLARK: But it's not separate. That's what you're missing. It is not separate. . . . Now, the tobacco company's got a national reputation to preserve, so they would never, never even permit it or ever advise or never even [think] about letting a consultant talk to a juror. But see, you don't have to talk to a juror when the juror's mother is sitting there and the juror's sisters and brothers are sitting there and you're wining and dining them every day. You don't have to talk to the juror, Pat. See what I'm saying? Do you get my point?

BARRETT: Oh, yeah.

CLARK: Okay? If the father was sitting there, you take him to dinner every day, you pay for his dinner, you go take him shopping, you — if the mother's sitting there, you take her shopping and go and buy her lunch every day, you let her keep the tip on the table, [if] the brother's sitting there, take the brother to dinner and give him cash in his pocket and pay him for the days he missed work. Okay? You don't have to talk — you don't have to touch no juror.

Proof of that kind of conduct, Barrett told Clark, "would be a bigger story than winning the case if we had won the case in January," it would "shake the rafters of the whole United States."

Getting that proof meant persuading Clark to become a witness for the Horton side. As spring moved into summer in 1988, the Barrett brothers held a series of meetings and phone calls with Clark, trying to reel him in. Each time, Clark offered fresh tidbits. He named other consultants. He described how he had talked to the pastors of six of the jurors, explaining American Tobacco's position in the case in the hope the message would be passed on to their congregations. Clark also said he made cash contributions to the churches. At one point he mentioned he had information "that would blow this case sky high," but said he couldn't reveal it because to do so would harm him more than anyone.

Clark was getting cold feet. He had heard that his visits to the Barrett law office had been reported to Ed Blackmon. Don Barrett worried during this period that his phone might be tapped, and Clark began to use a code name when he called. In the end, Clark balked at the idea of becoming a turncoat, telling the Barretts that there were "just too many people who are going to get hurt." Feeling they had no choice, the Barretts forced Clark to testify by subpoenaing him to appear at the jury-tampering hearings that began in late July. It was at this point that Clark learned his initial phone call to Pat Barrett had been secretly recorded. And he did what the Barretts had feared: He repudiated all the information he had been telling them.

The state highway patrol, meanwhile, had also come up empty-handed in their investigation of improper attempts to influence the jury, though some jurors had refused to talk to them. In the midst of all this, Judge Evans recused himself from the case. With the Horton team planning a retrial, American raised questions about Fred Clark, Don Barrett's cocounsel, having once served on Evans's campaign committee, a perfectly proper activity in Mississippi, but one that can lead to a recusal motion. Without waiting for such a motion, Evans happily seized the opportunity to step down, passing the case to his junior colleague, Judge Eugene Bogen. In addition to inheriting the retrial, Bogen, then forty-five, stepped in to preside over the misconduct allegations arising from the first trial. But he had little patience with the murky charges and countercharges, and quickly ruled that the Barretts' allegations had no basis.

To this day, Tom Bezanson and Jim Upshaw vehemently deny that the defense made any improper attempts to influence the jury. Upshaw says he has "never worked for any client who demanded such integrity and purity from me" as American.

Of seven jurors and one alternate reached for interviews, none could recall any outside effort to influence their vote. At the same time, none could offer any detailed description of the deliberations, combining a general reluctance to discuss the matter with protestations that their memories have been clouded by the passage of time. Asking about how initial votes were reached and then switched seemed akin to searching for a key dropped on a once bare field since grown thick with kudzu.

There was no hesitation in Don Barrett's mind about seeking a retrial. He felt he had been robbed of a victory, and was determined not to lose the second time around. At the first trial, Barrett and Davis had presented almost the entire case for their side, with Fred Clark putting in what amounted to a cameo appearance. For the next round, Barrett wanted a black attorney who could be a major, forceful presence in the courtroom. He put in a call to Victor McTeer, the civil rights lawyer who had once regarded Barrett as an enemy. Although McTeer, who now had a growing civil practice in Greenville, was wary about Barrett, he came to believe his former adversary had changed. "Without making Don seem like Mother Teresa, which is hard to do," McTeer recalls, "I was persuaded that he had come a long way." So he signed on to the team.

Lawyers on both sides of the case found a very different jurist at the helm of the case as it headed toward a retrial. As short and compact as Judge Evans was tall and gangly, Judge Bogen had close-cropped blond hair, blue eyes, and a ramrod-straight, almost military, demeanor. A native of Greenville, some sixty miles west of Lexington in Washington County, Bogen was the great-grandson of the man who came to the town in the 1870s and became the first rabbi at the synagogue there. Bogen's mother, though, was a Methodist, and he was raised principally in that faith. After attending college at the University of Virginia, he returned to Mississippi for law school and to practice law. As a judge, he ran a tight courtroom, brooking no nonsense from attorneys. He also took his duties as a jurist seriously, issuing thoughtful written opinions on matters many of his colleagues saw fit to address in single-page orders.

Even Bogen, though, was not able to remove the hex that seemed to have attached itself to the Horton case, at least when it came to assembling a jury free of controversy. In February 1990, just two months prior to the scheduled start of the retrial, the clerk of the Holmes County court reported that someone had broken into the courthouse over the weekend. A few dollars had been removed from a cancer fund box. The only other thing that had been disturbed was a locked metal box that held the names of 2,500 prospective jurors typed on individual slips of paper. The box had been pried open, and a number of juror names were left scattered on the floor. It was possible, the clerk reported, that some juror names may have been taken from the box, or that new typed names could have been added. Judge Bogen decided that the Horton trial would move forward as scheduled, although, at the clerk's suggestion, he did have an additional 350 names added to the jury pool and ordered that the Horton jurors be chosen from the new group.

Then, on April 24, the day jury selection was getting under way, the judge learned something that convinced him it would be impossible to impanel an untainted jury in Holmes County. About two weeks prior to the start of the trial, Fred Clark had delivered glossy black folders to a number of Holmes County residents. Labeled "Horton vs. American Tobacco Company News Kit and Litigation Summary," the folders contained newspaper articles about efforts of cigarette companies to target black smokers and detailed the health toll inflicted on blacks by smoking. The packet also contained a "position paper" prepared by the Horton legal team quoting Louis Sullivan, then the secretary of the U.S. Department of Health and Human Services, saying, "We must resist the unworthy efforts of the tobacco merchants to earn profits at the expense and well-being of poor and minority citizens. This trade-off between profits and good health must stop. And it will stop if, around the country, our citizens rise up and say: 'Enough, no more.' " The Horton family lawyers, the position paper continued, "are committed to the pursuit of such accountability," and it noted that the 1988 trial of the family's claims "ended in a hung jury, amid charges that the tobacco company had tampered with the jury." Clark asked the recipients of the news kits to copy the material and to distribute it to others in Holmes County. He also sent a copy to the *Jackson Advocate,* a newspaper for the black community, which ran a story based on the contents.

This information campaign was misguided in both its conception and its execution, for it was almost certain to come to the attention of the defense. Which it did, and American's lawyers filed a motion for a change of venue, attaching a copy of the news kit as an exhibit, on the day jury selection began. Judge Bogen was livid. Excoriating the plaintiffs for their "blatant attempt to make an appeal on the basis of race to the persons in Holmes County, and thus indirectly to the jury pool," he immediately declared a mistrial and granted the defense request to move the proceedings. Thanks to this clumsy ploy by the Horton team, the defendants had at last succeeded at something they had been trying to do from the earliest days of the lawsuit: getting it moved out of Holmes County.

Judge Bogen set September 4, 1990, as the new trial date, and decided the case would be tried in Oxford, seat of Lafayette County (pronounced La-FAY-ette by Mississippians), about a hundred miles north of Lexington. Not that he thought moving the trial would assure an end to the lawyers' shenanigans. Even though he usually kept a tight rein on cases before him, Bogen knew the Horton matter would require particular vigilance. So he imposed a gag order on the lawyers, prohibiting them from talking to the press about the case. And when American sought permission to add two prominent Oxford physicians as expert witnesses at the retrial, Bogen refused, calling the request a ploy to curry favor with a Lafayette County jury. When, during the trial, the judge learned that one of the doctors was sitting on a bench at the front of the courtroom reserved for members of the defense team, he ordered him to sit with the rest of the spectators.

As in Lexington, the courthouse in Oxford is a two-story, late-nineteenth-century building that sits in the middle of the town square, surrounded by shops. A Confederate war monument — this one paying tribute to those who "gave their lives in a just and holy cause" — stands outside the building, while traffic whirls around the perimeter. Like Lexington, Oxford is the urban hub of a predominantly rural county. But no one would ever confuse the two towns. As the home of the University of Mississippi, Oxford is bustling and thriving, vibrant with youthful energy. The shops and restaurants around the square do a brisk business catering to students and faculty, and everywhere one looks is the droopy-mustached visage of Colonel Reb, a symbol of Confederate resistance and, to the dismay of many blacks, the mascot of Ole Miss. The overall look of the square and its environs suggests a Disney theme park re-creation of a small Mississippi town. Everything seems just a bit too tidy, the paint just a bit too fresh. As the Faulkner quotation on its south wall reminds us, the courthouse is at the center of it all, and it, too, furthers the impression of fabricated reality. The whitewashed structure is so pristine and elegant, it looks like part of a movie set.

The differences between the two towns were mirrored in the differences between the juries selected for the two trials. Ten whites and two blacks were selected to sit on the Oxford jury, and three or four had college degrees. Six of the jurors — twice as many as in Lexington — smoked. Given the failure of a predominantly black jury to decide in favor of Nathan Horton, it seemed pointless to speculate about where the sympathies of a majority-white jury would lie. But as journalists and stock analysts once again descended to report on the proceedings, they did note that a new legal ruling in the case appeared to offer a significant boost to the plaintiffs. Judge Bogen had restored the plaintiffs' strict-liability claim based on Section 402A of the *Restatement*, which states that anyone who sells a defective product that is "unreasonably dangerous" is liable to the consumer for damages. At the same time, he rejected the language of Comment *i*, which explicitly immunized "good tobacco," and instead said that it would be up to the jury to decide whether cigarettes were an "unreasonably dangerous" product. The jurors would thus be able to consider the dangers of tobacco itself, not just the additives. On other fronts, Judge Bogen did hand the tobacco company some minor victories. For example, he refused to let the plaintiffs delete the N-word from Walter Dickerson's taped deposition. And he ruled that American's lawyers could ask Dr. Ginzel about his service in Hitler's army.

The trial got under way the day after Labor Day. It was broiling hot, with afternoon temperatures soaring to 100 degrees, and the courthouse air conditioning simply couldn't keep up. Judge Bogen recessed each day around four o'clock so people could seek refuge at their better-cooled hotels and offices. For the most part, the lawyers for each side presented testimony very similar to that offered at the first trial, much of it from the same witnesses. At the end of three weeks, the case went to the jury. After six hours of deliberation, the jurors returned with a verdict that surprised virtually everyone. The American Tobacco Company, the jury concluded, was liable for the death of Nathan Horton, but they were awarding zero dollars in damages.

It was a compromise verdict. Jury foreman David Roach, forty-four years old at the time of the trial and the head of the University of Mississippi's computer center, recalls that "most people by far thought [Horton] exercised his own judgment, made his own choices" about smoking, and thus were not inclined to award him compensation. The smokers on the jury, he says, were least supportive of Horton's case. On the other hand, there was widespread agreement among the jurors that smoking caused illness. "I think that we probably all felt that it caused him to be sick, but he was an adult, he knew what he was doing, there was information at that time," says Barbara McGregor, who was fifty-five and worked as a secretary, though she had a master's in education. When one juror recalled a case in which there had been a finding of liability but no damages, that was it. "It really struck a chord with a lot of us as being a reasonable thing to do," Roach recalls.

The jury may have seen its verdict as a compromise, but Wall Street read it as another victory for the industry. Tobacco company stocks rose, and a stock analyst told *Newsday* that the verdict would "slow plaintiffs' cases to even less than a trickle."

As the lawyers filed out of the courtroom, Don Barrett was approached by reporters, who, naturally, wanted to know what he thought. Barrett, seldom at a loss for words, eventually found a way to capture his emotions. "It's kind of like watching your mother-in-law drive your new Cadillac off a cliff," he said. "You have mixed feelings about it."

Part 2

"Things Up My Sleeve"

13

On January 4, 1988, the day the Horton trial began in Lexington, Mississippi, Merrell Williams started a new job in Louisville, Kentucky, hoping to begin rebuilding his life. He had no way of knowing that his new position would put his life and Don Barrett's on intersecting trajectories.

Things had hit bottom for Williams a year earlier. At the beginning of 1987, his wife, Mollie, gave him a watch to commemorate their ten-year wedding anniversary. But it was more of a good-bye present. In July she filed for divorce. After consulting a lawyer, Williams decided he could best protect his interests by refusing to leave the modest two-bedroom house they shared in a middle-class section of Louisville. This strategy had a major flaw, however: He and Mollie were renting the house, and the landlord was Mollie's father. One day in August, Williams drove up to the house and noticed a BMW parked out front. A heavyset man got out, walked up with his arm extended, as though to introduce himself, and slapped an eviction notice into Williams's hand. That night, Mollie took their two daughters, ages seven and nine, and moved in with her parents.

To drive the eviction message home, members of Mollie's family showed up a number of days later with weed eaters and mowed down the huge vegetable garden Williams had planted, leaving a carnage of tomatoes, corn, okra, and peppers rotting in the late summer sun. "It was like something out of Sherman's march," says Williams, horrified to this day at the slaughter. "Merrell had trashed the place and my family came over and cleaned it up" was Mollie's version. He moved out in September.

Mollie was a twenty-year-old music major at the University of Mississippi when they first met, in Oxford in 1976. Williams was thirty-five and at the end of his marriage to his first wife, whom he had met and married in the space of four days in 1966. A Ph.D. in theater, Williams was a restless academic. Bored by teaching at Jackson State University, in Jackson, Mississippi, he took courses on rebuilding cars and launched what he called a "hobby-business," taking trips to England, buying vintage autos, and shipping them home. After restoring the cars, he sold them for a modest profit. When Mollie met him, Williams was tooling around in a Bentley and embarking on another venture. On one trip to England he hadn't found any cars to his liking, so instead he brought back the fixtures for an English pub, including a stand-up elm bar, a brass cash register, and even a "what the butler saw" device that patrons would crank to view naughty pictures. He installed his imported pub in a building just off the main square in Oxford (named after the English Oxford in 1837 in the specific hope that the Mississippi legislature would locate the state's first university there). He called it Abbey's Irish Rose, after the Abbey theater in Dublin.

Attracted to his good looks and rakish ways, Mollie married Merrell in 1977. "He seemed like a fascinating person with all these many experiences," she recalled. Marriage "seemed like it was going to be a wild adventure." Instead, she said, "it turned out to be a hand-to-mouth existence." By his own admission, Williams was a terrible businessman. What he loved was theater; that had been true ever since he got his first part at age fourteen in a Christmas production, playing a thief. Four years later he won accolades for his role in Tennessee Williams's *Glass Menagerie*, in which he played Tom, the defiant but conflicted would-be writer straining to break free. Offstage, Merrell Williams's approach to life was improvisational, and he marched through experiences as though they all had the transience of a theatrical production. Abbey's Irish Rose was but one example. "I just wanted to put in the set and then leave," Williams reflected years later. The pub quickly ran to ruin.

The couple moved to Denver, where Williams did a stint as a dishwasher and salad maker. Things looked up a bit when he landed a job at a car dealership selling Rolls-Royces. Then academia beckoned. Through contacts at the University of Denver, where he had earned his Ph.D., Williams got a teaching position at William Penn College in Oskaloosa, Iowa. Mollie and Merrell, baby daughter Jennifer in tow, settled in to what seemed like an ideal Midwestern-college-town life. The students, Mollie recalled, loved Williams. But, as was the case in job after job, Williams couldn't get along with his colleagues, in this instance the college president and his department head. His contract wasn't renewed, and it was back to Mississippi for a position at Hinds Junior College outside Jackson. "That's going down, not up," noted Williams, who enjoys annotating the events of his life with droll commentary.

Here, too, Williams clashed with his colleagues. The school just wanted him to do South Pacific and My Fair Lady, Mollie said. Instead, he mounted experimental productions that nobody wanted to see. For Williams's part, he was less than pleased to be called upon for such chores as handling the lighting for a fashion show put on by the college president's wife. Once again, there was a parting of ways.

The Mississippi Gulf Coast had always been a place of sanctuary and opportunity for Williams. His grandmother's cottage in Ocean Springs, an affluent, arty community adjoining the gaudier and grittier gambling mecca of Biloxi to the west, was a frequent vacation spot when he was a child. As he grew older, he came to the Mississippi Sound to sail, and performed in summer stock theater in Pascagoula. So it was to the coast that Merrell and Mollie, now with two young girls, repaired in 1981, hoping to make a go of something new. Williams decided on shrimping. He traded his '71 Fiat for a twenty-seven-foot boat, and spent much of a summer converting it to a shrimper. To help him along, other shrimpers gave him flounder that came up in their nets. While his boat sat idle, Williams also worked at the Biloxi Yacht Club, until he was fired, accused of having a bad attitude. Somehow the shrimping never panned out either, and Williams tended bar and dug ditches at construction sites.

Through it all, Mollie recalled, Williams was always "on the make for the big score." Early in their marriage, she said, he had been impressed by a large award someone had won in a lawsuit, and he remarked in passing that it would be a nice way to cash in. He also wrote plays and sent them off to agents, but they were invariably rejected. Mollie was getting fed up. Williams's failed ventures and troubled employment history left them penniless, relying on food stamps and other public assistance to survive. What's more, Williams had a drinking problem, and while he was never a violent drunk, he would frequently become withdrawn and cantankerous. Mollie was starting to feel she was married to a Tennessee Williams character: "intelligent, charming, persuasive, and . . . hopeless," in her words.

In 1982, at Mollie's insistence, they moved to her hometown of Louisville so she could be near her family. Here, too, Williams bumped from job to job, mostly selling cars. Coworkers from this period remember him fondly. He was a bit of an eccentric in their ranks, tweedy and academic, even smoking a pipe to complete the image, but he knew cars. "Merrell seemed to operate in his own sphere," recalled Tom Payette, owner of a Buick dealership where Williams worked. "He was a kind, gentle person who you couldn't rush or push." Williams worked for Payette for about a year and a half, left on his own accord to sell Nissans for a few months, then left that job, too.

By this time, Mollie was done waiting for things to improve. Having received her master's in speech pathology in 1986, she felt for the first time that she could get a job that would provide for herself and the children. "Things that had been barely tolerable before had become intolerable," she said. After she left him, she did a tally of their life together. In their ten years of marriage, they had lived in seven places and Williams had held twenty-three jobs.

So by late summer of 1987, Williams had lost his wife and children and been evicted from his home. Creditors were pursuing him in Kentucky courts. Even his Renault Le Car had broken down. Getting on a bicycle, which had one working brake, he wheeled over to Tom Payette Buick to see if he could get his old job back. Nothing was open in sales, so Williams took what was to be had: For $4.50 an hour, he cleaned oil out of the dealership's service bays. On weekends, he earned extra cash raking leaves at the home of one of the salesmen.

In November Williams got a phone call. "How would you like to make nine dollars an hour?" asked a woman from the Louisville Bar Association. Williams had taken some paralegal courses at the University of Louisville and had registered at the bar association's placement office. The woman sent him for an interview at Wyatt, Tarrant & Combs.

One of the oldest and largest law firms in Kentucky, Wyatt traced its history to frontier Louisville in 1812. By the late 1980s, its two hundred lawyers engaged in typical large-firm practice, ranging from antitrust and securities law to public finance and commercial lending. Among its blue-chip clients were the likes of General Electric, Ford, Metropolitan Life, and Pfizer. Still, there were some aspects of the practice that were distinctive to Kentucky. Some Wyatt lawyers, for example, specialized in equine law, advising clients on such things as racing regulations and buying and selling horses.

In a series of employment interviews, Williams learned little about the specifics of the available job. He does, however, recall with particular clarity one question he was asked: "Do you have any problems with smoking?" one of the interviewers inquired.

"I smoke, but I can quit," Williams replied.

In retrospect, it was the perfect answer.

The letter from Wyatt, Tarrant & Combs congratulating Williams on being hired informed him that he would be working on a document-screening project for one of the firm's biggest clients, Brown & Williamson Tobacco Corporation. That didn't mean much to Williams, who knew only that B&W was a large local employer. In fact, it had been a major presence in the city since the late 1920s, when it built a cigarette manufacturing plant and moved its headquarters there from North Carolina. In 1927, B&W was acquired by the London-based British-American Tobacco Company (BAT), one of the largest cigarette makers in the world. BAT itself had been created in a turn-of-the-century merger between American Tobacco and Great Britain's Imperial Tobacco

Company. Later, when U.S. trustbusters broke up American, BAT was spun off on its own.

Brown & Williamson got BAT back into the American market. The company's better-known brands included Raleigh, Kool (introduced in 1933 to compete with another mentholated brand known as Spud), and later, Viceroy and Belair. By 1986, B&W had consolidated all of its cigarette manufacturing in Macon, Georgia, but its headquarters and other operations remained in Louisville.

As directed, Merrell Williams showed up for his first day of paralegal work at the Brown & Williamson tower in downtown Louisville. There he found himself amid several dozen other paralegals and lawyers who had been mustered for a massive task. Brown & Williamson's attorneys had decided to create a database with detailed descriptive information on hundreds of thousands of internal company documents. The purpose of the database was to help the lawyers defend the company against product-liability lawsuits similar to the one Nathan Horton had filed against American Tobacco in Mississippi. B&W did not face as many suits as American, thanks to its smaller market share over the years, but as more smokers of B&W brands got sick, and as the ranks of plaintiffs' attorneys swelled, tobacco litigation seemed certain to be a growth industry.

In order to comply with discovery requests in this litigation, tobacco company lawyers needed to know what documents the company in fact possessed. Just as important, the lawyers needed to know what documents they did *not* have to turn over, based on a claim that under law they were "privileged" — involving, for example, communications between a lawyer and client. (In the case of a business, both the lawyer and the client may be individual employees of the business.)

The beauty of a database was that with a few computer keystrokes, a lawyer or law clerk could call up information on a document and determine its status. First, though, someone had to code and enter all that data. Williams and the others gathered at the Brown & Williamson tower that day were about to be trained for that task. Not all of his cohorts were Kentuckians. Two of Brown & Williamson's other principal law firms, King & Spalding, based in Atlanta, and Vinson & Elkins, based in Houston, had sent employees for the training session. The three firms had agreed to divide the document-coding process, with King & Spalding handling biological studies, Vinson & Elkins handling marketing documents, and Wyatt, as the home firm, taking corporate files from B&W's headquarters.

The lawyers and paralegals involved in the coding process were made to feel appreciated. Before the end of the training period, they were feted with a party at the Seelbach Hotel, a redoubt of restored elegance in the heart of Louisville. Such gestures were not lost on Merrell Williams. "I was a poor person, very poor, and I really wanted some kind of respect," he recalls.

Williams and his fellow coders initially received instructions in "objective" coding, the rote task of entering the date of a document, then names of the people who authored it and received it, and so forth. After just a couple of weeks, though, Williams was transferred to a smaller team of paralegals, who were told they were about to be inducted into an elite group responsible for "subjective" coding. In this process, the coders would need to read through a document and evaluate its contents, paying particular attention to its potential import in litigation. Although the subjective interpretation of each paralegal would determine the codes assigned to the document, the need for consistency and reliability required that this be a highly guided process. So Williams and the other subjective coders received a new round of intensive training.

In developing a coding procedure for its documents, Brown & Williamson was not reinventing the wheel. As Williams understood it, other tobacco companies, including Philip Morris and Liggett & Myers, had already coded their documents under a system developed by Shook Hardy & Bacon, a Kansas City law firm that had represented the industry since cigarette liability cases were first filed in the 1950s. Ruthless rivals in the marketplace, tobacco companies closed ranks and cooperated extensively in a number of areas deemed beneficial to the industry as a whole. This included lobbying, public relations, some forms of scientific research, and legal strategy. While a number of the most prominent law firms in the country have had long-standing relationships with individual cigarette manufacturers, the Shook Hardy firm has served as a kind of command central for tobacco litigation for decades. Indeed, it was Shook Hardy lawyers and scientists who came to Louisville to explain the subjective coding "taxonomy" developed for Brown & Williamson.

For a full week Merrell Williams and his coworkers attended lectures on a range of topics, from the corporate structure of Brown & Williamson and its parent, British-American Tobacco, to industry-sponsored scientific research projects. At one point, a biologist who was addressing the trainees made reference to something called "Special Account 4," and said, "I'm sure the plaintiffs would love to know about this," according to Williams's recollection. That piqued Williams's curiosity, and he realized that this job might be more interesting than he'd anticipated.

There was plenty else to foster a sense of adventure, a feeling that the document coders were embarking on something high-stakes and clandestine. Supervisors admonished coders to maintain secrecy, even suggesting that they not tell anyone where they worked. And then there was the taxonomy itself, whose complexities were discussed in a guide full of intriguing references. Some sample topic excerpts from the guide:

CONFIRMATION OF CAUSATION

The "MA; Confirmation of Causation" codes are intended to capture documents suggesting that research results confirm or supplement the alleged evidence that smoking causes disease. The objective is to capture documents which plaintiff's counsel could use to show that anyone's, especially Brown & Williamson's or BAT's, research produced results confirming that smoking causes disease.

INDUSTRY COMPETITION

Documents coded to "MK; Industry Competition" should discuss smoking and health issues in relation to research. Specifically look for any statement that research was performed in order to get a competitive edge or anything that implies that research was secondary to marketing. A document that suggests that a product should be designed to (subconsciously) cause a smoker to adjust his smoking habits (e.g., compensate) to obtain greater delivery of nicotine is an example. Another example would be not removing an allegedly carcinogenic substance from the product because removal would adversely affect the product's taste, thus giving other unaltered (better tasting) products a competitive edge. . . . Unfortunate statements not related to smoking and health should not be coded to "MK."

PROJECT MADHATTER
Sir Charles Ellis performed nicotine research in Project MAD-HATTER and in Project HIPPO. MADHATTER was a precursor to Project ARIEL (the Ellis patent). The MADHATTER project occurred in the early 1960s. Collect all references to Project MAD-HATTER and forward them to [a lawyer at King & Spalding in Atlanta] as soon as possible.

The litany of topics ran to fifty-seven pages. And to help the coders further, there were organization charts, personnel lists, project summaries, and glossaries galore — all designed to give as much discipline and direction as possible to the "subjective" coding process. Still, it was not meant to be a completely mechanical exercise. Williams and his fellow subjective coders had been selected specifically to *think* about what they were reading. One of the most important things they could do as they reviewed a document, they were told, was to evaluate whether it might be something the opposing side in lawsuit would want.

"Think like a plaintiff," they were told over and again.

In February 1988 the document-coding effort was moved to a different building, Brown & Williamson's Research, Development & Engineering center in an industrial area southwest of Louisville's downtown. It was not the best of neighborhoods. The parking lot in back of the four-story building was surrounded by a fence topped with barbed wire, and anyone entering or leaving the building had to pass a guard station on the first floor. The coding operation was set up on the second floor in a cavernous room filled with temporary tables. Immediately above them, on the third floor, were the labs, and occasionally, as Williams remembers it, various aromas would drift down through the vents.

With training finished, the coding process now got under way in earnest. At forty-seven, Williams was one of the older paralegals on the project. The supervising paralegal, Ernest Clements, was in his mid-twenties. He had a sprightly, Jerry Lewis–like sense of humor, according to Williams, and was a member of Mensa, the genius society. Assisting Clements in overseeing the coding crew was Barbara Boiarsky, who, at age forty-three, was also somewhat older than the rest of the crowd. She and Williams quickly took a liking to each other. Williams had a daughter the same age as hers, and he began to confide in Boiarsky about his divorce proceedings. Despite his maudlin moments, Boiarsky found him charming and enjoyed his dry sense of humor. By the fall of 1988, they were dating.

Document review can be a wearisome, eye-blearing task, and the coders would take frequent breaks, often organizing pickup games of miniature golf in the back of the room, putting into Styrofoam cups. Williams bantered easily with his coworkers, whom he found to be an amiable bunch. He also joined the B&W baseball team, a move that engendered some discussion, since he was technically a Wyatt employee. Increasingly, though, Williams found that he didn't have to look to activities outside work for diversion. He was finding plenty of interest in the documents he had been assigned to code.

An early group that grabbed his attention detailed efforts by Brown & Williamson to have its cigarettes appear in movies. Product placement, as such advertising is known, is hardly limited to cigarettes; the most famous example was the appearance of Reese's Pieces in the movie *E.T.* in 1982. Under that arrangement, Hershey Foods agreed to sponsor a tie-in promotion after the movie's release, and as a result saw sales of the candy soar. Often, though, manufacturers pay a fee to get their product — or the product's brand name or logo — featured. Brown & Williamson hired an agency, Associated Film Promotion, to help with this process, leading Williams to find the following letter in B&W's files from Sylvester Stallone to the president of AFP, Robert Kovaloff:

April 28, 1983

Dear Bob:

As discussed, I guarantee that I will use Brown & Williamson tobacco products in no less than five feature films.

It is my understanding that Brown & Williamson will pay a fee of $500,000.00.

Hoping to hear from you soon;

Sincerely,
Sylvester Stallone

There is nothing illegal about product placement per se, but cigarettes raise special concerns. A congressional ban on television commercials for cigarettes took effect in January 1971. Films that open in movie theaters, of course, often end up on television, as those involved in product placement were well aware.

External events, meanwhile, continued to feed the suspicion Williams was developing about the industry he worked for. The Horton case in Mississippi had attracted his attention, and shortly after it the Cipollone tobacco trial started in New Jersey. The original plaintiff in that case, Rose Cipollone, had sued three cigarette makers, having smoked each of their brands. On April 21, 1988, federal district judge H. Lee Sarokin issued a ruling denying a request by the tobacco companies to have the Cipollone case thrown out. In his opinion, Judge Sarokin wrote: "The evidence presented . . . permits the jury to find a tobacco industry conspiracy, vast in its scope, devious in its purpose and devastating in its results." He found that the jury could "reasonably conclude" that the cigarette makers had conspired to mislead the public "with full knowledge" and with "callous, wanton, willful and reckless disregard . . . for the illness and death it would cause." In June 1988, the jury did award the widower of Rose Cipollone $400,000 in damages, the first such award against cigarette makers, though it was later overturned on appeal.

Merrell Williams, too, had come to feel that the tobacco companies were hiding information from the public, and that he needed to get the information out. He just didn't know how. "By the middle of the summer I was a spy, no question about it," he recalled. His acts of espionage began modestly. He jotted notes about topics that interested him on scraps of paper and smuggled them out in the bottom of his shoe or in a coat pocket. "Yesterday — went through Brand Switching Studies," he scribbled on the back of a letter. "The Ind. St. [Industry Studies] show a statistic for 16–21 year olds, and I have seen this time & again. If they are in the studies why any interest if not to market to them?" Separately, he noted: "Read numerous abstracts on harmful effects of smoking 1985. Mag [Magazine]: *Chest, Mutagenesis* — how can so many scientists be wrong? 'The facts are not conclusive' is bullshit." The article abstracts, Williams explained later, were prepared for distribution to B&W lawyers.

No one suspected that Williams had become a mole. In May 1988, his supervisor Ernest Clements signed an evaluation letter — drafted by Williams — which was sent to the director of the paralegal program at the University of Louisville, where Williams was finishing a course. "Mr. Williams is punctual, reliable, follows directions, and has shown a healthy initiative throughout his employment," the letter stated. "At present, I have no suggestion for improvement regarding Mr. Williams' performance. I recommend the grade of A." Later Williams wrote a letter for Clements when he was seeking a promotion.

On a warm day in the fall of 1988, Williams walked out of the building with his first document. The item he selected for removal was one of the numerous guides prepared specifically for the document coders to help them understand what they were reading. The thirty-five-page guide, titled "Chronology of Brown & Williamson Smoking and Health Research," summarized B&W research projects from the 1940s into the 1980s. Nearly every entry in the chronology contained a citation to a specific document or series of documents by "Bates number." Bates numbers are to litigation documents what Social Security numbers are to people: unique numerical tags used for identification and tracing. Every page of every document slated for review by the subjective coders had a Bates-number stamp, usually on the lower right corner.

Ultimately, Williams would use the Bates-number references in the chronology as a road map to guide him to the cited documents for removal and copying. Initially, though, he had a concern. He wondered whether some kind of security feature might be incorporated into the Bates-stamp ink — a magnetic substance, for instance. The research chronology was not Bates-stamped, since it was not an actual internal Brown & Williamson document. So on the day he decided to take the chronology home, Williams also took a random B&W document that had been stamped to see if any alarms would go off.

At lunch hour, he folded the documents, stuffed them down the front of his pants, and headed out of the building. Nothing happened as he passed the guard station, walked into the parking lot, and got into his car. Shortly after he turned out of the lot onto Hill Street, though, Williams noticed a police car in his rearview mirror and was sure he was being stopped. "You're gone, you're gone," he said to himself as he pulled to the side of the road. The police car drove right by.

With the test run a success, Williams started systematically removing documents in December 1988. His smuggling techniques tended more toward the comical than the sophisticated. He bought a pair of baggy pants at a thrift shop to accommodate larger caches of paper, and occasionally carried a bag of potato chips on his way out of the building, hoping his crinkling the bag would mask any rustling sounds. At times he strapped on a rubber corset that he had bought during a paunchy period in the mid-seventies and essentially used it as a rubber band to secure documents to his body. In addition to being uncomfortable, the corset smelled awful. More prosaically, Williams sometimes simply brought a briefcase to work, filled it with documents, and then walked out with it at the end of the day.

Hours for paralegals working on document coding were somewhat flexible, and Williams started most of his workdays at 5:30 or 6:00 in the morning and left by mid-afternoon. The paralegals also had access to the building on weekends, and Williams used this time in particular to remove documents. After copying the documents, he returned the originals to B&W, smuggling them in the same way he got them out. Over time, Williams made a number of copies of the documents he accumulated, depositing varying sets in different locations around the country, a fact that would later bedevil B&W lawyers as they tried to reconstruct the document trail.

Plowing through B&W's files, Williams grew increasingly troubled about the way he felt the tobacco industry was manipulating and misleading the public. He also became alarmed on a personal level because of his own experience with smoking. Both his parents had smoked, even though that aggravated the asthma he suffered while growing up. His condition was severe enough that the family heeded a doctor's recommendation and moved from Baton Rouge, Louisiana, to west Texas for the drier climate. Other remedies were also tried: On one occasion as a child Williams was actually told to smoke small brown "medicinal" cigarettes to help his breathing. He didn't pick up a real cigarette until 1959, when he was eighteen and starring at the Pascagoula Playhouse as Tom in *The Glass Menagerie*. The stage directions for the first scene call for Tom to walk onstage and light up. Then he utters his opening line, one that would seem apt years later, when Williams was working at B&W: "Yes, I have tricks in my pocket, I have things up my sleeve."

For that play, the cigarette was merely a prop, which Williams readily abandoned. The following year, as a student at Baylor University in Waco, Texas, he landed a part in a play called *A Whistle in the Night* as a frustrated ad executive who yearned to be a playwright. The character chainsmoked, and this time life and art merged. Onstage and off, Williams became a heavy smoker of Kools, a Brown & Williamson brand. Around this time, Williams's father began what became an annual tradition, giving Merrell two cartons of Kools for Christmas.

Although he continued to smoke heavily for a number of years after college, Williams was also able to put cigarettes aside for long stretches. At his paralegal job, he bought B&W's Richland cigarettes on the cheap from vending machines at the office. But he didn't buy them for long, despite the cut-rate prices. Motivated by what he was reading about smoking and disease, he quit cold turkey on September 27, 1989.

That same week, he drove his first load of documents out of Louisville to Jackson, Mississippi, leaving the box temporarily with a friend, who had no idea of the contents. Accompanying Williams on the journey was Barbara Boiarsky, his supervisor, who had practically become his fiancée. The two had been dating seriously and had discussed marriage, and Williams wanted her to meet his mother, who lived in Jackson. This trip marked the high point in their relationship, which deteriorated over the next several months.

Boiarsky had begun to notice Williams's dark side. While she suspected he had some problems with alcohol, she was amazed during one visit to his apartment to find empty beer cans stuffed under the couch and piled in the linen closet. One day she was with him, he drank an entire case of beer. Boiarsky also began to feel she was being used. During the trip to Jackson, for example, Williams asked if he could buy furniture with her charge card. Williams says he was developing his own reservations about her — one problem was that she smoked, while he had quit. At no point, Boiarsky says, did she ever know that Williams was smuggling documents.

14

Day by day, the coding team moved steadily through the files of various departments located at Brown & Williamson's corporate headquarters. And almost everywhere Merrell Williams looked, he found evidence buttressing his conviction that the company he was working for was engaged in a dirty business, and knew it.

In the 1950s, as evidence linking smoking and cancer began to mount, company documents started referring to cancer by a code word: Zephyr. Even though the industry dismissed the validity of the mouse-painting experiments that looked at the effects of cigarette smoke condensate, B&W's parent, British-American Tobacco, commissioned precisely this kind of research as part of "Project Janus." And while industry officials and lawyers would contend — and still do contend — that there is debate about whether smoking causes illness, a set of meeting minutes from a 1978 conference of B&W and BAT scientists states the opposite: "There has been no change in the scientific basis for the case against smoking," states the first paragraph of the minutes. "Additional evidence of smoke-dose related incidence of some diseases associated with smoking has been published.

But generally this has long ceased to be an area for scientific contro-versy."

Similarly, BAT — and through it, B&W — gained early and substan-tial knowledge about the pharmacological effects of nicotine. A 1963 report titled "The Fate of Nicotine in the Body" described in great detail how the body absorbs, distributes, and eliminates the substance. Other studies documented its effectiveness as a mild tranquilizer, perhaps more effective in this regard than anything any pharmaceutical companies had developed. That led B&W's general counsel, Addison Yeaman — who had also received reports of a possible breakthrough in filter tech-nology — to propose in a memo that cigarettes could be recast as a prod-uct sold specifically for this effect.

"Moreover, nicotine is addictive," he stated flatly, before setting forth his vision of B&W's new market niche: "We are, then, in the business of selling nicotine, an addictive drug effective in the release of stress mech-anisms." Of course that is precisely the business Brown & Williamson and other cigarette makers were engaged in, but they would never publicly acknowledge it, claiming, to the contrary, that nicotine's only intended function in a cigarette was to enhance its taste.

Certain things Williams discovered particularly stuck in his craw: evi-dence of marketing to kids, for example, and the use of product placement in movies. Nothing, though, shocked him more than a group of files doc-umenting the extensive role played by tobacco industry lawyers over the years in controlling the research into smoking and health conducted by the industry and in selectively screening the results. Given the increasing concerns over product-liability litigation, the lawyers' role at cigarette companies became central and pervasive. In Williams's view it became improper as well.

A series of documents unearthed by Williams chronicle the efforts of B&W's in-house attorneys to assure that scientific research conducted by the company, and especially by BAT, came under attorney–client privi-lege or the "work product" privilege, so it would not have to be produced in liability suits. The attorney–client exemption applies to communica-tions between a lawyer and client related to a legal matter; the work prod-uct rule to material prepared specifically at the behest of a lawyer in anticipation of litigation. Reports of routine scientific research clearly don't qualify under either, but in a November 1979 memo to B&W general counsel Ernest Pebbles, in-house attorney J. Kendrick Wells III appeared to suggest steps to establish a privilege for sensitive BAT reports on smoking and health. "Appropriate paper work should be established with BAT," he wrote, "to establish that documents of a certain nature are prepared for B&W in anticipation of litigation."

A few years later, Wells discussed concerns about Project Rio, a BAT investigation into making a "safer" cigarette. The idea of a manufacturer announcing development of a safer cigarette terrified tobacco defense lawyers, because it would amount to an acknowledgment that the previous product was not safe, thus opening a floodgate of product-liability litigation. So in a June 1984 memo to the file, Wells wrote: "If Project Rio must continue, restructuring probably will be required to control the risk of generating adverse evidence admissible in U.S. lawsuits. . . . Direct lawyer involvement is needed in all BAT activities pertaining to smoking and health from conception through every step of the activity." On another subject in the same memo, he fretted: "The problem posed by BAT scientists and frequently used consultants who believe cause [of disease by smoking] is proven is difficult," and he ruminated about ways senior management could distance themselves from such conclusions.

Much as they would have liked to, B&W's lawyers realized they couldn't completely shut down the flow of information from BAT, but they tried as much as possible to play gatekeeper. In a February 1986 memo Wells commented on a series of projects in which the B&W scientific staff had expressed interest. For what was called an "aerosol testing" project, he wrote:

> Among things of interest, the project apparently intends to investigate the retention of smoke particles in the respiratory tract. Such data could be used by the plaintiff. I have taken under advisement whether B&W should receive reports from this project. I propose to suggest to RD&E [Research, Development, and Engineering] that we ask for more information before we decide. The work will occur in Germany, and the German scientist who designed the program should seek counsel before providing the additional information. Hopefully, the problem area will disappear.

An investigation of "nicotine within the smoker" drew this comment:

> RD&E is interested in information pertaining to the role of nicotine in the smoker's subjective perception of smoke quality. If the reports stick to research data, the reports would be interesting. However, if the reports include discussion of pharmacological effects of nicotine, the information will not be interesting and would be helpful to the plaintiff. RD&E will begin receiving reports from this activity and be prepared to inform BAT to cease sending the data to B&W if the science is not interesting.

"Interesting" to Wells seemed to mean "innocuous in the event of litigation."

Industry lawyers didn't just vet scientific research, they commissioned it. In public pronouncements and in trials, cigarette company representatives pointed proudly to their funding of "independent" scientific studies on the health effects of smoking through the Council for Tobacco Research (CTR) and its "independent" Scientific Advisory Board. At the Horton trial, for example, American Tobacco executive Preston Leake had boasted of the CTR's devotion to finding out the truth about smoking and health.

Williams, however, unearthed evidence of another side to the CTR. Apart from the Scientific Advisory Board, a group of industry lawyers operated outside the public view, funding "special projects." The primary purpose of these studies was to generate data that could be used to support the industry's position on health issues in courts or before legislatures. Other research was underwritten by industry law firms through programs with cloak-and-dagger names such as "Special Account 4." One Special Account 4 project, for example, funded a look at "a possible genetic component in disease" based on data from Scotland's Orkney Islands, presumably part of an industry effort to establish that you get some illnesses from your ancestors, not your cigarettes. It was these special accounts that Williams had been told during his training sessions plaintiffs would "love to know about." Merely learning of the existence of this shadow research program would be important to antitobacco forces, because it belied the industry's 1954 promise of full and frank disclosure of information about smoking and health.

When Merrell Williams began smuggling Brown & Williamson's documents, he had no plan about what to do with them, only a feeling that he possessed information that needed to get out, a story that needed telling. Yet he was afraid. The very act of removing the documents was risky enough. Actually disseminating the information seemed suicidal. Williams, though, contemplated taking this step. In his mind the tobacco companies had become more than just devious corporate miscreants. Together with their law firms they had become forces of unalloyed evil, capable of doing almost anything to sell a deadly product — and to keep their secrets under wraps. But he didn't know what to do.

Then, in what Williams acknowledges sounds like a biblical experience, he had a revelation in the mountains. In January 1990, he and Barbara Boiarsky drove to Natural Bridge park, part of the Daniel Boone National Forest in eastern Kentucky, and rented a cabin for a weekend. It was the dead of winter, the trees were covered in ice, and Williams decided to take a walk alone. Many things were weighing on his mind. His ex-wife Mollie was about to get married and move with his kids to Indiana. At the same time, his child support payments had gone up, and he had to move to a cheaper apartment to make ends meet. And he knew his relationship with Barbara was deteriorating. "I really felt terribly isolated about everything," he recalls. The one thing that emerged as the center for his life was the documents. "While things seemed to be breaking apart in other areas, this was kind of a continuity," he says. That's when the revelation came. "The word 'God' comes to mind," he says. "It was just an overwhelming moment. . . . I just had to do something about this one thing." At that moment, he says, "I made a decision that, come hell or high water, I was going to start talking with the enemy" — meaning opponents of tobacco.

His first call was to Tom Eagan. A Mississippian who had moved to Louisville, Eagan, at the age of forty-nine, had just earned a law degree and passed the Kentucky bar. Because Eagan was an attorney, Williams had some hope that their conversations would be protected by the attorney-client privilege. The tale Williams spun of a monstrous tobacco company conspiracy to deceive the American public struck Eagan as off the wall and, at the same time, completely in keeping with the kinds of stories Williams would concoct when they had first met in Jackson in the mid-1970s.

Eagan had been artistic director of the Jackson Little Theater at that time and Williams was teaching drama at Jackson State. They met when Eagan caught sight of Williams in a Rolls-Royce and asked if he could sit in the car, just to see how it felt. In short order they became collaborators on some writing projects. Williams, Eagan came to find, was moody, irascible, and antisocial — not someone he particularly wanted to hang out with. At the same time, Eagan was drawn to Williams's creative intellect, with its flair for drama and dark humor. In Eagan's view, Williams was a "genius," whose abilities and limitations were a perfect complement to his own. "He's a writer [who] said he could never complete things," Eagan recalls, "and I'm a hack writer — I complete things." Williams's storylines veered toward the sinister and conspiratorial, while Eagan liked things light and sugary.

One of their collaborations was a novel (never published) about a Nazi U-boat in the Gulf of Mexico that is ordered up the Mississippi River. The crew's mission is to free members of Germany's elite Africa Corps, who are imprisoned in Natchez, Mississippi (on the banks of the river), and somewhere along the way, they are supposed to steal the secrets to the atomic bomb. Eagan also set out to produce a play Williams had written called *The Skinner Box,* which features a group of professors at a small college who come to learn that the new president of the college has no academic degrees and is a former used-car salesman. What's more, the president has landed a federal grant to admit "certifiable morons" to the college to see whether they can be educated. The production never got off the ground.

The storylines for both the novel and the play derived from experiences in Williams's life, the novel from stories Williams's father heard when he worked at a naval base near New Orleans during World War II, and the play from Williams's own teaching experience. But now, listening to Williams talk about tobacco, Eagan felt incapable of separating fact from fantasy, and he wondered if Williams was having the same problem.

It was certainly too much for a newly minted lawyer practicing on his own to get involved in, Eagan decided.

It was clear, though, that Williams was genuinely afraid, so Eagan reluctantly agreed to serve as an intermediary to put him in touch with another lawyer. Williams came up with the name of Richard Daynard, the law professor and antitobacco activist who had helped Don Barrett hook up with Don Davis to try the Horton case. Now Eagan called Daynard, saying he was an attorney representing a client, whom he couldn't name, who had important information about the tobacco industry. But various efforts to set up a meeting foundered, including a proposal from Williams to rendezvous at the Shakespeare festival in Stratford, Ontario. Daynard also received various written communications with a Louisville post office box as the return address, signed with a woman's name, asking if Daynard would be interested in receiving some damning information about tobacco companies. Daynard wrote back to say he would be, under the right circumstances. Bemused by the cloak-and-dagger communications, Daynard himself observed his own precautions. His wife, he says, would not let him travel to Louisville, B&W's home turf.

Although a meeting proved elusive, Daynard was able to refer Williams to another attorney, named — appropriately, for these circumstances — George Covert, who had a small practice in Baton Rouge. Covert had started out as a business and real estate lawyer; then, when asbestos litigation burgeoned in the eighties, he began representing workers with claims against asbestos manufacturers. In 1988, Covert's first wife died of lung cancer, and when Williams called him in February 1990, his office was pursuing lawsuits for her death as well as cases on behalf of two other smokers. Williams sounded "scared shitless," Covert recalls. Saying he feared his phone might be tapped, Williams arranged a meeting in Jackson, Mississippi, at the Old Tyme Deli, a well-known establishment where you can get everything from pastrami to catfish pâté. Covert showed up accompanied by his second wife, but her presence seemed to make an already edgy Williams more nervous. So Williams and Covert drove down the road to a tennis club, where they sat on a bench while Williams talked about what he had been reading.

Covert asked Williams if he had any documents, but Williams was wary, not entirely sure who he was dealing with. Maybe, was his answer.

Covert suggested that any documents that did exist could simply be left on his doorstep. But that wasn't satisfactory to Williams. Once the documents became public, he was sure they would be traced to him, so any plan to turn them over, he felt, had to include provisions for his own legal defense. Overall, Williams thought that Covert just didn't seem to appreciate what he had to offer. Years later, Covert agreed. "I probably made a tactical mistake," he said in retrospect, "but I was trying to keep it so simple at the time that I really didn't want to go into anything else."

The meeting ended inconclusively, but a month or so later the two agreed to meet again. The appointed place this time was Mary Mahoney's restaurant in Biloxi. The fabled establishment, popular with tourists and locals alike, would become even more famous six years later with the publication of John Grisham's *Runaway Jury*. The upstart jurors in the thriller — which, it so happens, is about a tobacco lawsuit in Mississippi — demanded to be fed at the landmark restaurant. There would be no thrills on the day of Williams's appointed meeting with Covert, however. Williams waited for two hours, and then left in disgust. Recalling the day years later, Covert said he was delayed by a rainstorm.

Williams had told Barbara Boiarsky that the reason for his trip to the Gulf Coast was to look for a teaching job there. False though it was, the explanation certainly demonstrated a lack of commitment to their sputtering relationship, and the two soon split up. Meeting women was never a problem for Williams, however. In the summer of 1990 he was walking his dog near his apartment complex when he happened upon Sherry Gibson, who was walking hers. "I love your dress, I love those Oriental designs," Williams told her. What a line, thought Gibson, who felt she happened to be wearing one of her least attractive outfits that day. Still, the two stood and chatted for nearly an hour and a half. Williams launched into a soliloquy about literature, and Gibson was dazzled. "I was just astounded at his intellect," she recalls.

Forty-three at the time and divorced, Gibson was also wary of Williams, who seemed fascinating, but a bit odd. He was persistent, though, leaving two or three messages on her answering machine over the next several weeks, and he finally persuaded her to come to his place for dinner. An accomplished cook, whose repertoire includes everything from Cajun dishes to chicken parmigiana, Williams won her over with cuisine and conversation. She had never met anybody who engaged in such wide-ranging discourse. When it came to discussing his work, though, Williams clammed up. At the beginning of their relationship he told her only that he was a "legal analyst" involved in a special project that he couldn't discuss. Later he acknowledged that he did research for Wyatt, Tarrant & Combs, but said that a confidentiality agreement prevented him from divulging anything else.

Of course, Williams was desperate to talk about his work — if only he could find the right person. With Tom Eagan tired of fronting for him, Williams turned to Nina Selz, who had been his friend and confidante since they had met as students at Baylor in the early sixties. There they had both been drawn into a small group of students who shared intellectual pretension and social disaffection, but didn't know quite what to do with themselves. Too late to be beatniks and too early to be hippies, they called themselves the Brazos River Society (after the river that runs through Waco, Texas, where the university is located) and spent a lot of time drinking Jack Daniel's. Selz emerged from this milieu to pursue a fairly steady course through life. After two years in the Peace Corps in Turkey, she went on to get a doctorate in psychology from the University of Texas, and has since held a series of jobs in the area of learning research and, more recently, computer-based training for businesses and the military.

Selz recognized that Williams was prone to adopt the dissolute ways of the Brazos River crowd as a permanent form of existence, and in 1963 she encouraged her friend to join the Army as a way to get some discipline in his life. He did, but never made it past basic training. Wearing full gear in the broiling sun at the rifle range at Fort Gordon, Georgia, Williams called for a medic after noticing that a fellow soldier had mangled his thumb in the chamber of an M-1 rifle. The drill sergeant was unsympathetic; his response to Williams's insistent pleas was to order him to hit the ground and do fifty push-ups. After complying, Williams again asked for aid for his comrade. Fifty more push-ups, came the order. Williams ripped off his helmet and charged the sergeant, swinging wildly at him with the helmet.

The incident was ultimately excused because it was decided that Williams had been suffering from heatstroke. His last memories of military life are of sitting in an Army hospital reading *Moby Dick.* He was discharged — honorably — after about four months of service. "It was not Colin Powell's story," Williams noted. He drifted off to New York, where he landed some off-Broadway roles, and then headed for Denver for graduate school in theater.

Over the years, Selz came to regard Williams as family. Although her career took her to various places around the country and Williams pursued his own peripatetic path, they kept in touch, speaking by phone and visiting when they could. Selz has known each of Williams's wives, is a godparent to his daughters, and is friends with his mother. In 1990 she visited him in Louisville, and found him agitated. He let her in on part of his secret. He was reading things at work that disturbed him tremendously, he told her. Things that made him think of his father, puffing on a cigarette even as he waited for an ambulance after a heart attack. Things that enraged him about how tobacco companies were trying to appeal to children. Things about smoking and health that had been known by the cigarette manufacturers years before they became public knowledge. He did not mention that he was smuggling documents.

At Williams's request, Selz revived efforts to set up a meeting with Dick Daynard. Frustrated after his experience with Covert, Williams felt that Daynard had the kind of antitobacco credentials he was looking for. Williams knew, for example, that Daynard was on the board of a nonprofit organization called Stop Teenage Addiction to Tobacco.

For his part, Daynard had about given up on the mystery informant who had tried to contact him. After fielding furtive phone calls and sending responses to strange P.O. boxes, only to see communications die out, Daynard had begun to wonder if he was actually dealing with someone from the tobacco industry, trying to dupe him into something. Then came the call from Nina Selz. She offered her Florida home as a meeting spot, and in September Daynard flew down to Orlando. Selz wore a carnation when she met him at the airport, lest he have trouble spotting her. It wasn't until he arrived at Selz's house that Daynard learned Merrell Williams's name.

Despite the nuttiness leading up to their get-together, Daynard's gut told him that he was meeting someone who had genuinely important information about the secret world of tobacco, he recalls. When Daynard learned about Williams's documents, he realized just how important that information might be. He also understood how perilous it was to possess it. He was relieved, therefore, that Williams didn't offer him any documents during the course of the meeting, because he wasn't sure what he would have done with them.

What *Williams* should do with the material was the subject of their conversation through the afternoon and into the night. One option they discussed was for Williams to turn over the documents anonymously to an antismoking organization. Another was for him to take the material to someone on Capitol Hill. Finally, there was the idea of Williams writing a book about the papers. This was the option Williams seemed most eager to pursue. After all, if there was a story to be told, why shouldn't he do the telling? Daynard's advice, however, was discouraging under any scenario.

For starters, Williams would lose his job. Even if he proceeded anonymously, Daynard and Williams reckoned, it wouldn't take long for Brown & Williamson to identify him. The loss of his livelihood, of course, was a concern to Williams. In addition to his own welfare, there were his children to consider, and he had recently hired an attorney to win custody of his daughters from Mollie. Williams did wonder if somehow the documents could be a source of income to him, but it wasn't Daynard's impression that Williams's principal aim was to cash in on his trove.

Money, moreover, might be the least of his problems. If his aim was to get the story out, Brown & Williamson could sabotage that effort by denying the authenticity of the documents, and he might be hard-pressed to prove otherwise. Most dangerous and most likely of all, B&W could go on the offensive, pursuing Williams on civil and maybe even criminal charges. No one on Capitol Hill could shield him from prosecution in the Kentucky courts, Daynard told him. So he would need good defense counsel, and unfortunately, Daynard's organization at Northeastern University law school didn't have the financial resources to offer that.

In the end, the best Daynard could do for Williams was the same thing he had done before: offer him a name. This time it was not a lawyer, but a journalist, someone who might be willing to assume the risk of helping Williams tell his story. Following their lengthy conversation, they slept at Selz's house and rode together to the airport in the morning. As they said their good-byes, Daynard told Williams: "You're a good man." Hearing that meant a lot to Williams. As much as he felt a moral imperative to expose Brown & Williamson's secrets, at times he was wracked by guilt and doubt. He was, after all, engaged in deceit and betrayal. For years to come, he would remember and cherish these parting words from Daynard.

15

Morton Mintz left the *Washington Post* in 1988 after a thirty-year career with the newspaper. He covered the pharmaceutical industry for the paper, and, pursuing his particular interest in birth control, had authored a book about the Pill and another on the Dalkon shield intrauterine device. During two periods, once in the mid-sixties and again in the mid-eighties, he wrote about tobacco for the *Post.* Indeed, in his last year on the job he had covered the Horton and Cipollone trials.

In the fall of 1990, he was looking for a big project to occupy him in his retirement, so he welcomed Richard Daynard's call putting him in touch with Merrell Williams. Unlike Daynard, Mintz had no qualms about visiting Louisville, and on a weekend in late November he flew into town and checked into an airport hotel. Williams met him there.

The chemistry was bad from the start. According to Williams's account, Mintz was skeptical and abrupt, peppering him with questions that evinced doubt about the authenticity of what Williams was telling him and about whether the information was really anything new. Recalling the meeting, Mintz disagreed that he was hostile. He thought Williams's information might be fascinating and terribly important, but he noted that, at that time, Williams wasn't showing him anything. Mintz wanted to get his hands on the documents to see if there was a book to be written.

The two entered into an uneasy alliance. Williams started mailing Mintz batches of documents, but seemed irritated that Mintz wasn't dropping all his other projects to focus on them. When he saw the documents, Mintz acknowledged that they were indeed extremely important, but he sensed that Williams thought they would bring down the whole tobacco industry. That view, Mintz felt, was grandiose.

Over the course of about a year Williams sent roughly a dozen packages of material to Mintz's Chevy Chase, Maryland, home. They never met again, but communicated by letter and phone, taking certain minimal precautions. If Mintz answered one of Williams's calls on a cordless phone, for example, he switched to one with a cord. Where he could do so without blowing Williams's cover, Mintz used information from the documents to guide further research. He filed Freedom of Information Act requests seeking data on cigarette product placement in movies, for example. To a great extent, however, the need for secrecy stymied him. And all along he knew that if he were ever to write something about the documents, he would have to contact Brown & Williamson to get their comment, but for a time Mintz simply swept that concern under the rug.

Many months into his dealings with Williams, Mintz decided to get this issue resolved. He sought two legal opinions, the first from the Government Accountability Project, a Washington, D.C., public-interest group, the second from Alan Morrison, a Washington attorney seasoned in constitutional law and public policy. Morrison also had antitobacco credentials: He'd worked on the Cipollone case and had testified before Congress as a proponent of regulating tobacco advertising. Both opinions were unequivocal and devastating: Mintz was playing with fire, he was told. He might well be violating Kentucky and Maryland law, and could face civil and criminal liability. Indeed, the lawyers told him, all this could happen *before* he even got to publish a word.

That was it for Mintz. No longer affiliated with the *Post*, he didn't have a large media organization backing him. Legal fees and damages would be his alone to bear, and he wasn't about to risk his retirement nest egg for that. Or while away his golden years in prison. He shipped all the Brown & Williamson documents back to Williams.

Fortunately for Williams, his string of disappointments in trying to unload the Brown & Williamson documents was paralleled by a dramatic improvement in his personal life. Not only were he and Sherry Gibson hitting it off, she and his daughters were becoming fast friends. On weekends, when Jennifer and Sarah, now twelve and ten, were visiting Williams, they would hang out for girl talk at Sherry's apartment. Williams was also moving forward with his efforts to win custody of the girls. It wasn't long before he and Sherry began to talk about marriage. In early 1991, they began to do some house hunting in Louisville, looking for a place that would be big enough for a family of four. Standing in the basement of one home that they liked on a quiet cul-de-sac, Williams said he thought they should take it. And then, in front of the surprised seller, he turned to Sherry and said, "And why don't we get married? Will you marry me?"

"Are you serious?" she replied.

The wedding took place in April 1991 in a small chapel overlooking a lake and garden outside of Louisville. The chapel is located on the grounds of a cemetery, and during weddings the bride and groom actually stand on the grave of someone buried in the church floor. Sherry and Merrell took their vows on the tomb, with Sarah and Jennifer at their side and about thirty guests looking on. The newlyweds then left for a honeymoon cruise in the Bahamas.

Just before the wedding, Williams had filed for bankruptcy, something he had done in 1977, the year he married Mollie. It was a way of jettisoning the past and making a clean start, never mind how many jilted creditors were left paying for what he abandoned. In 1991, though, it really did seem that life was beginning anew for Williams. Just weeks after the wedding, a court awarded him temporary custody of his daughters, and he, Sherry, and the girls all moved into the contemporary five-bedroom home where he had proposed, and which Sherry had purchased, just a few months before. They bought clothes and bedroom furniture for Jennifer and Sarah, enrolled them in Catholic school, and settled into family life. Even financial security, something that had eluded Williams for so long, seemed at hand. Sherry, a one-time nurse, had launched a successful business that offered consulting services and written material to hospitals, hospices, and funeral homes to help them help their clientele deal with grief and loss. As for Williams, in addition to seeing his pay rise to eleven dollars an hour, he found that Wyatt seemed to need him for as many hours as he could give. One year he earned $27,000, more than he ever had in his life.

At home, Williams was initially happy. He planted a bed of roses and perennials, along with his usual enormous vegetable garden. When a bounty of hot peppers ripened on the vines, he pickled some and dried others. The family took camping trips together, and Williams cooked chili and other dishes over an open fire. He played tennis and volleyball with Jennifer and Sarah, and when the girls brought friends over, he would give them acting lessons, teaching them to read evocatively from a list of names in the phone book.

But the topic of tobacco steadily consumed Williams and darkened his outlook. It had been frightening to see how frightened others were of his smuggled documents, as one attempt after another to unload them foundered. But Williams refused to put the genie back in the bottle. If anything, he became more systematic in his espionage, seeking out specific documents from B&W's files to help tell coherent stories. Almost every week he spirited out additional material. He also began to do extracurricular research, going to the public library to get copies of patents for various cigarette manufacturing processes, and sending away for copies of congressional hearings on tobacco. For a time, Morton Mintz fed Williams results of his own research, particularly having to do with the appearance of cigarettes in films.

It wasn't long before Williams's obsession spilled over into his home life. His family found that they couldn't sit down and watch a rented movie without him interrupting to rant about one scene or another that featured tobacco. At a play they attended in which one of the lead characters smoked, Williams again launched into a diatribe. "Come on, Dad, we're just trying to enjoy this," Jennifer told him with exasperation. She became furious when she learned he had canceled her subscription to a music magazine and had written a letter to the publisher excoriating the company for taking cigarette advertisements.

Privately with Sherry, Williams agonized over what he was seeing at work, though he refused to offer specifics. Sherry was no stranger to the world of tobacco. Her mother, aunt, grandmother, and grandfather had all worked for Brown & Williamson. And in years of working as a nurse in both cardiac and oncology wards, she had seen plenty of evidence of what smoking could do. But when she pressed Williams for details, he told her he didn't want to get her involved in a conspiracy, one in which he was beginning to feel he had some complicity, because of his silence. "What if you knew that somebody was doing something that was hurting a lot of people, but you promised not to tell?" he asked her. "What would you do?"

Whatever he wanted to do, Sherry told him, she would support. If he wanted to blow the whistle on B&W, she would be there for him. If he wanted to keep working and keep quiet, that was fine, too. Or he could quit, and walk away from it all. Over the course of several trips, Williams had consolidated a set of the B&W documents at Nina Selz's house in Florida. But beyond that, he couldn't decide what to do, and his mood began to deteriorate. As he had in previous funks, he became withdrawn and refused to socialize. This time, though, alcohol did not become a problem, according to Sherry. Still, he was clearly in a downward spiral.

On a rainy Sunday in February 1992, Williams's dog crawled under the porch and died. Williams fell apart. He wept and wept, and as Sherry tried to console him, he told her that a few days earlier, he had lost his job. Wyatt had informed him and two other paralegals that they were being let go as of the middle of March. Williams's smuggling activities hadn't been discovered; Wyatt simply needed to trim back its cadre of coders. In addition to the month's notice, Wyatt told Williams, it would also give him two weeks' severance.

His last day of work was Friday March 13. After saying some farewells, he packed up a box of personal effects, and slipped in one final batch of Brown & Williamson documents. "Do you want to check the box?" he asked supervisor Ernest Clements on his way out. Clements waved him on.

The following week, Williams filed for unemployment and registered once again with the Louisville Bar Association, which had placed him at Wyatt. But when none of the bar association leads turned up any work, and then the leads themselves stopped coming, Williams decided that Wyatt had blackballed him. As defeatism overtook him, tension grew with Sherry, who had no patience for his torpor. "Come on, get off your ass and do something," she told him.

In September, he surprised her for her birthday: He bought her a sailboat and took her out for an evening cruise on the Ohio River. The gesture got a decidedly mixed reception from Sherry. While she and Williams had talked about getting a sailboat someday, she had thought of it as a long-range dream. How could they possibly afford it now? she wondered. The answer was upsetting: Williams had made a lump-sum withdrawal of his retirement money from Wyatt, and plunked down $5,200 for the boat, a twenty-two-foot Hunter. During the birthday sail, moreover, Williams spent much of the time ranting about the cigarette industry.

Still, Williams made no move to air his documents. Instead, he focused on keeping his life together, as it was clear that both his domestic tranquillity and financial security were crumbling. With his unemployment payments running out by the end of the year, Williams finally got a job selling cars at a Mercury dealer. His three-week training class was filled with smokers, and he came home coughing and wheezing and reeking of tobacco. He quit before selling a single car.

Although he hadn't smoked for more than a year, Williams was not the picture of health. Gardening, camping, and light sports kept him more active than most Americans, but he still could put away a six-pack of beer while mowing the lawn. Not surprisingly, he was a bit overweight. And Sherry noticed that he often seemed short of breath and took antacids a lot. Both Sherry and his own physician were worried that the stress he was under was a further threat to his health, and they encouraged him to see a therapist. After months of nagging, Williams relented, and went to see a clinical social worker.

During the first few sessions, in late February and early March 1993, Williams's therapist found him to be articulate and intense, but caught up in feelings of helplessness and failure.* Williams admitted to having an "obsession" with tobacco, and then couldn't resist venting on one of his

---

* Williams gave his therapist, Jan G. Horton Sr. of Louisville, written permission to discuss their sessions for use in this book.

special concerns. During his research at Wyatt, he said, he had learned that some cigarette makers used Freon to "puff" tobacco. Some B&W documents discussed the concern that, when burned, Freon can turn into phosgene, a poisonous gas that had been used in World War I. One document noted that a number of scientific analyses concluded that no dangerous quantities of phosgene were released. But Williams said that he planned to write a book about this and other industry secrets to get the story out and to try to make some money. In his notes the therapist wrote that while it was possible Williams was driven by fantasy or paranoia, his accounts were "convincing," with references to names, dates, and places as well as to individual documents, which Williams said were in a safe location.

The therapy sessions were interrupted by events beginning in the early morning hours of March 4, when Williams woke Sherry up and told her he'd been suffering chest pain for several hours. Although he usually brushed off any of her efforts to monitor his health, this time he let her take his blood pressure and his pulse, which was racing. A checkup at the hospital indicated nothing serious, but they kept him overnight for observation and some further tests. Sherry had just returned from dropping the girls off at school in the morning when the phone rang. Williams's condition had deteriorated and he was being rushed to surgery. He had a quintuple bypass.

"God sent me a message," Williams later said. "He tried to kill me." It was enough to spur Williams to action, and now he had a new plan. Convinced that his cigarette smoking was at least partly to blame for his brush with death, he decided that he would bring a personal-injury claim against Brown & Williamson, whose Kool brand he smoked for many years — exactly the kind of lawsuit he'd been hired to help the company defend. On April 29, at his first therapy appointment since his surgery, Williams's demeanor was distinctly cheerier. He smiled more, his therapist noticed. And in addition to explaining his litigation plans, Williams also outlined a longer-range course of action. He wanted to move to Florida, he said, get a boat and a teaching job, and start a new life. As he had done so often in the past, Williams was preparing to cut and run.

16

To discuss a lawsuit against Brown & Williamson, Merrell Williams went to a Louisville lawyer named J. Fox DeMoisey, who had represented him in his contest to gain custody of his daughters. DeMoisey is a strapping former college basketball player who runs his own practice. Almost totally bald, with a bushy brown mustache, he looks as though he might have stepped out of a barbershop quartet.

The court had awarded Williams permanent custody at the end of 1992, and DeMoisey recalls that at one of the final hearings in that proceeding, Williams had said to him, "When this thing is over, I have a real troublesome thing I want to talk to you about." Months passed, and when Williams, still in the throes of recovering from his heart surgery, walked into DeMoisey's office in the spring of 1993, the lawyer, who was forty-five at the time, was startled. "He looked like fifty miles of bad weather," DeMoisey recalls. Williams pulled up a chair and told the lawyer about his experience at Wyatt, and about what he thought was a scheme by the tobacco companies to hide information, duck discovery, and mislead the public. Would DeMoisey represent him in a personal-injury suit against B&W? Williams wanted to know.

This is a particularly weighty question for a Kentucky lawyer. Taking on the tobacco industry, with its armies of lawyers and limitless funds, is an enormous endeavor for any attorney, particularly a solo practitioner, like Fox DeMoisey, who has limited personnel and financial resources. Suing Brown & Williamson in its tobacco-friendly home state required a special degree of courage. Then there were the documents. Williams referred to them in describing the basis for his lawsuit, but he didn't bring any, and he didn't go into any detail. The mere mention of them, though, set off alarm bells in DeMoisey's mind. Wading into them without a careful plan, he realized, would land him in an ethical quagmire. Chain-smoking Marlboro Lights through their conversation and stubbing them out in an enormous circular ashtray on his desk, DeMoisey said he needed some time to think.

Over the next few months, Williams and DeMoisey discussed various options, including simply throwing the documents away. At the other extreme was filing a personal-injury claim for Williams's damaged health, and making the documents part of that proceeding. Williams, though, was worried about the impact such a public fight might have on his family. In June 1993, Williams worried that DeMoisey might drop the matter; DeMoisey recalls that Williams "teeter-tottered back and forth." Finally they decided on a course of action, one designed to let Williams seek a settlement of his personal-injury claim in a nonpublic fashion and give B&W a chance to regain custody of its documents.

On July 9, DeMoisey sent the following letter to Gordon Davidson, then the managing partner of Wyatt, Tarrant & Combs:

> Please be advised that I have been retained to represent an individual who, at one time, was an employee of Wyatt, Tarrant and Combs. During that period of employment, my client was exposed to information concerning the tobacco industry in general, and Brown and Williamson Tobacco Company in particular. Also, this exposure included information concerning other tobacco companies, CTR [Council for Tobacco Research], and other law firms.

Being a smoker (and a smoker of Brown and Williamson products), my client became tremendously distressed over the information available to him. Apparently, this information devastated him, not only on a personal and direct basis (i.e., smoking), but also on a moral and "civil consciousness" basis. In other words, my client was shocked at the fraud and hoax being perpetrated upon the government and the American people.

Apparently, during this employment period, my client made copies of documents and removed them from your firm's offices. After reviewing the subject employment contract and the above described scenario, I have advised my client to "box up" the documents for the purpose of returning these documents to your offices. My client has agreed with this advice.

Therefore, tendered with this letter is a box with the above described documents; I presume this to be so as I have not seen these documents, nor have I seen the contents of the box. However, my client assures me that all the documents taken are now contained in the tendered box. I believe this tender brings my client back into compliance with the subject employment contract.

However, after my client left the employment with the firm, he has suffered greatly — physically and emotionally — from *both* the effects of his decades of smoking Brown and Williamson products *and* from the psychological fall-out from:

(1) Being unwillingly made a "co-conspirator" in the deception, deceit and cover-ups being perpetrated by the tobacco companies and CTR, and their agents;

(2) Knowing the physical damage done to his person and the environment by smoking these adulterated products; and

(3) Now knowing that he was purposefully and knowingly addicted to nicotine, etc., by the tobacco companies;

(4) The ongoing and constant dynamic tension between feeling compelled to public disclosure of this information so as to stop the ongoing damage being done to fellow human beings and to the environment, and fear of reprisals from the tobacco companies and their agents.

The crush of this "Gordian knot" dilemma finally has taken its toll in the form of major surgery. My client's life expectancy has statistically been dramatically shortened.

My client has taken the option to return the subject documents, and to simply seek recovery for *his* injuries — through settlement if possible, and through suit, if necessary. . . .

I must respectfully demand that the box and its contents be physically maintained separately in its present form. If settlement cannot be achieved, then it is my intention to file suit and immediately demand production of the box and its contents. Obviously, if suit is necessary, my client would consider and assert that the box and its contents would be, in and of itself, *evidence* to be used in the case. . . .

However pure Williams's original motives in copying B&W documents, however much his real interest was to make the information public, the course of action he and DeMoisey had embarked on would look to Wyatt and to Brown & Williamson — and ultimately to the world at large — like blackmail.

DeMoisey left for a ten-day vacation as soon as the letter went out, and he advised Williams to leave town as well. Sore-subject sailboat in tow, Williams drove down to the Mississippi coast. Tied up to a pylon off the Gulf Island National Seashore in the pouring rain, he read a book Sherry had finished and passed on to him, *The Firm* by John Grisham.

The faxed reply to DeMoisey's letter arrived on July 19, the day DeMoisey returned to work. It was signed not by Gordon Davidson, but by K. Gregory Haynes, a litigation partner at Wyatt who had been one of DeMoisey's college fraternity brothers. Haynes was polite, but pointed. He called DeMoisey's letter extortionate, and cautioned DeMoisey that he was venturing into an area "fraught with ethical considerations for all concerned, particularly the lawyers," a not very veiled threat directed at DeMoisey. "Consistent with long-standing industry practice," Haynes added, "Brown and Williamson has a strict policy against settlement of smoking and health claims. . . . The fact that your client has stolen documents that he feels provide him with damaging evidence will not change that policy." Haynes expressed concern that additional documents might remain at large, and threatened to get a court order requiring their return. Then he noted: "Although you were not at liberty to confirm the fact, we already know that your client is Mr. Merrell Williams."

The battle had been joined and, though DeMoisey refused to confirm the identity of his client, Williams had been exposed — and he was terror-stricken, fearing for his life. There never was and never would be any evidence of an attempt on Williams's life, but DeMoisey didn't help Williams's state of mind by mentioning that he'd heard, through some criminal work he'd done, that a hit man could be hired in Louisville for as little as $2,000. Aware of Williams's anxiety, DeMoisey encouraged him to write down what he knew, and style it as an "affidavit in expectation of death." The idea was to deliver a copy to Wyatt as a kind of insurance policy. Williams had already begun writing some things down, prompted to do so at one point because he thought he might be working with Morton Mintz on a book, and at another by Sherry, who thought keeping a journal might be a good outlet for his stress. Working on a home computer, he gave what now became his affidavit a best-seller-style title, "Intent to Deceive."

He also began to act like a character out of a paperback novel. He was sure that phones were bugged and that he was being followed. And he and DeMoisey agreed on a fake name he would use when he returned from his trip to Mississippi. Even with Sherry, Williams would talk about the matter only if they were in a restaurant or their backyard. They were not just reading Grisham, they were *living* it, Sherry mused some years later. Wyatt was not even the law firm Williams feared the most. To him, the real-world analogue to the sinister Bendini, Lambert & Locke of *The Firm* was Shook Hardy & Bacon, the Kansas City outfit that had represented the tobacco industry for decades.

Of course, Williams's penchant for the dramatic magnified his fears, and he began to imagine killers lurking in every shadow. DeMoisey, too, got spooked. One day in late July or early August, as he drove around town doing errands, he became convinced he was being followed. At a stoplight he leaped out of his car and strode to a vehicle two cars behind him. Bending his six-foot-three-inch frame down, he told the driver, "You better hope that I don't see you again or I will personally pull you out of your car and beat you to a pulp." There was, in fact, good reason to be worried — though not about hit men. Williams had put himself in a position where he was certain to draw the full fury of Brown & Williamson and its attorneys. For the moment, though, there was an eerie calm as the parties negotiated and plotted their next moves.

For two months DeMoisey talked on the phone and exchanged correspondence with Wyatt's Haynes, who, on Brown & Williamson's behalf, was intransigent in refusing to pay any sort of settlement. But he did leave the door open to disposing of the matter quietly, particularly if Wyatt could be assured that all documents had been returned. Even while insisting on the documents' return and stressing their confidential nature, Haynes tried to play down their significance. Much of the information, he said, had already been made public in various forums, including the Cipollone case. B&W's subsequent ferocious efforts to keep the documents under wraps gave the lie to this nonchalance. For his part, DeMoisey pressed home his client's desire to be compensated for his injuries without stepping into the public arena, but he continued to threaten a lawsuit if that failed.

The pace of the discussions frustrated Williams. In July, he told his therapist that he foresaw his agony over tobacco ending by September. On August 30, he told him: "I can't stand the stagnation." His therapist tried to get him to focus on the bigger picture, to compartmentalize the tobacco issue and set some goals for his life. But Williams seemed uninterested in almost anything else, and emotionally detached from his family. Even after Sherry was hospitalized with heart problems of her own, all Williams wanted to talk about was tobacco.

By the middle of September 1993, his therapist concluded that his obsession with tobacco had almost overwhelmed his ability to deal with his family or other issues in his life, and he suggested that antidepressants might be helpful. Growing impatient, meanwhile, Williams pressed DeMoisey to file a lawsuit. Throughout their negotiations, Wyatt objected to the idea of allowing DeMoisey to review the box of documents that Williams had sent them, and, to avoid any effort to disqualify him based on a claim that he had seen privileged material, DeMoisey refrained from discussing the substance of the material with Williams. In a letter to Haynes on September 22, though, DeMoisey wrote: "My client has drafted a narrative by which he tells me he has 'put all the pieces together.' " Enclosing a sealed copy of the affidavit that Williams had been working on, DeMoisey told Haynes that he had not read it. But, he said, he planned to do so on October 1 and file suit by October 4.

Wyatt had had enough. On September 29, the firm filed its own suit in Jefferson County Circuit Court in Louisville. The very caption of the complaint — the part that states who's suing whom — symbolized the David-and-Goliath nature of the battle that had begun. On one side of the *v* was a list, in seniority order, of all ninety-six Wyatt, Tarrant & Combs partners. On the other side, just squeezed in at the bottom of the page, was "UNKNOWN DEFENDANT, by his Attorney, J. Fox DeMoisey." Wyatt charged Williams with breaching a signed confidentiality agreement as well as fiduciary duties he owed to the law firm and its clients.

This preemptive strike completely blindsided Williams. On the day Wyatt went to court, he had helped Sherry with a mailing project, spent a little time working on the sailboat, and gone for a therapy appointment. That afternoon, sheriff's cars pulled into the cul-de-sac where Williams lived, and an officer began knocking on doors, asking if anyone knew his whereabouts. When Williams finally drove up, his daughters came running out of the house, terrified. But their dad was not being arrested. At 1:35 P.M., Judge Thomas Wine had given Wyatt's partners what they wanted: a restraining order barring Williams from disclosing to anyone any information learned in connection with his paralegal job, including, of course, the contents of the B&W documents or the documents themselves. The sheriff was there to serve Williams with the ruling.

Five days after Wyatt filed suit, Brown & Williamson joined the case, known as *Maddox et al. v. Unknown Defendant.* (Maddox was a senior partner at Wyatt.) Within days, Merrell Williams's name surfaced in the press, and he quickly became a named defendant in court papers as well.

This wasn't the way things were supposed to work out. Williams was supposed to be the *plaintiff;* he was the one who was supposed to be making allegations of misconduct. But if he were to detail his claims now in a complaint, it would almost certainly violate the terms of the restraining order. In fact, if read literally, Judge Wine's order did not even permit Williams to talk to his own lawyer about the substance of the charges he was now being called on to defend himself against. Wine confirmed this absurdity in court, and although DeMoisey won a brief reversal on appeal, the Kentucky Supreme Court reinstated Wine's ruling, after deciding that DeMoisey's appeal had come too late. Williams began to feel he had fallen into a play by Ionesco.

Meanwhile, he had to sit mute as he was branded a thief in legal filings and newspaper articles. Wyatt even got some of his fellow paralegals to file affidavits attacking his character. "In my opinion, Williams is a conniving opportunist with an ulterior motive for everything he does," one declared in her sworn statement. "I do not believe that he is trustworthy and would not believe him under oath." Another called Williams "devious and dishonest," and recounted that Williams suggested she falsify medical information in order to obtain a large settlement after she was in an automobile accident, and advised her on another occasion to sue Wyatt "over an extremely insignificant and petty matter." She concluded: "He frequently made up things to glorify his image, which later turned out to be false."

Former girlfriend Barbara Boiarsky stated: "During a portion of the time that Mr. Williams worked at Wyatt, Tarrant & Combs, he and I dated. Based on my experience with him at work and during the time that we dated, I know Merrell Williams to be a dishonest person. He frequently lied to me. I would not believe him under oath." A few months later she was laid off, the result, she believes, of her relationship with Williams.

In his own court filings, Williams took to referring to himself as "Dr. Merrell Williams, Ph.D."

Wyatt's worries that Williams had not returned all of the B&W documents in his possession were confirmed by Williams's narrative. Ernest Clements, Williams's former supervisor, noted that a number of documents cited in the narrative were not among those in the box forwarded by DeMoisey. Judge Wine ordered Williams to appear for a deposition on October 5 to answer questions about where any remaining documents might be. DeMoisey didn't know what to do. He didn't know how to defend a client he couldn't talk to. One possible defense to charges that Williams had made off with privileged documents was what is known as the "crime–fraud exception" to the privilege. A court may find that a claim of attorney–client privilege does not apply if it determines that the privilege is being asserted to conceal criminal or fraudulent activity. But DeMoisey didn't know what was in Brown & Williamson's documents. Of more immediate concern, he also didn't know what questions Wyatt and B&W might ask Williams that could get Williams in deeper trouble. Right now this was a civil case, but, given allegations of "stolen" documents, criminal charges were certainly possible.

At 1:00 P.M. on October 5, 1993 — six days after obtaining the restraining order against Williams — five lawyers for Wyatt and Brown & Williamson assembled in a conference room at a Louisville law firm to take Merrell Williams's deposition. Williams, though, was a no-show. The lawyers sat there for an hour and a half, at which point John Ballantine, the attorney retained by Wyatt, placed a call to Fox DeMoisey. Very politely, and in a long-winded, lawyerly way, Ballantine told DeMoisey that he believed Williams to be in contempt of court for having failed to appear in response to the deposition subpoena, and that Wyatt and B&W would "take all appropriate steps relating thereto." DeMoisey was in the process of appealing Judge Wine's order, and was not about to make any irrevocable missteps by delivering Williams — who was sitting in his office when Ballantine called — into the hands of an inquisition. Explaining his position — also very politely — DeMoisey told the assembled forces listening in on a speaker phone, "My apologies to you gentlemen. I didn't certainly mean for you-all to wait around."

Ballantine immediately went back to Judge Wine and got an order directing Williams to appear the next day. DeMoisey felt he had little choice about complying with such a direct order, but there were other ways of assuring that Wyatt and B&W didn't get anything of substance out of his client.

"State your name for the record, please," Ballantine began the deposition the next morning, October 6, after DeMoisey and Williams showed up about forty minutes late.

"Merrell Williams Jr. And that's doctor. I have a Ph.D. I'd like that on the record," Williams said.

The first thing Ballantine wanted to know was why Williams had not brought to the deposition — as the subpoena had demanded — any documents, computer disks, or other material containing information he had obtained during his employment at Wyatt, Tarrant & Combs.

"I assert the Fifth Amendment privilege to remain silent," Williams responded.

Did Williams even have such material in his possession? Ballantine asked.

Once again, Williams took the Fifth. "As we have previously discussed," DeMoisey explained, "there is an outstanding allegation, although somewhat unspecified . . . that my client may have committed a criminal act in this case. . . . It is felt that to produce any documents at this time or testimony about any of the actions taken at this time would be subject to the Fifth Amendment right to remain silent."

Even in the face of this obstacle, Ballantine was determined to press forward. Williams seemed equally determined not to let him. Pulling out the complaint that Wyatt had filed to get the restraining order, Ballantine pointed to a paragraph that quoted from DeMoisey's letter of July 9 stating that he was transmitting a box of documents to Wyatt. "Do you recall that what is set out in that paragraph did occur and that he transmitted with that letter to the Wyatt law firm a box of materials, sealed, that you had turned over to him?" Ballantine queried.

Williams compared the section of the complaint quoting DeMoisey's letter with a copy of the actual letter. "There appears to be one — two errors that delineates this one from that one," he said after examining the documents. "A minor error, the word 'has' is eliminated or added in your complaint." He also pointed out that the words "box up" in DeMoisey's letter were typed with double quotation marks, while in the complaint the same words were typed with just single quotation marks.

After spending several minutes clarifying these discrepancies, Ballantine got back to his original question.

"I assert the Fifth Amendment privilege and remain silent," Williams responded.

Ballantine turned his questioning to the narrative that Williams had authored, the one in which he had supposedly "put all the pieces together." But DeMoisey was getting increasingly nervous about allowing the questioning to continue. "I certainly am not being disrespectful to counsel, but I'm in an impossible circumstance," he told Ballantine. "This is just getting more and more deep, and I feel more and more inadequate at this point to advise my client," he said, pointing out that he had not read the narrative himself. If anything established what a surreal and absurd exercise everyone was engaged in, it was Ballantine's response. "I don't know what's in the narrative any more than you do," he said, even as a sealed copy sat in his office.

The deposition sputtered to a close. But it was clear that Wyatt's and B&W's pursuit of Williams had only just begun. DeMoisey, hoping to avoid a full-fledged war, kept trying to negotiate a settlement, and set forth the terms of a deal to Ballantine. Williams would drop his plans to sue and would go away quietly in exchange for an immediate payment of $750,000, another $750,000 to be paid periodically during Williams's life, and $1 million to be paid to his beneficiaries upon his death. DeMoisey himself sought $1 million in attorney's fees. No deal, Ballantine replied. He made a counteroffer: B&W would not pay Williams a cent. It would, however, refrain from initiating any further legal proceedings against him, including criminal prosecution, if he would forgo his personal-injury claim and agree to a permanent injunction similar to the restraining order then in effect. The company also wanted DeMoisey to be bound by the same injunction, so he couldn't use any knowledge he might have gleaned from Williams to file suit on someone else's behalf. DeMoisey was willing to live with that limitation, with one proviso: that it not preclude him from someday filing a suit on his *own* behalf against Philip Morris, the maker of the brand he smoked. As for the rest of it, he would have to check with his client.

On October 20 Williams visited his therapist and told him of the settlement discussions. Williams mentioned that his older daughter, Jennifer, now fifteen, had encouraged him not to settle with Brown & Williamson if it would mean he couldn't talk about what he knew. She wanted him to take a moral stand, and that made him feel good, he said.

There would be no deal, Williams told DeMoisey.

With settlement talk over, Williams now faced an all-out assault by Brown & Williamson. Concerned that DeMoisey didn't have the firepower to mount an adequate defense, Williams set out to bring in reinforcements. His first call went to John Banzaf III, a Columbia law school graduate who heads a Washington organization called Action on Smoking and Health (ASH). In the late sixties, Banzaf almost single-handedly prodded the Federal Communications Commission to rule that its own "fairness doctrine" required broadcasters to air antismoking messages to counterbalance the cigarette commercials that then saturated the public airwaves. He is known for an arrogant and abrasive manner, and for never shirking a fight. To Williams's shock, though, Banzaf turned him down cold, citing the restraining order.

Williams's next call went to Joe Cherner, the antitobacco activist who had put up a bounty for the plaintiffs' team in the Horton case. Reaching Cherner at his New York–based organization, Smoke Free Educational Services, Williams asked for help financing his legal battle. Cherner was intrigued, but wanted to get some more information. And he wanted to see some Brown & Williamson documents. That made Williams very nervous. Cherner was asking him the same kinds of questions the tobacco industry lawyers had asked, Williams told him, saying he wondered who Cherner really worked for. Williams hung up without leaving his phone number.

In November an envelope arrived at DeMoisey's office. The contents offered Williams a fragment of hope that he would cling to even as legal and family pressures mounted and his mood deteriorated over the next few months. The U.S. Department of Justice was in the midst of investigating whether Brown & Williamson and its competitors had colluded to restrict research and development of so-called "fire-safe" cigarettes — ones less likely to cause fires if left unattended on upholstery or other combustible surfaces. (Nearly six years later, no charges had been filed.) Public health officials and some members of Congress had pressed for such a product, given that cigarettes start 40,000 fires each year, and those fires cause more than 1,500 deaths. And in the 1980s Philip Morris did some promising research in the area in a study dubbed Project Hamlet ("to burn or not to burn"). But Philip Morris and the rest of the industry opposed any legislation, which might have required changes in cigarette design. The industry lobbied instead for public education, and enlisted support from, of all places, the International Association of Fire Chiefs and other firefighter organizations. These same groups received millions of dollars in grants and equipment from the tobacco industry.

Williams's cache of documents included a memo that discussed efforts to cultivate the fire chiefs' association. And when he worked at Brown & Williamson's R&D building, Williams had noted with bemusement that directly across the street from the facility was a training center for firefighters on land donated by B&W.

When Williams's name surfaced in the press in the fall of 1993, Justice Department investigators decided he might be worth talking to. They sent DeMoisey a "civil investigative demand" — essentially a subpoena — seeking to take Williams's deposition. At last, Williams thought, here was a chance to tell government authorities *everything*. Federal authorities would soon take his problem out of his hands, he told his therapist in December.

There was one problem: Judge Wine's restraining order. Months passed before Justice Department lawyers filed a formal request asking the judge to let them question Williams. Wyatt and B&W, meanwhile, pressed on. On January 7, 1994, they got Judge Wine to extend the terms of the restraining order by issuing a "temporary injunction," which, although called temporary, would remain in force for years. The judge once again ordered Williams and DeMoisey to turn over any remaining material they had that was removed from B&W, as well as anything containing notes or summaries derived from this material. At this point, DeMoisey felt he could no longer resist such an order and, on January 12, John Ballantine, the lawyer representing Wyatt, arrived at DeMoisey's downtown Louisville office. There Williams and DeMoisey had three sealed packages for him: an envelope with another copy of Williams's narrative, a box containing Williams's computer, and a second box of unspecified material.

Ballantine again sought assurance that Williams was really turning over *everything* Judge Wine had directed to be turned over, and he brought along a court reporter to make an official record of the meeting.

"You are Merrell Williams, the defendant in this action?" Ballantine began the formalities.

"I am Merrell Williams Jr., Ph.D.," Williams answered.

DeMoisey then pointed out the materials being handed over, but when Ballantine asked for Williams to state under oath that the material constituted his compliance with Judge Wine's order, things bogged down. DeMoisey objected to Ballantine trying to turn the hand-over proceeding into a deposition, and as he and Ballantine argued back and forth, Williams became progressively more agitated. Suddenly he interrupted the lawyers and said, "May I respectfully point out that I'm going to have to leave the room. I've had heart surgery. And I'm going to have to leave the room right now."

He returned shortly and agreed to sign and date the packages. But when Ballantine asked him, "Do these three containers represent your compliance with the court order?" Williams said, "It represents what it is. It is what it is." When Ballantine said he would have to get a court order compelling an answer to the question and that he would "move for sanctions in their fullest regard," Williams once again got up and left.

Ballantine did go back to Judge Wine, who directed that Williams "shall answer directly the pending deposition question as to whether or not the three sealed containers provided by him and his counsel . . . constitute his compliance with this Court's Temporary Injunction entered on January 7, 1994."

Litigating against Wyatt and B&W was proving to be at least as stressful for Williams as working for them had been. What's more, his health had become fragile and his family's financial situation precarious. His bypass surgery had cost $70,000, and while Sherry's insurance had covered most of it, there was still between $15,000 and $20,000 left to pay off. And he was unemployed. His fear that the tobacco industry might retaliate against him *outside* the courtroom rekindled. While there was no evidence of any attempt to harm him, he does recall events that made him anxious. At the end of December 1993 the family had received an anonymous telephone call wishing them "Merry Christmas from Brown and Williamson and Wyatt, Tarrant and Combs." One day in the schoolyard, a boy told his younger daughter Sarah that there was a hit man out for her dad. Williams became fearful for his family's safety, as well as his own. "It'll be my children, and then it'll be you," he told Sherry. "Oh, Merrell, come on," she responded, "this is too public." Not convinced of that, he sent Nina Selz a sealed envelope, with instructions on who to contact in the event of his death. Those people were also to receive the boxes stored at Selz's house. Williams's physician gave him a prescription for Ativan, an antianxiety medication, and by the end of January recommended antidepressants as well.

It was all becoming too much. Mentally and logistically, Williams began preparing his exit. During therapy sessions he repeated his desire to relocate to the South, and said he simply wanted to hang out at the beach and sail. He would work just enough to subsist, he told his therapist. In February Williams assembled Sherry, Jennifer, and Sara and told them he couldn't stand living in Kentucky anymore and that he was moving to the Gulf Coast. The girls could come with him or go back to their mother, he said. What about Sherry? his daughters wanted to know. He hoped she would join him, he replied, but said that was up to her. Sherry was devastated, but hardly surprised. She would wait until he got settled, she told him, and then she would explore what opportunities there might be for her.

As ordered by Judge Wine, Williams showed up at Ballantine's office on March 3 to answer his one question. Although Ballantine tried to be surgically efficient, Williams would have none of it:

BALLANTINE: Now then, do you agree, sir, that those two boxes and the envelope are your compliance with the court's temporary injunction in this case?

WILLIAMS: And I'm assuming you're referring to the same statement on page 11 of the other deposition, "Do you agree, sir, that your signature on the two boxes and dated signature on the two boxes and this envelope will constitute your representation that these three containers are your compliance with the court order?"

BALLANTINE: I don't understand what you just assumed.

WILLIAMS: Well, I was just quoting what was similar to what you said before.

BALLANTINE: I understand. My question to you at the moment is, are the two boxes and the envelope that were present at your deposition on January 12, 1994, in your lawyer's office, are they your compliance with the temporary injunction in this case?

WILLIAMS: And I refer you to page 19 of the deposition and the answer that was provided at the time, "It represents what it is. It is what it is." That's line one, page 19. And I also state further on page 19, line 12, "I have no further answer."

BALLANTINE: I can read what the transcript of that deposition says. My question —

WILLIAMS: That, sir, represents my compliance with the court in accordance with this statement here. I might also add that I'm very confused, because really I am not able to consult with counsel. I am confused by what appears to be an order as I see it which is interpreted by the verbal statements of Judge Wine on January 10, 1994. I have made a transcript of that on the typewriter. And there seems to be some contradictory statements that don't actually meet with the word "all information." As a layperson, sir, I can't understand this. I have no knowledge of how to interpret this. And I guess what I'm saying is that I've given your answer to you. You've asked it, and I've answered it. Now, for example, does "all information" mean the information that I have found in the public record? . . . I'm representing to you that the first document you are holding is from the Cipollone documents. They are in the public record. I'm representing to you that the second document — I can't really see it from here, and I can't represent it — is a book which I recently checked out of the library, and I believe that was published in 1964. And I have read it.

Now, the document right there is the 1965 hearings. Is that correct? Cigarette Labeling and Advertising Part I and II, public document. And I have a real difficult time interpreting exactly what you mean. What you have — what you just had your hands on was H.R. 2147, which is a bill which is — was introduced by Senator Mike Synar [Synar was actually a congressman from Oklahoma]. And I have a very confused concept of what exactly — well, for example, patents. Here I was watching a show the other day, and it was a fascinating piece on *Day One*. Mentioned a patent. And since I have a Ph.D. and am very capable of doing research, I was very fascinated by this possibility of finding this patent. And through no knowledge that I gained through my employment at all, I found the document, which [discusses] nicotine transfer. And I was quite shocked by that.

But — and here is a document which is also public, and it deals with something that just is fascinating to me. And it is a patent on a process for increasing the filling capacity of tobacco. I don't know that I am acquainted with this process or have been through my knowledge. But "all information" might cover this. For example [reading from the document], "The process of example one was repeated employing Freon-11," which is a class one substance. And I am very shocked by that. You can put that in the record.

Williams went on and on. "Are you through?" Ballantine asked when the monologue finally seemed at an end.

"I'm through," Williams said. Ballantine asked his question again.

"Asked and answered," Williams snapped. The deposition got nowhere.

The next day — March 4, 1994 — presented Williams with an anniversary and a deadline. It had been a year since his heart operation, and that meant that under a statute of limitations for personal-injury suits in Kentucky, he now had to set forth his own allegations about injuries caused to his health from smoking and his work at Wyatt, or risk forever losing the right to litigate them. Hamstrung though they were by the injunction, DeMoisey and Williams were not about to forfeit the opportunity to sue. Williams himself worked on drafting the complaint, which opened by stating misleadingly that he had smoked continuously for twenty-nine years. He then charged that smoking had harmed his health, that the tobacco industry had fraudulently concealed information on the addictive properties and adverse health effects of cigarettes, and that Wyatt and B&W had fraudulently induced him into working on a project that caused him extreme emotional distress. The harm had been compounded, Williams charged, by the injunction, "which continues to deny the Counterclaim Plaintiff the cathartic and emotional release of being able to turn over the truth about the tobacco industry to the public."

For the foreseeable future, Williams knew, Judge Wine's injunction would deny him the emotional release he was looking for. His best hope to get his story out, he felt, was to talk to the Department of Justice investigators. But where were they?

17

One day in late February 1994, the fax machine in Don Barrett's law office had begun humming, spitting out copies of some newspaper articles about Merrell Williams and his battle in the Kentucky courts. Nothing identified the sender. A few days later, an unsigned note arrived by fax, which stated, "One of these days I may call you. We ought to talk." This time Barrett inspected the numbers printed at the top of the paper by the transmitting fax machine, and he placed a call to Louisville. A woman answered, and, on a hunch, Barrett asked, "Could I speak to Merrell Williams?" Williams came to the phone.

They spoke briefly, with Williams — who was at Sherry's office — explaining why he had contacted Barrett. Whenever he drove through Mississippi, he said, he thought of people there he admired. Oxford brought to mind Faulkner and Grisham; Jackson, Eudora Welty; and whenever he passed the sign on the interstate for Lexington, he thought of Barrett and his battle in the Horton case, which Williams had followed as he was starting his job at B&W six years earlier. Now he wanted to move back to Mississippi, and he thought perhaps Barrett could help. Williams ended the conversation by hanging up abruptly, saying his phone was probably bugged. "He was like a scared little deer," Barrett recalls.

A few weeks passed before they spoke again. This time Williams called Barrett's office and left a message. Barrett called back, and agreed to meet Williams in Jackson at what seemed to be Williams's favorite spot for such rendezvous, the Old Tyme Deli. On March 8, a Tuesday, Williams left Louisville early in the morning, making the eleven-hour drive to Jackson in Sherry's pickup. It was cool outside when he arrived at the deli, so he went in and took a table in the center of the dimly lit main eating area. The dinner hour was just beginning and the place was bustling. He ordered a beer and waited. After about a half hour, a man who he thought looked like a lawyer came in and looked searchingly around the room. Williams got up and introduced himself to Don Barrett. They sat down and were joined shortly by a man whose last name Williams heard as "Scaggs."

Unbeknownst to Williams, Barrett's involvement in cigarette litigation had not ended with the Horton case. Indeed, for the previous eight months, he, Dick Scruggs (not Scaggs), and a group of other lawyers had been plotting a whole new legal assault on the tobacco industry. It was clear from press accounts of the proceedings in Kentucky that Wyatt and B&W feared Williams might still possess tobacco industry secrets. That's why Barrett and Scruggs had rushed to meet a stranger at the Old Tyme Deli — Scruggs drove four hours from the coast in a nasty rain.

Forty-seven at the time, Scruggs had emerged as one of the most successful plaintiffs' lawyers in Mississippi. Throughout his life, opportunity seemed to have a way of finding him, and he found a way to make the most of it. Tall and trim, with thinning silver-streaked hair, he is regularly described as a "gentleman" by people who know him. He is also a fierce competitor, and he combines the two qualities with a kind of "right stuff" calm and confidence that is just what you would expect from a former fighter pilot. Even his voice, more notable for its timbre than its drawl, is the kind you'd imagine coming over the PA from the cockpit, reassuring you that the engine fire you see out your window is just a *small* one and that you should sit back and enjoy your flight.

Seated at a table in the restaurant, however, Williams did not find

In cigarettes, as in coast defense guns, it's modern design that makes the big difference!

"*Yes, Colonel*—Pall Mall's modern design filters the smoke—lessens throat irritation!"

Of traditionally fine tobaccos

• Modern design has made a vast difference in coast defense—has given these streamlined railway guns a new kind of performance. That's important—for lives may depend on their range and accuracy—their modern design.

Listen to the men who direct these guns. They'll tell you that in cigarettes, as in coast defense guns, it's modern design that makes the big difference.

Pall Mall's modern design brings you an entirely new kind of smoking pleasure. For this streamlined cigarette is deliberately designed to give you a much smoother, less irritating smoke. You see, tobacco is its own natural filter. In Pall Mall the smoke is measurably filtered—filtered over a 20% longer route of Pall Mall's traditionally fine tobaccos.

Pall Mall's modern design also means a definitely cooler smoke. The additional length travels the smoke further—gets rid of heat and bite on the way.

Now, at last—thanks to modern design—a truly fine cigarette provides in fact what other cigarettes claim in theory—a smoother, less irritating smoke—Pall Mall.

Prove it! Yourself, try Pall Mall critically. See if you, too, don't agree that—

"Pall Mall's modern design filters the smoke—lessens throat irritation."

"WHEREVER PARTICULAR PEOPLE CONGREGATE"

A 1941 magazine ad for Pall Mall cigarettes, Nathan Horton's brand. Typical of ads of that era, the text makes what borders on health claims by referring to the way the extra length gives consumers "a much smoother, less irritating smoke."

Nathan Horton, his wife Ella (both seated on couch), and other family members in December 1986, about six weeks before Horton died.

Don Barrett in front of the Confederate war memorial in Lexington, Mississippi.

Jim Upshaw.

Don Barrett and Fred Clark in front of the courthouse in Lexington, Mississippi.

Merrell Williams on the Mississippi Gulf Coast.

The Brazos River Society at Baylor University, circa 1960. Merrell Williams standing, far left; Nina Selz seated, far right.

The house in Ocean Springs, Mississippi, that
Dick Scruggs bought for Merrell Williams.

A surveillance photo of Merrell Williams taken
by investigators for Brown & Williamson's law
firm, King & Spalding, in December 1994.

King & Spalding attorney
Gordon Smith.

Dick Scruggs.

Jeffrey Wigand.

Mike Moore.

Joe R. Colingo.

Scruggs's presence reassuring. Barrett started off the conversation by telling Williams that he had read about his battles with Wyatt and B&W and that he thought Williams was a hero. That made Williams feel good. Scruggs, though, didn't say much of anything. That made Williams nervous. Was he an FBI agent? Williams wondered, worried that he was in trouble with the law. Scruggs thought Williams looked frightened, but decided the best thing to do would be to listen. And Williams *did* talk, rambling, as was his way, from his concerns about the tobacco industry to his recent deposition to worries that he might be headed toward yet another divorce. He also pulled out a copy of his freshly filed counterclaim.

Eventually, Williams turned the conversation from tobacco to his need for a job, ideally on the Gulf Coast. To his surprise, Scruggs offered to help, noting that he was from Pascagoula and knew a college dean in the area. Scruggs also said he might be able to get Williams a job at a law firm. Maybe, Williams decided, this guy "Scaggs" was someone he should trust after all, and he handed him a copy of his résumé.

Williams didn't mention his B&W documents, and the lawyers didn't ask about them. But in the parking lot, after the meeting ended, Williams handed Scruggs a chapter from his "narrative" (which in total was about three hundred pages long) dealing with product placement in films. "I hope you're not with the FBI," he told him.

After the meeting, Scruggs and Barrett looked at each other in befuddlement. They couldn't get a read on Williams or what he wanted, but decided to keep talking to him if he ever called again.

Although he was still hoping for some kind of break in the case against him in Kentucky, Williams's principal purpose in coming to Mississippi was to find a job. While staying at his mother's house in Jackson, he engaged in a few more days of networking, including meetings with a former teaching colleague and even the woman he had taken to his high school prom. Then he dragged the boat he had given Sherry out of the mud in his mother's yard — having left it there on a previous trip — hooked it up to Sherry's truck, and headed south.

The boat needed work, which Williams decided to do himself. In a marina in Biloxi's back bay, he sanded and painted by day, and slept on board at night. Scruggs had told Williams to call when he arrived on the coast, and, after a few days, Williams phoned Barrett's office to get Scruggs's number, as well as his correct name. Calling from a pay phone at a Popeye's chicken restaurant, Williams learned that Scruggs was out of the office. But Scruggs's secretary took the number of the pay phone and told Williams to stand by. A few moments later, Scruggs called from Bermuda, where he had taken his yacht for a pleasure cruise. How would Williams like a job working for a law firm? Scruggs wanted to know. As long as it didn't involve tobacco, Williams said, he'd take it. Scruggs told him he could arrange something, and that Williams could start any time he was ready.

At long last, on March 17, lawyers for the Department of Justice filed papers requesting that Judge Wine allow them to question Williams. Williams went back to Louisville for the hearing on the matter, only to have Judge Wine reject the DOJ plea. It was at once a dashing of Williams's last hope and the birth of new resolve. Over the next two weeks he hatched what he would later refer to as "the turnover concept."

Returning to Mississippi, Williams now set about building his new life in earnest. He sailed his Hunter 22 out of the boatyard in Biloxi, through the shallow waters abutting the Mississippi Sound, and tied up at the docks of the Fort Bayou apartments in Ocean Springs. A two-bedroom duplex apartment was available, and Williams filled out the rental application in the name of his mother, explaining that she liked to come down to the coast to sail. He didn't mention that she was eighty-three, or that if he had used his own name, he never would have passed a credit check. He moved in himself, but was flat broke. Once again, he called Scruggs and set up a meeting.

Scruggs's office was located in the heart of Pascagoula, in a low-slung brick building that once housed a discount clothing store. Retail establishments had largely vacated the downtown area, just as they had in Lexington, and about all that was left were empty storefronts and law offices. Around April 6, Williams arrived to discuss his job. Scruggs had arranged a position at Barton & Williams, a Pascagoula law firm that, like Scruggs's, primarily did asbestos work. Since Williams wouldn't be getting a paycheck for several weeks, Scruggs gave him something to tide him over: an envelope with $3,000 in cash.

"It was 'Give it back when you can' — that was my understanding of it," Williams explained later. The fact is, though, that this payment was only the beginning of what turned out to be astounding largesse by Scruggs, all of which he and Williams described as "loans," despite the absence of anything documenting the debt, or any apparent way for Williams to repay it. In court filings ten months later, Brown & Williamson offered their own version of the kind of understanding Scruggs and Williams may have reached. But in April 1994, B&W had no idea where Williams was.

Over the next several weeks, Williams met repeatedly with Scruggs and with Scruggs's law partner and longtime friend Steve Bozeman. Aware that they were planning on filing a major tobacco lawsuit, Williams told them he wanted to help, and he began to disclose things he had learned at B&W. But he did so nervously. When they met at restaurants and other lawyers would come up and say hello to Scruggs and Bozeman, they would introduce him as "Mr. Jones." Bozeman had been a prosecutor in the Navy and had dealt with undercover informants whose identity needed protecting. Williams had the same scared manner as those informants, Bozeman recalled years later.

At one of these sessions, around April 13, Williams decided to take the plunge. He met Scruggs and Bozeman for lunch at the La Font Inn, a motel with a frozen-in-time-circa-1969 look and feel that sits on Highway 90, the main east–west road through Pascagoula. Sitting at a window table overlooking the motel's enormous pool, Williams told them about the stash of Brown & Williamson documents he had left at the house of his old college friend, Nina Selz, in Florida. He was increasingly worried, he said, that Selz might face problems if it became known that she possessed the material, even though they had never discussed the specific content of the boxes. And he wanted to find a way to get them into the hands of public authorities.

No problem, said Scruggs. He would fly Williams to Florida to pick them up.

For Scruggs to do this was certain to unleash myriad troubles. But he paid that no heed. Scruggs is "a man of action," Williams said afterward. "He does not go haltingly into anything."

Two days later, on April 15, 1994, Nina Selz stood at the Orlando Executive Airport, a small airfield for private planes, and watched a Learjet descend out of the blue Florida sky. She cut a striking figure, six feet tall with straight black hair streaked with gray. Wearing a light jacket and slacks, she fixed her eyes skyward as the plane made its final approach.

Since their student days together at Baylor University, Selz and Williams had seldom lived in the same part of the country. But over the years, Williams had a way of showing up at her place unannounced, sometimes to visit and catch up, other times just to leave things for her to store. Once he had left her a box with holes punched in the sides and a sign on top that said "feed me." It held a puppy.

Now Williams had called and asked her to bring three other boxes to the airport, and they sat, sealed tight with tape, in her blue Mitsubishi hatchback. Selz knew that for the past seven months, Brown & Williamson had been pursuing her friend in court, charging that he had stolen sensitive documents. And Selz knew that he was fearful for his life. While he hadn't sounded under duress when he had called her from Mississippi, she was concerned. She told him she would hand over his boxes only if she saw him get off the airplane of his own free will, without anyone holding a gun to his back.

The Lear taxied right up to the terminal, just a few feet from where she had parked her car. When the door opened and the steps folded down, Williams clambered out — freely — and, standing on the tarmac, said a terse hello. Ignoring his gruffness, Selz bent over Williams's five-foot-eight frame and gave him a kiss. He had been movie-star handsome in his younger days, but now, at fifty-three, he had gone a bit pudgy around the middle and his face was puffy. He did not look well.

The pilots loaded the document boxes onto the plane. After a quick lunch at the airport, Selz joined Williams on board for the return trip, so they could spend the weekend together in Mississippi. Also on board were Scruggs and his wife, Diane, and the plane dropped the two of them off at Destin, a resort town on Florida's panhandle where they have a condominium. Then it flew on to Pascagoula, as Williams and Selz sat in the back sharing some stiff drinks.

When the plane landed in Pascagoula, Tammy Cauley, a paralegal who worked for Scruggs, loaded the boxes into a car and drove them to a building in the center of town that once housed a bank but now served as an annex for Scruggs's law office.

Although Williams was giving Scruggs custody of his documents, there was at least a tacit understanding that Scruggs would not do anything with them without Williams's approval. Cauley knew that Williams was contemplating writing a book about them — essentially an expansion of his "narrative" — and that, at the very least, he wanted to be the one to lead Scruggs and Don Barrett through the material.

But Scruggs and Barrett didn't want to wait for that, and Cauley was under orders to start copying the material that night, without letting Williams know. She was foiled, however, by the amount of tape Williams had wrapped around each box — there was no way she could open the cartons without it being obvious. So Cauley decided to put the boxes in the old bank's safe. The hour was late, and as she struggled to get the vault open, her activity in the building caught the attention of the police, who stopped by to investigate. The cops, of course, had no way of knowing that they had stumbled onto hotly contested contraband. After they left, Cauley stashed the material away and swung the vault's heavy steel door shut.

The following weekend in April, Scruggs had Williams come to the old bank building to start leading him, his colleague Steve Bozeman, and Don Barrett through the documents. Another man also showed up to have a look at the material: Mississippi Attorney General Mike Moore. Williams was so skittish that part of him wondered whether Moore would prosecute him for taking the Brown & Williamson documents.

Quite to the contrary, Williams learned. Moore had deputized Scruggs, Barrett, and a team of other lawyers to investigate filing a novel lawsuit against the tobacco industry on behalf of the State of Mississippi. Williams's documents could not have arrived at a better time, and, in a brief meeting, Moore assured Williams that he had done nothing wrong in turning them over.

On Sunday afternoon, Barrett took Williams out to lunch at a fancy

Gulf Coast restaurant, where they dined on oyster stew. As they drove in a Mercedes coupe borrowed from Scruggs, Barrett spoke in religious terms of his efforts to battle the cigarette makers, saying that he felt his fight against the industry was God's work. "I'm not easily persuaded when someone says 'religion' and talks about God," Williams remembered later. "But with this man I was convinced."

Meanwhile, back at the bank building, where some of the choicest B&W documents had been laid out in stacks on a table, Tammy Cauley quickly copied the material and then put it back so it would look undisturbed. It wasn't long, though, before Williams gave permission for the whole cache to be copied.

18

One of the most enduring tableaus of the tobacco wars is the image of the senior executives of seven tobacco companies raising their right hands and swearing to a congressional subcommittee that they did not believe nicotine was addictive.

"I believe nicotine is not addictive," William Campbell, the president and CEO of Philip Morris USA, told members of the House Subcommittee on Health and the Environment on April 14, 1994.

"Cigarettes and nicotine clearly do not meet the classic definitions of addiction," said James W. Johnston, chairman and CEO of R. J. Reynolds Tobacco Company.

"I believe nicotine is not addictive," intoned Thomas E. Sandefur Jr., the chairman and CEO of Brown & Williamson.

And so it went, down the line.

For two months, the tobacco industry had found itself unexpectedly on the defensive. In February, David Kessler, the commissioner of the Food and Drug Administration, sent a letter to the Coalition on Smoking or Health, a Washington, D.C., antismoking organization. "Evidence brought to our attention is accumulating that suggests that cigarette manufacturers may intend that their products contain nicotine to satisfy an addiction on the part of some of their customers," Kessler wrote. He also said that cigarette companies might be adding nicotine to cigarettes so as to deliver specific amounts of the addictive substance. If that proved true, Kessler wrote, it would give the FDA a legal basis to begin regulating the product.

For the tobacco industry, this was an assault from an unexpected quarter. Ever since its establishment in 1906, the FDA had treated tobacco products as beyond its purview. Even after Congress expanded the definition of a drug eligible for FDA review in 1938, by including nonfood products "intended to affect the structure and function of the body," the FDA maintained its hands-off approach. The rationale was that the cigarette companies were not making any explicit health claims. The reality was that the agency didn't have the stomach to take on the politically powerful industry. That changed with Kessler, a Harvard-trained doctor who also had a law degree from the University of Chicago. He assembled a team of investigators, including lawyers and scientists, to explore the FDA's right to regulate cigarettes as devices "intended to affect the structure and function of the body" — in this case, the central nervous system — even if the manufacturers did not state this as an intention.

At the same time that FDA staffers were at work, Walt Bogdanich, a producer for ABC News's *Day One*, was pursuing a story about nicotine manipulation by the cigarette industry. Clifford Douglas, then a lobbyist for the American Cancer Society, had put Bogdanich in touch with a former RJR manager, who was willing to talk — anonymously — about the use of nicotine extract in the cigarette manufacturing process. Douglas also arranged for FDA investigators to talk to the RJR source, who soon became known as "Deep Cough." By early 1994, Bogdanich and the FDA were in a race. On February 24, ABC issued a press release announcing that its *Day One* program on February 28 would examine nicotine manipulation by the cigarette industry. The next day, the 25th, David Kessler issued his letter.

On Capitol Hill, meanwhile, Representative Henry Waxman cranked up hearings on tobacco in March. A nine-term Democratic congressman from Los Angeles, Waxman had been an implacable foe of the industry ever since he gained the chairmanship of the Health and the Environment subcommittee in 1979. In the early 1980s, Waxman had worked with Matthew Myers, a lobbyist at the Coalition on Smoking or Health, to get legislation passed that required a new series of rotating health warnings on cigarette packages. One warning the industry managed to kill during the legislative process stated that smoking was addictive. Periodically over the next decade, Waxman continued to hold hearings on smoking and health. The tobacco industry had enough friends on the Hill to keep further antismoking bills bottled up, but they couldn't deny Waxman his forum for airing concerns about the marketing of cigarettes and the consequences of smoking.

If this wasn't enough for the industry, on March 29 a group of plaintiffs' lawyers from around the country filed a class-action lawsuit in federal court in New Orleans against cigarette makers. Picking up on the nicotine theme, they fashioned a novel claim, seeking damages on behalf of all current and former smokers who were, or had been, addicted to cigarettes. It was an attempt at an end run around the personal-choice defense used so successfully by the tobacco industry in one trial after another. If a person was hooked on a product, her decision to continue using it could not reasonably be said to be a choice. The approach also offered a way to sidestep the tortuous, costly, and frequently unsuccessful effort to prove that smoking caused a particular plaintiff's disease. Rather, the plaintiffs' lawyers said, *addiction itself* was an injury worthy of compensation, and with much hoopla announced that the class of potential claimants might approach 90 million people.

If a jury found the tobacco companies liable for fraud, conspiracy, and other charges, the plaintiffs' lawyers proposed, in what became known as the Castano case, that an administrative process could be set up to determine who was eligible to receive damages. No way, the tobacco companies declared. Each case had to be considered on its own; 90 million claimants would mean 90 million mini-trials, and that would tie up the courts well into the next millennium. Taking individuals on one at a time, grinding them down with superior resources, confounding juries with alternate theories of disease causation, and hammering home a particular claimant's freely made decision to smoke — that was how cigarette companies won their cases. When the trial court judge in New Orleans approved the Castano suit as a class action, the tobacco companies appealed.

The industry fought back on other fronts as well. On March 24, Philip Morris sued ABC for libel, objecting to statements made in the *Day One* programs aired in February and March. The company disputed the reports' claims that it "spiked" its cigarettes, adding nicotine from sources outside the original leaf. (While the show's producer and correspondent defended the report, ABC ended up settling with Philip Morris, issuing a humiliating on-air apology and paying the cigarette maker $15 million.) One month later, Philip Morris was embarrassed by new revelations from the Waxman hearings. Victor DeNoble, a behavioral psychologist, testified about his work at the company in the early 1980s, investigating the effect of nicotine on rats. When reports he prepared showed nicotine acting very much like an addictive substance, Philip Morris terminated the work he and a colleague were doing, shut down their lab, and killed the rats. Nicotine was a touchy subject.

Into this supercharged atmosphere came the Merrell Williams documents. Within days after Dick Scruggs, Don Barrett, and Mississippi Attorney General Mike Moore had reviewed the collection in the old bank building in Pascagoula, Barrett, who was a member of the Castano team, circulated some of the choicer selections to a few of his cocounsel in that case. Some of the documents then made their way to Washington, and Scruggs and Moore ultimately flew a complete set there, handing them to Henry Waxman. Their arrival was timely, given the recent testimony about nicotine by the tobacco executives (the "Seven Dwarfs," Williams called them), for they included B&W general counsel Addison Yeaman's 1963 memo calling nicotine an addictive drug, as well as other references to nicotine's habit-forming ways.

Barrett was eager for the documents to get maximum exposure, and in a hotel room in Wichita, Kansas, in late April, he delivered a stack of them to Walt Bogdanich and his associate producer Keith Summa of ABC News. ABC was a logical choice, having recently aired its two *Day One* pieces on the cigarette industry, and Bogdanich and Summa immediately started preparing another segment for the show. As was routine for sensitive stories, Bogdanich informed ABC's in-house lawyers about what they were working on. He was stunned at the reaction. The lawyers first tried to convince the *Day One* team that the documents weren't interesting — in essence, that there was no story. Bogdanich suggested that perhaps the attorneys weren't qualified to make such a judgment. Then the lawyers voiced their concern that it be clear Merrell Williams was not the source of the documents. Would it be possible to identify Barrett in some fashion — perhaps as a "government source," since he was representing the state of Mississippi? — the lawyers wanted to know. When Barrett refused, the ABC lawyers would brook no debate. Pointing to Judge Wine's injunction requiring Williams to return everything he had from his paralegal work and to disclose none of it, they ordered Bogdanich to drop the story.

The injunction might be unconstitutional, Bogdanich argued. And any risks associated with violating it had to be balanced against the opportunity to air what he regarded as an extraordinarily important story, one that was crucial to an ongoing public debate. But the lawyers didn't see risks, they saw apocalypse. Even possessing the documents, they said, might be a criminal act. Thomas Murphy, the chairman of Capital Cities/ABC, could end up in jail, they said. A court might levy huge daily fines that could ultimately bankrupt the company. The ABC lawyers told Bogdanich that they had consulted two outside law firms, who concurred that the story had to die. Philip Morris's just-filed suit against ABC also had to be weighing on the lawyers' minds. Appalled, Bogdanich watched lawyers from his own company haul away the documents and check to make sure that no one had any related material on computer disks.

ABC lost its scoop to Philip J. Hilts, then a science and health reporter in the Washington bureau of the *New York Times.* Some of Williams's B&W documents had made their way to Capitol Hill, and in early May, a government source let Hilts review a pile about a foot tall and take copies of what he wanted. Hilts walked away with about a two-inch stack and began preparing his story. This time the lawyers weren't a problem. As the *Times*'s counsel saw it, Judge Wine's injunction applied only to the parties involved in the lawsuit in his court, and no one else.

Hilts had not been informed that Merrell Williams was the source of the documents, and he was worried that Brown & Williamson might deny their authenticity. When he called the company for comment, though, they immediately told him that the documents he was talking about had been stolen from company files. That was all the confirmation he needed.

All during the first week of May 1994, the newspapers in Kentucky were filled with stories about the upcoming 120th Kentucky Derby. But on Saturday May 7, the day of the famous horse race, there was another big story as well. "You're all over the paper," his wife told Merrell Williams in a call from Louisville. Hilts's 2,100-word story, headlined "Tobacco Company Was Silent on Hazards," ran in the *Times* that day, and the *Courier-Journal* in Louisville had picked it up from its wire service. It was just the beginning. In succeeding days the *Wall Street Journal,* the *Washington Post,* and *USA Today* all carried stories. Williams's name appeared in some of the accounts, but none of the papers was able to locate him for comment.

Brown & Williamson quickly went back to court, seeking an order allowing them to question Williams about how the documents got leaked to the press. "It seems like the cat is out of the bag," Judge Wine said before ordering Williams to appear for a deposition. "The cat's not just out of the bag, it's having kittens," DeMoisey remarked later. After agreeing to return to Louisville for his deposition on May 14, Williams failed to show. DeMoisey explained that Williams felt B&W simply wanted to gather evidence to use in future criminal proceedings against him, and that he had retained counsel in Mississippi to deal with any criminal charges.

But Williams's being AWOL was the least of B&W's troubles. On May 12, a package had arrived at the doorstep of Stanton Glantz, a professor on the medical faculty at the University of California at San Francisco and a seasoned antitobacco crusader. The box had no return address, and listed as the sender "Mr. Butts," the name of the talking cigarette in the comic strip "Doonesbury." Glantz decided a good spot for the nearly four thousand pages of documents was the UCSF library, and soon the entire collection was available there for the public at large to review.

Desperately, B&W tried to plug the holes in the dike. It hired Barbara Caulfield, a former federal judge who had become a partner in a high-powered California law firm, who went to court in San Francisco seeking an order forcing UCSF to return the Merrell Williams collection. B&W hired investigators to stake out the area of the university library where the papers were kept, and also asked the court to have the library turn over the names of people who had checked out the material. In depositions, the company tried to determine who had sent the documents to Glantz. "Do you know anybody named Mr. Butts — B–U–T–T–S?" Caulfield asked Richard Heimann, a San Francisco plaintiffs' lawyer involved in the Castano case. "If you mean do I know a living person by that name, no," Heimann answered. Three years would pass before Heimann learned that Mr. Butts was none other than his colleague on the Castano legal team, Don Barrett.

Perhaps appropriately for litigation against a university, the debate over the documents in the San Francisco court veered toward the philosophical, and even the metaphysical. Whether the Mr. Butts documents at the UCSF library really constituted "stolen" material was one issue debated. After all, the documents were *copies,* not originals. B&W commissioned a big-name Deep Thinker to counter this argument. "I contend that for information-intensive products, especially in the contemporary 'Information Era,' a product owner's property interest should reside not exclusively or even primarily in the sheer physicality of the product — the assemblage of molecules that comprise it — but primarily in its information content," Robert E. McGinn, a Stanford University ethics professor, stated in an affidavit. McGinn was hardly a typical tobacco industry expert. His scholarly publications, listed in a curriculum vitae appended to his affidavit, included "In Defense of Intangibles: The Feasibility-Responsibility Dilemma in Modern Technological Innovation" and "Nietzsche on Technology."

The California court was not impressed. It ruled that the UCSF library could keep the documents, and sent Brown & Williamson home empty-handed. On other fronts, too, B&W was losing badly. It sent out a slew of subpoenas to newspapers and congressional offices seeking recovery of its documents and to question recipients about how they obtained the material. But courts in Washington, D.C., and Virginia quashed those efforts. Even Judge Wine in Kentucky refused to enforce subpoenas sent to the *Courier-Journal* and *USA Today*. Brown & Williamson's attorney–client privilege was "not as strong as the right of the public to know whether or not B&W has withheld information concerning the dangers of smoking," he ruled.

Then came the ultimate nightmare for anyone trying to limit the dissemination of information. On July 1, 1995, Stanton Glantz and a team of researchers at UCSF put the documents, indexed and annotated, on the Internet (http://www.library.ucsf.edu/tobacco).

As Dick Scruggs had promised, in the spring of 1994 Merrell Williams was put on the payroll of Barton & Williams, the Pascagoula law firm, as a paralegal. But he didn't spend a lot of time at work. Instead, he went shopping.

The first item on his list was a house, and after less than a day of look-ing with a broker from Century 21, he picked out a contemporary, wood-sided home in a quiet subdivision of Ocean Springs. It was perfect for his family, he thought, hoping they would be joining him over the summer. It was also less than a mile from the Ocean Springs hospital, a plus given the state of his health. On April 26, he made a cash offer at the agreed price of $109,600, explaining to the broker that another party would actually take title to the house and provide the funds for the transaction.

Sure enough, at the closing on May 11 — which Williams did not attend — the sellers received a check for the full amount from an "M&S Enterprises." In July Williams moved into the house, stiffing the landlord of his apartment building for $987 in unpaid rent and other charges. On July 20, M&S transferred title to the house to Williams's name.

In succeeding months, Williams bought a 1991 Mustang convertible for $6,500 and a new Dodge Neon, which cost about $13,000. The Neon was for his daughter Jennifer, who had just reached driving age. With the help of a lawyer friend in Jackson, Williams incorporated a business, the Island Wind Sailing Company, and, using a loan from the SouthTrust Bank, he bought, in the name of the corporation, a thirty-foot Morgan sailboat for $17,500. His idea was to set up a charter business, running tourists out on wine-and-cheese trips to the barrier islands in the Mississippi Sound. It was only after he bought the boat that he learned it was too small for that use. Still, the spending didn't stop. The owner of a sixteen-foot catamaran noticed Williams admiring the boat one day at the Ocean Springs Yacht Club. Would he like to buy it? the owner asked. Sure, Williams said, on a whim, forking over $500. He never used it, and one day a waterspout — a kind of liquid tornado — picked it up off the sand and smashed it on the road.

How on earth could he afford all this? Sherry wanted to know, looking around the new house when she and the girls came down for a visit during the summer of 1994. Sherry liked the house and began to imagine living there. With a hospital up the street, maybe she would sell her business and go back to nursing, she thought. But she was in a financial mess at home, still trying to pay off medical bills from Williams's heart surgery and facing tax problems thanks to his impulsive plundering of his 401K to buy her a sailboat (which had soon become his). She needed Williams's cooperation so she could start sorting things out. Could he give her some pay stubs, so she could calculate estimated tax payments for 1994? she asked. He refused, and also wouldn't explain how he'd funded his recent shopping spree.

In August, Sherry rented a van and drove Jennifer and Sarah and some furniture from Louisville to Ocean Springs. The girls were going to take a stab at becoming Mississippians. Sherry's own intentions were heading in the other direction. Her husband's refusal to help her and his secretiveness about his financial affairs had broken a bond of trust that had endured through all their other troubles, she felt. They even fought over whether Williams owed her money for the rental van and other costs connected with moving the girls to Mississippi.

Things worsened in the fall. With the start of the school year, the girls realized how much they missed their friends back home, and, after just a few months, they moved back to Louisville, returning to the custody of Mollie, their mother. In November, Sherry filed for divorce; she was so devastated financially that she had to sell her house in Louisville. Williams succumbed once again to the demons of depression and fear. After his daughters left, he found himself at times weeping uncontrollably. He started seeing a psychiatrist and resumed taking antidepressants.

One day, while walking at the Ocean Springs running track, Williams heard what sounded like a gunshot, and was convinced it was intended for him. While Williams imagined threats to his life, there was no question that Brown & Williamson's Atlanta law firm, King & Spalding, had tracked him to Mississippi. Private investigators for the firm were quizzing real estate brokers and insurance salesmen and combing land deeds and motor vehicle registrations for information about Williams's dealings. Williams was sure he was under surveillance. He had his home swept for bugs, though none were found.

It wasn't long before King & Spalding's lawyers had pieced together a chronology of Williams's life on the Gulf Coast. They also figured out who was underwriting it, and on February 14, 1995, the firm filed a lawsuit on behalf of Brown & Williamson in federal district court in Biloxi, detailing their theory of how and why Williams transferred a cache of the company's documents. As B&W and King & Spalding saw it, Dick Scruggs had furnished Williams with the house, the cars, and the sailboat as an inducement for him to turn over the documents — documents that Scruggs and his pals in the plaintiffs' bar could then use in personal-injury suits against B&W. In short, it was a payoff.

In addition to naming Williams as a defendant, the Biloxi suit named M&S Enterprises, as well as other persons identified only as "[John] Does 1 through 10." While Scruggs was not specifically named, the allegations in the complaint made it clear that B&W considered him, and perhaps other plaintiffs' lawyers as well, to be among the Does. Exhibits appended to the forty-page complaint showed that in documents relating to the sale of the house, the phone number for M&S Enterprises was Scruggs's office number. When M&S transferred the house to Williams, the deed was executed by Charlene Bosarge, Scruggs's secretary.

However well documented the financial relationship between Williams and Scruggs, the basis of the relationship, the motivation of each man for entering into it, was only a matter of conjecture by B&W. Still, the conjecture seemed well founded. The juxtaposition in time of the document transfer and the spending spree *looked* bad. There was also Williams's previous behavior to consider. However pure his original intent in collecting the Brown & Williamson documents, his offer in the summer of 1993 to give them back to the company in return for a substantial sum of money had every appearance of extortion or blackmail. But whistle-blowers are rarely saints. While they may act to reveal information that is in the public interest, their motivation may be, in small or large part, self-interest. Such was certainly the case with Williams.

Inevitably folded into an analysis of a whistle-blower's conduct is the nature of the information made public. The more it appears that the secrets revealed are ones the public has a right to know, the more forgiving people tend to be of any treachery involved in revealing it. Given the content of the Brown & Williamson documents, Williams came to be viewed in many circles as someone who had done something heroic, not horrific. His minor misdeeds were canceled by the monstrous ones he uncovered.

In defending his own conduct, Dick Scruggs similarly sought cover behind the wrongdoing he felt was revealed in the documents, as well as in B&W's failure to disclose them. And he said he did exactly what a lawyer who comes into possession of such material should do: He turned it over to government authorities, namely to Mike Moore, Mississippi's attorney general, and to Congress. As to the material and financial assistance he provided Williams — the "loans" — he and Williams both said that the aid was in no way a quid pro quo for the documents. It was in a series of conversations in the late spring of 1994 — *after* Williams had given Scruggs the documents — that he told Scruggs of his hopes of establishing a safe and secure home on the Mississippi coast for his family. Scruggs said that he simply decided to help Williams get back on his feet, knowing he was down on his luck and had sacrificed a lot in his battle with Brown & Williamson.

In all of this, Scruggs was, at the very least, treading on murky ethical ground. As a lawyer about to be engaged in litigation against the very party whose stolen documents he had received, he was hardly disinterested in their disposition. The people he passed them on to, moreover — an attorney general about to sue the cigarette industry, and antitobacco lawmakers — were similarly not in a position to render an impartial decision about whether the material had rightly been made public. In a July 1994 ethics opinion involving another matter, the American Bar Association suggested that a lawyer in Scruggs's position ought to turn the documents over to a court for "a definitive resolution of the proper disposition of the materials." This, the ABA opinion said, "would afford the adverse party a reasonable and timely opportunity to resort to judicial remedies to determine the rights and allow the receiving lawyer, under appropriate circumstances, to use relevant materials in the prosecution or defense of an action." That would have been the cautious course of action. As Brown & Williamson soon learned, though, caution was hardly the byword of those the company was up against in Mississippi.

On the same day in 1995 that Brown & Williamson filed its suit in Biloxi — Valentine's Day, Williams pointed out — the company went back to court in Kentucky with a motion to hold Williams in contempt of court. The motion papers spelled out the litany of frustrations B&W and its attorneys had endured in their pursuit of information from Williams and in their failed efforts to contain the documents. Because Williams had "blatantly and repeatedly" defied the court's orders, the motion requested that he be incarcerated for up to six months for contempt. For the first time, a stint in jail seemed more than a theoretical possibility for Williams. Outwardly, at least, he met the prospect with his usual wryness: "I'll write poems, read Baudelaire, and teach the other inmates how to interpret *Waiting for Godot*," he joked at the time.

19

The second Horton trial, in which the jury found the American Tobacco Company liable, but awarded zero dollars in damages, had been the last straw for Don Barrett's cocounsel from Texas, Don Davis. Davis's firm had invested $365,000 in the lawsuit, not including the value of his time, and the September 1990 verdict in Oxford led him to conclude that litigating against Big Tobacco was lousy business. Deciding to cut his losses, he abandoned the Horton suit and decided he would no longer pursue cigarette litigation. That made the Horton verdict a far more significant victory for the industry as a whole than anyone at the time appreciated.

Davis was hardly alone in his discouragement. In case after case around the country, plaintiffs' lawyers had gone down to defeat, outgunned by the industry's superior resources and unable to neutralize the he-chose-to-smoke defense that proved so appealing to juries. And few had the willingness or wherewithal to continue the fight. What's more, in June 1992, the U.S. Supreme Court handed down its decision in the Cipollone case, nine years after it was filed in New Jersey. While the court left open the right of plaintiffs to sue cigarette makers on a number of theories, it ruled that claims alleging the companies had provided inadequate warnings about the dangers of their product had been preempted by federal legislation that mandated warnings on cigarette packs and advertisements. At that point, the Cipollone lawyers threw in the towel and dropped the case. The second wave of tobacco litigation was over.

But Don Barrett wasn't done. "I felt that I was doing something the Lord would honor," he said years later, echoing what he had told Williams shortly after he had turned over the B&W documents. In December 1987, just days before the start of the first Horton trial, he had filed a second cigarette suit, but it had languished while the Horton matter dragged on. Once *Horton* was out of the way, though, Barrett turned his attention to the second suit. The case bore many similarities to *Horton:* It was brought on behalf of a black man, Anderson Smith Jr., who lived in Kosciusko (pronounced Kazz-ee-ES-ko), about thirty miles east of Lexington, in Attala County. Like Horton, Smith had left Mississippi for a period of his life, served in the armed forces, and even worked at the John Deere tractor works in Waterloo, Iowa. Once again, the defendant was American Tobacco Company and the product at issue was Pall Mall cigarettes.

This was not a coincidence; in taking on a second case, Barrett was looking to piggyback on the discovery he had done in *Horton*, rather than having to start from scratch the exhaustive process of extracting information from a new company. The cause of Smith's death in 1986, according to the complaint filed in the name of his daughter, Jeanette Wilks, was cancer and emphysema. The Wilks case, as it was known, was assigned to Judge Eugene Bogen, who had presided over the second Horton trial.

For all the similarities, there was a critical difference between *Horton* and *Wilks*, one Barrett thought made *Wilks* an almost certain winner: "We took the Anderson Smith case," he explained years later, "because Anderson Smith had the mental age of a nine-year-old, and he had been in mental institutions practically all his adult life, for forty-something years." Smith had been declared mentally incompetent while in the Army, which is where he began smoking. This, Barrett figured, meant American Tobacco could not possibly rely on the he-chose-to-smoke defense that it had used with such consistent success in other lawsuits. As a mental incompetent — not only was he mentally retarded, he was a diagnosed paranoid schizophrenic — Anderson Smith could not be deemed to have made a rational choice to do anything.

It is hard to say which was more perverse, the tobacco industry's use of the assumption-of-risk defense, even as it denied the risk, or Barrett dredging up a plaintiff with the requisite disabilities to disarm such a defense. But on May 11, 1993, Judge Bogen issued a decision in the case that rendered the assumption-of-risk defense, as well as Smith's impairment, irrelevant. In a seven-page opinion that stunned everyone involved in *Wilks* and generated headlines around the country, he wrote:

> Once again this Court is called upon to decide the standard of tort liability to which the manufacturer of cigarettes is held. The Court has considered this matter anew and concludes that cigarettes are, as a matter of law, defective and unreasonably dangerous for human consumption. Cigarettes are defective because when used as intended, they cause cancer, emphysema, heart disease and other illnesses. That the result reached here imposes absolute liability on the manufacturers of cigarettes for injuries arising from the use of their products is not a departure from the doctrine of strict liability, rather the logical extension of the doctrine in the light of present day scientific and medical knowledge and the enormous burden which cigarettes place on the nation's economy and its health care system in particular.
>
> Cigarettes are the most lethal product which may be legally sold in this country. According to the Affidavit of Dr. David Burns, Senior Reviewer of several Surgeon General's Reports, cigarettes kill approximately 435,000 persons annually from cancer, emphysema and heart disease. Cigarettes kill more Americans each year than AIDS, automobile accidents, alcohol, fires, heroin, morphine, cocaine, suicide and homicide combined. One in four two-pack-per-day smokers will die of lung cancer. Cigarettes kill 40% of the people who smoke them. The health costs associated with cigarette smoking fall upon everyone, the smoker and his family, non-smokers, insurance companies, employers, employees, physicians, hospitals, and the taxpayers who pay the bills for many of those hospitals. Everyone, that is, except the cigarette manufacturer. . . .
>
> It is clear that to effectuate the policy objectives underlying the

doctrine of strict liability — the reduction of hazards to life and health and placing responsibility on the manufacturer for injuries caused by his defective products — cigarette manufacturers must be held liable for the deaths and disease arising from the use of their products.

With this groundbreaking ruling, the judge transformed the upcoming trial. Gone as a question for the jury was whether cigarettes cause illness and death. As a general proposition, Bogen ruled, they did. All the jurors would have to decide was whether cigarette smoking had been the cause of Anderson Smith's death in particular, and, if so, what damages his heirs were entitled to. As if that weren't bad enough for American Tobacco, Judge Bogen also granted the plaintiffs' motion to strike the defenses of assumption of risk and comparative fault. Assumption of risk, he ruled, had been subsumed within the doctrine of comparative fault in Mississippi, but comparative fault could be asserted only if evidence showed that the injured person had misused or abnormally handled the product. "No such claim is made here," Bogen wrote. Smith "did with Pall Mall cigarettes what Defendants intended to be done, he smoked them."

Jim Upshaw, reprising the role he had assumed in *Horton* as lead local counsel for American Tobacco, remembers his jaw dropping when he learned of the ruling. "If you were a comedian, it's kind of like getting hit with a shit pie," he said. At a hearing following the decision, he accused Judge Bogen of having created America's "first smokers' compensation law." Don Barrett thought Bogen's decision was "a perfect ruling," and that the industry had received a "body blow."

On the eve of trial, the case had suddenly been vastly simplified. Getting it that far, however, had been the same arduous, financially taxing process for Barrett that *Horton* had been — and that every case against the tobacco industry had always been. In fact, in the early stages of *Wilks*, with Don Davis no longer at his side, Barrett wasn't sure he had the wherewithal to move the case forward. Desperate for support, he placed a call to Pascagoula and got Dick Scruggs on the phone. "I was just out of money and worn out physically," Barrett recounted. "Dickie's my old friend, and I called him up and told him that. I said, 'Dickie, I'm out of money, I'm tired, I'm emotionally worn out, and I can't believe I've taken this thing so far and everybody else has bailed out and nobody else in the country is doin' these things. And if I quit, that's going to be the end of it, and you've just got to help me.' And he said, 'I'll help you. That's great; let's do it.' And he jumped in and financed the rest of the case. I doubt that I could ever have gone to trial without him."

Although the case had been filed in Lexington, Judge Bogen moved the proceedings sixty miles west, to his hometown of Greenville. None of the parties objected, given their previous experiences in Holmes County. Greenville, population 45,000, sits defiantly and precariously on one of the many hairpin turns carved by the powerful Mississippi River, which also serves as the border with Arkansas. While one imagines most towns perched on banks *above* a river, Greenville literally sits below the Mississippi, with the heart of the town shadowed by a tall protective levee. The only real signs of vitality come from the casinos that have sprung up atop the levee since the Mississippi legislature authorized dockside gambling. Just a few blocks from the glittering gambling palaces sits the Washington County courthouse, a well-scrubbed, three-story stone structure.

It was here, in a courtroom on the second floor, that the Wilks trial began in June 1993. Judge Bogen began the proceedings by having potential jurors fill out an extensive questionnaire about their backgrounds and attitudes. When one well-dressed female juror was asked during voir dire why she had written that the Wilks suit was "stupid," she said it was because she hadn't been sure how to spell "asinine." Needless to say, she was dismissed. Whatever skepticism jurors in general might have harbored about the idea of compensating smokers for the consequences of their habit, Judge Bogen's pretrial rulings gave little opportunity for doubts on that score to come into play. This was to be a case of medical causation in a specific individual, not an epistemological discussion of what it takes to prove that smoking can cause cancer or a morality play about responsibility and personal choice.

Victor McTeer, whom Barrett had called on to help with the retrial of *Horton*, again stepped in to help present the plaintiffs' case. So did Dick Scruggs, who drew on his experience in asbestos litigation to handle some of the testimony by medical experts. But when it came to proof of medical causation, the weak underside of the plaintiffs' case became suddenly clear. In a trial that lasted less than five days, American's lawyers presented convincing evidence that Anderson Smith had died from a pulmonary embolism following urinary tract surgery, an event, their experts testified, that was unrelated to his lung cancer and emphysema. Jim Upshaw called this the "preposition" defense: Smith died *with* cancer, not *of* it.

In his closing argument, Don Barrett stepped back from the narrowly focused medical facts of the case and tried to convey, in emotional terms, the enormity of the wrongdoing committed by cigarette makers. He read jurors the story of the Emperor's New Clothes, to point out, he explained later, that "we ignore the obvious. Here's a product that kills all these people, and we say that's okay." He also read a passage from the Bible's book of Jeremiah which referred to evildoers, turning to look at American's lawyers as he did. Spreading his hands in a gesture of perplexity, Upshaw said, "Why is he looking at me, Judge?" producing laughter in the courtroom. To Barrett, though, it was no laughing matter. He had come to view his battle with the tobacco industry in biblical terms. The Bible, he once noted, is "filled with admonitions" to people with intelligence, wealth, or "other gifts from God" to use those attributes to help the less fortunate. So tobacco litigation, in his mind, was a "high calling," and the cigarette companies were truly forces of evil to be vanquished.

"We are a sick people," Barrett said in a conversation years after the Wilks trial. "The human race is a fallen race. And it's easy to do monstrous things simply by redefining the terms." To his mind, it was no stretch to compare tobacco merchants to Hitler, Stalin, or the Khmer Rouge, though, he noted, "at least in their minds what they were doing would improve things, however perverted their reasoning." Singling out tobacco industry lawyers, he said, "Those bastards are doing it for the money."

But the Wilks jurors would not join Barrett's jihad. After just two hours of deliberation, they found for American Tobacco, concluding that Smith's death had not been caused by smoking.

At this point one might have thought Barrett would follow Don Davis's lead and abandon the fight against the tobacco industry. If the Wilks case made anything clear, it was that in suits by individual smokers, there were myriad weaknesses cigarette makers could exploit in their defense. For all the developments in product-liability law over the course of the twentieth century, it seemed that if there was to be any real hope of defeating the industry, a new approach to tobacco litigation would have to be found.

That new idea, it so happens, popped into the head of Mike Lewis just as the Wilks case was heading to trial. Lewis was born and raised in the Delta town of Belzoni, Mississippi, which bills itself as the Catfish Capital of the World, thanks to the vast catfish-farm ponds that are steadily replacing cotton fields in the region. After a stint in the Air Force, he settled in Clarksdale, another Delta town further north, and set up a small general law practice with his wife Pauline. Clarksdale is dirt poor, but the Lewises had done fairly well there, enough to buy nice cars, a single-engine plane that Mike used to zip around the state, and an elegant old house in the center of town that they converted into their law office.

In March 1993, Lewis drove to Baptist Memorial Hospital in Memphis to visit Jackie Thompson, the mother of his law secretary Alice Craven. At forty-nine — one year younger than Lewis — Thompson was dying from heart disease. She had smoked Salems for decades, at times up to three packs a day, and doctors blamed this for her illness. In 1988, she had a major heart attack, which was followed over the next few years by three or four more. Angioplasty and triple bypass surgery had failed to reverse her condition, and by 1993 her lungs had become so weakened that she was awaiting a combined heart–lung transplant. The disease had taken a devastating toll. Thompson's body was emaciated and pierced with tubes; her family was emotionally shattered by her premature and precipitate decline. And the financial costs of her illness were staggering. After her private insurance ran out, Medicaid, health insurance for the indigent funded by the state and federal governments, had stepped in to pay the bills, which totaled over $1 million by the time of her death in June 1994. Although she was hospitalized in Memphis, Thompson was a resident of Mississippi.

Prior to Lewis's visit, he had talked to Thompson's daughter about the idea of videotaping her. Thompson thought it might serve to educate young people on the dangers of smoking. Lewis thought it might educate a jury. But by the day of his visit, Thompson was in no shape for it, and

Lewis put the idea aside. He found the visit to the hospital wrenching. "The emotion that I was really feeling was a desire for revenge, for vindication," Lewis recalled three years after Thompson's death. "I wanted to destroy the tobacco industry, to put them out of business." But Lewis knew that jury after jury had failed to offer anyone that kind of satisfaction.

It was after he left Jackie Thompson's bedside and got in the elevator to head down that the idea hit him. When it came to *financial* harm caused by smoking, he realized, a primary victim in Thompson's case was the government, which spent taxpayer dollars on her huge medical bills. Cigarette companies had created a mess, and the state paid to clean it up, plain and simple. Why shouldn't the industry have to pay the state back? For Lewis, it was an epiphany. And the more he thought about it, the better it sounded. Cigarette makers, he realized, wouldn't be able to point at the state and say *it* chose to smoke. By the time he got into his dark-blue Cadillac to begin the seventy-mile journey home, Lewis was so excited by the idea that he couldn't concentrate on driving and had to pull to the side of the road to collect his thoughts.

Over the next several days, Lewis, mild-mannered and modest, wondered if his idea was too grandiose, and he felt a bit embarrassed about it. His wife liked it, though, and he couldn't get it out of his mind. After a couple of weeks he picked up the phone and called his Ole Miss law school classmate Mike Moore, who was in his second term as Mississippi's attorney general. "I presented [the idea] to him in an apologetic way," Lewis recalls, but Moore was intrigued. "Get down here," he told Lewis. A few days later, Mike and Pauline Lewis met with Moore at his office in Jackson. What especially interested Moore about going after the tobacco industry, says Lewis, was the idea of protecting children. As attorney general, Moore had made illegal drug use by children a particular focus, and he felt a campaign against underage smoking fit naturally into that effort. As for developing the idea further, Moore told Mike Lewis to talk to Dick Scruggs.

When Lewis caught up with Scruggs, he was in the middle of helping Don Barrett try the Wilks case. Over breakfast in Greenville, Lewis met the two men and outlined his idea. Just a few months earlier, Scruggs had thought of something similar. Knowing that Anderson Smith had been a veteran and had been treated at Veterans Administration hospitals, Scruggs wondered if there was a way to bring a claim for the federal government on behalf of all veterans who had fallen ill due to smoking. He even asked his law partner Steve Bozeman to research the idea, but they couldn't figure out how to make it work.

Judge Bogen also seemed to dance around the idea in his pretrial ruling in the Wilks case that imposed absolute liability on American Tobacco. He had referred to "the enormous burden which cigarettes place on the nation's economy and its health care system in particular," and mentioned that it was often "taxpayers who pay the bills." Even the nation's leading cigarette maker had worried about a claim based on this notion. A November 1978 Philip Morris memo that plaintiffs' lawyers learned about years later noted:

> More industry antagonists are using an economic argument against cigarettes — i.e., cigarettes cause disease; disease requires treatment; major health costs are borne by the government; the taxpayers pay in the end.
>
> Thus, as health costs rise astronomically, the opposition becomes armed with more potent weapons. We must be prepared to counter this line of argument.

When, fifteen years later, Mike Lewis presented his idea to Scruggs and Barrett, they were bowled over by the concept. While the Wilks case would end in disappointment, they emerged more determined than ever to hold the tobacco industry accountable. And now, they thought, they had a sure-fire way.

Part 3

Mississippi First

20

Rivers in Mississippi fall into two categories: ones with names you can pronounce, and ones with names you can't. There's the Pearl, Red, Deer, and Big Black, for example. And then there's the Nanawaya, the Yockanookany, and the Tchoutacabouffa. Sometimes two rivers that start far apart meander and curve toward one another until they merge into one. For example, in the boggy woodlands of George County, about forty-five miles north of the coast, the Leaf and the Chickasawhay join to form the Pascagoula, which flows south into the Gulf.

Developments in tobacco litigation in Mississippi seemed to follow a similar course. Disparate people and events — Don Barrett with his Horton and Wilks cases, Merrell Williams with his documents, Mike Lewis with his idea — merged in a single stream. When Lewis contacted Mike Moore in the spring of 1993 and Moore said to bring in Dick Scruggs, that stream took a decisive turn south.

Both Moore and Scruggs grew up and launched their careers in Pascagoula, and under the leadership of these two men, that city on the sea became the staging ground for an assault on cigarette makers unlike anything the industry had ever seen.

Pascagoula, population 26,000, just thirty-five miles west of Mobile, near the Mississippi–Alabama state line, takes its name from the river that runs through it into the Mississippi Sound. The river, in turn, is named for a small tribe of Indians that inhabited the region when French explorers arrived there in 1699. It is also sometimes referred to as the "Singing River" because, a local guidebook explains, "of a mysterious singing sound associated with the waters."

Throughout the colonial period, the Mississippi coast remained a sparsely populated backwater. Hopes of finding gold and pearls there foundered. And the environment was utterly inhospitable. Steaming hot summers were sometimes followed by winter chills cold enough to kill carefully nurtured sugarcane and fruit trees. Swamps nurtured alligators, snakes, and mosquitoes in droves, and the mosquitoes periodically spread yellow fever. From time to time, hurricanes pounded the coast.

Still, through the eighteenth and early nineteenth centuries, France, Spain, and England jockeyed for dominion in the area. From New Orleans in the west to Mobile in the east — with Pascagoula in between — flags rose and fell and territory was divided and renamed as alliances shifted and wars were fought among the great powers of Europe.

One bit of agricultural history during the colonial period is worth mentioning, though it took place not on the coast, but in the Natchez district, on the banks of the Mississippi, just across from what is now the state of Louisiana. A 1967 article in the *Journal of Mississippi History* relates what happened:

> When the Spanish moved into the area in 1778, one of their first steps was to provide for the inspection and governmental purchase of tobacco, of which the production in 1787 was nearly 590,000 pounds. But Mississippi tobacco was not of first quality; its growers prepared it for market carelessly and fraudulently; and the Spanish permitted competition from Kentucky. By 1792, production was down to 75,000

pounds, the planters were ruined, and the Spanish governor had to protect them from their creditors. The planters tried to fill the void with indigo, but it was messy in its preparation, polluting water courses and attracting even larger hordes of flies than usual, and it required capital for equipment. In 1793 insects ravaged almost the entire crop. The royal government had finally to suspend executions against debtors for five years. . . .

In this extremity, cotton came to the rescue and fastened its tyranny on the colony and then the state. The Whitney-type cotton-gin arrived in 1795. By 1797 cotton was clearly the staple crop.

Even with statehood in 1817, the coast remained of marginal importance in Mississippi, thanks to the emergence of the cotton economy of the Delta. It was this "white gold" that made Mississippi the fifth-richest state in the Union on the eve of the Civil War, and it was the Delta planters who dominated the politics and economics of the state well into the twentieth century. Indeed, when Mike Moore was elected attorney general in 1987, he was the first politician from the coast to win a major statewide office in fifty years.

It was twentieth-century industry that put Pascagoula on the map, and the industry that has defined the town more than any other is shipbuilding. From the time local Indians burned out trunks of fallen cypress trees to make dugout canoes, inhabitants of the coast had made boats. Small boatyards, for the most part family-run operations, dotted area bayous, turning out whatever met the commercial needs of the day, from fishing craft to freight schooners.

Then, in 1938, Robert Ingersoll Ingalls came to town. Ingalls, a Yankee from Ohio, had established a steel business in Birmingham, Alabama, where he manufactured tanks, and a small shipyard just outside Mobile, where he built steel barges. But Ingalls wanted to get into shipbuilding in a bigger way, and chose Pascagoula as the site for his new yard. Ingalls's plan was to compete for contracts for new passenger and cargo ships from the U.S. Maritime Commission, which was seeking to rebuild America's shipping capacity. His timing proved exquisite: Just three years later, the United States entered World War II, and Ingalls Shipbuilding Corporation, as the new operation was called, was swamped with orders.

Suddenly, instead of producing commercial vessels, Ingalls was turning out escort aircraft carriers, submarine tenders, and troopships. Production ran around the clock and workers flooded the town. Pascagoula's population skyrocketed from 5,900 in 1940 to 35,000 in 1943, with many people living in hastily thrown-together government houses, or even tents and trailers.

From the time its first ship was launched in June 1940, Ingalls employed a revolutionary manufacturing technique: The giant steel plates that form a ship's hull were welded together, rather than riveted. Not only was welding a far faster — and cheaper — process, it produced a stronger vessel.

Still, shipbuilding was hard and gritty work. The inside of a ship's hull was a punishing place, often sweltering hot, and almost always filled with dust and ear-splitting noise. Wide use was made of materials containing asbestos. With a name derived from a Greek word meaning "inextinguishable," asbestos is a mineral whose properties have been appreciated from ancient times. Containing fibers soft enough to be woven into cloth, it remains impervious to heat and flame. The Romans reportedly used asbestos to make napkins, which they would clean by tossing into the fire, and the Tatars showed Marco Polo asbestos fabric during his thirteenth-century trip through their empire. But it was with the Industrial Revolution that asbestos came into widespread use, invaluable as insulation and fireproofing in everything from boilers to roof tiles.

Nowhere was asbestos of greater utility than in a modern ship. Insulation workers mixed a special cement that contained asbestos and used asbestos firebrick to line the steam boilers, turbines, and electrical generators in the belly of the vessel. And they used asbestos insulation to sheathe the spaghetti-maze of pipes that ran for miles throughout the ship. They then wrapped the pipe insulation with cloth comprised of 90 percent asbestos fiber, while sheetmetal workers wrapped the same material around heating and air conditioning vents. Further up in the ship, workers mixed giant batches of decking compound in which asbestos was a major ingredient, which they spread on decks, along passageways, and inside ammunition magazines and cargo holds. Others lined living quarters with fireproof composite sheets containing 50 percent asbestos.

Asbestos was also of great use in the shipbuilding *process,* which itself generated torrents of heat and sparks and molten slag. Workers wrapped themselves in A-cloth for protection against the heat of a welding torch or hot, dripping metal; they wore asbestos gloves to shield their hands; and when the scorching summer sun made the decks too hot to stand on, they laid asbestos cloth down on them. On rainy days they even used it to make ponchos. In similar ways painters and welders employed it as a drop-cloth so no harm would come to surrounding equipment.

As virtually everyone now knows, harm was being done, not to equipment, but to men. Every time asbestos cloth was used — whether as a body wrap or a floor covering — it left a powdery white residue. Every time asbestos gloves were clapped, fibers were sent flying into the air, and every time bags of asbestos material were mixed or fireproof board was sawed or drilled, it produced clouds of dust. Myriad blowers used to ventilate the labyrinth of holds and compartments on each ship kept the particles airborne, almost assuring that those inside would breathe them in. The steady accumulation of the needlelike asbestos fibers in the workers' lungs would ultimately produce widespread illness and death. But employees at Ingalls — and at shipyards and construction sites throughout the country — would not learn that for decades. So the work went on.

When World War II ended, orders at the shipyard dropped dramatically. But local political leaders were not about to let Pascagoula revert to being famous only for its pecans, large groves of which had been planted in the area around the turn of the century. In 1955, voters elected a state legislator who ran on the slogan "Vote Industry In." Another local politician, Edward Khayat, was already putting that notion into practice. The son of Lebanese immigrants, Khayat (pronounced KY-yaht) had come to Moss Point, the town adjoining Pascagoula to the north, as a schoolteacher and football coach before moving into business. In 1947, he was elected to the board of supervisors, the leaders of county government in Mississippi.

After just a few years in office, Khayat had emerged as a one-man chamber of commerce and industrial development authority. As he saw it, what was good for business was good for Jackson County, and he was a relentless booster of every enterprise in the area. Thanks in good part to his efforts, an area known as Bayou Casotte was turned from grazing land for cows into an industrial park, and it is now home to fertilizer and chemical companies, as well as a vast Chevron Corporation oil refinery. Some of the industry in the area quite literally stinks. On the not infrequent occasion that a stench blankets Pascagoula, residents will tell you the wind is blowing the wrong way from either the paper mill or the pogy plant. Pogy is what locals call menhaden, a small, oily deepwater fish that is processed into raw material for use in products ranging from cosmetics to chicken feed. But when newcomers to the area commented on the odors, Khayat would tell them it smelled "just like money in the bank."

While he hobnobbed with captains of industry, Eddie Khayat was also a consummate populist politician, who adeptly tended to the needs of his constituents. Voters in Jackson County clearly appreciated the attention, not to mention the employment and relative prosperity Khayat helped bring to the area, repeatedly returning to office. In time he came to be the most powerful political figure Jackson County has ever known, and though he never ran for statewide office, he became tremendously influential in the state, serving nearly ten years as the head of the Mississippi Association of Supervisors. In some circles he was known as the "boss" of Jackson County, a double-edged term that evokes the big-city political bosses of the North and the Huey Long–style Southern version. Like many of these counterparts, Khayat was a benevolent patriarch who wielded his power for the public good. But at the same time, he perpetuated and fostered a system of corruption that placed himself and a few of his cronies above the law and abused the public treasury and trust.

With its industry and its politics, Pascagoula sometimes seemed to have more in common with Chicago than with Holmes County. On matters of race, Jackson and Holmes counties also seemed worlds apart. It is true that the antisegregation editorials of a young newspaper editor in Pascagoula earned him both a Pulitzer Prize and a burning cross on his lawn — an experience paralleling that of Hazel Brannon Smith's in Holmes County. Yet overall, the level of trepidation and racial hostility among whites in Pascagoula was nothing like what it was in Lexington. As Don Barrett explained, whites in and around the Delta felt the civil rights movement threatened their whole way of existence and would turn their world upside down. They lived, after all, in "a black sea," he said. White hatemongers in Jackson County may have hurled plenty of invective, but they had little to fear. For starters, whites had always been a significant majority of the population — about 78 percent today — so there was no reason for concern about being outnumbered, either in schools or at the polls. But Jackson County also had something else: prosperity. Ingalls and other enterprises offered abundant jobs to whites and blacks alike, and poverty, the root of so much prejudice, was relatively low.

As Pascagoula drew new industry in the 1950s, immigrants from all corners of Mississippi and beyond flocked to the town and it grew and thrived. Even Ingalls, after a postwar dip, regained its bearings and was turning out a mixture of standard military and commercial ships, as well as more exotic vessels, such as icebreakers and nuclear submarines. One of those drawn to the booming town was Helen Scruggs.

Born in 1910, Helen Furlow Scruggs still lives in Pascagoula today, her hearing failing a bit but her mind sharp and playful. When she's not at home, chances are she's out playing bridge. She takes great pride in the accomplishments of her only child, Dick, and deserves no small credit for giving him a stable, secure childhood despite some difficult circumstances.

Helen grew up well educated and independent. After graduating from Millsaps College in Jackson, she worked for a time as a hostess — much like a flight attendant — on the Gulf, Mobile & Ohio railroad, riding a train called the *Rebel* from New Orleans to East St. Louis. In her thirties, she married, divorced, then remarried Tom Scruggs, a Texan she had met in Mobile, but the relationship didn't work out the second time around either, and they divorced again. Their only child, Richard, was born in 1946. Thirty-six and a single mother, Helen took a job as a secretary in the town of Brookhaven, Mississippi, to support herself and her young son. Fortunately her brother, William Furlow, also lived in Brookhaven and had three kids, which provided an extended family. But in 1957 the accountant Helen worked for was on the verge of retiring, and she needed to find new employment. Through a friend, she landed a secretarial job at Ingalls, and moved to Pascagoula, leaving Dick with her brother while she tried to find a place to live.

People's need for housing brought Hugh Moore, Mike Moore's father, to Pascagoula around the same time. Hugh's grandfather, Benjamin Dowd Moore, owned a number of sawmills in southern Mississippi, and lent his name to a company town, Ben Moore, in Perry County, whose sole reason for existence was the mill operating there. (The town, which once appeared on maps, is now just a few cement slabs in the middle of the woods.) Located on a spur of the Illinois Central, the Ben Moore mill sent most of its wood north to Chicago, where International Harvester made it into wagon tongues. Hugh was born there in 1920, "just about the time that the sawmill . . . cut out," he says. He decided to go into the real estate business, initially settling in Jackson until the economic bustle on the coast caught his attention. "The shipyard was going full blast, and they needed homes, lots of homes," he recalled. So he moved his family to Pascagoula.

The first day Helen Scruggs reported to work at Ingalls in December 1957, a ship launching was taking place, which she attended. The ship was the *Brasil,* one of the last luxury passenger liners built in the United States. Lavishly appointed, with swimming pools, theaters, an ornate ballroom, and a covered solarium, it would sail for the Moore-McCormack Lines from New York to South America. "It was a beautiful ship," Helen Scruggs remembers. The liner, however, was laden with asbestos, and thirty-six years later, the *Brasil* would receive star billing in a massive personal-injury trial in Pascagoula. Dick Scruggs, age eleven at the time of its launch, would be one of the lead lawyers for the plaintiffs.

At the launching ceremony, Helen Scruggs ran into an old friend from Millsaps College: Eddie Khayat. Decades later, Khayat, too, would face his day of reckoning. It would come at the hands of Mike Moore.

21

Dick Scruggs did not actually move to Pascagoula until 1959; housing was so tight that it took his mother a year and a half to find the modest house she bought in the Pinecrest subdivision, the same development the Moores settled in about the same time. Despite their proximity, Mike Moore and Dick Scruggs were six years apart in age, and for nearly thirty years, they would lead parallel but separate lives, until a mixture of friendship, politics, and the law united them.

Initially, there was not much reason to think their paths would converge. Scruggs attended public school in Pascagoula through tenth grade, and finished his final two years of high school at the Georgia Military Academy (now called Woodward Academy) near Atlanta. He did so not out of any particular interest in the military, but because the school had a national-class swim team, and he loved competitive swimming.

Moore attended Catholic school and liked baseball. While Scruggs ran on the edges of a rough crowd, Moore led a milk-and-cookies existence. Scruggs was an only child raised by a single mother, while Moore grew up as the eldest of five in a house that seemed like something out of the *Brady Bunch*. Moore, who let his curly locks grow to his shoulders, even looked like Greg Brady for a time. He played keyboard in a rock-and-roll band with his friends, which enjoyed a good deal of success landing gigs along the coast. Scruggs kept his hair short and didn't play an instrument.

Moore didn't particularly excel at anything. "Mike had average talent. He was an average baseball player, an average piano player, and an average student," his father Hugh told the local Pascagoula newspaper in 1996, adding that his son "managed to succeed in everything because of a lot of grit and determination." Initially, though, Mike Moore didn't show much in the way of ambition. Dick Scruggs, on the other hand, did well at both academics and athletics. And he was driven.

In the fall of 1973, Moore and Scruggs could not have been at more different stations in life. Moore was a student at Ole Miss, where he had transferred after two years at a community college on the coast. His main passion in life continued to be music, and he quickly formed another band. Scruggs was in the Mediterranean, about to face down World War III.

Upon entering Ole Miss in 1965, Scruggs had signed up for ROTC with the Navy. But after fulfilling his two-year commitment, he signed on for two more. "I said, 'Hell, if I'm going to go [to Vietnam], I might as well go as an officer,' " he recalls. In the summer between his junior and senior years, he was sent to San Diego, where he spent time on an aircraft carrier and got exposed to aviators. "It was a whole different life," Scruggs remembers thinking. "These guys were wild and crazy and everybody respected them. . . . I said, 'Damn, I'm going to do that. I'm going to fly.' "

Scruggs narrowly missed being sent to Vietnam, and in the fall of 1973 was aboard the aircraft carrier U.S.S. *Roosevelt* in the Mediterranean on what should have been a quiet tour. But in October, Egypt attacked Israel, and for the next few months, Scruggs flew reconnaissance missions and escorted groups of new fighter-bombers into Israeli airspace, as the United States helped resupply the Israeli air force. But things got really tense when the tide changed in the war and Israeli general Ariel Sharon crossed the Suez Canal and seemed poised to wipe out the Egyptian Third Army. The Russians, Scruggs recalls, looked like they were going to mobilize their own forces to try to stop the Israelis. "When that word got out," he says, "we went to war footing. We had targets for nuclear attack all over Eastern Europe and Western Russia. . . . The carrier even went to the vicinity of its launch point, the point in the Mediterranean where we were going to launch our strikes, and stayed there for about three days. It was *really* scary." The A-6, which Scruggs flew, can carry three nuclear weapons. To this day Scruggs recalls that one of his targets was an intelligence facility in the heart of Prague.

Even outside of combat, the day-to-day flying done by carrier pilots contained plenty of peril. There is, for example, the routine task of landing a plane on a carrier deck, hard enough on its own, and made even more challenging on a moonless night with a pitching sea. Or midair refueling, in which a pilot brings his aircraft alongside a tanker plane and takes a "plug" through a hose, a maneuver Scruggs says he performed two or three times a week.

The character traits required of naval aviators are a propensity for risk, steely nerves, and a capacity for instantaneous decision-making. In Scruggs's case, he has brought them to the practice of law.

Why Scruggs decided to go into law isn't clear. "I can't tell you why," he says. "Basically, all my life I've thought one day I was going to be a lawyer." Joining him at the University of Mississippi's law school was Mike Moore, whose stated reason for being there squares with his do-gooder image. For years, he says, he thought being a lawyer was the best job to have if you wanted "to help people" and "to make a difference." At the Catholic school he attended, he notes, "that was pounded into us, that you're put on this earth to help people. . . . A lot of us came out of there being mission oriented." Still, there was little to suggest that Scruggs and Moore would launch any missions together.

"Mike was a long-haired child when I met him," recalls Mike Lewis, who in 1993 would bring the idea for the Medicaid suit to Moore and Scruggs. Fresh out of the Air Force, Lewis and others who had been in the military considered themselves men, he says. By contrast, Moore was "a happy, fun-loving, casual law student," who lived by the maxim "cooperate and graduate," Lewis says. Single and living in a rented house with friends, Moore was more interested in "girls, music, and stuff like that," says one classmate. Scruggs, who had married fellow Pascagoulan Diane

Thompson in 1971, had a young child and had bought a house in Oxford he couldn't afford. To make ends meet, Diane got a secretarial job on campus and Dick became a weekend warrior, flying in the naval reserves out of a base near Memphis. School itself, for Scruggs, was a grind. He studied all the time and "hated every day of it," he says.

While Moore may have seemed fun-oriented at law school, things began to change quickly after he graduated. Upon taking a job with the Jackson County district attorney's office in Pascagoula, Moore grew up fast. In 1977, just as he was beginning to enjoy his new job "prosecuting the bad guys," in his words, the district attorney who had hired him, Clinton Lockhard, became a state court judge, and the governor named Roy Pike as the new DA. Moore and Pike had clashing styles, and Moore thought he had no future as a prosecutor working for him. "I made a decision that I wanted to keep doing what I was doing," Moore recalls. So when election time rolled around, Moore ran against Pike. After losing the special election to fill Lockhard's unexpired term, Moore ran again in the general election in 1979 and won. He was twenty-seven.

In January 1980, shortly after Moore was sworn in, a visitor dropped by his courthouse office in Pascagoula. It was Eddie Khayat, come to pay his respects and to deliver what Moore calls the "Where-were-you-in-1948?" speech, in which he reviewed his own role in making Jackson County an economic powerhouse. He also asked Moore if he wanted his office refurbished.

And there was someone else interested in meeting Moore. Royce Hignight, a ruddy Oklahoman, was an FBI agent who had been assigned to the Bureau's Pascagoula office in 1977. Rumors of political corruption had swirled around Jackson County for much of the seventies. In 1973, Khayat had pleaded no contest to federal tax evasion charges, but had refused to reveal publicly the source of his undisclosed income. Later in the decade, press reports called attention to large purchases of seashells by Jackson County supervisors. Shells dredged from area waters had long been used in the area to prevent dirt roads from turning muddy in the rain, but the supervisors were delivering many shells to constituents for use on their private roads and driveways. Questions were also raised about the county's leasing of construction equipment.

Hignight had begun to investigate apparent improprieties, and found that county officials were failing to comply with state statutes governing contracting and bidding procedures. Moreover, an inventory of county-owned equipment that was supposed to be on file in the chancery court clerk's office was missing. When Hignight pressed for it in late 1979, the clerk told him the supervisors had said that "the FBI don't run Jackson County." It was just a few weeks later that Moore took office. "So I marched myself up to the young district attorney and told [him] that they weren't abiding by the law and I wanted to know what he was going to do about it," recalls Hignight, who is now retired from the FBI.

Mike Moore had been elected in part on a clean-government platform, but Jackson County voters obviously had some ambivalence on the subject, since they continued to elect Khayat to office even after his tax troubles. Moore, though, had no hesitation about fulfilling his campaign pledge; working closely with Hignight and other investigators, he began documenting widespread corruption. From early on, it was clear that Khayat and other supervisors would become a focal point of the probe. But those who knew Moore at the time say he was undaunted in taking on the area's entrenched political honchos. Dan Goodgame, who knew Moore while growing up in Pascagoula and is now a senior editor at *Time* magazine, says that "while [Moore] got along with a lot of people, he wasn't afraid to not get along, and that was something that distinguished him from most people in politics in Pascagoula."

While there were those who supported the effort to root out corruption, plenty of people in the county benefited from the established way of doing business, and an intimidating atmosphere developed. Moore received a variety of threats, ranging from comments that he would be a one-term DA to more serious ones suggesting he wouldn't live to see his next birthday. Louis Guirola, an assistant district attorney who had been an agent with the Mississippi Bureau of Narcotics, gave his boss a .357 Magnum and taught him how to use it at a local firing range. Moore says he still has the gun and keeps it in his truck.

Guirola, Moore, and the only other assistant DA, Kathy King Jackson, formed a congenial trio. Single and in their late twenties, the three both worked and played together, occasionally escaping for weekends of water-skiing and boating at a small condominium Moore owned on the Florida panhandle, just a few hours to the east of Pascagoula. Moore and Guirola both ribbed Jackson about her smoking habit, telling her that when she died, they were going to place a carton of cigarettes in her casket.

The media, to a great extent, became an ally of Moore's during this period. His willingness to talk to the press drew criticism, but he also garnered statewide publicity. A 1981 article in the Jackson *Clarion-Ledger* captured the mood. Headlined "Something old meeting something new in Jackson County government, politics," the piece quoted Moore on his dealings with the press. "Maybe I'm not as cautious as I should be," he said. But then he added, "Who's going to tell [the public]? I don't like a public official who shies away from the media."

In June 1981, a grand jury convened by Moore indicted four of Jackson County's five supervisors, including Eddie Khayat, for fraud. Given the nature and scale of political corruption that has occurred elsewhere in this country, the charges brought in Jackson County seem, at first blush, like a litany of petty and near-petty offenses. Khayat, for example, was charged with having had steaks delivered to auditors reviewing the county books, and of having the market that delivered the T-bones and ribeyes cover the cost by billing the county $1,006 for electrical services. Allegations concerning the purchase of shells and rental of construction equipment showed little if any money ending up in the accused supervisors' pockets.

At the beginning of the probe, FBI agent Hignight says, investigators had looked for payment of large kickbacks. But "what we learned was that you couldn't look at the amounts they were taking, but at the amounts they were misspending." The recipient of a $10,000 contract, for example, might simply reward a supervisor with personal favors. The county, meanwhile, was getting ripped off, paying more than it should have for something or even paying for nothing at all. A private company in one supervisor's district, for instance, was getting paid to cut grass in the dead of winter. And the purchase of shells — often at above-market rates — had cost the county millions of dollars over the years.

The relatively small amounts involved in the specific criminal charges,

Hignight admits, didn't have much "sex appeal or jury appeal." That fact, combined with Khayat's enormous voter appeal, may explain why he was acquitted in an October 1981 fraud trial and won a hung jury in a second trial the following March. Under intense pressure, Moore was sustained during this period by his faith. During the trial, he said, he would go to the Catholic church near the courthouse to pray and ask for strength, and "then go back across the street and let it rip." He succeeded in winning the conviction of one supervisor and methodically converting some non-supervisor defendants into witnesses against the remaining members of the board. "It was a case of tumbling bricks," Moore recalls, and in May 1982, the biggest brick of all fell. Eddie Khayat agreed to plead guilty to misdemeanor charges and to resign from the board. Two of his colleagues did the same thing.

The toppling of the board of supervisors had significance well beyond Jackson County, and not just because Khayat had been one of the most influential figures in the state. The success of Moore's prosecution spurred the FBI in Jackson, Mississippi, to launch a statewide probe of county government corruption in an investigation called Operation Pretense. Hignight recalls that the agent in charge of the Bureau's Jackson office had initially been concerned about the seemingly nominal amounts of money at issue. But, drawing on his experience in Jackson County, Hignight explained the need to focus less on illegal personal gains and more on improper public expenditures. Over the course of the mid-eighties, Operation Pretense led to the conviction of dozens of county supervisors around the state.

While Moore would not seek statewide office until 1987, his prosecution of the Jackson County board in 1981 garnered him TV and print exposure throughout Mississippi. The shaggy, happy-go-lucky rock-and-roller had emerged as a poised, telegenic, and focused public official. Not that the experience totally eliminated the boy in Mike Moore: The crime-fighter who jailed murderers and thieves and the corruption-buster who vanquished Eddie Khayat and his cronies still lived at home in Pascagoula with his mom and dad.

22

If the years immediately following law school were a time of growth and extraordinary responsibility for Mike Moore, for Dick Scruggs it must have seemed that things were heading in the other direction. Having done very well in law school, he was recruited in 1976 by William Winter, a former lieutenant governor of Mississippi and a future governor, to work at one of the largest and most prestigious law firms in Jackson. Winter himself was the "main reason" he joined the firm, Scruggs notes. "He was a very progressive Democrat, and when I was growing up in Mississippi, he was sort of the ideal for people of my generation who thought of themselves as being a little more progressive on the racial issues and that sort of thing."

Yet for all the prestige attendant on joining Winter's firm, the reality of working there offered a kind of comeuppance. Scruggs, who just a few years before had been a Navy lieutenant flying his own jet off an aircraft carrier, was now a junior associate in the hierarchical and often mind-numbingly dull world of a large law firm.

What's more, as much as he admired Winter, Scruggs

clashed with Arnold Pyle, who was the firm's managing partner and headed the litigation department. A former judge, Pyle was irascible and difficult to get along with. One day, Scruggs and Pyle were at a lunch meeting with a client, when Pyle made a remark that Scruggs felt undermined and embarrassed him in front of the client. Later that afternoon, Scruggs walked into Pyle's office, shut the door, and had it out with the senior partner, telling him that he never expected to be treated that way again. Not surprisingly, a parting of the ways quickly ensued, and Scruggs moved to another Jackson defense firm.

At his new firm, Watkins & Eager, Scruggs wasn't entirely happy either. For one thing, he thought his compensation should reflect the fact that he had brought the firm a client — Frigitemp Marine Corporation, a large subcontractor at the Ingalls shipyard — but the firm disagreed, and continued to pay him the salary it set for associate attorneys with his experience. Beyond that, Scruggs didn't like taking orders, particularly from those who, because of his five years in the Navy, were younger than him. "I just didn't work well in harness in a big firm," Scruggs recalls, and in the summer of 1980 he finally returned to Pascagoula to launch his own practice.

The years in Jackson, though, were hardly a waste. In particular, Scruggs got some experience trying cases. One of his first assignments upon arriving at Watkins & Eager was to defend an electric power company against claims that sparks from its lines had set a house on fire. The case was in Holmes County, and the lawyer representing the plaintiff, a black mother who had escaped the blaze with her children, was Don Barrett. Scruggs had known Barrett in passing at Ole Miss, when they were undergraduates. This case gave them a chance to become reacquainted, and they developed a lasting friendship.

Of course, this hardly meant that Barrett was going to give Scruggs a break at trial. After picking a predominantly black jury, Barrett went to work. "I knew I was in trouble from the opening argument," Scruggs remembers, laughing, years later. "It was one of these church things: When Don was telling them what happened and how terrible the company was, they were giving amens and all this sort of thing on the jury, so after that, I was just along for the ride. . . . I got the shit kicked out of me." The plaintiff won $15,000 in compensatory and $50,000 in punitive damages. "It was the longest ride I ever took back to Jackson," Scruggs says. "I thought I made a mistake practicing law."

Although Scruggs's plan after moving back home to Pascagoula was simply to open a law office and take virtually anything that came in the door, he did not start out with a completely empty file drawer. In May 1979, a court put New York attorney Lawson Bernstein in charge of the affairs of Frigitemp Marine, which had gone bankrupt, in good part due to problems in its relationship with Ingalls. When Scruggs confided in him that he was thinking of striking out on his own, Bernstein encouraged him. "I told him, 'Dick, these guys [at the big firms] are not for you. You've got too much ability to be wearing someone else's collar.'" When Scruggs left Watkins & Eager, Bernstein gave him the Frigitemp account.

By the mid-1980s, Scruggs was pursuing a healthy, though unremarkable, general practice, still fed in part by Frigitemp work. In early 1984, he tried a product-liability case against Black & Decker Corporation in federal court in Biloxi. The plaintiff was a former Frigitemp employee who had rigged a circular sander to hold a wood-saw blade and then tried to cut brick with it for a fireplace he was building at his home. The blade shattered, crushing his cheekbone and ripping a gash in his face that required more than two hundred stitches. "He wanted to sue somebody, and I was stupid enough at the time to take it on," Scruggs recalls. "In retrospect it was sort of a dumb idea, but I thought I'd give it a roll anyway, maybe it'd settle or something. But they wouldn't offer a penny." With good reason. After a brief trial, the jury determined the plaintiff had intentionally misused the tool, and found for the defendant.

Sitting at home nursing a gin and tonic the evening after the verdict was delivered, Scruggs got a phone call. It was from a man named Lonnie Parden, who wondered whether Scruggs could help him with a couple of legal matters. "He said, 'Don't you remember who I am?'" Scruggs recounts. "I said, 'Well, your name is really familiar, Mr. Parden, but to tell you the truth I can't place you.' He said, 'I was on your jury over there in federal court for the past three days.' I said, 'Well, man, you got the wrong lawyer. You must have got me mixed up with the guy who *won* the case.'"

Parden, however, insisted it was Scruggs he wanted. Scruggs's client had had a lousy claim, he explained, but Parden liked the way Scruggs had handled himself in the courtroom. Forty-eight at the time, Parden had worked at Ingalls Shipbuilding for twenty years, and one of the matters he wanted to discuss with Scruggs was the breathing difficulties he'd been having. Utterly unwittingly, Scruggs had landed his first asbestos case.

Viewed on its own, Parden's claim was no different from any other product-liability lawsuit, in which a plaintiff alleges his injuries were caused by a defective product. But by 1984, it was impossible to consider any asbestos case on its own — asbestos litigation had become a "mass tort." The ranks of Ingalls employees and ex-employees had become studded with ailing and dying men. Most of the afflicted were hobbled by asbestosis, pulmonary scarring caused by asbestos fibers, which diminished lung capacity and usually worsened over time. A number found it hard to walk or even to talk without becoming winded. For some, this condition would progress into lung cancer, while the most unfortunate few — as if lung cancer wasn't bad enough — would get mesothelioma, a horribly painful, invariably fatal cancer of the lining of the lung.

For workers at construction sites, shipyards, and refineries around the country, the story was the same. All told, according to one government figure, between 8 million and 11 million Americans had been exposed to asbestos since the beginning of World War II, but because asbestos-related disease has a long latency period, symptoms often didn't appear until two or three decades after exposure. It struck broadly, but indiscriminately: A woman whose only exposure was washing her sons' work clothes died of asbestos illness, while men who spent their whole working lives inside ships' hulls remained disease free.

The litigation began with a trickle. In 1969, a lawyer in east Texas had filed an asbestos suit in that state on behalf of a shipyard insulation worker, and in a 1971 trial won $79,000 in damages. The verdict was upheld on appeal, and eventually other lawyers around the country began pursuing claims against asbestos manufacturers. Initially, though, the industry had great success keeping evidence and depositions in individual cases under seal, making them unavailable to plaintiffs as a group. And, for a time, the defendants won a significant number of cases, enough so that Johns-Manville Corporation, the world's largest asbestos company, stated in its 1979 annual report: "In the opinion of Management, the Company has substantial defenses to these [asbestos-related] legal actions, resulting in part from prompt warnings of the possible hazards of exposure to asbestos fiber . . . following the 1964 publication of scientific studies." Throughout the 1980s, cigarette makers' annual reports contained similar confident language regarding the legal threat they faced, and even relied on a similar defense: that the publication, also in 1964, of the first Surgeon General's report on the dangers of smoking helped immunize them against liability.

Another section of Manville's 1979 annual report is worth noting. Citing the steadily increasing number of asbestos suits being filed, the report said:

> Johns-Manville is seeking a recognition that the occupational disease problems associated with excessive asbestos exposure . . . constitute a significant and growing societal problem. In all its aspects, it is a prob-lem more appropriately resolved by uniform, comprehensive legislation than continuing litigation.

That never happened, but a decade and a half later, when tobacco litiga-tion put cigarette makers' feet to the fire, the idea of a legislative resolu-tion, this time to deal with burgeoning tobacco-related claims, surfaced once again.

For all these parallels, asbestos and cigarette makers were not corpo-rate bedfellows. To the contrary, one tactic used by asbestos defense lawyers was to blame the plaintiffs' lung disease on cigarette smoking, a strategy known as the "empty chair" defense, since they would literally point to an empty chair in the courtroom and suggest that the *real* defen-dant wasn't present. It was true that a vast majority of asbestos workers seem to have smoked, and that smoking significantly increased the chance that asbestosis would become lung cancer. It also made it harder to say which carcinogen caused the illness.

Even as Johns-Manville was issuing its confident legal pronounce-ments, the tide was beginning to turn. Despite an effort by asbestos mak-ers to shield information about their early knowledge of the dangers of their product, a dogged group of plaintiffs' lawyers began unearthing one damning set of documents after another. Perhaps the most famous cache to come to light is the so-called Sumner Simpson papers, named for the man who created the asbestos company Raybestos–Manhattan in 1929. The papers were a treasure trove, revealing that as far back as 1933 Raybestos and Johns–Manville had shared information about the dangers of exposure to asbestos dust. In fact, in 1929 the asbestos industry had commissioned the Metropolitan Life Insurance Company to study the occupational hazards of asbestos, but the companies sought to keep the resulting reports confidential, and their lawyers suggested language to soften the conclusions.

That kind of legal involvement in, and control of, basic health research appears quite similar to what Merrell Williams found lawyers doing at cigarette companies nearly sixty years later. The reverberating common chords with tobacco only grew louder. In 1978, Ronald Motley, a South Carolina lawyer, then thirty-four, who had met with mixed success in a series of asbestos suits, got his hands on the Sumner Simpson papers and filed them in a case in New Jersey. After reviewing the documents, the trial judge ruled that correspondence between Johns–Manville and Raybestos "reflects a conscious effort by the industry in the 1930s to downplay, or arguably suppress, the dissemination of information to employees and the public for fear of the promotion of law suits." Fourteen years later, the very firm that had represented Manville won a ruling from New Jersey federal court judge H. Lee Sarokin stating that the tobacco industry "may be the king of concealment and disinformation" and that it may have abused the attorney–client privilege to shield damaging documents. (An appeals court removed Sarokin from tobacco cases, finding that his language gave the appearance of bias against the industry.)

Using the Sumner Simpson papers and other incriminating files, plaintiffs' lawyers began to inflict serious harm. Ronald Motley in particular came to be viewed by asbestos companies and their insurers "with a mixture of awe, hatred, and dread," writes Paul Brodeur in his book *Outrageous Misconduct*. Motley had acquired a thorough knowledge of the science of asbestos disease, and had grown intimately familiar with the industry skeletons' hiding places. Combining this knowledge with a fluid, folksy style that one observer likened to that of a Southern tent preacher, he riveted juries. As other plaintiffs' lawyers around the country filed asbestos lawsuits, they often "associated" Motley, who would swoop in if a case got to trial.

In July 1981, Motley helped a Florida man win a $1.8 million verdict against Johns-Manville, an amount that included $750,000 in punitive damages. And in June 1982, Motley and a team of lawyers won $1 million in federal court in Biloxi for James L. Jackson, a former sheetmetal worker at Ingalls who had asbestosis. That verdict, against both Manville and Raybestos-Manhattan, included a $500,000 punitive award. Now there was blood in the water, and all over the country, lawyers filed tens of thousands of claims. A number of asbestos defendants began settling cases, but the cases most likely to be settled were the ones closest to trial, and herein lay a problem for the plaintiffs. As the number of asbestos cases exploded, court dockets became jammed, and the pace at which suits moved forward slowed to a crawl.

In some sense, then, asbestos litigation presented Dick Scruggs with as many obstacles as opportunities. But Scruggs was not the type to merely file and fiddle. Through a series of deft legal and tactical maneuvers, he parlayed Lonnie Parden's chance call into a caseload of thousands and then outflanked many of those attorneys who had gotten to the courthouse before him. Within a few years, he became one of the richest lawyers in Mississippi.

The first thing Scruggs did was front some of his own money to have Parden checked out by a pulmonologist. Getting a medical diagnosis showing some kind of impairment was a necessary first step to filing a claim, but other lawyers in the area were not paying for the testing of their clients at the time. Parden referred some of his friends from the shipyard, and, Scruggs recalls, "after about a month, I started having fifteen, twenty, thirty guys come in a day. After I'd spent ten thousand dollars and borrowed another ten thousand, I realized why I was so popular all of a sudden — I was paying for the tests," Scruggs says, laughing.

But having a large number of cases wasn't any good if they couldn't be moved forward. Scruggs's first effort at an end run around the backlog in federal court in Biloxi was to file his cases in federal court for the Northern District of Mississippi. Although the defendants were eventually successful in getting the cases bounced back to Biloxi, Scruggs's temporary front-of-the-docket status made him a force to be reckoned with, as asbestos defendants increasingly sought to cut deals. In 1986, Raybestos–Manhattan offered asbestos claimants around the country $4,000 apiece to settle their cases. The Sumner Simpson papers had made Raybestos a "target defendant" for plaintiffs' lawyers, who saw the company as an easy mark for big punitive awards, and it was desperately trying to contain its spiraling liability.

William Reed, a friend of Scruggs's from college and law school, was representing Raybestos–Manhattan in Mississippi and a number of other states. In a conversation at the University Club in Jackson, Reed told Scruggs that Raybestos was in terrible financial straits and that there was no way the settlement offer would go higher. Scruggs had reason to take Reed seriously. In 1982, Johns–Manville, announcing it was overwhelmed by the number of asbestos suits it faced, had filed for protection under the bankruptcy code and halted all payments to claimants. But most plaintiffs' lawyers were skeptical of Raybestos's plea of penury. "The senior members of the asbestos bar scoffed at [the company's offer], and really would not even listen to the presentation," Reed recalls. But Scruggs took it and, with a caseload of roughly 600, walked off with about $2.4 million (60 percent of which went to the clients).

One of those who had spurned Raybestos's offer was Pascagoula attorney Lowry Lomax. One day, during a trip to New York City, Lomax decided to take a train to the company's suburban Connecticut headquarters to get his own sense of its financial situation. He found a nearly deserted office building, with the cafeteria shuttered and boxes of office equipment piled in the halls. Placing a call to Reed from the train platform, Lomax said he would take the $4,000. Sorry, Reed told him, the amount had dropped to $2,800. In 1989, the successor company to Raybestos's asbestos business entered bankruptcy.

A settlement with a single defendant didn't close a client's file. Given the huge number of asbestos products used at the shipyard, there were many others against whom claims could be made. So even as Scruggs took on new asbestos clients, he continued to pursue claims for those he'd signed on before. When his cases were finally sent back to federal court in Biloxi, however, he once again found himself in a bind. "Hell, this isn't going to work," Scruggs remembers thinking. "If my cases are all [in] federal court, I'm in line behind several hundred or even over a thousand other cases. I've got to do something to put pressure on these companies to either try or settle my cases." He decided to try to get his cases into *state* court. "I thought the state court judges, being elected judges, would be more responsive, considering the number of people in the communities who were being affected by this," he explains. He was also mindful, as Barrett was in *Horton,* that in state court it took just nine of twelve jurors to win a verdict, not all twelve as in federal court.

For years, though, in Mississippi, out-of-state defendants had been able to get cases "removed" to federal court under "diversity" jurisdiction. The idea is that federal court is more neutral territory. But if a plaintiff could come up with a basis for suing a local defendant along with one from out of state, then the suit could stay in state court. The more neutral federal forum wouldn't be needed because an in-state party would be on each side of the dispute.

In Mississippi, however, plaintiffs' lawyers had trouble coming up with ways to sue in-state companies in strict-liability cases — all because of Mrs. Carrie Barlow's shoe. During her lunch hour one day in January 1970, Barlow had gone out and bought a pair of "Young Set" shoes from the Sam Shainberg store in Jackson. Leaving work later that day, wearing her new purchase, Barlow fell on a staircase, an accident she believed was caused by the heel of her left shoe coming off. Barlow sued both the shoe manufacturer — an out-of-state corporation — and Shainberg's. But in a 1972 opinion, the Mississippi Supreme Court dismissed Shainberg's as a defendant, ruling that if the seller is "a mere conduit of the product which he has purchased from a reputable manufacturer," then he cannot be liable for defects in the product. With local distributors freed from such liability, out-of-state corporations — which included all major asbestos manufacturers — could not be hauled into state court in Mississippi.

Then, in 1986, in yet another landmark tort case, involving Coca-Cola, the Mississippi Supreme Court shifted course and allowed a product-liability suit against an in-state Coca-Cola bottler. That opened the door for national companies' once again becoming subject to suit in state courts when their products passed through a Mississippi distributor. By suing a local cigarette distributor along with American Tobacco, Don Barrett was able to keep the Horton case in state court. And Dick Scruggs also seized on the Coca-Cola ruling. By adding local asbestos distributors as defendants, he got his cases against the major asbestos makers shifted to state court in his district. Instantly he went from the back of the line behind hundreds of cases on a barely moving docket to first in line in the courtroom of Darwin Maples, a populist judge intent on speeding matters along.

As a "country" judge, Maples, who retired from the bench in 1991 at the age of 65, seemed straight from central casting. Tall, with a full head of white hair and bright blue eyes, he has a bearing at once magisterial and down-to-earth, commanding and compassionate. One of ten children born to a logger in George County, immediately to Jackson County's north, Maples says he got his first name because "when my daddy saw me first, he said, 'He looks so much like a monkey, we'll have to call him Darwin.' " The young Maples evolved into a progressive-minded public servant, first as a state legislator and then as a judge. Construing his judicial powers broadly, he often took steps for which he could point to no explicit legal authority. One of his favorite phrases to justify these actions was, "I felt I had the inherent authority." For example, he helped establish a pioneering public defender program in his district and experimented with vocational rehabilitation for offenders he felt had learning disabilities. These measures won him plaudits from the Mississippi legislature, which in 1994 issued a resolution honoring his service. Some of his other actions were more controversial, such as his practice of unilaterally reducing sentences for prisoners while they were serving time. Another one of his favorite phrases, the legislative resolution notes, was "I may be in error but never in doubt."

Maples knew the Ingalls shipyard well. One of his brothers had worked there and, he says, emerged "asbestos free." His wife's father worked there during World War II, and died of lung cancer in the early 1950s — probably too soon for asbestos to have been the cause. Maples recalls visiting University Hospital in Jackson, where doctors showed him a machine that puffed a cigarette and suggested that smoking may have produced the cancer. As time went on, though, Maples came to know many victims of asbestos-related disease. "I kind of grew up with it and it was very close to me," he said years later. "I had a lot of sympathy with the victims."

When Scruggs's cases hit his docket, Maples tried to move them forward expeditiously. But as Scruggs added plaintiffs and other lawyers eventually followed his lead into state court, the caseload mushroomed and Maples was overwhelmed. Part of the problem was there was no mechanism under Mississippi court rules to try groups of cases in a single proceeding, such as the class action available in federal court. Another problem, Maples notes, was that the two other judges in his circuit were dying. One, Robert Mills, had worked at Ingalls briefly while in college in the late fifties and early sixties. In November 1988, he was diagnosed with mesothelioma and he died two and a half years later at age fifty-three, though not before filing his own claim against the asbestos makers. The other judge, Clinton Lockhard, whose ascendancy to the bench had paved the way for Mike Moore to become Jackson County district attorney, had been a two-pack-a-day smoker, and after a lengthy bout with lung cancer, he died in January 1993 at sixty-three.

Pressed by criminal cases, which could not be delayed because of speedy-trial rules, the burgeoning number of asbestos claims, and other civil cases, Maples found himself under siege. He pleaded with the governor's office and the state Supreme Court for more judges and staff, but was turned down. All the while, he says, he fielded phone calls at his office and his home from anguished shipyard workers, who, laboring for breath, would "beg to get their case disposed of before they died." It was "so disheartening," Maples says.

Dick Scruggs was frustrated, too. Encouraged by Judge Maples to come up with a more expeditious approach, Scruggs crafted a novel trial structure. The idea was to consolidate the thousands of claims then pending in Jackson County and conduct a "common issues" trial, in which a jury would be asked to decide certain basic issues, such as whether asbestos caused asbestosis and cancer, and whether a certain defendant's products were used in the shipyard. If it found any defendants liable on these common issues, the jury would then award damages to a representative group of plaintiffs, chosen for their differing illnesses, and the amount awarded would be extrapolated to all other claimants who were similarly ill.

It was to be an all-or-nothing roll of the dice. If the plaintiffs won against a particular defendant, then that defendant would be on the hook to pay damages to a vast group of claimants. But if a jury found a defendant not liable, then that defendant was lost for everyone. In essence, Scruggs proposed creating a class action, even though Mississippi law made no provision for one, and Maples — Mr. Inherent Authority — signed off on the plan. "We didn't mind plowing new ground and doing what was necessary to get the job done," he says. Scruggs explains, "The idea [was] to raise the stakes so high that neither the plaintiffs nor the defendants can afford to lose. And when you get the stakes that high, then you generally resolve the cases — you settle."

Sure enough, that's what happened. Prior to the scheduled start of the trial in June 1991, all but one defendant, Owens-Corning Fiberglas Corporation (called OCF), settled. Judge Maples arranged for the trial to take place in his hometown of Lucedale, and as jury selection got under way, Scruggs and OCF lawyer Donald Beebe of Mobile began driving to the town in used cars to hide their affluence. Beebe thought the whole approach to the trial was of dubious validity under Mississippi law, and that if his client lost, he would have good grounds for appeal. At the same time, OCF, which made pipe insulation, felt that it had repeatedly been called on to pay more than its fair share of damages to those injured by asbestos exposure, and that other makers of asbestos products not even named in lawsuits ought to bear some of the burden.

On the day trial was set to begin, Beebe told Maples he wanted to talk to Scruggs alone. Beebe respected Scruggs, noting years later that he is "not personal about things," "doesn't threaten or bully," and "approaches matters from a business perspective." Maples put the two men in a room and even stationed a deputy outside so they wouldn't be bothered. A few hours later they emerged with a deal. Once again, notes Walter Watkins, an asbestos defense lawyer from Jackson, a number of plaintiffs' lawyers thought the settlement Scruggs had agreed to was "ridiculous." It certainly was innovative. OCF agreed to pay the plaintiffs a hefty amount of money — up to $90 million. But OCF also agreed to fund discovery aimed at unearthing additional defendants, and amounts the plaintiffs recovered from those new defendants would be used to reduce OCF's payment.

Watkins notes that Scruggs could do deals with companies because he understood something critical about them: their need for financial certainty and predictability. By settling large groups of cases, asbestos companies could establish a cost or cost range for their total liability, and then explain to shareholders how that might be covered through such things as insurance and product price increases. It wouldn't be long before Scruggs would bring the same understanding to his dealings with the tobacco industry.

23

Without trying a single asbestos case, Dick Scruggs had emerged as one of the most successful asbestos lawyers in Mississippi. It was time to move to the beach. In 1967 a local writer, Ira Harkey, had described the significance of such a move:

> Whatever else a Gulf Coast town is, it is a dichotomy of Beach and non-Beach. In territory, Beach is a one-block long strip along the Gulf, as little as one-fiftieth of a town's area. In substance — economic, political, [and] cultural . . . it *is* the town. In the beginning Beach was desirable because one who lived along it could breathe in the summer. There was a breeze in the evening, flowing from the sea, cooling the blistering day and making sleep possible. The rest of the town sweltered. . . . Like the hill in a mine town, the suburbs in a mill city, the Gulf Coast is Nirvana, attainable only by the superlative few who, upon achieving it, thenceforth in a feat of inversion proclaim their occupancy as final proof that it is indeed the abode of the blessed.

The beach in Pascagoula is a two-mile crescent of elegant and affluent homes, flanked by the Ingalls shipyard on the west and the Chevron refinery to the east. Beach Boulevard, a two-lane road and jogging path, separates the mansions from the shore, which features imported sand, polluted water, and shimmering views south into the Gulf. The front lawns of the beachfront homes are mostly treeless, testament to those occasions when offshore breezes have turned to hurricanes. But in back, and stretching for a block or two inland, the neighborhood is studded with ancient and magnificent live oaks, their gnarly, moss–draped limbs, thicker around than the trunks of most trees, spreading horizontally across entire yards.

Pascagoulans of stature and wealth have been making the beach their home for generations. When Dick Scruggs arrived in town as a boy, the grandest house on the beach, a stately white colonial, belonged to Johnny Walker, who ran a small but highly profitable shipyard, which specialized in commercial craft such as seismograph vessels used for undersea oil exploration. In the early and mid-sixties, the Walkers' Beach Boulevard house became a frequent hangout for Scruggs, since his good friend Louis Harkey was dating Walker's daughter Linda. Louis and Linda went on double dates with Dick, and on one outing Linda recalls lending Dick a couple of dollars for a movie. Nearly thirty years later, there had been a dramatic reversal of fortune. After Johnny Walker's death, his shipyard was badly mismanaged, and the family lost its money. As Scruggs amassed his wealth, Linda Walker went to work as a paralegal. In 1991, the Walker house was put up for sale, and Scruggs decided to buy it. Before he made the purchase, Linda notes appreciatively, he called her to see how she would feel about him living in her old family home. It would be just fine, she told him.

One could track Scruggs's upward mobility not only on land, but in the air and at sea as well. Since the mid–eighties, Scruggs has made effective use of private planes to get anywhere, anytime, at a moment's notice. He started with a four-seat, single-engine Mooney, so rudimentary that it had a "Johnson bar," a lever that the pilot uses to physically raise and lower the landing gear. As asbestos money started to flow, Scruggs steadily upgraded, and traveled by Learjet in 1994. Although Scruggs flew its predecessors himself, by the time he got the Lear he was too busy to spend hours in the cockpit, and he now employs pilots.

With boats, the story has been similar. From the time he moved back to Pascagoula, Scruggs has owned thirty-foot sailboats, which he loves to race. In 1989, after a major asbestos settlement, he added a fifty-three-foot Hatteras motor yacht to his fleet. A few years later, he upgraded to a sixty-one-foot model by the same maker. And that would not be the end of it.

Scruggs was hardly the only plaintiffs' lawyer to profit handsomely from asbestos. Around the country, particularly in industrial areas where the product had been widely used, scores of attorneys grew rich from suing asbestos makers, some extremely rich. This was bad news for the tobacco industry. As the wave of asbestos cases crested, some of these lawyers, flush with cash and experience in mass tort litigation, went in search of bigger quarry.

While they had only been passing acquaintances while in law school, Mike Moore and Dick Scruggs became friendly as they launched their very different legal careers in Pascagoula. Early on, when Scruggs was handling a high-profile whistle-blower claim against Ingalls, involving allegations that Ingalls had overbilled the Navy, he ran into Moore, who was in the midst of prosecuting the county supervisors. "We appreciate your taking some of the heat off us," Scruggs remembers Moore saying at the time. Their contacts after that were primarily social, but when Moore decided to run for state attorney general in 1987, Scruggs actively supported him. He not only gave money to Moore's campaign, he flew him to appearances around the state in his Mooney. Scruggs did the same thing for Ray Mabus, another classmate from Ole Miss, who was running for governor. When Moore, Mabus, and other young Democrats swept into office in 1988, they were featured on the cover of the *New York Times Magazine* in an article titled "The Yuppies of Mississippi — How They Took Over the Statehouse."

Scruggs's own politics had come to be driven more by pragmatism than ideology. As a Navy pilot, he was "conservative and a Nixon Republican," he says, noting that "most people in the officer corps were during that time." Over time, he says, "I've become far more of a Democrat than I ever was. . . . My clients are workingmen, who generally get the shaft by big business politics, and Republicans unfortunately [are] pretty closely identified with big business interests. And I owe it to my clients to represent their interests." Still, he eschews party labels, not a bad idea when you have friends from different parties headed to high places. He backed Republican Trent Lott in his successful run for the U.S. Senate in 1988, for example. That certainly helps smooth things out at Thanksgiving dinners, since Lott is married to Diane Scruggs's older sister.

Scruggs's ties to Moore paid immediate dividends. In 1988, the year Moore took office, he awarded Scruggs the job of bringing claims on behalf of the state to have asbestos makers cover the cost of removing their product from public buildings. Scruggs would come to view the rip-out cases, as they became known, as a mixed blessing. Although his firm recovered about $20 million for the state, press accounts focused on Scruggs's 25 percent cut of that amount, and other public officials criticized Moore for cronyism and questioned his authority to hire a lawyer under a contingent fee (whereby a lawyer takes a percentage of a client's award). "Both of us thought we were going to get a ticker tape parade; instead, we got pilloried," Scruggs recalls.

It was also in 1988 that Scruggs made his first foray into cigarette litigation. In January of that year, Don Barrett, who had trounced him in Holmes County in the electric company case ten years before, was trying to do the same to American Tobacco in the Horton trial. Immediately after the mistrial was declared at the end of January, Scruggs called Barrett to offer his condolences. A few days later he and Barrett got together for dinner in Destin, the Florida panhandle resort where each of them owns a condominium, and they spoke well into the night about the trial. "For some reason it just sort of fascinated me," Scruggs recalls. "He *had* these guys, and what happened? Why didn't he nail them?" Barrett offered his view that the case had been bought from under him, that American Tobacco had gotten to enough prominent people in Holmes County — and perhaps the jury itself — to assure it would not lose. He had maintained this view despite having failed to prove any such charges at hearings following the trial.

Scruggs was not the only asbestos lawyer intrigued by *Horton*. Walter Watkins, the Jackson attorney who represented asbestos companies, had ample experience presenting the case against smoking as part of defending his clients. Actually suing the tobacco companies on behalf of smokers seemed like a natural next step, so much so that he sent a young associate to observe the Horton trial and meet some of the witnesses. When the trial ended, he too sat down with Barrett over a lengthy meal and dissected what had happened. "We tried to figure out what had gone wrong," Watkins remembers.

It wasn't long before Watkins, Scruggs, and Barrett were all talking, and an idea hatched. Why not steal a page from the tobacco industry playbook (or at least what they viewed as the playbook)? Why not go into a county before even filing a suit and "preempt the field," in Scruggs's words? Why not hire all the influential political and community leaders before the industry could get to them? Over the course of 1988, the lawyers set their plan in motion. The place they settled on was the tiny town of Raleigh, Mississippi, the seat of Smith County, about an hour's drive southeast from Jackson. The region is predominantly white, but, like Holmes County, it is poor and rural. And just as the Barretts have dominated law practice for decades in Holmes County, a lawyer named Eugene Tullos and his family have played a similar role in Smith County. The Tullos law office, like the Barretts', sits on the town square, directly across from the courthouse. After Scruggs and Watkins visited Raleigh and outlined the plan, Tullos signed on.

All they needed was a plaintiff, but Tullos could take care of that. As Scruggs and Watkins sat in Tullos's office, he picked up the phone and called a local doctor to ask if he had any lung cancer patients. "He was screening cases right there in front of us on the phone with a doc," Scruggs marveled years later. "That's the system down there." Although Tullos came up with several good prospects, the plan fell apart when one of Watkins's partners got cold feet about the expense of litigating against Big Tobacco. With the Watkins firm out, the plan foundered. Barrett went back to pursuing the retrial of *Horton*, and Scruggs returned to asbestos.

Four years later, when Barrett called and pleaded for help in the Wilks case, Scruggs was nearing the climax of his asbestos work. The settlements with Owens-Corning and other manufacturers in 1991 set the stage for trial against an even larger group of defendants — many uncovered through discovery paid for Owens-Corning — in 1993. The Abrams case, as it was known, would be only the third asbestos suit to reach trial in

Mississippi. Because no courtroom in Pascagoula could accommodate a proceeding of this size, it was moved to a building on the county fairgrounds known as Fair Hall. Attorneys for both sides worked out of trailers stationed nearby. It was at the Abrams trial, which ran from April through August of 1993, that workers testified about installing asbestos-laden products on the *Brasil*, the luxury liner Helen Scruggs had seen slip into the sea more than three decades earlier.

With opening arguments set for early June 1993 — smack in the middle of *Abrams* — the Wilks trial could not have come at a worse time for Scruggs. "It was not a prudent thing to do, given what we had at stake in *Abrams*," Scruggs admits, "but Don was pretty damn insistent that I actually get involved in the trial." With Ron Motley taking the lead in *Abrams,* and other cocounsel providing support, Scruggs felt the case was well enough in hand, and he slipped away to Greenville to help Barrett in his quest against tobacco.

Motley gave Scruggs a commiserating hug when he returned from *Wilks* empty-handed. But when, during the next trial day in *Abrams,* Scruggs leaned over at the counsel table and quietly told Motley of the idea of the state's bringing a Medicaid reimbursement suit against tobacco makers, "Motley almost exploded," Scruggs recalls. "It was just, 'Eureka!' . . . From that point on, at every spare moment, that's all we talked about."

The eureka chorus that greeted the idea had much to do with the power and simplicity of the concept. But it would not have resonated as it did were it not for the previous experiences of those who heard it.

Don Barrett's efforts in *Horton* and *Wilks,* which served as a laboratory and training ground for his colleagues in the state, had demonstrated the utter futility of pursuing lawsuits on behalf of individual smokers. Cigarette companies were too strong to be taken on one case at a time. They had too many ways of casting doubt on the cause of illness in a particular person. Cases about illness in individuals, they could accurately contend, could not be proved with statistics about illness in populations. Most devastating of all, juries bought their defense of personal choice. A Medicaid suit would get around all that. It would be about smoking-related illness in a population, and it would seek recovery not for an individual, but for the state.

Dick Scruggs's experience with asbestos offered its own lessons. There were some striking parallels to consider: Asbestos and tobacco both caused serious illness, but with long latency periods. Millions of Americans had been exposed to each product, making individual claims resolution utterly impracticable. And in the case of both asbestos and cigarettes, there was substantial evidence that the companies producing them had extensive information about the health hazards their products posed, but acted to suppress that information. There was, of course, one huge difference: No one would say workers at shipyards and other sites where asbestos was used knowingly and voluntarily exposed themselves to a known health hazard.

In his asbestos practice, Scruggs had quickly realized the advantages of aggregating large numbers of claims as part of a single case, not only for its efficiency, but because of the magnitude of the threat it presented to a defendant. A Medicaid recovery suit did just that, handing cigarette makers, in one fell swoop, a bill for treatment of tens of thousands of smokers. And while smokers may voluntarily have taken up cigarettes, the state could argue that it never voluntarily undertook the cost of treating cigarette-related illnesses.

Finally, there was Mike Moore. Even in a non-tobacco-producing state like Mississippi, taking on the cigarette makers was not something to be done lightly. And in a conservative state like Mississippi, litigating health claims against a legitimate industry was certain to generate political opposition. But, as he had shown early in his career when he took on Eddie Khayat, Moore was not easily deterred from a course of action that might prove unpopular. "I just decided that it would be the most important case I could ever get involved in and it was worth doing," Moore recalls. "To me it was just the right thing to do, pure and simple."

24

The Abrams asbestos trial ended in August 1993 with mixed results. Jackson County jurors awarded $9.26 million in actual damages to six Ingalls employees, and then threw in a relatively paltry 10 percent of that for punitives. Of the ten defendants who went to a verdict, the jury found seven not liable at all. Still, the plaintiffs' lawyers did just fine. Dozens of other defendants had settled before or during the trial, not just with the plaintiffs whose claims were tried but with thousands of others whom Dick Scruggs and other attorneys had assembled as part of the consolidated proceedings. That produced millions in attorneys' fees.

One might wonder why anyone with this kind of golden goose practice would want to turn his energies to anything else, much less tobacco litigation, which had yielded plaintiffs' lawyers precisely nothing. Certainly Ron Motley's partners at his Charleston law firm wondered as much when he presented them with the idea of the Medicaid suit. It wasn't until he threatened to leave the firm that they finally came around.

Scruggs explains: "Guys like Motley — and perhaps me, although it's hard to analyze yourself — get involved in cases like [tobacco] because they have a need to be approved, they have a need for professional fulfillment and achievement, they need to be recognized by their peers as having done something that nobody else can do. It's a constant, insatiable desire of most successful men. . . . The prospect of making huge sums of money was always there. But the challenge was the professional and intellectual challenge of doing this for the first time. . . . We knew [the tobacco companies are] diabolical, they're guileful, they're savvy, they'd spent years preparing their defense."

By the autumn of 1993, preparations for attacking those defenses were in full swing. The first order of business was lining up the Medicaid legal team. As attorney general, Mike Moore would be commander-in-chief of the effort, but he knew the planned lawsuit was too politically sensitive for him to spend taxpayer dollars and staff it out of his own office. So he decided to have the state represented by outside attorneys, and the nucleus of that group — Dick Scruggs, Don Barrett, Ron Motley, and Mike Lewis — was already in place. Over the next few months, the team expanded to include a number of Scruggs's asbestos colleagues on the Mississippi coast, as well as a few others.

The group drafted a joint-venture agreement that spelled out in elaborate detail the duties each of the lawyers would perform. It also set forth what percentage of the cost of the litigation each lawyer (or law firm) would pay. Scruggs undertook to cover 25 percent, Motley 22.5, and Barrett and Lewis each took 10. Various other lawyers, including some of Scruggs's colleagues from the asbestos plaintiffs' bar, also chipped in small amounts. Scruggs estimated that the cost of the litigation — out-of-pocket expenses for everything from travel to expert-witness fees to photocopying, but not the value of lawyers' time — would be $5 million. He was about $8 million too low.

The expenses, the lawyers knew, would be real. Far more hypothetically, the joint-venture agreement also spelled out what each lawyer (or firm) would receive in the event they won and the cigarette makers had to pay damages. These, too, were stated as percentages, and the amounts for the most part mirrored the expense contributions. When Barrett insisted that Fred Clark and Victor McTeer, his comrades from *Horton* and *Wilks*, should also be part of the Medicaid team, the other lawyers told him that was fine, but that their cut would have to come out of Barrett's share. His 10 percent was thus divided three ways.

While willing to take a big gamble on tobacco litigation, Dick Scruggs also took steps to protect his bet. Chastened by the attacks he and Moore had endured following the fees he earned on the asbestos rip-out cases, Scruggs sought to head off any similar criticism. Some of the earlier attacks, he felt, grew out of jealousy among members of the Mississippi trial bar who were not offered a seat on what they saw as a gravy train. So Scruggs made sure to offer members of prominent trial firms around the state a chance to join the action. Most refused, since litigating against the tobacco industry looked more like an invitation to a train wreck.

Critics had said it was improper for Moore to have hired Scruggs on a contingent fee to handle the asbestos rip-out work. Although he disagreed, Scruggs wasn't going to take any chances this time around. He hired Pete Johnson, a former state auditor and Republican gubernatorial candidate in Mississippi, to persuade state legislators to slip a minor wording change into a bill; the change authorized the attorney general to hire counsel for a contingent fee. Johnson had to do this without alerting the lawmakers to the contemplated Medicaid suit, since Scruggs feared that would trigger an effort by conservatives to kill it even before it got started. "Under the cover of darkness," Johnson notes, he "came up with two paragraphs embedded deeply in a long document" — a bill already in conference committee — and the change was made with hardly anybody knowing what they had done. Scruggs didn't inform Moore about much of his backroom politicking. In the end, though, Moore decided that it was still too politically risky to hire outside counsel on a contingent-fee basis. Instead, he agreed that if the Medicaid team won — and only if they won — he would join them in asking the court to order the cigarette makers to pay the team's attorneys' fees. As with a contingent-fee arrangement, if the state lost its case, the lawyers would get nothing.

Even though Johnson's stealthy maneuvering proved unnecessary, it indicates the lengths to which Scruggs was willing to go to pave the way for success. And throughout late 1993 and early 1994, he took other steps to defuse possible opposition to the Medicaid suit in political circles, holding discussions with various movers and shakers around the state to ensure they would not make any trouble. Sometimes it took more than a discussion. "There were [some] people who had political connections, that I'm not even at liberty to tell you who they are, that had to be touched, that had to be talked to, that had to be given a stake in [the litigation]," Scruggs says. He retained two or three of these mystery consultants to run political interference. "These guys have lots of friends and connections with the legislature," he explains. "These are people who are lobbyists, but they're not really registered lobbyists. It's really sort of the dark side of the force." Over the course of the litigation, Scruggs says, he paid these individuals well over $500,000.

Beyond all these behind-the-scenes machinations, a more basic issue had to be resolved: what kind of complaint to file. The idea of bringing a Medicaid recovery action was just a starting point. Deciding the kinds of claims a state could assert against tobacco makers, determining what the basis of alleged liability would be, was a huge task, with no precedent to follow. To research this, Scruggs turned to his law partner Steve Bozeman, who in April 1994 would be present at the lunch where Merrell Williams decided to offer up his Brown & Williamson documents.

Stout and compact, with shaggy red hair, Bozeman had been a Navy ROTC buddy of Scruggs's in college. By pure coincidence, after stints in the service, they reunited at Ole Miss for law school, where they were joined at the hip, taking nearly every class together. After law school, Bozeman returned to the Navy as a prosecutor, ending up, at the end of his service, in Pensacola, Florida, just a couple of hours from Pascagoula. During this period, Bozeman moonlighted on weekends, helping Scruggs set up a computer system in his office to track his clients. The two men were personally close — Bozeman says that if he could have another brother, it would be Scruggs — and, in the summer of 1989, Bozeman came to work for Scruggs. Scruggs thought that nobody wrote better than Bozeman, and that his research was "impeccable." He had done much of the heavy intellectual lifting for briefs filed in the asbestos litigation, and in the fall of 1993, Scruggs set him to work developing claims for the Medicaid case.

Bozeman did not work alone. Other lawyers on the Medicaid team contributed thoughts, and brainstorming sessions were held at Ron Motley's beach house on Kiawah Island, in South Carolina. Academics were also consulted, for everyone realized it would be a landmark case.

Laurence Tribe, an eminent professor at Harvard Law School, who usually commands handsome fees for his advice, helped the Mississippi Medicaid lawyers free of charge. Walking through Harvard Yard with Scruggs and Moore, on their way to visit Tribe, Bozeman looked at his Ole Miss classmates and said, "Who'd have thunk it, guys?"

The Medicaid team wrestled not only with what kind of claim to file, but where in Mississippi to file it. Two obvious possibilities were Jackson, where the attorney general's office was located, and Pascagoula, Moore's and Scruggs's hometown and the site of Scruggs's office. But an old idea resurfaced: filing suit in Smith County, or a similar rural jurisdiction, just as Scruggs had thought of doing five years earlier for an individual-smoker case. The logic was the same as it had been before. Scruggs explains: "I figured, if we were going to try a jury case, that was the place to go. We'd have the most control. That jury pool would probably be the least corruptible by the industry. If we went in there and sewed up those who were corruptible, then we wouldn't have to worry about them buying the jury out from under us." Moore, however, rejected that idea. He was not about to have the state get involved in anything like that.

Even before Moore's veto, information on another front was complicating strategy in the case. In the fall of 1993, Scruggs decided to poll potential jurors to gauge the public's attitude toward a suit by the state — rather than by an individual — against the tobacco industry. To do the polling, Scruggs hired Dick Morris, the political consultant who went on to become an adviser to President Bill Clinton before flaming out in a sex scandal in the summer of 1996. In the late eighties, Trent Lott had hooked Scruggs up with Morris when Scruggs needed jury research done prior to an asbestos trial. Now, for the Medicaid suit, Scruggs asked Morris to poll four counties: Hinds, Jackson, Smith, and Jones. Jones, a rural county in the southeastern part of the state, had long had a reputation for independence. During the Civil War, it seceded from the Confederacy, and Mississippians today still refer to it with a chuckle as "the Free State of Jones."

Around Thanksgiving, Morris presented his results to the Medicaid team at the Royal Sonesta Hotel in New Orleans. Scruggs met him at the elevator on the way up. "I said, 'How'd it look, man' — I thought it was

gonna be great," Scruggs recalls. "He said, 'It doesn't look good.' "
Morris's people had spoken by telephone to 800 registered voters in the
four counties. When the pollsters explained the basic idea of a lawsuit by
the state to recover health care expenses, 55 percent of those surveyed
opposed it. Those most strongly disagreeing with the idea were smokers
and the elderly. When the respondents were presented with arguments on
both sides of such a case, sentiment shifted in favor of the state. But even
if just the opinions of nonsmoking, nonelderly residents were considered,
the ranks approving the suit rose to only 69 percent. "That might win an
election, but it doesn't win a jury," Scruggs notes. (Nine of twelve jurors
is 75 percent.) The results were consistent across all four counties.

Scruggs had been so confident that the suit would have wide appeal,
he thought there was a problem with Morris's data. So he commissioned
an additional survey to weed out people who just plain hated lawsuits,
period (even though there is no guarantee of keeping such people off a
jury). "There is no co-relation between dislike of lawsuits in general and
a decision to oppose plaintiff's position in the contemplated tobacco lawsuit," Morris reported back after completing the additional polling.

The Medicaid team had a problem.

In a May 1953 ruling, the Mississippi Supreme Court summarized the
allegations in a case before it:

> The defendants operate a fish reduction plant on the south bank of
> Sioux Bayou, on the Pascagoula River, in Jackson County. During the
> period from May to October of each year, menhaden or pogie fish are
> taken in the Gulf of Mexico and are reduced to oils and solids. In the
> process, large quantities of vapors, gases and minute particles of the fish
> are discharged into the atmosphere as waste matter. The odors are nox-
> ious, nauseating and revolting to the senses. Foul and putrid waste is
> dumped into the bayou, polluting and ruining it and the lower stretches
> of the Pascagoula River for fishing. The area for several miles is blan-
> keted with these deleterious and sickening odors. The people in the
> vicinity are unable to enjoy the comforts of their homes or the food

which is served at their tables. They are nauseated, made sick, and are unable to sleep at night. The value of nearby property has been greatly depreciated. Such conditions are detrimental to the health of the community.

These circumstances, the court ruled, created a "public nuisance," which the court, quoting from an old English treatise, defined as "a species of offense against the public order and economical regimen of the state; being either the doing of a thing to the annoyance of all the king's subjects, or the neglecting to do a thing, which the common good requires."

Forty-one years later, Steve Bozeman looked at the pogy case with interest. He could certainly have some fun making a comparison between putrid pogies and cigarettes. The language in the decision about the fish odors being a detriment to the "health of the community" was also useful. More important than the facts of the case, though, was what the Supreme Court said was the remedy: The district attorney could seek an order in chancery court enjoining the offending conduct.

Every county in Mississippi has two trial courts: a circuit court, which is considered a court of "law," and a chancery court, which is considered a court of "equity." The roots of this division are ancient. In thirteenth-century England, the king retained power to administer justice independent of the system of common-law courts that had developed in that country. In particular, the king entertained petitions when a remedy in the courts was unavailable. As the number of these petitions mounted, it fell to the king's chancellor, a member of the powerful privy council, to develop a system for handling these claims, and by the fifteenth century, a separate system of justice had arisen within what was known as the Chancery.

Chancery courts became known as courts of "conscience" or "equity" because the chancellor, not bound by the rigid rules of common law, could seek to render true justice in individual cases. When Mississippi joined the Union in 1817 it, like many other states, adopted the dual court system. England, and most states, ultimately combined the law courts and the equity courts, because, over time, so many principles and procedures developed in chancery that, as one book puts it, "equity hardened into law." In most states, unified courts still entertain claims that are said to be "equitable," rather than strictly "legal," and a few states, including Mississippi, have retained separate courts of equity. In these courts, the notion endures that the chancellor (as the chancery court judge is known) has more freedom to fashion justice than his counterpart in a "law" court, and that he will consider fairness more than formality in an effort to "do right."

A less charitable view of chancery jurisdiction was pithily stated by John Selden, a distinguished jurist and commentator in seventeenth-century England: "Equity in law [is the same as] spirit is in Religion, what ever one pleases to make it." He quipped that having a chancellor look to his own conscience to determine equity was like having him look to his own foot to determine the measurement of a foot. This was certainly a view of equity the tobacco companies came to share.

To the members of the Medicaid team, though, there was much to recommend a suit in chancery court. As they saw it, the history of cigarette litigation pointed up the inadequacies of the common law: There had been a clear wrong, and no remedy. What's more, they figured, a suit seeking reimbursement of taxpayer funds expended on treating illness caused by cigarette makers at the very least had fairness on its side. In addition to the public-nuisance claim derived from the case of the putrid pogies, the lawyers came up with other "equitable" theories of recovery, among them "restitution" and "unjust enrichment." A complaint drawn up by Bozeman stated:

> Many of the State's citizens who are afflicted with tobacco-related diseases are poor, undereducated, and unable to provide for their own medical care. These citizens rely upon the State to provide their medical care, which reliance results in an extreme burden on the taxpayers and the financial resources of this State. Yet, these very citizens, along with our youth, are targeted by tobacco promotional techniques. Mississippi taxpayers have thus . . . expended hundreds of millions of dollars in caring for their fellow citizens who have and are suffering from lung cancer; cardiovascular disease; emphysema; chronic obstructive pulmonary disease; and a variety of other cancers and diseases that were and are caused by cigarettes. While Mississippi is perhaps the

poorest state in the Union in per capita income, Mississippians lead the nation in their incidence of coronary heart disease, a disease which is directly related to cigarette smoking. . . .

The defendants are able legally to promote the sale of their cigarettes to the citizens of Mississippi by continuing to misinform the federal and State authorities about the true carcinogenic, pathologic and addictive qualities of cigarettes. Instead of honestly disclosing the genuine health risks of smoking cigarettes, the tobacco companies have spent billions in slick, sophisticated marketing tactics designed to make smoking appear to be glamorous to our youngsters.

In equity and fairness, it is the defendants, not the taxpayers of Mississippi, who should bear the costs of tobacco inflicted diseases.

By early 1994, Bozeman had also drafted a complaint for filing in circuit court (the "law" court), since Moore and Scruggs had yet to choose where to file the case. Dick Morris's polling results would prove decisive in this choice. If a jury seemed certain to be hostile to the state's claims, the obvious solution was to avoid a jury.

Chancery court had no juries.

The core idea behind a Medicaid suit was to recoup money paid out by the state, but from the very beginning, Moore wanted it to have another objective as well: curtailing the marketing of tobacco products to children. Thus, as the state's complaint began to take shape, it made this issue a focal point, noting, for example, that "each day, more than 3,000 young people in the U.S. begin to smoke — or more than 1 million each year." Further alleging that "about 90% of smokers born since 1935 started smoking before age 21 and almost 50% started before age 18," the complaint accused the cigarette makers of "targeting minors with sophisticated promotional schemes designed to create successive generations of addicted customers," and asked for an injunction to halt the promotion and sale of cigarettes to children.

For evidence of the extent to which kids smoked, Moore need only have visited the high school in his hometown. In a survey of seniors graduating from Pascagoula High School in 1997, 31 percent identified themselves as smokers (201 of 216 seniors responded to the questionnaire, which allowed them to remain anonymous). Anecdotal evidence, based on interviews with students and administrators, indicates the percentage of smokers may have been significantly higher. One school security official described raids he and his colleagues would conduct on students smoking in parking lots near the school. "It's six grown men playing like they're cops," he said. "Sometimes we'll catch a whole group of them smoking and we'll sort of descend on them Elliot Ness style." The kids, who had obviously watched plenty of crime shows, would jettison the evidence, tossing their cigarettes and lighters on the ground.

It is not far from Pascagoula High School to Jerry Lee's supermarket, where one could get a capsule demonstration of just how pervasive tobacco promotion and advertising had become. For a visitor in 1996, it started in the parking lot. Along the full length of the grocery store was a fire lane, lined with a dozen orange traffic cones signaling cars to keep away. On top of each cone was a sign touting Marlboros as the "low price leader." Walking between the cones and into the entrance of the store, customers passed sand ashtrays mounted atop two-foot-high replicas of packs of Basic cigarettes. Just inside, the stand holding shopping baskets was decorated with a placard picturing an attractive young woman in a leather jacket — a Virginia Slims ad. Shoppers were then channeled past the customer service booth, which sported two back-lit ads touting Marlboro "gear" (hats, jackets, duffel bags), and then toward a rack holding coupon flyers, mounted with a Marlboro placard at toddler height.

Arriving in the produce section, shoppers at last reached a tobacco-free zone, but when they circled around to the checkout lines, they found a twenty-five-foot-long case of cigarettes and chewing tobacco, with the walls around it adorned with ads for Winston Select, Camel, and Marlboro. An electronic sign running like a stock ticker read: "Come to where the flavor is — Marlboro . . . Thank you for shopping Jerry Lee's."

Just as the tobacco industry maintained that it opposed the sale of cigarettes to minors, it also denied advertising the product to kids. Yet the scope of promotional efforts at places like Jerry Lee's guaranteed that children from infancy on were inundated with the logos, slogans, and iconography of cigarettes. Mike Moore thus had good reason to make limiting this activity a major thrust of his lawsuit. Above all, this strategy made political sense, because, however little sympathy the public felt for adult smokers, however much criticism their suit against the industry might engender, the aim of protecting kids would prove unassailable. And as the assault on the industry escalated from 1994 onward, it created pressure in an area where the cigarette makers ultimately felt they had to give ground.

25

Although Dick Scruggs and Mike Moore tried to keep plans for their suit under wraps, it was inevitable that word would leak out, especially as Scruggs invited other lawyers in Mississippi to join the effort. Rumors of something pending were strong enough to send R. J. Reynolds to Pascagoula to hire a defense lawyer. Attorneys from Jones, Day, Reavis & Pogue, a giant law firm serving as national counsel to RJR, recommended that the company talk to Joe Colingo.

Jones, Day had worked successfully with Colingo in Mississippi to defend International Paper and Georgia Pacific in toxic tort litigation. Plaintiffs' lawyers in the state had filed a number of cases against the paper companies starting in the late eighties, alleging that wastewater discharged from their mills contained trace amounts of dioxin, a potent carcinogen, which had contaminated the Pascagoula River and a tributary, the Leaf. But there is widespread disagreement in the medical community about what amount of dioxin causes harm, and none of thousands of plaintiffs in the various suits could point to any medical symptoms resulting from their living near or eating fish from the allegedly contaminated rivers. Ever enterprising, the plaintiffs' lawyers asserted claims for their clients' "fear" of getting cancer, and while they initially won a few large verdicts, the Mississippi Supreme Court ultimately rejected this theory of recovery, and the cases went away.

Of medium height, with a squarish build and hairline, Colingo bears a resemblance to Fred Flintstone. Well before the dioxin litigation, Colingo had established a reputation as an able trial attorney, defending companies against product-liability claims and doctors in medical malpractice cases. His most famous work, though, at least in local circles, was on behalf of Charles Hickson and Calvin Parker. On the night of October 11, 1973, Hickson, then forty-two, and Parker, then nineteen, were fishing at the site of an abandoned shipyard on the Pascagoula River. Both men worked at the Walker shipyard, which was directly across the river from their fishing spot. According to a book coauthored by Hickson, he was getting ready to rebait his hook when he heard a "zipping sound" that made him stop in his tracks. As Hickson tells it, he and his fishing buddy were then set upon by aliens, who dragged them into a football-shaped spacecraft, analyzed them, and then deposited them back outside.

The two men showed up for work the next day at the Walker shipyard, but Hickson was still so shaken that he spilled his coffee and began to cry. As their story got out, and reporters from around the nation clamored to interview them, Johnny Walker decided they might benefit from legal counsel. Walker's oldest daughter, Johnette, was married to Joe Colingo, so Walker called his son-in-law, who came right to the shipyard. Hickson was concerned about radiation contamination, so Colingo arranged for the two men to be rushed to Keesler Air Force Base in Biloxi for testing. He also decided that the best way to answer skeptics would be to have the two men take a polygraph test, which Hickson did the next day. "And, shit, he passed!" Colingo recalls. On the same day, two professors, one from Northwestern University, the other from the University of California, put Hickson and Parker under hypnosis. The professors pronounced the men's story true. Today, Colingo seems slightly embarrassed by the episode, but he keeps a copy of Hickson's book prominently displayed on a shelf in his office, and it's obvious that he still thinks something very out of the ordinary happened to these men. "I'm satisfied they didn't make it up," he says.

Around the time Colingo was handling the UFO matter, a young Navy flier asked him whether a career in law would make a good next step. Colingo told the man to stay put, saying it would take him too many years in law to catch up to what he was making in the Navy. The flier, of course, was Dick Scruggs. And twenty years later — having ignored Colingo's advice — Scruggs was bankrolling a case that was about to bring Colingo one of the biggest assignments of his career.

Acting on the recommendations of lawyers at Jones, Day, an in-house attorney at RJR, Sharon Johe (pronounced YO-hee), flew down to Pascagoula to meet with Colingo. "Do you mind if I smoke?" Colingo asked her. "No," said Johe, "but you're smoking the wrong brand." Colingo smoked Marlboros, made by RJR's archrival, Philip Morris. Later, when Colingo was driving Johe around Pascagoula to give her a tour of the area, the air conditioning in his Jaguar broke. "It was about 110 degrees," Colingo recalls. Nevertheless, RJR hired him.

Of course, part of the reason RJR hired Colingo was that it was presumed the state's lawsuit was going to be filed in Pascagoula. When word got out that the plaintiffs were looking at other jurisdictions, two local political officials contacted Scruggs and suggested to him that filing a major lawsuit in Jackson County would be good for the area's economy. It was a pitch that would have made Eddie Khayat proud.

By May 1994, Moore and Scruggs had decided they would indeed bring the Medicaid suit in their hometown. In a deeply conservative state, a team of lawyers was about to file never-before-asserted legal claims against an industry that was one of the most economically and politically powerful in the country — and that had never had to pay a penny in a smoking-related case. The plaintiffs would have to put up the enormous cost of the action themselves, would earn nothing if they lost, and could not even say for sure that they would get anything if they won.

For Moore, there were also the political minefields to consider. He recalls telling his comrades, "If I was going to risk everything I had accomplished to date, I wanted to know that they were going to be with me." So, on the eve of filing, Moore gathered members of the Medicaid team in his office in Jackson and asked for a demonstrative statement of their commitment to follow through with the litigation, no matter what the obstacles, no matter how long the odds. In *The Alamo*, a 1960 movie about a group of soldiers defending their small Texas fort against the Mexican army, Colonel William Travis draws a line in the sand for his troops. Those committed to fight to the end were to step across it; everyone else could walk away. Moore drew a line in his carpet, and to a man, all those assembled stepped across.

On May 23, 1994, David McCormick, a Pascagoula asbestos plaintiffs' lawyer who had joined the team, walked across the street from his office and filed Mississippi's Medicaid complaint in Jackson County Chancery Court. When word came that the complaint had been filed, Steve Bozeman turned to Moore, Scruggs, and others who were preparing to announce the suit and said, "Boys, we've swatted the beast."

One could forgive the tobacco industry for taking umbrage at Mississippi's suit. Certainly the state had known for decades about the harm associated with smoking, and could have banned cigarette sales if it wished. Far from doing that, however, Mississippi allowed, benefited from, and participated in their sale: The state licensed, and collected fees from, vendors who sold them, collected excise and sales taxes on them, and even sold cigarettes to inmates in the state prison. Now, in 1994, the attorney general was marching into a court of equity to vilify the product and its makers, seeking nearly a billion dollars in "restitution," as well as punitive damages. Could that be "fair"?

The apparent hypocrisy of the state's action reflects an ambivalence that has come to characterize the attitude of many in recent years toward cigarettes and what to do about them. The unique nature of cigarettes as products, and the unique position — political, economic, and social — tobacco has occupied in America from its earliest days forces many people to adopt internally contradictory positions over what to do about this legal scourge. Years of duplicity and double-talk from cigarette makers can complicate one's feelings on the subject even more. Perhaps no one captures the conflicted thinking and feeling on the issue better than David Owen, a professor at the University of South Carolina School of Law. Owen is a distinguished product-liability scholar, coauthor of the most respected legal treatise on torts and of one of the leading casebooks on product-liability law. He served briefly as a consultant to the Mississippi

Medicaid team as it prepared its complaint, and subsequently submitted an affidavit in support of the State of Florida, when it filed a similar action.

In a later interview, Owen noted: "I have trouble addressing the merits of claims against tobacco makers on a scholarly basis because my strong initial reaction is as a citizen and a former smoker, who regards the cigarette manufacturers with a substantial dislike. So I would be pleased to see the tobacco companies reduced to financial shambles, as a citizen. As a legal scholar, the problem is much more complex, and I have some difficulties allowing the destruction of an industry that's been allowed to produce its products by litigation based on the unwholesomeness of cigarette smoking."

The industry would take aim at what it saw as the unfairness of the state's claims, but the primary thrust of the defense would be to challenge the mechanics of the suit. The suit, the cigarette makers argued, should be recognized for what it really was: a giant subrogation claim. Under subrogation, the state, having made payments on behalf of an ill smoker, could step into that smoker's shoes and assert any claims he might have against a cigarette maker (just as an insurance company might do if it has paid a policyholder but believes there may be a right of recovery against a third party). In the Medicaid case, the cigarette makers argued, the state could assert product-liability claims, and would have to prove all the things any *individual* plaintiff would in such a suit, including that a particular illness was in fact caused by smoking. At the same time, the industry could present its usual affirmative defenses, specifically comparative fault and assumption of risk. Come after us if you want, the industry said, just do it the right way: File and prove a product-liability case on behalf of each Medicaid recipient alleged to have smoking-related illness. Let a thousand Horton cases bloom.

The industry had made a similar argument in the Castano case, the giant class action in New Orleans, which sought damages on behalf of tens of millions of people for their addiction to cigarettes. There, too, the industry had argued that the only way to adjudicate those allegations would be through tens of millions of mini-trials, a number of individual trials so large that all the plaintiffs' lawyers in the country wouldn't have the money or manpower to pursue them, and the judicial system wouldn't have the time or resources to handle them. In a way, the industry was saying that if the magnitude of their wrongdoing was great enough, it bought them immunity. Was that "fair"?

In the fall of 1994, the state Medicaid team filed what at first blush appeared to be a dry procedural motion: to "strike challenges to the sufficiency of the complaint and the subject matter jurisdiction of the chancery court." In fact, it was a preemptive strike, aimed at getting a ruling on whether the state's claims would remain in chancery court or be transferred to circuit court. If the tobacco companies won a transfer, it would be a victory on two fronts: The state would have to pursue a product–liability case, and it would be decided by a jury. That would be a death knell for the plaintiffs. The plaintiffs' team decided to force the issue at the beginning of the lawsuit because "if we were going to lose, we wanted to lose early and cheap," Scruggs explains.

In subsequent years, tobacco company lawyers and PR representatives would gripe about Mike Moore and his "handpicked" judge in Pascagoula. That wasn't exactly true. Once the Medicaid team decided to file in chancery court, they did choose to file in Jackson County for the convenience of being near Scruggs's office. But the chancery court there has three judges, and when a case is filed, a computer randomly assigns it to one. The Medicaid suit was originally assigned to Chancellor Glen Barlow, but he recused himself because a lawyer involved in the Medicaid suit had served on his campaign committee. The case then got sent to Chancellor Kenneth Robertson, but he and Mike Moore had had their differences. In 1989, Moore had entered a consent decree with the U.S. Justice Department, agreeing to judicial redistricting in Mississippi, with the aim of bringing more blacks onto the bench. Robertson, as head of a committee of chancery court judges advising on the matter, opposed the plan and publicly called it an "unconditional surrender." He, too, stepped aside and, by default, the case then went to Chancellor William Myers.

Myers, fifty-three when the suit was filed, proved to be something of a stealth judge. Although he had practiced law in Pascagoula, no one in town could say whether he had leanings that were pro–defense or pro–plaintiff. Nor was he well known personally, since he lived in Ocean Springs and seemed to socialize little. He had been appointed to the bench by Mississippi's ultraconservative Governor Kirk Fordice. (Fordice was still in office and would soon make his own trouble for Moore.)

On December 19, 1994, Chancellor Myers held a hearing on the crucial motion pending before him. Mike Moore spoke first:

> The State of Mississippi believes that this is the most important public health care case ever brought in America. Standing in this courtroom reminds me of the kinds of cases that I used to try here. Cases against cocaine cartels and cases against marijuana growers, and cases against folks who sold heroin. Last year in this country, less than twenty thousand people died from all illegal drugs . . . and all the violent behavior and murders associated with them. Four hundred and nineteen thousand people died from tobacco-related diseases.

Scruggs went next. Turning the Medicaid case into a subrogation action, he argued, was unworkable. "There are not enough courts, judges, juries, or lawyers in the State of Mississippi — probably in the United States — to conduct" the tens of thousands of trials that would result. "If you send us to circuit court for individual trials and force the State to stand in the shoes of the smoker, you are saying we have no remedy at all for the health care costs that this enterprise has inflicted on the State of Mississippi." Then he noted that "the whole purpose of equity . . . jurisprudence is to fill in the gaps and the voids where the law is inadequate."

Joe Colingo, leading off for the defense, urged the judge to look at the substance, not the form, of the suit. "The plaintiffs have charged the defendants in numerous sections of the bill of complaint with manufacture, distribution, and sale of a defective and hazardous product, i.e., cigarettes. What is that? That is a claim in products liability."

Jim Upshaw, American Tobacco's counsel in *Horton* and *Wilks*, also spoke for the defense, though overall he would play a minor role in the Medicaid case. Characteristically, he began with an abrasive — though in this case apt — remark. "[Attorney] General Moore made a real good, bombastic political speech that you would expect to hear at the Neshoba County fair, were one running for something," he said. He also couldn't seem to avoid making an ethnic reference. Addressing the suit's efforts to enjoin sales to children, he said, "How are [the tobacco companies] going to stop these Vietnamese grocery stores down here from selling cigarettes to a minor?"

At the time, the argument Dick Scruggs feared most from the industry was that the issues presented in the Medicaid suit constituted a "political question," something more appropriately dealt with in the legislature, not the courts. Upshaw did raise that point. Quoting from a 1981 Mississippi Supreme Court decision, he noted: "In modern times the trend to turn to the judicial department for a solution to all of the real or imagined ills of our society has increased, sometimes to the point of requesting the courts to usurp the legislative power." Later he added, "If there is any conduct on the part of these defendants that we represent here today that General Moore thinks is a violation of public policy, he knows exactly where he should go. He is even up there in the capital city. He could walk right across the street. The doors of the legislature are open to him."

Chancellor Myers apparently didn't think much of that argument — or any other contention of the defendants. On February 21, 1995, he ruled that the state's claims could go forward in his court. His single-page order (like Judge Gray Evans in the Horton case, Myers offered no explanation for his rulings) was a huge victory for the plaintiffs. When word reached members of the Medicaid team, Scruggs recalls, "that's when we did our celebrating." If Myers had decided to keep the case, Scruggs thought, "he's keeping it for a reason. He's not keeping it to try a case like that to be the eight hundredth judge in America to rule for the tobacco industry."

Of course, the case was far from over. In the Horton case, American Tobacco had lost some crucial rulings early in the pretrial phase, only to come back and get those orders reversed, thanks to exhaustive discovery and relentless lawyering. In the Medicaid suit, industry lawyers would try everything they could to overturn Myers's early decisions. To an extent, they also ignored them. Right through to the end, the defendants acted as though they were defending a tort suit brought on behalf of individuals.

Although Scruggs had worked to neutralize political forces in the state that might have leaped to the industry's defense, one person he couldn't dissuade was the governor. A day after the Medicaid action was filed, Kirk

Fordice attacked it, and said the number of product-liability lawsuits in general made him "want to throw up." In early 1996 the governor followed in the footsteps of the tobacco industry and filed an unusual suit directly in the state supreme court to try to halt the litigation. As a result of these challenges, the Medicaid case moved forward in Pascagoula with a sword of Damocles hanging over it, the possibility that the Mississippi high court could stop it dead at any minute. Two years would pass before the court issued its decision.

26

As the time had neared for the filing of the Medicaid suit in May 1994, Merrell Williams had become steadily more apprehensive. Events were undermining his idea of making Mississippi his sanctuary. Of course, he had set some of those events in motion himself, by handing the Brown & Williamson documents over to Dick Scruggs in mid-April. But he hadn't really imagined that, three weeks later, they'd end up on the front page of the *New York Times.* In subsequent press reports, B&W had identified Williams as the person who had smuggled out the documents, but it took them a while to make the link to Scruggs. The filing of the Medicaid suit in Pascagoula, Williams knew, would turn a spotlight on the Mississippi coast.

As best he could, Williams tried to lay low. When he spoke to Tammy Cauley, the paralegal at Scruggs's firm who had shuttled the documents from the plane to the bank vault, he identified himself on the phone as "Mr. Jones." And when she had to deliver something to him, she would call him and say, "Mr. Jones, do you want to go to lunch?" That was a signal to meet at a Taco Bell in Gautier (pronounced GO-shay), the town just west of

Pascagoula. "I would get there and park and Merrell would drive around for ten minutes to make sure no one had followed me," Cauley remembers.

In a meeting with Scruggs, Williams made known his anxiety over the filing of the Medicaid suit, and discussed the possibility of hiding somewhere, such as Puerto Rico. But in the end Williams didn't want to be a fugitive. He wanted to start rebuilding his life and reunite his family. One day he returned to his apartment in Ocean Springs to find the door opened. Although nothing was disturbed inside, he was sure it had been broken into. That prompted him to mention to Scruggs his desire to find someplace secure for himself and his family, and that, Williams says, led Scruggs to offer to buy Williams a house and "lease" it to him. The two cars and even the sailboat (which he'd planned to run as a business) were an outgrowth of the same idea: helping Williams make a fresh start. "Why didn't you buy him a plane?" one of Scruggs's colleagues asked him, jokingly, when all this assistance came to light. "He didn't ask," Scruggs joked back.

When, in February 1995, Brown & Williamson did finally "out" Williams by filing the lawsuit in Biloxi and a contempt motion in Louisville, reporters began calling, and slowly and cautiously, Williams emerged from the shadows. Over the course of 1995 and 1996, a series of increasingly detailed magazine and newspaper profiles chronicled his battle with Brown & Williamson. During this period, he struck up a relationship with Philip Hilts, the *New York Times* reporter whose Derby Day story in May 1994 had first described Williams's documents. At the time he wrote that piece, Hilts was unaware that Williams had been the original source of the material. When he did finally learn that, he went down to Mississippi and wrote a short profile of him. He also began to feel sorry for him. Hilts saw people swooping in to do stories about Williams, and Williams getting nothing out of it. "He was being left behind," Hilts recalls. "I didn't feel that was right."

So Hilts began to advise Williams, suggesting that he tell his own story in articles or in a play. Hilts also began exploring writing a book, possibly in collaboration with Williams. Despite mutual respect, their relationship became as troubled as that between Williams and Morton Mintz, the former *Washington Post* reporter who started, and then abandoned, a book.

"He's hard to talk to, and at any given moment you can't be sure if he's liking you or hating you," Hilts says of Williams. When Hilts finally wrote a book on his own (*Smokescreen*, published in 1996), he notes, Williams "got pretty pissed at me." Their relations got worse when HBO, seeking to do a docudrama, bought the rights to Hilts's book, which contained a chapter on Williams. Hilts offered Williams part of the option payment, and more if HBO followed through with the project, but Williams became suspicious that Hilts was trying to rob Williams of the rights to his own story.

Williams had, in fact, begun to think that a film deal might be his salvation. As press interest in his story — and the tobacco story in general — grew, he entertained visions of a large six-figure check that, he thought, would let him pay back Scruggs for all his help, and then some. There were expressions of interest, and Williams even engaged a Hollywood agent to represent him. The best he could do, though, was to get Jim Dollarhide, a Mississippi-based director, to pay him $30,000 to option the rights to his story for a year.

"Mr. Williams, for the record, please sir, state your full name."

"My name is Merrell, M-E-R-R-E-L-L Williams, W-I-L-L-I-A-M-S, Junior, Doctor."

Brown & Williamson, of course, still very much wanted Williams to tell his story. Four months after opening a new front against him with its lawsuit in Biloxi, the company was using the Kentucky proceedings to put pressure on him as well. Thus, in June 1995, it had begun its sixth attempt to take Williams's deposition, this time with Gordon Smith of King & Spalding asking the questions. Williams had driven up to Louisville the evening before the deposition in the Dodge Neon financed by Dick Scruggs. He had brought along his two small dogs, which he deposited with Mollie, and he took his daughter Sara and one of her friends out to a fancy hamburger restaurant for dinner. Then he returned to his room at a Motel 8 to prepare for his grilling the next day.

Just two months earlier, Judge Thomas Wine had modified his restraining order, permitting Williams to talk to his counsel. The deposition got off to a promising start. In response to Gordon Smith's questions about how he came to move from Kentucky to Mississippi, Williams told, for the first time, about his exchange of faxes and phone calls with Don Barrett. Smith pinned down the fact that Williams was still in Kentucky when he made his initial contact with Barrett. As to why Barrett was someone he would call, Williams explained that he knew of Barrett's involvement in the Horton case. "I admire certain lawyers. Certain lawyers I find to be not admirable," Williams added, looking hard at Smith. But when Smith asked who was present at the meeting at the Old Tyme Deli, Fox DeMoisey, Williams's lawyer, objected.

"Could you state the basis of your objection as to who was present at a meeting?" Smith asked.

DeMoisey said he felt compelled to object because he hadn't been able to talk to Williams about this meeting, and thus didn't know whether Williams should be asserting any Fifth Amendment privilege. Smith was puzzled. Hadn't Judge Wine removed any limitations on DeMoisey's freedom to talk to his client?

The judge's order, DeMoisey replied, was a "trap." While permitting him to talk to Williams, the judge had declined to review the B&W documents and rule on whether they were, in fact, protected by attorney–client or work product privilege. So DeMoisey feared that if he read them or talked to Williams about them, he still might face disqualification from the case. Later he characterized the ruling as saying, in effect, "You can go through the minefield now, but I'm not going to give you a map, you'll just have to tap dance your way through, and at the end I'll tell you if you've stepped on any mines." DeMoisey also remained concerned about possible criminal charges against Williams.

Smith was incredulous: "Now you have chosen, after seeking an order for — for months and months and months to talk to your client, and incredibly you just told us on the record that you've chosen not to do that, even though that's what the — you've now been allowed to and — and — after delaying the deposition so that you . . . would have time to meet with your client, you've now told us on the record that . . . you have [not] talked to him."

"After much deliberation, that is correct," DeMoisey replied.

Any remaining civility quickly evaporated, as Smith attempted to press ahead with his questioning, and DeMoisey advised Williams not to respond to most questions.

When Smith made it clear that he would continue with the deposition as long as he needed to get answers, Williams became very agitated, and launched into a tirade about the time and expense of attending a deposition in Louisville, far from his new home. He noted that his doctors — "who wear shoes in Mississippi, they do, they actually do" — had warned him to avoid stressful situations, and he virtually threatened to have a coronary on the spot. "I'm not comfortable to continue under the circumstances," he said.

> I've been particularly ordered not to come here by my physicians. You are, your firm, I would assume in some way would be in some risk if something happened to me, because you've been apprised of this. I don't know the law on this, I'm not a lawyer, thank God, but I will say this: It is not convenient for me to remain for another two hours, another three hours, simply because medically it just doesn't feel good to me right now. You have elevated my blood pressure. You have changed my stress factor. If you have any knowledge of what stress and coronary disease is about, then — then we can just assume that it's not just about that particular item [indicating cigarettes] causes cancer, but it [also causes] heart disease.

Smith quickly backed off, offering to stop the deposition immediately. But Williams continued venting. "Stop," said Smith. "Please stop." And again: "Please stop."

After finally getting Williams out of the room and calmed down a bit, DeMoisey stepped back in to suggest a two-hour break to see whether the deposition could continue. They agreed to reconvene at 3:30.

At 4:05, John Ballantine, who, as an attorney for B&W and Wyatt, Tarrant & Combs, was assisting Smith at the deposition, made a statement for the record. With the video camera that was recording the proceedings aimed at Williams's empty chair, Ballantine said he had just learned that DeMoisey and Williams were not coming back.

Smith, too, spoke his final piece for the stenographer:

> Once again Brown & Williamson is unable to ask the questions that
> it has the right to ask. . . . We have no indication that the deposition
> couldn't have been completed tomorrow, either in the afternoon or
> some other time at the convenience of the witness and Mr. DeMoisey.
> It is obvious that they simply don't want to have these questions asked.

Williams at this moment was making like a bandit for the border.
Agitated and afraid, he wanted to get as far away from Kentucky as he
could. Driving into the night, he was back on the Mississippi coast by 1:00
A.M. and fell into bed. When he woke up, he embarked on a binge. Since
moving to the Gulf Coast, he had struggled with his drinking problem,
and had begun to attend meetings of Alcoholics Anonymous. He started
this morning, though, with a beer, then bought a bottle of vodka and drank
half of it. Totally drunk, he drove to a billiard club in Biloxi, called
Scruggs, and told him he wanted to leave the country. Scruggs drove over
and talked him down.

After Scruggs left, Williams realized he hadn't eaten anything, so he
walked over to a casino to get a meal. His state was such that the guards
wouldn't let him in, "which is really something for a casino," he noted
later, "because they want you there drunk." Williams got belligerent and
ended up in jail, leading to another call to Scruggs, who sent Rocky Bond,
his boat captain, to bail him out and take him home.

For most people, doing battle with the tobacco industry is all-consuming,
leaving little time or energy to deal with other conflicts in life. But following the filing of the Medicaid suit, Dick Scruggs resembled a swords-
man in a B movie, fending off multiple attackers simultaneously as he
parried and thrust his way forward, for he found himself fighting not only
the cigarette makers, but his present and former law partners and his
neighbors as well.

When Scruggs had entered asbestos litigation in the mid-eighties, the
defendants were shifting from a posture of fighting everything to settling,
and Scruggs's strategic acumen had enabled him to move his cases to the
front of the payout line. But the key to a lawyer's really cashing in on
asbestos was accumulating large numbers of clients; it took no more effort

to settle a thousand cases than it did a hundred, and the attorney's fees were ten times greater. The result was a great deal of jockeying and maneuvering among lawyers as they entered joint-venture or cocounsel relationships with one another, or moved from one firm to another, cases in tow. Inevitably, conflict arose: charges of shady dealing, underhandedness, and betrayal. "I don't think you can do this without leaving a trail of blood," observes Danny Cupit, a lawyer in Jackson who was probably the first in Mississippi to file an asbestos suit.

Scruggs was particularly aggressive about building his client base, and he entered and dissolved a number of relationships with other lawyers as his practice developed. In 1994, two of those lawyers, Alwyn Luckey and William Roberts Wilson, sued Scruggs, claiming he had kept millions of dollars in asbestos fees that was rightly theirs. In counterclaims he filed, Scruggs revealed how ruthless he can be when the gloves come off in court. Going after his former colleagues personally, he asserted in pleadings that Wilson's professed expertise in asbestos litigation "proved to be either vastly exaggerated or untrue," and claimed that Luckey had been "abusive and arbitrary" to staff and that Scruggs had dismissed Luckey for "highly improper" conduct. He also charged that Luckey and Wilson "rarely, if ever, participated in the material aspects of the asbestos litigation," and claimed they freeloaded on the efforts of Scruggs and other attorneys. (Luckey and Wilson deny these allegations in reply papers.) Scruggs further contended that Luckey and Wilson actually owed *him* money. Most of the court filings have been sealed (at Scruggs's request), and it is impossible to judge the merits of the claims based on the pleadings alone.

Whatever the merits, the suit is notable because it is the product of what have been a series of acrimonious partings Scruggs has had with people with whom he has practiced, events that seem out of character for someone widely described as easygoing and congenial. "I'm probably not the best person in the world to work with others on a coequal basis," Scruggs admits. "I like to make decisions and call the shots." His firm in Pascagoula is certainly structured to let him do that. Although there are other partners (technically shareholders) among the nine lawyers working with him, Scruggs retains a 68 percent interest in the firm, giving him absolute control. The way he exercises that control, though, often rankles even those who are loyal to him.

In November 1994, Scruggs slashed his partners' base pay — the amount of money they took home before any year-end bonuses were determined. Scruggs's partner and longtime friend Steve Bozeman was furious about what he felt was the unilateral and peremptory manner in which the cuts were made. To prevent a fight over money from destroying his friendship with Scruggs, he decided to quit the firm. Scruggs recalls that the cuts were "done with discussion, but it was not consultation. I did it the honorable way," he says, "but they didn't like it very much." He also says that once bonuses were paid, his partners' total compensation was more than restored.

Given the enormous settlements Scruggs had reached in asbestos litigation, it's surprising that he felt he had to resort to belt tightening. According to financial information provided by Scruggs, his practice won about $100 million from asbestos defendants between 1991 and 1997, and perhaps $10 million to $15 million in previous years. Sixty percent of that went to the clients, and some went to associated counsel, or was plowed into funding new litigation, such as tobacco. That would still seem to leave a healthy amount for Scruggs and his colleagues, but Scruggs says he ran into cash flow problems. "We had a lot of money accrued, but didn't have it in hand," he says, noting that many of his firm's files on his asbestos clients were in terrible shape and had to be brought up to date before asbestos makers would process settlements for them.

Steve Bozeman's departure came just as the Medicaid team was preparing to argue its motion that the case ought to remain in chancery court. After the team won the crucial ruling in February 1995, Mike Moore called Bozeman — who had done much of the research and brief-writing — and encouraged him to patch things up with Scruggs. A few days later, Scruggs called and said, "Let's just say we called each other and said let's try to work things out." Soon Bozeman was back on board.

There was to be no such rapprochement with Luckey and Wilson, Scruggs's former cocounsel in asbestos litigation. Indeed, as the fee fight between Scruggs and his ex-colleagues progressed, it grew more heated. During a deposition at Scruggs's office, the lawyers tussled over a document and nearly came to blows. The police were called, and three squad cars pulled up as Luckey, Wilson, and their lawyers spilled out onto the sidewalk. (No one was arrested.)

Then there was the battle at the beach. In 1993, two years after he bought the Walker house, Scruggs bought another storied home on the shore. He paid $200,000 for what was known as the Longfellow House, a name it acquired after a legend arose that Henry Wadsworth Longfellow had written a poem, "The Building of the Ship," there in the mid-1800s. One line in the poem refers to "Pascagoula's sunny bay." The poem was actually published five years before the house was built, but the property has a place in the hearts of many Pascagoulans.

A New Orleans sea captain and slave trader built the mansion in 1854, and legend has it his wife was so cruel to her personal slaves, the house became haunted by the ghost of one who died on the property. After changing hands several times, the Greek revival structure and its beautiful grounds were acquired by Robert Ingersoll Ingalls, the shipping magnate, in the 1940s. Ingalls wanted an elegant place where he could host executives and dignitaries, and he had lodgings and a first-class restaurant built on the premises.

In the fifties and sixties, Ingalls Shipbuilding turned the house and surrounding grounds into a country club, and a broad spectrum of the white community were members. Elegant meals were served inside, while outside, peacocks perched on the limbs of live oaks. Dick Scruggs and his high school friends also hung out at Longfellow, which had a pool and a six-hole golf course. His wife Diane remembers a long pier, since destroyed, that jutted into the Mississippi Sound. From a telephone at the end of the pier, she and her friends would order hamburgers and pink lemonade, which would be delivered by a waiter on a bicycle.

By the early 1990s, Longfellow had been bought by a developer, who was threatening to tear it down. This dismayed many Pascagoulans, who had fond memories of time spent there in their youth. So Scruggs bought Longfellow, and then proceeded to spend $800,000 more to restore it. His plan was to donate the house to the community, to be used as a hall for weddings, receptions, and other functions. This kind of benevolence was not uncharacteristic of Scruggs, who is a generous supporter of organizations such as the Boy Scouts and March of Dimes. He is also known for helping individuals, whether by making his plane available to transport accident victims or by giving college kids jobs at his firm, whether he needs them or not. One person who ended up on Scruggs's payroll was Eddie Khayat. After Mike Moore ran him out of office in 1982, Khayat fell on hard times, burdened in part by legal bills. Scruggs says he "felt sorry" for Khayat, and paid him "a monthly stipend, if you will, just to help him out." (Khayat died in 1993.)

In the case of the Longfellow House, however, not everyone was pleased with Scruggs's planned munificence. Over the years, property surrounding the house had been sold off and developed into upscale homes, and the residents worried about noise and traffic problems that might develop. "Some of them are concerned the bubbas will be down there having beer parties and peeing in their flower beds," Scruggs said in early 1996, describing the "running gunfight" he was having with the homeowners. Two of Scruggs's principal opponents in the fight were Joe Colingo, R. J. Reynolds's lead local lawyer in the Medicaid litigation, and Jerry St. Pé, president of Ingalls Shipbuilding. But Scruggs threw himself into this conflict with the same vigor and confidence that characterized his fight against the tobacco industry. Some in town came to wonder which was the bigger fight.

27

"Good afternoon, Mr. Williams. How are you?" So began Gordon Smith on the afternoon of January 15, 1996. It was round seven in the effort to depose Merrell Williams, and the lawyer for Brown & Williamson finally had his quarry just where he wanted him: seated in a Louisville courtroom, with Judge Thomas Wine present to rule immediately on any objections and prevent any shenanigans.

"Mr. Williams is on medication, one of which is a diuretic," Williams's attorney Fox DeMoisey warned at the outset. "So from time to time he may have to, I suppose, just raise his hand if we have to take a short break for that."

But bathroom breaks would prove to be the least of Smith's problems. His substantive questioning began with what had been B&W's core concern since it first obtained an injunction against Williams in January 1994: Did Williams's handing over of the three packages constitute his full compliance with the judge's ruling? As he had before, Williams refused to answer, asserting his Fifth Amendment privilege against self-incrimination. When Judge Wine ruled that Williams could not use the

Fifth Amendment to avoid answering questions seeking to find if he was in contempt of a court order — since it did not put him in danger of criminal prosecution — DeMoisey objected. A finding of contempt could still lead to his client being incarcerated, he pointed out. What's more, Brown & Williamson might use Williams's answers in a contempt inquiry to support criminal charges against him. "The problem is . . . this case operates on many parallels," DeMoisey said.

Judge Wine was sufficiently uncertain of his own interpretation of the law that he wanted an appeals court to rule on the issue, and he said he would not seek to have Williams jailed until he got such a ruling. So the most the judge would do for Smith was state that Williams was in contempt each time he refused to answer questions about what he had done with B&W's documents, a small step forward for Smith, but hardly the compelled testimony he was looking for.

For a second time, Brown & Williamson had been hoist with its own petard. At first, the company's insistence that Judge Wine's restraining order and injunction prevented Williams from even talking to his own attorneys had given Williams an effective pretext for silence. Now B&W's threats that he could be prosecuted for theft or extortion gave added grounds for him to remain mute. Even Judge Wine seemed to see this as an unnecessary obstacle to progress. Addressing Smith, he said, "There might be a way to avoid all these Fifth Amendment claims if, as previously suggested, Brown & Williamson and Wyatt, Tarrant had made an agreement with various local law enforcement agencies not to prosecute the defendant on any potential criminal charges, which is frequently done and would eliminate all these claims about any privilege he may have."

"Your Honor," Smith replied, "I would say that my client shouldn't be placed in a position of waiving the ability to pursue one wrong in order to be able to prove another wrong."

It's hard to say what Smith and his client were hoping to gain from their pursuit of wrong. It had been one thing when, through the first few months of 1994, B&W thought aggressive legal action against Williams might deter any dissemination of the company's documents. When publication of the documents in newspapers and on the Internet vaporized that goal, however, the company continued its pursuit, with the only possible objective being to punish Williams and, perhaps, deter others from similar acts. But vengeance was proving costly, cumbersome, and elusive.

After getting a number of rulings from Judge Wine that Williams was in contempt for asserting the Fifth, Smith moved his questioning into other areas. Learning that Williams had met with Richard Daynard, the antitobacco law professor, Smith asked what they had discussed. One of the subjects, Williams replied, was labor law, and he proceeded to give Smith an earful about what he said was Wyatt's policy of giving paralegals comp time instead of overtime, and denying them paid holidays or sick leave. His time cards, Williams said, would help tell the story, and some of them were in one of the sealed boxes he had turned over in January 1994. Smith wasn't the least bit interested in the time cards, but he decided the moment was right to unseal the box. "Let's open it up and look," he said.

It had the makings of a dramatic scene, since Williams had been instructed to hand over anything he had taken while working at Brown & Williamson. But Smith grew impatient and tried to hurry the loquacious Williams along as he pulled out and described pens, pay stubs, memos on sick leave, photographs of his daughters, and assorted "Far Side" cartoons. Smith wasn't amused. "Let's finish going through this," he said, and pointed to something that looked promising. "Now you have another document entitled 'Formula' at the top," he said. "What is that?"

"Well, that's the formula for figuring child support," Williams replied.

"Why did you give that to Mr. Ballantine?" Smith asked, clearly exasperated.

"Well, because it was in — it was in the box that I took out [on his last day of work]. I mean, I put everything that was there that I could possibly get my hands on."

Valiantly, Smith pressed on, but, after five and a half hours of questioning, Williams couldn't take any more. "I'm dying up here," he said as the lawyers fenced over a pending question.

"Let's take a short break," Smith said. But Williams didn't return. "My client is ill," DeMoisey announced after the break, adding that he was trying to find a doctor to assess his client's condition. Williams, who hadn't eaten in hours, was indeed feeling ill, and the lights and heat in the room were making his head spin. All he wanted to do was go home, but the last flight of the day had already left. After having a hamburger and a couple of beers, he spent the night at a motel, and got the first flight back to Mississippi the next morning.

28

The Mississippi Medicaid suit nearly came to an end in a wooded field outside Topeka, Kansas. It was a Sunday afternoon in April 1996, and Dick Scruggs and Mike Moore had been in California, interviewing a potential witness. Now they were aboard one of Ron Motley's planes, heading to a meeting with Carla Stovall, the attorney general of Kansas, to explain the policy and procedures of bringing a Medicaid recovery action against cigarette makers.

The cloud cover was low, as the plane, a Citation III jet, approached for a landing. In a rear-facing seat, Scruggs looked out as they finally broke through the clouds, and was surprised to see how close the plane was to the ground. "I looked forward to see if there was any runway out there and what the shit these [pilots] were doing, and then I realized that they had blown their altitude," he recalls. "I turned and just screamed at them to pull up. . . . They sort of half-assed leveled off without pulling up and I looked out the window and I was looking directly out at trees. And I just thought to myself, God, we're dead."

Finally the pilots got the plane up to its assigned altitude of 5,000 feet, but, when Scruggs unbelted and came into the cockpit, he found the two pilots so shaken that they then missed their next approach to Topeka. Scruggs ordered them to Kansas City, sixty miles away, where the weather was better, and when they finally landed, the senior pilot had tears streaming down his face.

The planned meeting with Attorney General Stovall — which was rescheduled for another day — was part of an effort by Moore and Scruggs to tighten the screws on the tobacco industry by getting other states to join in the Medicaid litigation. Although they hadn't planned to do this when they filed the Mississippi case, it was becoming clear that the only way to bring real pressure on the industry was to widen the threat. In its suit, Mississippi was seeking just under $1 billion in damages. But, as tobacco stock analysts on Wall Street pointed out, all the industry had to do to cover a $1 billion judgment was raise cigarette prices five cents a pack for one year.

Not that Mississippi was completely alone. In August 1994, three months after Mississippi filed its action, the State of Minnesota also sued the industry. While the general aims of the two states' suits were similar, their strategies were very different. Moore and Scruggs had decided to pursue a lean, streamlined case against the industry. They wanted to get to trial fast and, in relative terms, cheap. That meant, for example, not naming the tobacco companies' parents as defendants in the lawsuit (BAT Industries, for example, parent of Brown & Williamson; or Philip Morris Companies Inc., a holding company that owns the tobacco subsidiary Philip Morris). The reason was that the parent companies always contested a court's jurisdiction over them in cigarette litigation, and fighting these side battles could be tedious, expensive, and distracting. The tobacco subsidiaries themselves, Scruggs and Moore were confident, had more than sufficient assets to satisfy any judgment that might be awarded against them.

In the same way, the Mississippi Medicaid team sought to limit the amount of discovery they conducted against the tobacco makers. They actually felt they had enough damning documents to try the industry on the day they filed their suit, and, while they would certainly seek more, they wanted to avoid having the process turn into a black hole. Not only would reviewing the documents be a monumental task, the industry would vigorously resist disclosing many of them, leading to more time wasted, more expense, and more distraction.

Minnesota took the opposite approach. For example, it sued BAT, convinced that B&W's parent harbored important documents. Minnesota, in fact, mounted the most ambitious discovery ever conducted against the industry, ultimately compiling 30 million industry documents. In aeronautical terms, Mississippi was a sleek fighter jet, hoping to make a swift but devastating strike on the cigarette makers; Minnesota was a lumbering B-52, readying to carpet bomb the industry into submission.

By the end of 1995, attorneys general in just three other states — West Virginia, Florida, and Massachusetts — had joined Mississippi and Minnesota in suing. It appeared that momentum had stalled. The industry was counterattacking, seeking to overturn the statute that had authorized Florida's suit, winning a ruling in West Virginia that gutted that state's case, and, in early 1996, supporting Mississippi Governor Fordice in his challenge to Moore in Mississippi's Supreme Court.

But the wind hadn't died, it had just shifted direction. This shift was occasioned by a combination of unrelated events that ratcheted up the pressure on the industry, and by a broad reassessment of strategy within the two largest cigarette makers, Philip Morris and RJR. By the spring of 1996, developments in the tobacco war began to move faster and farther than anyone could have imagined.

From the moment they filed their lawsuit in 1994, members of the Mississippi Medicaid team were on the lookout for tobacco industry whistle-blowers. Merrell Williams, of course, had been one. But his job was essentially finished when he handed over his documents. They largely spoke for themselves, and, if admitted in court, could be used to make Brown & Williamson executives speak about them. As a paralegal who had simply coded the documents, Williams had no role as a witness.

There was nothing systematic about the Medicaid team's efforts. Names would be passed to them from various sources, an investigation would be made, and usually nothing would come of it. There was, for example, a former RJR market researcher named D. W. Tredennick, who had written a memo in 1974 about "what causes smokers to select their first brand of cigarette." In the memo, Tredennick noted: "For legal reasons, we have been unable to directly survey smokers under 18 years of age (as will be shown most smokers begin smoking regularly and select a usual brand at or before the age of 18)." That sounded intriguing, and Scruggs and Moore flew to California to meet with him, but he didn't seem to remember much.

On the opposite coast, in Connecticut, Russell Stewart, a one-time vice president of brand management for Brown & Williamson, described that company's "Beetle Bug" campaign, an effort to get young owners of Volkswagen Beetles to decorate their cars with Kool cigarette brand decals. Stewart came to Scruggs courtesy of the Castano legal team. They had placed an ad in a North Carolina newspaper soliciting tobacco industry whistle-blowers, complete with a telephone number that they could call collect. But the industry promptly marched into court, accusing the plaintiffs' lawyers of breaching ethical rules governing attorney conduct and of attempting to induce current or former employees to violate confidentiality agreements. The industry won an injunction in North Carolina state court, and ultimately a federal magistrate in New Orleans, where the Castano case had been filed, also placed significant limits on the lawyers' ability to solicit industry employees. As a result, when Stewart wrote to the Castano team offering his services (not in response to the ad, but because he had heard about their case), they forwarded his letter to Scruggs.

Although Stewart proved helpful as a consultant in some areas, Scruggs recalls, he couldn't really document efforts to reach underage smokers. Scruggs also found that Stewart's help didn't come cheap, paying him close to $100,000 to serve as a consultant.

Then Jeffrey Wigand showed up. From 1989 until he was fired in 1993, Wigand, a Ph.D. in biochemistry, had worked as head of research and development at Brown & Williamson. That made him one of the highest-ranking executives in the company, presiding over its innermost sanctum. Wigand quickly learned that the company monitored and guarded activity in R&D to protect not just its trade secrets, but also its legal position. Shortly after he was hired, he was sent to an orientation session in Kansas City, at the offices of Shook Hardy & Bacon, where lawyers presented their interpretation of data on smoking and health. During his work at

B&W, he found that minutes of scientific meetings were vetted by company lawyers, and he would discover later — after he had left B&W and read the Merrell Williams documents — that the results of certain offshore research projects had been kept from him. He was the company's top scientist, but he was forced to work with blinders on.

To an extent, Wigand had put blinders on himself when he first took the job with a cigarette company after a career in the health care industry. He has claimed that part of the attraction of the job at B&W was the opportunity to develop a "safer" cigarette, but he quickly came to feel that there was no commitment to that idea within the company. On other fronts, too, he ran into disappointment, and he repeatedly clashed with B&W's president, Thomas Sandefur. In March 1993, two months after Sandefur had been promoted to CEO of the company, Wigand was fired.

As part of a two-year severance package, Wigand signed a confidentiality agreement, forbidding him to discuss his work at B&W. In addition to money, the package offered Wigand health insurance, something he regarded as essential, since his daughter had been diagnosed with spina bifida, a serious congenital deformity of the spine. Wigand would later argue that the confidentiality agreement had been obtained through duress, and very soon he began to break it.

In early 1994, he helped Lowell Bergman, a producer for CBS's *60 Minutes*, analyze a group of Philip Morris documents relating to that company's Project Hamlet, the effort to develop a fire-safe cigarette. CBS paid Wigand $12,000 for his work, which arguably was not a violation of his confidentiality agreement, since it dealt with another company's research. But the process proved a slippery slope. Bergman soon realized that Wigand had much to tell about his own work at B&W, and slowly began to draw him out on his experience there, with an eye toward producing additional material for CBS. At the same time, Wigand's name began to circulate quietly among government investigators and foes of the tobacco industry. A Justice Department lawyer came to Louisville and took Wigand's deposition as part of an investigation into whether cigarette makers had conspired to suppress a fire-safe product. It was this investigation that had prompted the Justice Department to subpoena Merrell Williams as well, and had led Williams to be so hopeful that he would have an outlet to tell his story, hopes that were dashed when Judge Thomas Wine refused to let Williams speak.

Accompanying Wigand at his deposition was an attorney for Brown & Williamson, and Wigand played the good soldier, denying that his former employer had engaged in any wrongdoing. But in ways that B&W didn't know, he had already become a turncoat. In a series of meetings where he introduced himself only by the code name "Research," he tutored experts at the FDA on a variety of hot-button issues. Especially valuable was his explanation of how tobacco companies enhance the delivery of nicotine to smokers by adding ammonia-based compounds to cigarettes. He walked agency officials through a copy of a B&W leaf-blenders' handbook that spelled out the basics of ammonia technology and how it boosts the pharmacological impact of nicotine. By 1995, he was advising lawyers defending ABC in the defamation suit filed by Philip Morris following ABC's report that tobacco companies added nicotine to cigarettes.

He also kept talking to CBS's Bergman, who was pressing him to go public with the story of what B&W knew about nicotine, and its lack of interest in producing safer cigarettes. Because of his confidentiality agreement, and the possibility of his testifying before various grand juries that were investigating the tobacco industry, Wigand, with Bergman's help, retained legal counsel: Ephraim Margolin, a criminal defense attorney in San Francisco. By the summer of 1995, Margolin had extracted from CBS a promise to cover Wigand's costs in the likely event that his appearance on *60 Minutes* led Brown & Williamson to sue him. The agreement, however, was not wholly satisfactory, and Margolin began to feel that he did not have the resources to handle Wigand's legal needs. In particular, he wanted to be assured that whatever legal predicament Wigand ended up in, the costs of his defense would be covered.

So Margolin did a search, and the name he came up with was Dick Scruggs, who recalls: "Margolin told me that here was a guy who wanted to come out and tell a story, and he needed a lawyer to protect him, because Brown and Williamson was going to come down on him like a herd of elephants." Even though Scruggs had a larger agenda — namely, representing Mississippi in the Medicaid suit — Margolin concluded he would vigorously represent Wigand's interests as well. Using the exact phrase

Merrell Williams had, Margolin described Scruggs as "a man of action," and in late October 1995 he arranged for Wigand and Scruggs to get acquainted.

Meeting and dining together a number of times over the course of a weekend in New York City, the two men hit it off. Wigand, who had spent time in Japan and spoke Japanese, took Scruggs to a sushi restaurant, and was amused when Scruggs jokingly referred to the food as "bait." Scruggs, Wigand recalls, "made me feel very comfortable that he would have my best interests at heart," and he signed on as his client.

A few days after the meeting, Scruggs sent Wigand a letter reiterating his agreement to represent him at no charge. He also outlined an aggressive strategy for dealing with Brown & Williamson, the cornerstone of which was calling Wigand as a "surprise witness" in proceedings in Mississippi to testify about the company's wrongdoing. In frank — and prescient — words, he then set forth what likely lay ahead if Wigand decided to proceed:

> Your testimony as the former vice-president of a major tobacco company is a mortal threat not only to B&W, but also to the entire tobacco industry. Obviously, they will resort to all means (legal and probably illegal) to discredit and intimidate you. B&W will almost certainly sue for millions in damages for breaking the confidentiality clauses, whether or not you are directed to so testify. B&W will seek an injunction against your communications, even with your own attorneys. We can only imagine the types of social and professional pressures that B&W will attempt to impose, but they will clearly be extreme.
>
> If we fully succeed in our litigation efforts, you will be free of restriction against communicating with third parties about B&W's unlawful activities. . . .
>
> If B&W fully succeeds, you could lose virtually everything through adverse judgments and injunctions against your engaging in certain types of employment. You already have potential liability for your cooperation with federal authorities and news organizations despite the confidentiality clause, and without notifying B&W. Accordingly, by not initiating pre-emptive litigation in a favorable forum, you risk B&W

suing you anyway in Kentucky, as set out above. There is always the chance, however, that B&W will "look the other way" and forgo suit if not further provoked.

Given the uncertainties, contentiousness and stakes, I am unable to give you good odds on success or failure. However, my willingness to undertake your representation free of charge should be some indication of my commitment and my assessment of your chances.

These are clearly tough choices for you and your wife. Given the magnitude of this decision, I cannot make a recommendation about whether you should act or risk inaction. I can only assure you of my commitment to prosecute and/or defend you to the full extent of my abilities, whichever decision you both make.

The letter was vintage Scruggs. His statement that he could not recommend whether Wigand "should act or risk inaction" makes Scruggs's bias clear. Over the course of a year and a half, the two most important whistle-blowers in the history of the war on tobacco — Merrell Williams and Jeff Wigand — had come to Dick Scruggs, and it was no accident. It was because he was a "man of action" that they had entrusted themselves to him. And while he ended up representing only Wigand, the steps he took on behalf of both men typified his hard-charging, damn-the-torpedoes style.

Williams and Wigand shared surprising similarities, not the least of which was that they couldn't be cast as pure sinner or pure saint. The men were about the same age; Williams turned forty-seven the month he started reviewing Brown & Williamson's files, and Wigand was forty-six when he started at B&W. Of the four years both men worked for the company, they overlapped for three. They even worked at the same building — Brown & Williamson's R&D facility in Louisville. Neither was easy to get along with: Williams could be sullen and churlish, Wigand was short-tempered and could be verbally abusive. And even before they ventured into the tobacco conflict both had endured strife at work and at home. By the time they connected with Scruggs, Williams and Wigand were both in the midst of failing third marriages, and, as a consequence of taking on B&W, both were afraid for the safety of themselves and their families.

B&W, in turn, feared what each man had to reveal, and the company's willingness and capacity to retaliate were amply demonstrated in its pursuit of Williams. What purpose that served once Williams's cache of documents had gone public was hard to divine. With Wigand, though, the situation would be different. B&W's first aim was to prevent him from speaking, but even after he had done so the company would have good reason to want to destroy him. While the value of Williams's information lay in the documents themselves, Wigand's value was primarily as a witness, a high-placed executive who could offer personal testament to what the industry knew — and covered up — about its product. So if B&W could impugn Wigand as a human being, casting doubt on his motives and veracity, it could significantly limit the damage he could do. Despite his predictions of B&W's impending wrath, even Scruggs would be surprised at the lengths to which B&W would go to crush his client.

Coaxed by CBS producer Lowell Bergman, Wigand told *60 Minutes* that B&W lawyers had edited documents to delete references to efforts to make a safer cigarette; that CEO Thomas Sandefur had perjured himself in April 1994 when he joined other tobacco executives in saying he believed nicotine was not addictive, because he had previously referred to cigarettes as "a delivery device for nicotine"; and that B&W had continued to use the vanillalike flavoring coumarin in pipe tobacco, even after learning of experiments in which it had caused liver cancer in mice. (B&W has said coumarin is not used in any company products today, and that when it was, the levels were safe. B&W attorney J. Kendrick Wells has denied that documents were improperly altered.)

These were explosive allegations, coming as they did from the company's one-time head of research, but CBS agreed not to air them without Wigand's consent. Before he gave that consent, Wigand wanted an ironclad indemnity agreement, and in November 1995, nailing one down became Scruggs's first order of business. CBS had initially offered to cover legal fees, expenses, and damages arising out of any claim for *defamation* that B&W might make as a result of Wigand's appearing on *60 Minutes*. But Scruggs didn't think that was good enough; he demanded that CBS cover *any* legal claim B&W might bring. It turned out that CBS's top lawyers were similarly concerned about some other kind of suit by B&W, in particular a claim for "tortious interference with contract" charging that the network induced Wigand to breach his confidentiality agreement. Such a suit in Kentucky courts, the lawyers feared, could produce a billion-dollar verdict, and in conjunction with CBS executives, they reached an extraordinary decision: to kill the Wigand piece.

This decision quickly became a news event in itself. There was much speculation about whether other interests were driving the decision. For example, Laurence Tisch was the chairman of CBS, and the Tisch family, through its Loews Corporation, controlled Lorillard, the country's fourth-largest cigarette maker. Also, CBS at the time was in the process of being bought by Westinghouse Electric, and Westinghouse shareholders would certainly not have been happy to acquire a billion-dollar lawsuit along with the network.

Caught at the center of this maelstrom was Jeff Wigand. As the media spotlight focused on CBS's smothered story, his anonymity evaporated. On November 9, Scruggs sent a stern letter to CBS's in-house lawyers:

> Please do not force us to take legal action against CBS. Numerous media sources are telling Dr. Wigand that CBS representatives have identified him as the former Brown & Williamson executive described in today's *New York Times* page one story. If these reports are true, CBS has violated its agreements with Dr. Wigand and exposed him to threats and punitive litigation by Brown & Williamson. He is now being deluged by press inquiries and harassing calls.
>
> You guys now need to do the right thing and sign the indemnity agreement I sent you this morning.

Whatever the consequences for Wigand, someone at CBS was intent on airing his allegations, and on Friday November 17, the *New York Daily News* published not only Wigand's name, but extensive selections from a transcript of his never-aired *60 Minutes* interview. That night, CBS lawyers called to confirm their intent to cover Wigand's legal costs. On November 21, B&W sued Wigand in Kentucky state court and obtained a restraining order against him. Despite the urgency of the situation, it would take nearly six months of negotiations and repeated threats from Scruggs of a lawsuit against CBS before a signed indemnity agreement was in place. (CBS's lawyers never backed off from the network's commitment, they just refused to hurry as they worked out the details.)

Even before Wigand's name was catapulted into the public arena, Scruggs was moving forward with his plan to get Wigand's story told in the Mississippi proceeding. He decided to take Wigand's deposition in the Medicaid case, and scheduled it to be done in Pascagoula on November 29, the Wednesday after Thanksgiving. As the day approached, Wigand's anxiety grew, especially after his name leaked to the press and — as Scruggs had predicted — B&W sued him. On Thanksgiving Day, Scruggs sent Wigand a fax, updating him on developments and trying to calm his worried client. "Relax today and let us work for you," he wrote. "You're on the right side of this fight; just hang in there; I know it's tough on your family, but you all will prevail."

Facing possible contempt proceedings and fearing for his personal safety, Wigand nonetheless showed up for his deposition. He stayed at Scruggs's house, protected by bodyguards and electronic security, and the next day walked into a courtroom crammed with thirty lawyers. Ron Motley would conduct the questioning, but before he began, Tom Bezanson, who had served on American Tobacco's defense team in the Horton case and was now appearing for Brown & Williamson, issued a series of admonitions to Wigand concerning his testimony, including the potential consequences of violating the Kentucky court's orders. By that point, though, Wigand said in a later interview, he was "resolute." A half hour before he had left for the courthouse, he and Scruggs had discussed one last time whether Wigand wanted to go through with it. "He said, 'I respect whatever decision you make. If you go forward, we'll be there for you. If you don't go forward, we'll be there for you,' " Wigand recalled.

The deposition proceeded, with Wigand essentially recounting the same allegations he had made to *60 Minutes.*

Wigand's appearance was a major setback for Brown & Williamson, but the cigarette maker was hardly done fighting, and its next attack on Wigand would not be in court. A few days before his deposition in Pascagoula, Wigand had faxed Scruggs an ominous note. "I have been informed that B&W has hired a private investigator," he wrote. "He has been asking a lot of questions and has been in Buffalo [where Wigand attended graduate school] so far. . . . They are digging for dirt!"

Using lawyers, private investigators, and John Scanlon, a self-described practitioner of "guerrilla" PR (Scruggs later said "gorilla" was more like it), Brown & Williamson was preparing a smear campaign. In December Scruggs got a call from a reporter at the *Washington Post,* seeking comment on allegations that Wigand had engaged in spousal abuse and shoplifting. Early in 1996, B&W delivered to journalists a 500-page dossier titled "The Misconduct of Jeffrey S. Wigand Available in the Public Record." The massive file was divided into sections, with headings including "Possible False or Fraudulent Claims," "Wigand's Lies About His Residence," "Wigand's Lies Under Oath," and "Other Lies by Wigand."

The fight over Jeffrey Wigand's character became one of the pivotal battles in the war against Big Tobacco, yet there was no reason this had to be so. True, he was the highest-level whistle-blower ever to emerge from the industry; as a witness who could offer personal testimony about cigarette makers' misdeeds, he had no peer. That gave Brown & Williamson a reason to want to flatten him. But it didn't stand to reason that if B&W succeeded, the result would be devastating to the forces arrayed against tobacco in Mississippi and elsewhere. They had already amassed a tremendous amount of damning information about the industry, and much of what Wigand had revealed could be corroborated independently.

But Wigand became more than a witness. He became a symbol for the antitobacco movement, a living embodiment of the righteousness of their cause. If B&W could hit him with a lethal blow, it would fell more than the man. Scruggs knew it. So as the new year of 1996 dawned, Scruggs marshaled the forces to fight back. Taking a recommendation from CBS producer Lowell Bergman, he hired Jack Palladino and Sandra Sutherland, a husband–wife team of private investigators from San Francisco, to run B&W's allegations to ground. Wigand's past wasn't in fact pristine. His wife did accuse him of spousal abuse, he was charged with shoplifting a bottle of Wild Turkey from a liquor store, and there were discrepancies in his résumé. Scruggs says the shoplifting charge was the result of a misunderstanding, and it was ultimately dismissed. The spouse-abuse charge was dropped, though Wigand did attend anger-control counseling. B&W's problem was that it documented Wigand's foibles with a heavy — and sloppy — hand.

It apparently never occurred to B&W's attack squad that some reporters might regard its massive campaign to discredit Wigand as itself being worthy of a story. That was certainly the case at the *Wall Street Journal*. And when reporters there began to comb through the allegations made against Wigand, they found numerous inaccuracies. The result was a page-one story in the *Journal* on February 1, 1996, focused on "the lengths [a company] may go to discredit a critic." The 2,600-word article noted that "a close look at the [500-page dossier], and independent research by this newspaper into its key claims, indicates that many of the serious allegations against Mr. Wigand are backed by scant or contradictory evidence. Some of the charges . . . are demonstrably untrue."

Although Wigand did not emerge untarnished, it was the cigarette maker that came out the clear loser.

Wigand's cause was helped even more when three additional whistle-blowers came forward, this time from Philip Morris. Two former Philip Morris scientists and a manager of a cigarette production plant submitted sworn affidavits to the FDA backing up Wigand's claims that cigarette makers worked to ensure that smokers received a certain level of nicotine and believed they were in the nicotine-delivery business. For example, William Farone, the director of applied research at Philip Morris from 1976 to 1984, stated: "It is well recognized within the cigarette industry that there is one principal reason why people smoke — to experience the effects of nicotine, a known pharmacologically active constituent in tobacco."

29

"For the record," Gordon Smith stated, "this is a continuation of the deposition of Merrell Williams, which was begun . . . in the courtroom of Judge Wine on January 15, 1996. Judge Wine is not present with us today, but indicated that he would review this transcript and make rulings on claims of privilege raised by the witness during the deposition."

It was March 20, 1996, and even as Brown & Williamson was working to discredit Jeffrey Wigand, it continued to pursue its first whistle-blower. There was every reason to believe this deposition would prove the same exercise in frustration for the company that previous ones had been. It was actually a different exercise in frustration. Rather than refusing to answer questions, Williams decided to answer them halfway.

A key objective for Smith was tracing the path of the stolen documents, and for the first time, Williams revealed to him that Scruggs had obtained them in Florida. Smith wanted details: "I want to know the route of those documents, from the time you took them from your employer until you arranged for Dick Scruggs to have them."

"I can't give the specific dates because I don't remember," Williams answered.

"I don't want dates," Smith said. "I want the route. I want how it happened. . . . I want to know, step by step, how those documents got to Florida."

These questions presumed a systematic, organized document thief, and that had hardly been the case. There was much that was haphazard in Williams's modus operandi, and he tried to explain this. "The documents were assorted documents, and I don't know if copies were made other than copies I had," Williams offered as part of his reply. "Some of these documents were thrown in trash cans."

"I'm only interested in the documents that got to Florida," Smith reiterated.

"If we could put the documents on the table —. Here is the problem I have," Williams said, "I don't know what documents you're talking about."

"Oh yes you do," said Smith.

"Oh no I don't," said Williams.

At another point in the deposition, Williams served up a mix of evasive answers as he initially tried to protect the identity of Nina Selz, the longtime friend to whom he had personally delivered boxes of B&W documents in Florida. "The documents," he told Smith, "ended up in, I believe, in some part of Florida, but I don't know exactly where."

"How did [they] end up in Florida?" Smith asked.

"I don't know the man's name," said Williams. "I really don't know his name because it was — I left it in a garage or a carport."

"Well, how —" Smith tried to cut in, but Williams kept going:

"And I knew the person who knew the person who knew the person. So it was sort of like a chain letter type thing."

After some more questions, though, Williams shifted course and named Selz as someone who had helped him. Smith then tried to clarify her role: "Dr. Selz eventually located a place for you to put these boxes that contained copies of documents you had taken while you were employed at Wyatt in a location in Florida; is that correct?"

"I do not know," Williams said.

"I thought you said you physically took the documents to Florida," Smith said.

"I do not know if she found a location," Williams dodged.

"How did you learn there was a location?" Smith pressed.

"Through the process of later asking Dick Scruggs to take custody," Williams said. "I investigated the matter."

Naturally, Smith was having a hard time getting it all to make sense. How, he asked, did Williams know where to take the documents in Florida in the first place?

"Well, I think it's sort of like going into my sister's garage," Williams ventured. "If I went into my sister's garage, by analogy, and put something in her garage, she wouldn't even know it's there."

At this point, even Fox DeMoisey could see his client was digging himself not one hole, but a field full of them. "Could we take a break?" he asked.

"We really need to take a break," Smith agreed.

When the parties returned from a brief recess, Williams had taken off his sweater, and Smith had a new problem to deal with.

SMITH: Before we go back on, I would object to your client wearing
        signage during the video deposition that I'm taking —
WILLIAMS: It's just a T-shirt.
SMITH: With the name of a deceased person who sued the tobacco
        industry some years ago. And this is my deposition, and I strongly
        object to him wearing any signage as some kind of statement in the
        deposition.

After a good deal of haggling, the two sides agreed that Smith would make a record of his objection, and Williams would put his sweater back on.

SMITH: The T-shirt says on the front of it, Sean Marsee, M-A-R-
        S-E-E, in yellow letters on a blue background T-shirt. On the back
        of the T-shirt, it has a date, and the date, I believe, if you will turn
        around, is 2 /25 /84 [the date of Marsee's death] . . .

WILLIAMS: Did he identify him as a 19-year-old who died of laryn-
    geal cancer? I don't know. Who had a year —

SMITH: Mr. Williams, there are no questions pending. This is a depo-
    sition where I am to ask you questions and you're to respond
    under oath. And I am not going to sit here and listen to you make a
    speech. It's my record and you can either answer my questions or
    not. And I'm going to start asking them.

Surprisingly, the rest of the deposition proceeded without incident,
and Williams offered a truthful and relatively coherent account of the
B&W documents' journey to Pascagoula.

Don Barrett, who had helped usher Merrell Williams's documents onto
the public stage, seemed to be trying his hand at every kind of tobacco
lawsuit there was. With *Horton* and *Wilks*, he had worked on behalf of
individuals alleging that smoking caused illness or death. In 1994, he
helped pioneer state health care recovery suits as part of the Mississippi
Medicaid team. That same year, he also joined the Castano group, which
filed the mammoth nicotine addiction class action in New Orleans. Also
in 1994, he and Ron Motley joined forces and brought a secondhand-
smoke case against cigarette makers in Jones County, Mississippi. That
suit was brought on behalf of the family of Burl Butler, a nonsmoker who
was exposed to smoke from other people's cigarettes while working as a
barber for thirty years, and who died of lung cancer at the age of sixty.

Fortunately for his finances, Barrett had not focused just on tobacco
when he returned to law practice in the mid-eighties after his stint
with the Farmers Home Administration. At that time, he decided that
environmental-contamination cases offered promise, and he filed a number of suits. In September 1988, eight months after the first Horton trial,
he won a case in Biloxi for a client who had bought land that had once
been the site of a factory where turpentine and rosin were extracted from
tree stumps and had found 4,500 leaking drums of chemicals on the property. The previous owner settled for $4.5 million. Barrett also got into
dioxin litigation, settling about four dozen cases before the Mississippi
Supreme Court quashed similar claims. And in May 1996, he won a $218

million verdict in Russellville, Kentucky, on behalf of seventy-seven land-owners who claimed that a tool-and-die operation of Rockwell International had contaminated the Mud River with PCBs. (Rockwell appealed the verdict, $210 million of which was for punitive damages.) In an amusing turn of events, Wyatt, Tarrant & Combs represented Rockwell, while a number of Barrett's clients were tobacco farmers.

Were it not for this diversified practice, Barrett might have missed being involved in the next milestone development in the tobacco wars. It grew out of a case involving leaky plastic plumbing. For years in competing cases in Alabama and Texas, lawyers had pursued claims on behalf of hundreds of thousands of homeowners who found that polybutylene water pipes installed in their homes leaked and had to be replaced. But efforts to resolve the cases, brought against large chemical concerns such as Shell Oil and Hoechst-Celanese, had foundered. Sensing an opportunity to steal a march on the other cases, Barrett and a group of other lawyers filed suit on behalf of the homeowners in Union City, Tennessee, got the case certified as a class action, and then moved quickly to settle it.

Toward the end of 1995, as the case was coming to a close, Barrett picked up Marc Kasowitz, a New York lawyer who represented Hoechst, at the airport in Memphis. The two then drove together to Union City, about two hours away, for a hearing. Chatting in the car, Kasowitz asked what other kind of work Barrett did, and he learned about his running battle with tobacco. "My reaction to that," Kasowitz recalls, "was that it must have been an unsuccessful and unprofitable venture." But, Kasowitz continues, "I remember he seemed to feel very strongly about the correctness of his position. Notwithstanding the fact that he hadn't made any money on it, he was still enthusiastic about it because he felt he was right."

Unbeknownst to Barrett, Kasowitz's firm represented Bennett LeBow, the majority shareholder of the Brooke Group Ltd., corporate parent of cigarette maker Liggett Group (once Liggett & Myers). Of the five major U.S. cigarette makers, Liggett was the runt of the litter, with only a 2.3 percent market share and a cluster of faded brands, including Chesterfield, L&M, and Lark. (It also sold cheap private-label brands.) Still, the company was running up legal bills of $10 million a year defending itself in smoking litigation, and one of Kasowitz's partners, Daniel

Benson, had begun to think that settling these suits under some sort of blanket deal might make good sense for Liggett.

There was more to the idea than saving legal fees. LeBow was not a typical tobacco executive — or a typical any kind of executive, for that matter. He was a corporate raider, who took stakes in companies for short periods, attempted to squeeze value out of them, and then sought to unload his interest for a profit. In late 1995, LeBow had launched a proxy fight to gain control of RJR Nabisco Holdings Corporation, parent of R. J. Reynolds Tobacco and of Nabisco foods. If LeBow could negotiate a favorable settlement of smoking cases for Liggett, with the understanding that he could bring those same terms to any company he merged Liggett into — such as RJR — then he could, in essence, create value in Liggett that shareholders of RJR might find too good to pass up.

Kasowitz thought the state Medicaid lawsuits, in particular, presented the tobacco industry with a genuine threat, which made the idea of settling them — and having those settlement terms be portable — even more compelling. LeBow was receptive to the idea, and authorized Kasowitz to explore it.

In early December 1995, Don Barrett came to New York to tie up some loose ends relating to the settlement of the plumbing case. He and one of his cocounsel in the case, Robert Lieff of San Francisco, were scheduled to meet Kasowitz in his office at 10:00 A.M. But the day before, Kasowitz called Barrett and asked if he could come at 7:00 A.M. and not tell Lieff. When Barrett arrived, Kasowitz told him of LeBow's interest in discussing a settlement of the state tobacco cases. Barrett was stunned. Kasowitz wanted to keep the negotiating teams as small as possible to maintain secrecy, but Barrett insisted on bringing in Lieff and one of Lieff's partners, Richard Heimann (the plaintiffs' lawyer who had not known, when asked by a B&W attorney, that Don Barrett was "Mr. Butts"). Barrett also wanted input from someone with a public health background, and called on David Burns, the San Diego physician who had helped prepare a number of Surgeon General's reports and who had testified for the plaintiffs in *Horton*.

For several weeks, Barrett and his colleagues held secret discussions to settle the claims against Liggett not only in the various state lawsuits, but also in the giant Castano class action as well. After about a month,

Barrett finally brought in Mike Moore and Dick Scruggs. The talks continued in New York and Houston, where Kasowitz's firm had offices, and in Miami, headquarters of LeBow's Brooke Group.

On March 13, 1996, Liggett became the first cigarette company ever to settle smoking-related lawsuits.

Joining Mississippi in settling were Florida, Louisiana, Massachusetts, and West Virginia. The agreement called for Liggett to pay the five states $1 million apiece, plus between 2 percent and 7 percent of its pretax income for twenty-four years, the amount depending on whether additional states joined the settlement. Liggett also agreed to phase in compliance with certain proposed FDA rules relating to smoking by children, including a prohibition on using cartoon characters in ads and limits on marketing to minors. Although Bennett LeBow won the right to have the terms of the settlement apply in the event Liggett merged with another cigarette maker, in the coming months his attempted run at RJR failed. In a separate agreement, LeBow settled the Castano case, too.

The agreements generated huge headlines and extensive coverage around the country. Articles spoke of how the deal "alters the legal battleground" and left other tobacco makers "rattled" and "reeling." This was somewhat overblown: Liggett under LeBow was already something of an industry pariah; add to that its minuscule market share, and the deal in itself was hardly likely to pressure the industry's larger players to consider anything similar. From the plaintiffs' perspective, the potential payoff was also minuscule: At existing earning levels, Liggett's *maximum* annual payout would be under $2 million.

Still, while it was possible to dismiss LeBow's move as a gambit to gain advantage in his takeover battle, other cigarette makers were not immune to the pressures of litigation. For starters, these included attorneys' fees, which even for the cash-rich cigarette makers were approaching staggering proportions. Wall Street's most respected tobacco analyst, Gary Black of Sanford C. Bernstein & Company, projected that the industry would spend $600 million on legal fees in 1997. That might have been well worth it if it guaranteed that the companies would never be hit with crippling verdicts. But there were no such guarantees, and, however unlikely, the risk of cataclysmic liability severely depressed cigarette company stock prices. According to analysts, tobacco stocks traded as much as 40 percent below their expected values, thanks to fear over litigation. Investors were also skittish. Two days after the Liggett deal became public, for example, Philip Morris shares dropped nearly 10 percent.

Just as investors were spooked, antitobacco forces were buoyed by news of Liggett's settlement, and it took on a symbolic importance out of proportion to what it actually produced. As Dick Scruggs saw it, one of the greatest benefits of the Liggett agreement was that it "validated" the state lawsuits. "Here was a tobacco company, albeit a small one, that was agreeing to pay money to settle these cases," he says. "Cash in hand fooleth no man," Mike Moore's father told him when Mississippi received its first payment under the deal.

And the Liggett settlement did not occur in isolation, but joined a stream of developments that were putting the tobacco industry on the defensive. The FDA, strengthened by the whistle-blower testimony on nicotine manipulation, was pressing forward with regulations on tobacco marketing and advertising, premising its jurisdiction on cigarettes being nicotine delivery devices. Grand juries were investigating possible fraud and antitrust violations by the industry and perjury allegations against its senior executives (for their statements to Congress that they believed nicotine was not addictive). In Florida, a one-time asbestos defense lawyer had filed scores of individual smoker suits against cigarette makers, and two class actions were also moving forward in the state.

One bright spot for the industry was the decision by a federal appeals court in May 1996 to throw out the nationwide class action in the Castano case. In one fell swoop, the single largest aggregation of claims against the industry was dismantled. But in the battle with the states, things were headed in the opposite direction. After two years of facing only five state health care recovery suits, cigarette makers found them popping up all over the map starting in the spring of 1996. Among them were Texas, which, with its huge population, presented the risk of Texas-sized damages. The movement had gone nationwide and bipartisan, and by the end of 1996, nineteen states had sued the industry, with more waiting in the wings.

The reasons for jumping on the bandwagon were various. Richard Ieyoub, Louisiana's attorney general, recalls that Moore and Scruggs both talked to him about bringing suit, and he found their public-health arguments persuasive. When word got out that he was considering such an action, he says, he was visited at his office by at least thirteen lawyers for the tobacco industry. "They ringed my conference room table," he says, and told him that a Medicaid case would be "a frivolous suit that would be unwinnable, [and] that they had never lost a case before to a jury." In addition, he said, "there were some veiled political threats that were made concerning my possible candidacy for the [U.S.] Senate." Ieyoub filed suit against the industry in March 1996.

Christine Gregoire, attorney general of Washington State, says she had considered bringing an action for some time, but needed to examine possible claims and muster the resources within her office. The last straw, she recalls, was when she saw a glossy magazine insert for Camel cigarettes. Opening the four-page insert, a reader encountered a pop-up figure of Joe Camel, holding concert tickets in his outstretched hand. In addition to offering discounts on tickets — obtained by redeeming "Camel Cash C-Notes" — a ten-page catalog taped to the back of the ad featured watches, boxer shorts, hiking boots, and sunglasses, all emblazoned with Joe Camel or the Camel logo. Like Ieyoub, she was visited by industry lobbyists, who tried to persuade her not to sue. But, pointing to the Camel ad, she told them: "You people put me over the edge; there is nothing that will stop you." She filed in June 1996.

Carla Stovall of Kansas and Grant Woods of Arizona became the first Republican attorneys general to file Medicaid claims against the industry, in August 1996. When she initially took office in January 1995, Stovall recalls, she "looked askance" at such suits, having "heard only the criticism." But as time went on, she saw that "the momentum was clearly changing," and events such as Jeffrey Wigand and other whistle-blowers coming forward as well as the Liggett settlement "caused me to sit down and look at [the idea of suing] seriously." Mike Moore, she concluded, was not the "loose cannon" critics painted him to be, but a "visionary."

Moore had called his prosecution of Eddie Khayat in Pascagoula a "case of tumbling bricks," as prosecution of underlings steadily toppled those higher up. Facing tobacco, Moore was trying to pile the bricks on, hoping that, at some point, the load would be too much for the industry to take.

30

Steven Goldstone had been a partner at one of the country's most prestigious law firms. Then, in February 1995, at the age of forty-nine, he joined one of his clients, RJR Nabisco, as its general counsel. By the end of the year, he had become the company's CEO. In his estimate, the Medicaid suits filed by attorneys general had no legal merit. Still, he felt that doing battle with the chief law enforcement officers of a growing number of states was contributing to the image of cigarette makers as an "outlaw industry."

And, as confident as he was of the industry's legal arguments, he couldn't be sure that those arguments would always carry the day. After all, these were cases brought by politically popular government officials against politically unpopular defendants, seeking revenue of behalf of taxpayers. Particularly in cases like Mississippi's that had been brought in state court, Goldstone was concerned more deference might be shown to politics than to law in deciding the outcome of these claims.

When it came to tobacco cases other than those filed by the states, Goldstone was similarly sure that the industry had the law on its side, but the mere existence of the suits, and the potential threat they presented, was a terrible drag on the prices of RJR's and other companies' stock. Even if the industry would ultimately prevail in all its litigation, it could still come out a loser.

Goldstone felt the ramparts the industry had built around itself had become too high and too thick for its own good. He understood that decades of litigation had forced the industry to surround itself with lawyers and even, to an extent, be run by lawyers. But that didn't do much for the industry's public image; it made it look defensive, made it look and act like it had things to hide. Its tremendous success over the decades in avoiding almost all government regulation, he thought, had also begun to backfire. When allegations surfaced about cigarettes, such as the claim that the industry adds nicotine, it would have been helpful to have industry denials backed up by government regulators responsible for overseeing the product. As it was, the industry's word had to stand on its own, and nobody believed it. A certain healthy amount of regulation might restore credibility to cigarette makers' statements about their products.

Goldstone figured there had to be something that could be done in a comprehensive way to solve these problems, and in March 1996, after talking the idea over with executives in his company, he floated his thoughts in a tentative, but calculated, way to the *Financial Times* of London. In a March 22 article, Goldstone was quoted as saying he would never consider simply settling pending litigation the way Bennett LeBow of Liggett had done, because that would just open a floodgate of additional claims. Then he said: "That doesn't mean that legislative, executive, political, social and other sources can't be brought together to resolve this issue. Nor does it mean that the tobacco industry has such a fight-to-the-death mentality that it would ignore eminently reasonable solutions." While he wouldn't specify the kind of resolution he had in mind, he suggested that part of it might include payments by the industry in return for immunity from further antismoking lawsuits.

After Goldstone's statement appeared, Dick Scruggs told Mike Moore that he wanted to sound out the industry position. Calling his wife's brother-in-law Trent Lott, whom he regarded as a tobacco-friendly senator, Scruggs asked if he knew of anybody who could serve as an intermediary with the cigarette companies. Lott gave him the names of John

Sears, a White House lawyer in the Nixon administration who had also served as a presidential campaign manager for Ronald Reagan, and Tommy Anderson, a Mississippi businessman who had formerly served as Lott's chief of staff for seventeen years and who was one of Lott's closest friends.

Over the next several months, a bizarre process got under way. Sears and Anderson held furtive meetings with officials from both Philip Morris and RJR, including, briefly, Steve Goldstone. Yet industry officials had a hard time knowing what to make of the two men, and what their agenda was. Meanwhile, the pair would report back to Scruggs with nuggets of information about what they thought the industry might be willing to accept, both financially and otherwise, in a package that would try achieve a global resolution of issues relating to tobacco. But it was impossible to tell whether the information they conveyed really came from the industry or was their interpretation of what the industry might say.

Even stranger, from Moore's point of view, was the fact that Sears and Anderson were willing to talk to Scruggs, but seemed to want to avoid Moore. "I didn't like the process, as Dickie knows. I just didn't like dealing that way," Moore recalls. "I was extremely uncomfortable. . . . I didn't know what it was. It was like talkin' to folks in the darkness." When Moore asked Scruggs what he was doing, Moore recalls, "He said 'Mike, trust me, there are just some things that are better if I don't tell you right now.' " So Moore let Scruggs go forward. "I don't think he would have been pushing it if he hadn't heard from somebody in the United States Senate that this was the way it could happen, you understand what I mean," Moore explains.

As Scruggs saw it — presumably based on conversations with Lott — the industry would never let itself be seen to be negotiating, and could never let it be known that it might agree to the kinds of measures that were being discussed, such as government regulation of tobacco. It was true that even as RJR's Goldstone dropped additional public hints about being amenable to an overall resolution to the industry's problems, he mixed them with public denials that his company was interested in such a process. So what Scruggs was looking to do was put together something that the industry would acquiesce to, even as it squealed in public protest.

The hope, says Scruggs, was to craft legislation that "the industry would hold its nose and swallow."

As 1996 progressed, the Mississippi Medicaid case was mired in the massive discovery process and procedural maneuverings that characterize any large lawsuit. Roughly once a month, lawyers descended on Pascagoula for hearings before Judge William Myers. They did not go to the chancery court building, however. Just months after the Medicaid suit was filed, workers gutted the two-story rectangular structure, stripping it down to its steel girders as part of an asbestos-removal project. And there it sat, as Jackson County supervisors bickered about how to put it back together. Some in Pascagoula felt the board had been indecisive and ineffectual ever since Mike Moore ran Eddie Khayat out of office, and they pined for the days of Khayat's forceful rule the way some Russians wax nostalgic about Stalin's no-nonsense reign.

The business of the court had to go on, nonetheless, and hearings on the fate of one of the largest, most powerful industries in the country were moved to a flimsy, single-story building on Market Street, once the commercial heart of Pascagoula but now a seedy stretch of low-end businesses, including pawnshops and gun shops, used car dealers, and game rooms.

As the Medicaid case moved forward, the defendants engaged in deliberate denial: No matter what Judge Myers ruled, they were going to treat the case like the tort action they thought it should be. While the plaintiffs talked about damages incurred by the state, to be proved by data relating to populations, the defendants resolutely sought information about individuals. Battles over discovery thus often mirrored a larger dispute about what kind of lawsuit was going to be tried.

When the tobacco companies asked to take the depositions of thirty Medicaid recipients "allegedly" treated for smoking-related disease, the state resisted. "Defendants will not accept this court's ruling that the state's case is a direct action, not in subrogation or in tort, and are attempting . . . to convert it into an individual smokers' lawsuit," stated a brief opposing the request. In response, the defendants as much as admitted that, noting "even the modest number of depositions now requested will demonstrate the overwhelming individuality of the claims and the impossibility of treating them fairly by . . . 'group proof.' " They quoted from a 1983 Mississippi Supreme Court decision (in a case unrelated to tobacco), noting that "the court made a comparison which is nicely applicable here":

> An apt analogy might run like this. The trier of the facts is charged to determine how many teeth are in a particular horse's mouth. One expert horse dentist says it's 36. Yet he acknowledges that he has not opened the horse's mouth to make an accurate count. He opines that the horse is suffering from severe neurosis and would suffer a psychological setback if subjected to the in-mouth count. Another horse dentist, however, perseveres in the face of the horse's neurosis, opens the mouth and counts only 32 teeth. . . .

The brief then continued:

> Plaintiff does not want to open the horse's mouth. Plaintiff wants to take a "national sample" of horses from all over the country and come up with some kind of an average or expert opinion about the number of teeth that are usually in a horse's mouth. But, as the Mississippi Supreme Court found, that is not good enough. Here, the only way to look in the horse's mouth is to see at least some of the allegedly injured persons: the Medicaid recipients. Defendants contend that, with the benefit of such discovery, they will be able to show that there are so many differences between the individual smokers and so many factors that may have contributed to their illnesses, that it is impossible to rely *solely* on statistics.

In response, the Medicaid team served up some analogies of their own:

> In seeking to engage in nonrepresentative patient discovery, Defendants are impliedly asking the Court to disregard the results of epidemiological studies of smoking and disease, and to substitute instead anecdotal testimony of a relative few Medicaid patients. A similar proposition would be that in order to determine the shape of the

earth, one should reject hundreds of satellite photographs, and instead conduct interviews of thirty people standing on the ground. Using the tobacco industry's methods, the earth would appear flat.

While Defendants may contend that every *individual* smoker is different, smoking populations *as groups* do not differ in their response to smoke: they predictably get sicker at rates that can be defined and quantified from existing scientific studies. . . . Just as surely as if Defendants had blown their poisonous smoke into the atmosphere, rather than encouraging individual smokers to inhale it, the harm of which this lawsuit complains is harm to the state's taxpayers *as a group.*

The state also saw the tobacco companies' desire to "open the horse's mouth" as a Trojan horse, a means of opening up the right to depose untold numbers of additional individuals. Statements made by defense counsel certainly seemed to leave that possibility open.

Judge Myers eventually ordered the state to make twenty Medicaid recipients available for deposition, but when the state dragged its feet in turning over those names, the tobacco companies pounced on the delay as an excuse to seek data on every person for whom the state was seeking reimbursement of health care expenses. At a minimum, that called for information on hundreds of thousands of individuals, and in addition to seeking their names, addresses, and Social Security numbers, the defendants also asked for their age, gender, tobacco consumption status (current or former), annual number of days spent in the hospital or nursing home, number of those days related to treatment of a smoking-related illness, annual number of physician visits, medical care costs, medication costs, and on and on. Full disclosure of this information, the defendants insisted, was "constitutionally required."

Compliance with this request would, as the defendants knew, have brought the case to a grinding halt, and the state never did produce the information.

The industry also treated Mississippi as though it were a person, and asserted defenses analogous to those raised in individual smoker cases, such as *Horton*. Just as American Tobacco argued that Nathan Horton knew full well the dangers associated with smoking, and thus assumed the risk of his conduct, the tobacco companies prepared to show that Mississippi officials were similarly aware, and yet never took steps to ban the sale of cigarettes.

As far back as 1604, a brief filed by the defendants notes, King James I of England issued his "Counter Blaste to Tobacco," in which he called smoking a "custome lothsome to the eye, hateful to the Nose, harmefull to the braine, dangerous to the Lungs, and the blacke stinking fume thereof, nearest resembling the horrible Stigian smoke of the pit that is bottomelesse." Surely three hundred–plus years later, the defendants reasoned, the sovereign — in this case the State of Mississippi — knew even more. In the 1920s, they noted, Mississippi "adopted textbooks that admonished students that smoking 'is a habit which may do serious damage to the health.' " By the 1950s, the brief continued, "many studies linking smoking with lung cancer and other diseases were reported in popular national magazines, such as *Time, Life* and *Reader's Digest*." And the 1964 Surgeon General's report, which "condemned smoking as a cause of cancer and other diseases," was "front page news throughout Mississippi."

What King James knew, what the State of Mississippi knew, what Nathan Horton knew, the tobacco companies themselves did *not* know, even in the 1990s. In a deposition taken in the Medicaid litigation, Ron Motley pressed Cathy Ellis, Philip Morris's senior vice president of research and development, on the point:

MOTLEY: You can't even tell the Court whether one person in America who smoked Marlboro for 30 years and died of lung cancer last year, that smoking Marlboros was the cause of his lung cancer?

ELLIS: Cigarette smoking has been identified as a risk. It's possible that one might have. But it is certainly impossible to determine whether anyone specifically has or what number. . . .

MOTLEY: Is the current position of Philip Morris that the case against cigarettes as a cause of lung cancer is still not proven?

ELLIS: Smoking is a risk factor.

It wasn't only what you knew about smoking that cigarette makers used against you, it was what you did besides smoke. Just as American Tobacco tried to establish that Nathan Horton had an unhealthy lifestyle, the tobacco defendants in the Medicaid suit assembled evidence that Mississippi was an unhealthy state. In November 1996, Peter Biersteker, a lawyer for RJR, took the deposition of Mary Currier, whose title at the Mississippi Department of Health was State Epidemiologist. Using various collections of statistics, Biersteker got Currier to agree that Mississippi was the poorest state in the nation; that it is one of the most poorly educated states in the nation; and that the quality of housing in the state is "well below the national average."

"Each of these factors — poverty, poor education, poor housing — adversely affects the status, the health status, of the citizens of the state, doesn't it?" Biersteker asked.

"Yes," Currier agreed.

Biersteker then read from a book with tables that documented the sorry state of Mississippians' health. The data showed that among the fifty states, Mississippi had:

- the highest birthrate among teenagers
- among the lowest percentage of mothers who got prenatal care during the first trimester of their pregnancy
- the sixth-highest overall death rate in the nation
- the highest death rate by injury
- the highest death rate by accidents and "adverse events"
- the highest death rate by motor vehicle accidents
- the second-highest death rate from homicide
- the second-highest death rate from tuberculosis
- the second-highest infant mortality rate
- the third-highest death rate from syphilis and the highest rate of syphilis
- the fourth-highest death rate from heart disease
- the highest percentage of adults who are overweight
- among the smallest percentage of overweight adults who are trying to lose weight

- the sixth-highest percentage of adults who live a sedentary lifestyle
- the lowest percentage of adults who consumed fruit and vegetables each day
- among the lowest in percentage of people who use seat belts

"We're the first state to file suit against the tobacco industry for health care expenditures, however," Charles Mikhail, a lawyer in Dick Scruggs's office representing Mississippi, piped up.

"That wasn't in this book," said Biersteker.

The defendants' aim in enumerating Mississippi's unhealthy ways stemmed from the plaintiffs' plans to use national statistics to calculate Mississippi's damages. If national data, for example, showed that on average 30 percent of heart disease was smoking-related, the defendants objected to having that figure applied to Mississippi, where the prevailing unwholesome lifestyle might mean factors other than smoking contributed to a far greater percentage of heart ailments.

The issue of damages took on unusually central importance as the Medicaid suit progressed, for two reasons. The issue of the defendants' liability — whether their products did in fact cause illness and death, and whether they had engaged in wrongful conduct, such as withholding information, suppressing development of less harmful cigarettes, and targeting minors — increasingly seemed like a foregone conclusion. Not that members of the Medicaid team weren't working hard to nail that case down, but substantial evidence was already available to prove such culpability on the day the suit was filed in May 1994. And as whistle-blowers came forward, government investigators pressed on with their inquiries, and discovery produced additional documents, that proof only grew stronger.

The second reason for the intense focus on damages was that in the context of a health care reimbursement suit, it was uncharted terrain. There was plenty of data available on Medicaid patients, and there were plenty of epidemiological methods to measure the effects of smoking on a population, but combining the two to produce reliable figures in support of the state's damage claims proved to be a monumental task. The aim was to figure out what portion of Mississippi's total Medicaid expenses were "smoking attributable." For example, under one method of analysis, of the $28.1 million the state spent in 1996 treating hypertension in Medicaid patients, smoking was responsible for $4.5 million of those expenditures. Of the $78,000 spent treating burns, $39,000 was attributable to smoking.

But salt contributes to hypertension as surely as smoking does. How did the analysis account for patients who liked both potato chips and cigarettes? And did Medicaid files indicate whether a patient's burns were caused by a cigarette-triggered fire, or was some percentage imputed to the data? In addition to attacking the whole notion of proving damages from population data, as opposed to looking at individuals, the tobacco defendants took aim at just about every aspect of the way the state proposed to calculate those damages. They found fault with the numbers that went into the calculations, fault with the numbers that came out, and fault with the black boxes in between: the "damage models" that crunched the data.

Dick Scruggs made damages one of his principal areas of focus in the Medicaid suit, and immersed himself in regression analysis and econometrics. In addition to relying on off-the-shelf methods for calculating smoking-related health care costs, the plaintiffs commissioned experts to come up with their own method for calculating these costs. But the models they created were constantly being revised and tweaked, and the defendants had a field day going after them. If the methods used by one plaintiffs' expert were correct, the defendants carped in a court filing, then "there are 1,009 women in Mississippi age 80 or older and pregnant." Even Scruggs had to admit at a hearing that the state had to "get the male hysterectomies out of the data."

"You would hope that would be a mistake," Judge Myers replied.

"Damages models are tough," Scruggs observed later. "They're hard to explain, they're easy to mischaracterize and easy to punch holes in any time you're doing modeling for a population like that. Science has not developed to the point that it's like fingerprints or actuarial tables." But as Scruggs saw it, the state had no choice: "The problem with the whole damages modeling was that it was the worst method for doing it, except for all the rest — there was just no other way of doing it."

31

Although Joe Colingo's client in the Mississippi Medicaid case was RJR, he had been designated "liaison counsel" for all the defendants. That was more an administrative assignment than an honor. His office handled the defendants' joint filings and made sure that all defense counsel received copies of all pleadings, depositions, correspondence, and other material generated in huge quantity by the litigation. Some fifty-five lawyers in twenty-seven offices were listed as defense counsel on court documents, with untold numbers of others laboring behind the scenes, and keeping them up to date kept Colingo's office humming. At one point, with the case in the middle of discovery, he noted he had already worn out two copy machines, and often had employees staying at his office until 2:00 A.M. operating the fax machine.

Colingo's role, though, was more than principal paper pusher. While attorneys from elite national firms jetted in for hearings, Colingo was the most regular presence at court on behalf of all defendants, and there was little doubt that if the case ever went to trial, he would have a prominent courtroom role.

In the spring of 1996, though, a new lawyer joined the

defense ranks. During a break in one of the first hearings he attended, he could be heard talking into his cell phone, reading the riot act to a prospective client who had dithered too long in deciding whether to hire him. Enough talk, he said, enough wasted time. His hourly rate was $550 — they could hire him or not. Click.

Abrasive, abrupt — and in demand. That was Stephen Susman, a fifty-six-year-old Houston litigator so sought after that he picked his clients as much as they picked him. And Philip Morris had just hired the tall, lanky Texan to represent the company in Mississippi.

Why was he needed, given the platoon of highly credentialed lawyers already representing Philip Morris and the other tobacco companies in the case?

"They're here to get rid of the case," Susman said at the time. "I'm here to try it."

It was true that the defendants' various efforts to derail the Medicaid suit — getting it transferred to federal or circuit court, or getting it dismissed altogether — had failed, and trial seemed like an increasingly likely possibility. At such moments, it's not unusual for defendants to parachute in a big-name trial attorney.

Susman was that. The founding partner of a forty-two-lawyer firm, he had built his reputation as a litigator handling major matters for clients ranging from Texas tycoon Nelson Bunker Hunt to Intel Corporation. His clients sang his praises, and when Susman was in the courtroom, it was not unusual for other lawyers to drop by just to watch him perform.

Still, Susman's I'm-in-charge-here attitude, combined with his brusque style of dealing with people, did not endear him to his fellow defense counsel, and friction quickly developed. Joe Colingo, in particular, bristled at Susman's self-proclaimed role as "lead counsel" for the tobacco companies. "I don't take my orders from Susman, and he doesn't take them from me," Colingo grumbled a few months prior to the scheduled Medicaid trial.

By late 1996, though, Susman was steadily taking control of the defense case, and he even moved physically onto Colingo's turf. He leased a suite of offices in the Ritz building, named for the movie theater that had once been housed there. Painted bright pink, like something out of Miami Beach, the building sat a stone's throw from Colingo's offices in the heart of Pascagoula. One of the only other tenants in the Ritz building was the local office of the state Division of Medicaid, and employees from that office occasionally joined Susman's secretary on the fire escape for cigarette breaks.

Susman also wanted a place for himself and others in his firm to stay when they came to town, and the local hotels were simply not up to snuff. Going out with a real estate broker to survey area homes for rent, he found the only place he liked was the broker's own house, an elegant turn-of-the-century residence on the beach, not far from Dick Scruggs's home. Although the broker originally had no intention of renting her house, Susman persuaded her and her family to move out and lease it to his firm.

Long a connoisseur of gracious living — he and his wife collected art, and their vacation home on Galveston Bay had won architectural awards — Susman had secured an oasis of comfort and tranquillity in Pascagoula in the event the Medicaid case went to trial. And as preparations for that trial proceeded, he and members of his team could be found there, poring over documents while soothing classical music was piped through speakers around the house, a maid circulated with fresh-brewed coffee, and the bright colors of fresh flowers were refracted in the glass of a chandelier.

Susman's behavior didn't always comport with his refined tastes and high-powered reputation. At court hearings in the Medicaid case, he would stick his long legs out, cowboy boots peeking from beneath his suit trousers, and twirl a toothpick in his mouth. On two successive days, while defending depositions of senior Philip Morris employees, Susman fell asleep, according to others who were in the room with him. ("I wasn't asleep," Susman maintains. "Nothing was happening.") On another occasion, he hopped aboard a shuttle at New York's La Guardia airport to attend a thirty-year reunion of Supreme Court clerks in Washington, D.C. (He clerked for Justice Hugo Black.) Only when he heard the pilot announce, "Well, the weather's looking pretty good in Boston," did he realize he'd boarded the wrong shuttle.

There was little doubt, though, that Susman would be in top form for the trial. If trials are performances, Susman was an Oscar-quality star. The only problem was the audience — or lack of one. Susman excelled at persuading juries to take his side. And in case after case for tobacco companies, juries had been the industry's best friend. In a bench trial, though, the dynamic was different. A judge was far more likely to look past razzle-dazzle theatrics and rhetoric to focus on the evidence and issues in the case.

In the Medicaid suit, Susman would have to put his clients' fate in the hands of a lone decision-maker, and he was openly apprehensive about it.

"I do fear a single judge — *any* single judge," he said, as the trial date drew near.

It is understandable that Philip Morris would want a commanding presence like Susman on the team of lawyers defending the industry in Mississippi. In the event of any damage award, Philip Morris would likely be on the hook for roughly half the amount, since, by the mid-nineties, it controlled 49 percent of the U.S. cigarette market. RJR was a distant second with a 24 percent share.

American Tobacco, once the industry colossus, had faded to just a 6 percent market share. In 1994, its parent company, American Brands, decided to get out of the U.S. tobacco business altogether, selling its American Tobacco unit to Brown & Williamson, boosting B&W's share of the market to 16 percent. As part of the deal, B&W had agreed to cover American Brands for any verdicts rendered against American Tobacco in product-liability litigation, a seemingly safe bet, given the industry's unblemished record in such suits.

On August 9, 1996, a jury in Jacksonville, Florida, ordered Brown & Williamson to pay $750,000 to Grady Carter, a former smoker who had lost part of a lung to cancer. The case was a double insult to B&W. First of all, Carter smoked Lucky Strikes, an American Tobacco brand that B&W didn't even own until after Carter quit his forty-year habit. Second, because B&W was the corporate successor to American Tobacco, the judge in the case allowed a number of Merrell Williams documents to be admitted at trial, even though it was American's conduct, not B&W's, that should have been at issue. And in press interviews after the trial, jurors in the case cited the B&W documents as a significant factor in their decision to find liability.

The decision to admit the documents was one of the grounds on which B&W lawyers appealed the Carter verdict. At the same time, they continued their pursuit of the man whose theft of the documents had come to cause the company so many headaches.

There would be no pleasantries, not even an on-the-record hello, as Gordon Smith began his questioning of Merrell Williams on September 16, 1996.

SMITH: Are you on any medication today?

WILLIAMS: Sir?

SMITH: Are you on any medication today?

WILLIAMS: Yes.

SMITH: Could you tell us what medication you're taking today?

WILLIAMS: The prescription medications are a generic Xanax, a diuretic, a Toprol, which is a blood pressure lowerer. Let's see. There is another one that's called — well, it's a beta-blocker. I don't know the name of it. And nonprescription, I've had an aspirin this morning. . . .

SMITH: The purpose of my asking about medication, of course, is to ensure that you are of sound mind today and are capable of understanding my questions and giving me your best recollection. Do you think that any of the medications you're taking would affect your ability to give me your best and truthful answer today, under oath?

WILLIAMS: I don't know the answer to that. . . .

SMITH: Do you feel any different today than you do on a typical normal day, other than perhaps being a little nervous?

WILLIAMS: I suppose so.

SMITH: You do feel okay today?

WILLIAMS: I have diarrhea.

Smith had deposed Williams many times as part of the lawsuit Brown & Williamson had filed in Kentucky, but this deposition was being taken as part of the federal suit B&W had filed in Biloxi in February 1995 against

Williams and Dick Scruggs. Instead of having Fox DeMoisey at his side, Williams was represented this time by Thomas Royals, a criminal defense attorney from Jackson. Royals's fees for representing Williams were being paid by Scruggs, who himself was represented by two lawyers at the deposition, which was being held at a law office in Biloxi. Before the deposition got under way, Scruggs's lawyer James Carroll got together with Royals and prepared a trap to spring on Brown & Williamson when the right moment arose.

Smith had the first go at the witness, and his questioning lasted the better part of two days. As in previous depositions, his questions elicited responses, but few answers, on many subjects. For example, a lengthy stretch of questions on the purchase of the house in Ocean Springs included the following:

SMITH: I simply want to confirm that you, indeed, did have conversations with Mr. Scruggs with regard to potentially obtaining a house for your use.

WILLIAMS: For my lease, yes.

SMITH: Now, you've said lease several times. There has never been a lease on that house, has there?

WILLIAMS: Not to my knowledge.

SMITH: And you've never made a lease payment, have you?

WILLIAMS: Not to my knowledge.

SMITH: So, in fact, the house wasn't bought to be leased, right?

WILLIAMS: No, sir. It was bought to be leased.

SMITH: Why wasn't it leased?

WILLIAMS: I have no answer for that.

SMITH: You don't.

WILLIAMS: The answer is, I don't know.

Equally mystifying was the $44,000 in loans Williams received from various Gulf Coast banks for the purchase of his two cars and the sailboat. He acknowledged that Scruggs paved the way for him to receive these loans, but couldn't say how this was done. Ultimately, Smith couldn't hide his bafflement:

SMITH: This is all very strange to me that you can go into a bank telling me that you know Mr. Scruggs agreed to cosign, and you understood that you would not have the ability to get these loans alone, but you can't tell me how Mr. Scruggs had any communications with the bank, how he arranged to cosign, where his signature appears or anything.

ROYALS: That's a statement. It doesn't require an answer, so I object to it.

WILLIAMS: I understand.

SMITH: Now, can you explain that to me?

WILLIAMS: I can't.

SMITH: It just happened?

ROYALS: Can he explain how you think it's strange? That's the question?

SMITH: Yes.

ROYALS: Can you tell this guy why he thinks something is strange? That's the question.

SMITH: Can you explain to me how you got a loan, three loans, when you understood your credit would not support them, when you have no knowledge of Mr. Scruggs signing anything?

WILLIAMS: This answer is, I don't know.

Williams testified that since June 1994 — two months after he turned over the documents — he had been getting paid $3,000 a month, initially by asbestos law firms that had relationships with Scruggs and then by Scruggs's own firm. At first Williams said he did various independent research projects for these firms, including scanning the Internet. But after a break, he admitted that he did no work at all for his pay.

Again, Smith couldn't contain his amazement. "Do you have any understanding of why Ardoin & Tanet [one of the law firms] would pay you $3,000 a month to do nothing?" he asked. After Royals objected and said, "Why keep lingering?" Smith sputtered, "I want this job, I guess, is why."

At times during the lengthy deposition, Williams baited Smith, and Smith bit. When Smith asked whether Williams had done any writing, Williams said, "I am writing three books." Smith followed up:

SMITH: And what three books are you writing?

WILLIAMS: Well, I'm writing about you right now, and you gentlemen right here, and you [gesturing to Smith and his colleagues] and the attacks on the — by the tobacco industry.

SMITH: I'm sorry. The what?

WILLIAMS: The attacks.

SMITH: On?

WILLIAMS: A professional defendant.

SMITH: You?

WILLIAMS: Yes.

SMITH: That's book number one. What's book number two?

WILLIAMS: Trying to survive the attacks of the tobacco industry.

SMITH: That's a separate book?

WILLIAMS: Well, it's in a format. It's not quite finished.

SMITH: All right, book number three?

WILLIAMS: Bypass surgery and the tobacco industry, and how to love your enemy, story of a foot soldier.

SMITH: Is that the title?

WILLIAMS: Yes, working title.

Day two of the deposition began with an exchange that captured the cordial hostility that had come to characterize the proceedings.

WILLIAMS: And there are a couple of things that I would like to say before, on the record. First of all, I would like to apologize to the court stenographer and to the court for the word "BS" yesterday. . . . And secondly, I don't know if this is a significant point with you, Mr. [Smith] — we've been — you've deposed me many times and I appreciate the strategy of your body language, but if you don't mind, would you kind of keep a distance from me a little bit? Because I realize that you may not feel that this is intimidating me, but it is, and maybe you do, maybe you don't. . . .

SMITH: Tell me what you mean. I want you to be comfortable. . . .

WILLIAMS: Well, you have a very high torso, and you tend to move

toward me like this. And it's a very minor point, I realize, with
you, but it seems to be that you're pressing on me a little bit.

SMITH: I'll try to sit back.

Smith hadn't resumed his questioning for long when Royals and
Carroll sprang their trap. They did it when Smith asked Williams when
he first began taking Brown & Williamson documents. "I think I will stop
you from going into anything about the documents," Royals objected.
"He's being made to look bad on the record with no chance whatever to
explain his position. [It's as though he said] 'I slapped my wife,' with no
chance to explain that she was running into a burning house."

"What about questions that have nothing to do with the contents of
the documents?" Smith wanted to know, pointing out that he only wanted
to ask about the "mechanics" of how Williams took the documents, not
about their substance.

"No, sir, not unless we can talk about what the documents were," said
Royals.

As orchestrated, Scruggs's lawyer Carroll then chimed in with his
piece. One of Scruggs's defenses to B&W's charges was that the documents he had received from Williams offered evidence of crime or fraud
by the company, and therefore B&W could not protect their confidentiality. But with B&W insisting that the terms of the Kentucky injunction
prevented any discussion of the substance of those documents, Scruggs
was unfairly hamstrung in developing that defense, Carroll contended. A
court would have to clarify whether "we are going to have to go forward
with one hand cuffed behind us," he said.

Days after the deposition, Carroll persuaded the federal magistrate
overseeing the case (Louis Guirola, the former assistant district attorney
who had helped Mike Moore prosecute Eddie Khayat) to move the matter to the inactive docket until the two sides could resolve the issue. That
bought both Scruggs and Williams valuable time.

Brown & Williamson's loss in the Carter case added impetus to the movement to reach a comprehensive settlement of tobacco claims. It was possible to view the Carter verdict as an aberration; two weeks later RJR won

a smoker suit in Indiana. But the same lawyer who won in *Carter* had hundreds of cases pending against the industry; other suits around the country, including the state Medicaid actions, were proceeding apace. Even if cigarette makers won a substantial number of these cases, it didn't take much imagination to conjure up a scenario similar to the one encountered by asbestos makers, in which the tide, turning slowly against them at first, gathered into a giant wave that would come crashing down with devastating results.

Sensing the industry's weakness, Dick Scruggs pressed forward with his behind-the-scenes effort to craft a resolution to the litigation that would offer cigarette makers peace and predictability in exchange for enormous sums of their money. Any plan that offered tobacco companies litigation immunity required an act of Congress, and in late August 1996, a draft legislative proposal was leaked to the *Wall Street Journal*. It called for the industry to pay $6 billion annually into a settlement fund starting in 1997, with the sum escalating over four years to about $10 billion, and continuing for a total of fifteen years. In addition to winning a reprieve from lawsuits, the industry could avoid regulation by the FDA, one of its greatest fears.

The leaked proposal instantly drew a mixture of astonishment and criticism. Attorneys general who had not been privy to the discussions chastised Mike Moore for his backroom deal-making, and some joined critics on Capitol Hill in charging that the plan was too soft on the industry. Others were upset that they had been left out of the process, including members of the public health community and trial lawyers from the Castano suit. Although the Castano national class action had been thrown out that summer, the lawyers had filed a number of statewide class-action suits (known as baby Castanos), and felt entitled to be present at the bargaining table.

Over the course of the fall and winter of late 1996 and early 1997, the number of groups involved in the discussions broadened considerably. The top executives of all the major tobacco companies met among themselves to discuss the issue, made contact with the White House, and hired high-powered advisers to help them out in Congress. In a way no one could have predicted even at the beginning of 1996, a fundamental shift had occurred in the tobacco landscape. For the first time, it appeared that some kind of peace conference might be in the offing. But whether it would really happen was far from certain, and whether it would succeed even less so. So the battles in the courtrooms had to rage on.

The cigarette makers had asked Judge Myers to delay the Medicaid case while the Mississippi Supreme Court considered petitions filed by the industry and Governor Fordice to block the suit. But in a July 1996 ruling, Judge Myers refused, and the best the defendants could do in succeeding months was get the trial date moved from March of 1997 to July.

So lawyers on both sides labored on, with the defense engaging in their trademark scorched-earth tactics. For example, they scheduled forty-three depositions of Mississippi state employees for the month of November alone. One area the defendants wanted to explore was efforts by Mississippi to enforce laws banning sale of alcohol to minors. At a hearing before Judge Myers, RJR attorney Peter Biersteker explained:

> I remember when I was younger, Judge, that it was a lot easier to go and buy a pack of cigarettes than it was to go and buy a six-pack. And why is that? That is what defendants want to explore. What were the successful enforcement measures that the State has used, for example, to restrict the sale of alcohol to individuals under the age of 21? And if those measures were successful with alcohol, why hasn't the State used them to enforce the restrictions on the sale of cigarettes to minors?

As the Medicaid team saw it, there was more than a bit of hypocrisy in Biersteker's argument about the unfairness of the state's singling out tobacco in its lawsuit ("That's not fair" being a legitimate ground of argument in a court of equity). One reason state enforcement against illegal tobacco use was weak was that the tobacco industry had worked effectively in the state legislature to assure it would be. Over the strenuous objections of the industry, lawyers for the state embarked on discovery that documented the scope and effect of the cigarette makers' lobbying over the years. "Their tentacles were everywhere," recalls Lee Young, a lawyer in Scruggs's firm.

Documents from the Tobacco Institute, the industry's principal lobbying organization, based in Washington, D.C., chronicled a coordinated effort at the state level to block cigarette tax increases, "fire-safe" cigarette requirements, curbs on smoking in particular locations, and restrictions on advertising, point of sale, and distribution of free samples. Lobbyists even worked to prevent smoking from being listed as a cause of death on state death certificates.

As to the matter Biersteker complained about, the industry played a major role. In the 1990s, when the federal government required states to pass laws limiting youth access to tobacco in order to be eligible for certain federal funds, industry lobbyists prepared drafts of youth-access legislation. In Mississippi, they got legislator D. Stephen Holland, an undertaker from Tupelo, to sponsor the measure. Holland, who sits on the state's Public Health and Welfare Committee, readily describes himself as a friend of the tobacco industry, and is a militant champion of smokers' rights. In one document the Medicaid team turned up during discovery, Holland wrote to a Tobacco Institute official: "The House [has] yet to ban smoking in the chamber, thanks to me and a few other 'assholes' who refuse to give in." The youth-access bill passed by the Mississippi legislature in 1994 contained a number of industry-suggested provisions that, in the view of public health advocates, guaranteed that enforcement would be weak.

As 1996 drew to a close, lawyers on both sides of the case waited for a decision from the Mississippi Supreme Court on the petitions filed there by the governor and the industry seeking to block the suit. Although the court was notorious for its foot-dragging — it took five years to dispense with appeals in the Horton case, for example — the delay here was excruciating, because both sides were pouring money and resources into the case, not knowing whether, at any moment, the plug would be pulled.

Dick Scruggs, who at times assumes the rest of the world follows his do-it-now approach to life, was sure the court would decide quickly after it heard oral arguments on the petitions in September 1996. Then he was positive a decision would come down by Thanksgiving. Then Christmas. By January 1997, all bets were off.

Finally, on March 13, 1997, the court ruled, rejecting on procedural grounds the challenges of both the governor and the industry. The Mississippi Medicaid case had a green light to go to trial.

Slow in coming as it was, the timing of the Mississippi Supreme Court ruling couldn't have been more propitious for the plaintiffs. Efforts to launch formal, face-to-face negotiations between the tobacco industry and its foes were on the verge of coalescing; the Mississippi court gave the cigarette makers a final push. News of the decision produced a sell-off in tobacco stocks, with shares of Philip Morris and RJR dropping 8 percent. More bad news for the tobacco companies soon followed. The U.S. Supreme Court refused to hear an industry appeal that claimed a special law authorizing Florida's Medicaid suit was unconstitutional. Trial in Florida was set to begin in August, just a month after the scheduled start of Mississippi's case.

Then, on March 20, Liggett's Bennett LeBow produced another surprise for his cigarette industry brethren. He broadened and expanded the settlement he'd entered a year earlier to include twenty-two states. In addition to upping the percentage of Liggett's profits he would pay to the states (though a larger percentage of next-to-nothing was still next-to-nothing), his real headline-grabbing concessions were on other fronts. LeBow agreed to acknowledge that smoking is addictive and to say so in warning labels; to acknowledge that smoking causes cancer; and to admit that tobacco companies had knowingly marketed to minors. Of particular concern to other cigarette makers, he also agreed to turn over thousands of pages of internal documents, including records of the Committee of Counsel, a group of top in-house lawyers from the major tobacco companies who met regularly over thirty years to discuss industry matters, including litigation.

The other tobacco makers immediately went to court in North Carolina and won a restraining order barring disclosure of the Committee of Counsel documents. They also issued a joint sneer at LeBow and his settlement, stating: "The only ones who potentially benefit from LeBow's latest shenanigans are plaintiffs' lawyers, who get nothing more than another free round of publicity and possibly some seed money to fund their illegitimate assaults on the remainder of the tobacco industry."

Sneer as they might, the publicity pushed tobacco stock prices down yet again, and more states were preparing to join the fray. LeBow may have been an industry outcast, but RJR chairman and CEO Steven Goldstone, and his counterpart at Philip Morris, Geoffrey Bible, were themselves preparing to sit down at the negotiating table. On April 3, 1997, the two men walked into a hotel conference room in suburban Washington, D.C., and announced to Mike Moore, Dick Scruggs, and others that the industry wanted to cut a deal.

32

In one sense, the cigarette companies were being held up with a toy gun. In courts around the country, the legal theories on which Mississippi had based its Medicaid claim were being rejected. Other states, and even some local governments, that had filed their own actions against the tobacco industry had modeled parts of their complaints on Mississippi's suit, but in cases filed by Florida, Maryland, San Francisco, and Washington State, judges struck down common-law claims that tried to sidestep traditional ways of recovering payments made on behalf of third parties. These suits didn't die altogether, because they asserted other claims as well, usually based on antitrust or consumer-protection statutes, or, in the case of Florida, a special law passed by the legislature authorizing a suit to recover health care costs.

However discredited around the country, the novel claims had been allowed to go forward in Mississippi, and as 1997 advanced, the cigarette makers found themselves facing potentially enormous damages at trial. In April 1997, Philip Morris attorney Stephen Susman, usually cocky and confident, didn't hide his pessimism about his client's prospects at trial. Facing a single judge, whose rulings to date had favored the plaintiffs, Susman considered an appeal his best chance of success. But there was one glimmer of hope remaining, one chance to mount a defense that Susman thought could win the case for the tobacco industry. And his opportunity to present that defense hinged on a motion that had been pending before Judge Myers for nearly two years.

It had to do with damages. If the plaintiffs' case was about reimbursing the state for the cost tobacco imposed on the public purse, then surely, Susman figured, cigarette makers could demonstrate the economic benefits that tobacco conferred on the state. One of these benefits was excise taxes levied on the sale of cigarettes. A second required the defense counsel to choose their words carefully. They referred to it variously as "medical expense savings due to smoking" and "lifetime medical costs of a smoker" versus a nonsmoker. What they meant was that smokers died earlier than nonsmokers. The plaintiffs called it an "early death premium," and worse.

These numbers could be significant. The excise tax alone generated about $45 million a year for Mississippi. And smokers, by dying twelve to fifteen years earlier on average than nonsmokers, saved the state significant amounts in everything from pension benefits to nursing home care to the routine medical care inevitably needed by the elderly. On a lifetime basis, defense lawyers argued, a smoker might cost the state no more than a nonsmoker did.

"The industry was showing all the signals of making this the cornerstone of their defense," Dick Scruggs recalls, "and they were starting to ask for huge chunks of discovery on that issue. We were afraid of getting into a battle over the economic benefits versus the economic detriment of tobacco. It'd become an economics case, as opposed to a health care reimbursement case. . . . We realized we were going to have to bring that to a head, . . . or be in a black hole of discovery that we could never get out of."

Scruggs came up with the idea of filing a motion *in limine* to preclude the cigarette makers from even raising the economic-benefit defense. It was an unusual tactic. Motions *in limine* are usually made on the eve of trial (*in limine* means "on the threshold"), and seek to prevent excessively prejudicial evidence from being presented to a jury (like Don Barrett's motion to keep evidence of Nathan Horton's dissolute ways out of that case). Scruggs's motion was made in July 1995, long before any trial date, and in a case to be heard by a judge; judges are typically deemed capable of keeping out or ignoring improper evidence on their own, without special motions. Scruggs, though, wanted to head the issue off early.

At a hearing on the motion, the Medicaid team argued that taxes are not a down payment on damages. Addressing Judge Myers, Scruggs said, "It would be as if I went out and broke the windows out of the courthouse and told Dale Harkey [the district attorney] to charge off my fine and the damages to the taxes I paid the state last year. That sounds simple, but that is exactly what they are trying to do."

The excise tax, the tobacco lawyers countered, was a special tax over and above taxes imposed on the sales of other products. The Medicaid complaint had alleged that "tax revenues generated by cigarette smokers help defray but a tiny fraction of the health care costs resulting from tobacco use in this state." This was wrong, according to the defendants, who wrote: "Plaintiff cannot have it both ways: he cannot allege that excise taxes 'help defray but a tiny fraction' of the State's costs, yet seek to deny defendants any discovery into the truth of that allegation." Citing a legal text on equity jurisprudence, the defendants wrote:

A court of equity is a court of conscience; it seeks to do justice and equity between all parties; it seeks to strike a balance of convenience as between all litigants; and it looks to the whole situation. . . . Here, the Court's duty to look at the "whole situation" requires the Court to look at the full economic impact of the sale of cigarettes on the State.

As to the claim about the money that smokers' premature deaths saved the state, the plaintiffs called it simply abhorrent. "The defendants' argument is indeed ghoulish," they said in their brief.

Seeking a credit for a purported economic benefit from early death is akin to robbing the graves of Mississippi smokers who died from tobacco-related illness. No court of law or equity should entertain such a defense or counterclaim. It is offensive to human decency, an affront to justice, uncharacteristic of civilized society, and unquestionably contrary to public policy.

It was hard for the tobacco firms to sound high-minded in seeking such a credit, although they correctly pointed out that it was routine in product-liability cases for a calculation of damages to include not only costs, such as medical expenses and lost wages of someone who died, but also savings resulting from not paying "personal maintenance" expenses. Indeed, the *plaintiffs'* own expert did just that in calculating the damages in the Horton case, subtracting $55,000 that Horton would have spent, but didn't, because of his early demise.

Scruggs entreated the judge not to open up the Pandora's box of economic balancing, and to "keep the case focused on what we filed." A frustrated Joe Sam Owen, local counsel for Philip Morris, complained about the chameleonlike nature of the state's case: "The plaintiff initially argued . . . that this was a case in which the objective was to balance the equities and to determine the state of Mississippi's net loss. Now for some reason we have vacillated away. We don't talk about economic loss any more. We talk about restitution." But the restitution claim, Owen argued, had an undefined, evanescent quality. "Issues in this case become non-issues every time the wind changes," he said. It was like boxing with a phantom. Every time the defendants swung at something — be it a tort claim or a claim for economic loss — the plaintiffs said it wasn't there.

Any hopes Scruggs had of dispensing with the economic-balance issue early were dashed: Judge Myers let the motion languish nearly two years. During that time, though, the plaintiffs' team resisted discovery on the topic. And the defendants kept their fingers crossed. Finally, on April 15, 1997, Judge Myers issued an eight-line ruling granting the plaintiffs' motion. By keeping the Medicaid suit in chancery court, Judge Myers appeared to have denied the cigarette makers the right to present standard tort defenses, such as assumption of risk. Now the economic-balance defense was out of bounds too. The defendants were headed to trial with both hands tied behind their back.

In a last-ditch attempt to regain advantage, the cigarette makers filed a motion on May 20, 1997, asking Myers to reconsider his earlier decision to keep the case in chancery court. "Defendants propose a procedure under Mississippi law that would permit transfer while preserving the trial date and retaining Chancellor Myers to preside over the trial," the motion stated. "The transfer would result in only one change: the placement of twelve Mississippi citizens in the jury box to ultimately decide this case." It was a jury the defendants desperately wanted. Every other Medicaid case scheduled for trial would be heard by a jury, they noted. "And for good reason. These cases all involve the exact same conduct and the exact same factual issue — issues that are recognized by all courts in this land as jury issues."

"Not so," the plaintiffs replied tersely. "The two courts in this land which matter most (the Chancery Court of Jackson County and the Mississippi Supreme Court) have ruled otherwise."

Judge Myers denied the defendants' motion.

As the Medicaid case headed toward trial in Pascagoula, and a foundation was being laid for national settlement talks, several boxes were delivered to Merrell Williams. Inside were copies of the thousands of pages of Brown & Williamson documents the company had accused him of stealing. For three and a half years B&W had doggedly fought to bar Williams from discussing their contents, to prevent them from being disseminated, to punish him and others for making them public, and to force him to give back any he might continue to harbor. Now, this set of the documents had been sent to Williams by Brown & Williamson's own attorneys.

This strange turn of events grew out of an effort to end the impasse in Brown & Williamson's suit against Williams and Scruggs in Mississippi. B&W's refusal to let Williams discuss the documents, even in a deposition, had led a federal magistrate to delay B&W's suit. If Williams could not describe the documents' contents, that seemed unfairly to crimp his and Scruggs's ability to argue that B&W couldn't protect the papers' confidentiality because they contained evidence of crime or fraud. To get the case moving again, B&W's lawyers decided to let Williams talk. A local rule in Mississippi federal courts also required plaintiffs — in this case, B&W — to turn over copies of all documents relevant to their complaint, but B&W had naturally balked at doing this in a case in which the central allegation was that the documents had been stolen. Assured by the magistrate that doing so would not preclude the company from claiming the documents were protected by the attorney–client privilege and that the papers would remain under seal in the case, B&W lawyers packed up the secret files and turned them over to the man they accused of stealing them. They even turned over copies of surveillance photos they had taken of Williams on the Gulf Coast in late 1994. (Williams had one enlarged and laminated for use as placemat.)

The questioning of Williams about the documents was scheduled for April 18, 1997, in Jackson, and Williams set about preparing for the deposition like a Ph.D. candidate preparing to defend his dissertation. In addition to reviewing the documents themselves, Williams assembled other material, particularly congressional hearing transcripts, that helped give them context. He wasn't just going to answer questions, he was planning to tell a story. Brown & Williamson's first hint that it was in for trouble at this deposition came when Williams requested that a blackboard be available.

Williams showed up wearing a Bugs Bunny tie, to which he had affixed, by means of a tie tack, a fresh clove of garlic — a gesture to let B&W lawyer Gordon Smith know what he thought of him. He also brought a bag of Gummi Bears, a tribute to testimony offered by James Morgan, president of Philip Morris USA, only days earlier in a Florida tobacco suit, that cigarettes were no more addictive than that chewy candy. Williams's deposition began with Dick Scruggs's lawyer James Carroll asking him if he recognized any documents summarized on a list prepared by Brown & Williamson.

"Just a brief statement that would include a landscape of the documents in a whole," Williams said.

> Before I get to the point of — I'm convinced, by just looking at a couple of the privilege log document analyses by Brown & Williamson, that there is a — has been a continuing fraud from at least 1954, continuing on until today. And with that in mind, I could certainly point this out. I would like to use the board up here, if it's available to me.

Williams was off and running. In his rambling and incoherent style, he set out to chronicle what he saw as a forty-year history of conspiracy and wrongdoing by the tobacco industry. With barely a question from counsel, Williams rattled on, filling nearly forty pages of transcript before Gordon Smith decided he had to say something.

"I have been quiet for the last hour and a half," Smith said.

This morning has been spent entirely with the witness stalking about the room giving uncontrolled and inappropriate statements that are really not in the nature of testimony. He's dealt with information he didn't have while he was at B&W. He's dealt with documents not stolen from and not at issue in this case, documents that relate to other entities that have nothing to do with B&W. He's gone so far as to give opinions on such matters as the False Claims Act and extensive quoting from congressional testimony. As of 11:30, he was still talking about 1954 matters.

Was this the way the deposition would proceed after lunch? Smith asked Carroll.

The questioning after lunch was far more guided, with Carroll striving to keep Williams focused on particular documents and the wrongdoing they suggested. For example, Carroll took an exhibit titled "A Tentative Hypothesis of Nicotine Addiction" and asked, "Is this one of the documents that you looked at that you testified about earlier this morning that convinced you that Brown & Williamson knew that nicotine was addictive while they were saying it wasn't?"

"Yes," said Williams.

"Is that one of the reasons you took it?" Carroll prompted.

"Yes, sir," said Williams.

Once Carroll finished his questioning, the fun was over for Williams. But Smith was not done with his questions, and when the deposition resumed a month later, on May 15, he started going over ground that he and Williams had been over many times before.

Williams's limited patience steadily eroded, and when Smith began asking about the flight from Florida to Mississippi after Dick Scruggs picked up the documents, Williams hit his boiling point.

Why, Smith wondered, did the plane's flight logs indicate that three passengers flew from Destin, Florida — where Scruggs and his wife had gotten out — to Pascagoula? Who else was on the plane besides Williams and his friend Nina Selz?

"Rod Serling was there, I remember, on the wing," snapped Williams, who had genuinely forgotten that paralegal Tammy Cauley had boarded in Destin.

Smith wouldn't relent. Was the flight log wrong? he wanted to know.

"Now, Gordon, you're asking stupid questions," Williams said, and walked out of the room.

"Let me tell you, if I can get a couple of straight answers, I'm pretty close to through, guys," Smith said to Carroll and to Williams's lawyer, Tom Royals.

"Let's see if we can help you do that and be through with it," offered Royals, who got his client back into the room.

But Williams wasn't in the mood to answer any more questions, and when Smith tried, he got a nonverbal response.

"Put this on the record," Smith said, leaping up from the table. "Let the record reflect that Mr. Williams intentionally threw a Coke onto my papers."

"Let's go," said Royals. The deposition was over.

The national settlement discussions had begun in secrecy, but there were those who had an inkling that something out of the ordinary was going on. Sitting at the counter at Scranton's restaurant in Pascagoula on April 14, 1997, Hugh Moore recounted a conversation he'd had the previous day with his son Mike, who was headed out of town.

"Where are you going?" Hugh had asked.

"I'm going north," Mike replied.

"Why are you going north when your case is south?"

"Well, Papa, sometimes you gotta go north to get south."

A few days later, Mike Moore could be less cryptic about his travel plans: On April 16 the *Wall Street Journal* broke the news of the settlement discussions, calling them "an extraordinary turning point in the four-decade-long controversy over cigarettes' toll on the nation's health."

These talks would continue at a furious pace for the next two months, with Moore and Scruggs leading the negotiations on behalf of what became the forty other states suing the industry. At various times, press reports pronounced the talks, which took place in Chicago, Dallas, and New York, before settling down in Washington, D.C., imperiled, snagged, stalled, and near collapse. They were. But through all the crises, progress was being made, as negotiators kept a nervous eye on Mississippi's looming July 7 trial date.

A phalanx of lawyers represented the tobacco companies at the talks. Strangely, though, Brown & Williamson chose to send no representative, deputizing attorneys for Philip Morris and RJR to do its bidding. But B&W monitored the negotiations closely, and when it objected to terms being discussed, it communicated its objections through the other companies' lawyers. This was "extremely awkward," says one of these lawyers, who notes that B&W "frequently took a harder line" than the other companies on some crucial issues, leaving them to do a lot of "patient explaining" of B&W's positions. As to the notion that B&W's bad-cop stance may have helped the industry hold its ground, he notes, "That kind of thing works better if you have somebody in the room to be the bad cop. When the good cop has to be the bad cop, it's more frustrating than effective."

On June 20, the negotiators reached an accord. The terms of the deal were astonishing in and of themselves; they were all the more so given the history of the industry that was agreeing to them. The most eye-popping element of the pact was the money: The cigarette makers agreed to pay $368.5 billion over twenty-five years to compensate states and individuals for smoking-related health costs. The tobacco companies also agreed to submit to a series of measures that would fundamentally alter the business, legal, and regulatory environment in which they operated. Most notable, they agreed that, with certain restrictions, the FDA would have the right to regulate nicotine as a drug. The deal also banned outdoor advertising of tobacco products and tobacco sponsorship of sporting events; barred the use of brand logos on T-shirts and promotional items; prohibited use of human and cartoon images in advertising, meaning that the days of the Marlboro Man and Joe Camel would be over. If certain goals on reducing youth smoking were not met, the cigarette makers could face fines of up to $2 billion a year.

By agreeing to these terms, the tobacco companies stood to settle forty of the state suits they faced (Minnesota refused to sign on), as well as a host of class-action suits brought by the Castano lawyers. The companies also would gain a ban on future class actions, the prohibition of punitive damages for past misconduct in new suits, and a $5 billion annual cap on damage awards against the industry. These liability protections fell short of the total immunity cigarette makers had originally sought in the negotiations, but provided them significant cover. By barring future class actions, the pact removed the most potent litigation threat. Facing only individual suits — without the possibility of punitive damages — the industry and its investors could consider major lawsuits a thing of the past.

As negotiators prepared to announce the terms of their historic accord on the afternoon of June 20, a last-minute hitch developed. Brown & Williamson refused to drop its lawsuit against Jeffrey Wigand, and when Mike Moore and his fellow attorneys general heard that, they threatened to walk away from the whole agreement. The tobacco lawyers scrambled up to the hotel room of Murray Bring, Philip Morris's general counsel, and patched together an extraordinary conference call. The attorneys joined the CEOs of Philip Morris, RJR, and Loews (parent of Lorillard), and got Martin Broughton, the recalcitrant chairman of BAT, B&W's parent, on the phone in Europe. It took them about fifteen minutes to persuade Broughton to give up his pursuit of Wigand in the interests of saving the deal.

At 3:30 in the afternoon, Mike Moore walked into the packed ballroom of the ANA Hotel in Washington, D.C., stepped to the microphone, and announced "the most historic public health agreement in history."

Given all the hoopla surrounding the national settlement, it was easy to forget that the deal on its own accomplished nothing. A number of its major provisions — specifically FDA regulation of nicotine and limitations on legal liability for cigarette makers — required congressional action, and until such time as Congress passed the necessary legislation and the president signed it, none of the terms of the agreement would take effect.

Industry representatives and their opposites at the bargaining table pledged to work together to get the provisions of the June 20 agreement enacted into law. But until they did, the cigarette makers did not have to cough up a penny, the Marlboro Man could continue to ride, and litigation, including the state suits, remained unresolved.

On at least one occasion during the national settlement discussions, Mississippi Medicaid team attorneys approached tobacco industry attorneys about the idea of settling the Mississippi Medicaid case. The tobacco companies rejected the idea, suggesting that the matter be dealt with after a national accord was reached. But the tables were turned, and it was the cigarette makers who found themselves displeased after June 20. They assumed that Moore would be willing to suspend his suit while Congress considered the proposed settlement. Moore and Scruggs, though, refused to do so.

From the day Mississippi had filed its suit in May 1994, it had been first in line among the states suing the industry. That position had put Mississippi's legal team in the driver's seat in the negotiations, and it assured that if they did go to trial and win, there would be solvent defendants from which to collect a judgment. They were not about to give up that status now. Even if Florida and Texas, the next states with trial dates, could also be persuaded to delay their suits, Minnesota was not a party to the national agreement, and had made it clear that it planned to go to trial on schedule in January 1998. Settle or go to trial in Pascagoula on July 7, Moore told the industry.

When tobacco executives learned of this ultimatum, one industry lawyer recalls, they weren't happy. The cigarette makers offered Mississippi $50 million to postpone the trial, but even that didn't budge Moore.

Once again, negotiating teams converged on Washington, this time to try to settle Mississippi's claims. And, as before, while the generals talked peace, the soldiers on the front lines prepared ever more frantically for war. Scruggs associate Charles Mikhail recalls that lawyers and paralegals in Scruggs's and Ron Motley's offices worked virtually around the clock in the final days of June, marking exhibits, preparing witness testimony, and drafting opening arguments, activity that was mirrored with equal intensity on the defense side.

As with every trial, there were last-minute motions to argue. Brown &

Williamson, for example, asked Judge Myers to exclude the Merrell Williams documents from trial. The plaintiffs' team not only opposed that motion, they filed their own "to preclude defendants from characterizing the Brown & Williamson documents as 'stolen.' " B&W "would be more honest were it to label the documents 'hidden' or 'withheld,' " they suggested in a court filing. B&W fired back, quoting Williams himself in various news stories saying "I was a thief and I knew I was a thief" and "You can call me Robin Hood, or you can call me a thief." Judge Myers denied the motion to exclude the documents from trial, but never ruled on whether they could be called "stolen."

There were other document skirmishes as well. Having encountered instances in discovery in which papers requested from defendants were described as lost or destroyed, the plaintiffs filed a motion requesting "that the jury be directed that the missing documents should be assumed to have contained information unfavorable to the defendants, and that their destruction is attributable to the nature of their contents."

"There is no jury in this case," the defendants pointed out in their response. "Why then was this motion filed?" they continued. "The answer is all too clear: to bring to the forefront the charges of document destruction that plaintiff hopes will generate substantial adverse press for defendants. Because there is no jury, this motion is improper and frivolous." (Judge Myers never ruled on this motion.)

On July 3, 1997 — four days before the scheduled start of the trial — Mike Moore, Dick Scruggs, Don Barrett, and the entire Medicaid team assembled in Jackson. They were not there, however, to map out their final strategy.

As he had done thirteen days earlier in Washington, Mike Moore stepped up to a bank of microphones, this time in the rotunda of the Mississippi state capitol, and made an announcement: "A little over three and a half years ago, now, way down south in Mississippi, not many people gave us much of a chance for this little ol' lawsuit. Matter of fact, some people here in this state said it probably wasn't worth a nickel.

"Well," he continued, "we have a settlement today that's worth 3.6 billion dollars." (The actual number was $3.366 billion.) With the lawyers behind him breaking into applause and grins, Moore noted that the first installment on that amount, $170 million, would be paid to the state on July 15.

Mississippi's settlement payment was based on a generous calculation of what the state would receive under the national accord. Scruggs and Moore also obtained a "most favored nation" clause, a term borrowed from diplomacy, guaranteeing that if the tobacco companies reached settlements with other states on more favorable terms, Mississippi would gain the benefit of those terms. That came into play a month later, when the cigarette makers settled Florida's Medicaid suit. In addition to paying Florida $11.3 billion (again, based on the state's share of the national settlement), the companies agreed to pull down their billboards, as well as their ads on mass transit and in stadiums. The billboards and ads then came down in Mississippi as well. Additional benefits flowed to Mississippi when Texas and Minnesota settled their Medicaid suits.

Mississippi, as the tobacco companies had been prepared to show at trial, was ranked last or near last on an embarrassing array of scales. But it had been first to file a Medicaid recovery suit, and Moore and Scruggs wanted the settlement to acknowledge — and reward — that pioneering role. So the companies agreed to create what the negotiators called a "lead dog fund," which promised to pay Mississippi up to an additional $70 million over and above the $3.366 billion already agreed to. (Florida and Texas also qualified for payments under the fund.)

Given the parameters set in the national accord, money was not a hotly debated issue in the Mississippi settlement discussions. The most-favored-nation and lead-dog clauses were more troublesome, but even in these areas the cigarette makers proved relatively accommodating. Except, that is, for Brown & Williamson, which continued not to have its own representative at the bargaining table, but readily communicated its objections to provisions it didn't like. "Brown & Williamson was the toughest nut throughout, in almost every phase of the negotiations, both national and state," says Scruggs. "They were just as contentious and cantankerous as they could be."

In a replay of what had happened in the national discussions, a final agreement on the Mississippi deal hit a snag when Brown & Williamson refused to drop its lawsuits against Scruggs and Merrell Williams, saying it would do so only when a national agreement was final. Once again, Moore threatened to walk out, and once again lawyers for Philip Morris and RJR scrambled to get B&W to back down in the interests of a larger goal. Finally, the company relented.

"I think that fundamentally Brown & Williamson didn't get it," Scruggs said nearly a year after the settlement, "and I still don't think they get it."

Epilogue

As Mike Moore stood triumphantly at his news conference on July 3, 1997, his multibillion-dollar settlement
for the State of Mississippi in hand, he addressed the
task that remained undone:

> My message to the president of the United States, and
> my message to members of the Congress — the sena-
> tors and representatives — is this: The clock starts
> ticking one more time. And it's a very, very important
> clock. Because every single day in this country, three
> thousand of these kids start smoking. . . . How much
> longer do we need to wait until we do something
> about this problem? The attorneys general of this
> country have done their job; the public health com-
> munity of this country have done their job; the trial
> lawyers of this country, in a very courageous manner,
> have done their job. Now it's up to the president of
> the United States and Congress to do their job.

He urged them to act quickly.

That did not happen. Disclosure of tobacco industry practices by Merrell Williams, Jeffrey Wigand, and

others had created deep distrust of the industry on Capitol Hill. There was little willingness in Washington to embrace a plan that not only extracted significant payments and concessions from cigarette makers but also seemed to offer them significant protections.

Throughout the second half of 1997 and into early 1998, Moore and Scruggs joined representatives of the industry in encouraging Congress to adhere as closely as possible to the terms of the June 20 deal, which they felt embodied about all the give-and-take both sides could bring to the issue. For a time, the settlement document did serve as a blueprint for further debate, but by April 1998 it had been shoved aside.

Like sharks smelling blood in the water, politicians came to see tobacco legislation as a tax vehicle through which cigarette makers could be made to fund all manner of social programs, from child care to education. The total cost to the industry of a bill that moved out of a Senate committee in June 1998 was $516 billion — up from the $368.5 billion in the June 20 proposal — and it offered cigarette makers no protection from further litigation. That was too much for RJR's CEO, Steve Goldstone. Two years earlier, he had been instrumental in getting the industry to the bargaining table. But as Congress toughened the terms of the deal, he declared industry cooperation at an end, and the cigarette makers mounted an all-out campaign to kill the pending legislation. On June 17, 1998, efforts to pass comprehensive tobacco legislation died on the Senate floor.

Given that outcome, Moore's decision to settle his Medicaid suit against the industry looked smart, at least for Mississippi. But that settlement did not achieve the marketing and advertising restrictions or the level of price increases that many hoped would reduce youth smoking. The absence of those and other public health provisions, Moore said, left a "little hollow space in my belly," and he continued to hope and work for a more comprehensive plan.

Moore's long absences from the state as he negotiated, and then tried to shepherd through, a national tobacco settlement did not seem to hurt his popularity at home. And just as his prosecution of Eddie Khayat in Jackson County had made him a political force statewide, his pursuit of the tobacco industry in Mississippi catapulted him onto the national political scene. He was touted as a possible U.S. attorney general, drug czar, or senator. But for the near future, Moore will pursue his ambitions on a Mississippi stage. After contemplating running for governor, he announced he would run for a fourth term as state attorney general in 1999.

When, at his news conference, Moore introduced the lawyers who had worked with him on the Medicaid case, he turned first to Don Barrett. Barrett, he said, was "the only lawyer in this country who's tried three cases against the tobacco industry. He lost all three of them . . . But today," he said, giving the grinning Barrett a high five, "you won a case."

An hour or so to the north, in Holmes County, things looked pretty much the same as when Don Barrett took on Nathan Horton's tobacco claim in 1986. In fact, the area probably looked much as it had decades ago, when Horton and Barrett were growing up, leading lives that seemed unlikely ever to converge. The county was still about as poor as it could be: A report released in 1998 showed 62.2 percent of children there living in poverty, third-highest of all counties in the nation. It remained segregated as well: The private schools founded by whites in response to court-ordered integration were still 100 percent white, while the public schools in the county were nearly 100 percent black.

The Barrett presence in the county, though, has grown ever more dynastic. In 1997 the family law offices expanded along the north side of Lexington's town square, taking over and refurbishing an adjacent three-story building that once housed a hardware and furniture store. Pat Barrett Sr. died at the end of 1998, but Don Barrett and his brother Pat continue to practice together. And all three of Don Barrett's children have joined the bar. Two joined the family practice in Lexington, while the other took a job in New York City, at the law firm run by Marc Kasowitz, the lawyer with whom Don Barrett negotiated the Liggett settlement.

For twelve years, Barrett had fought the tobacco makers without earning a penny for his efforts. In 1998, that would change dramatically. Under the terms of the settlement of Mississippi's Medicaid suit, the tobacco industry agreed to pay attorneys' fees in an amount to be set by a panel of arbitrators. In mid-1998, the industry made a down payment of $100 million. That itself was a large sum, but it would be dwarfed a few months later when the panel awarded Mississippi's Medicaid team $1.43 billion to be paid out over twenty-five years. Under the terms agreed to by the team to divide up the cash, Barrett's share of that, originally 10 percent, ended up a mere $47 million because of his decision to divide his portion with Fred Clark and Victor McTeer. As cocounsel to a number of other states, Barrett stands to earn additional amounts from those cases, too.

For Barrett, though, litigating against the tobacco industry has always been about more than money. As he told Merrell Williams in the spring of 1994, the "one last thing" he wanted to do was beat the cigarette makers. Three years later, he had, and he could barely believe it. "It was like a dream world," he said. "It's hard for the reality of it to sink in . . . that we actually defeated them, that we actually did."

In early 1998 Dick Scruggs traded in his sixty-one-foot Hatteras motor yacht for a ninety-one-foot Berger, whose master stateroom sports two marble-lined bathrooms. He also bought a bigger plane. He made these purchases before receiving any fees for the tobacco litigation, although in 1997 cigarette makers did reimburse members of the Mississippi Medicaid team $12.5 million for their out-of-pocket expenses in pursuing the case. Included in that figure was a $227,000 item Scruggs had listed as an expense. That was the amount he paid Tom Royals for representing Merrell Williams in the suit brought by Brown & Williamson in Biloxi. Scruggs submitted the amount he paid his own lawyer in that litigation, too.

Scruggs's firm had originally been entitled to about 24 percent of the fees in the Mississippi Medicaid case, but as the litigation progressed, Scruggs gave away a portion of that to lawyers who helped fund the plaintiffs' efforts. Still, his final take of about 15 percent would yield his firm roughly $215 million over twenty-five years. And that was just Mississippi. Although a division of the spoils had not been finalized, in January 1999 Scruggs said his firm might be entitled to about 15 percent of the $3.43 billion in fees awarded in Florida — or about $514 million —

and about 5 percent of the $3.3 billion awarded in Texas — $165 million. That brings the amount to $894 million. Cocounsel in twenty-nine other states as well, the firm is likely to see many millions more flowing into its coffers.

In addition to upgrading his planes and boats, Scruggs bought himself a $200,000 Bentley. When he drives around Pascagoula, he told the *Wall Street Journal,* people look at the "B" on the hood and ask, "What kind of Buick is that?" Scruggs also pledged $25 million over twenty-five years to the University of Mississippi, alma mater of eight of the attorneys on Mississippi's Medicaid team.

Even after the Mississippi suit ended, the other battles in Scruggs's life raged on. As he and Moore shuttled to Washington to try to hold the national settlement agreement — or some form of it — together, lawyers from his firm continued to prepare for trials against the tobacco industry across the country throughout most of 1998.

The suit against Scruggs by his former colleagues seeking millions in asbestos fees continued, and a new suit by one of his former partners alleging unfair financial treatment was filed in the spring of 1998. "As my profile has been increased, I've become a sort of giant piñata for everybody to swing at these days," he said calmly, like a pilot who has hit mild turbulence.

On the beach, meanwhile, Scruggs's feud with his neighbors over the Longfellow House intensified. In September 1997, Joe Colingo and others went before Pascagoula City Council and won an order limiting the number of weekend events that could be held on the grounds of the house. The next month, Scruggs took the matter to court. He also replaced an iron fence along the back of the property with a nine-foot-tall cement wall that blocks the beach view for his backyard neighbor — Joe Colingo's daughter.

When Mike Moore announced the proposed national settlement, he explained that the whole deal had almost collapsed when Brown & Williamson refused to drop its litigation against Jeffrey Wigand. But the attorneys general, Moore said, wanted "to make sure that we didn't leave any prisoners or hostages on the beach," so they held firm and forced B&W to relent.

Hearing the news at his home in Mississippi, Merrell Williams wondered if perhaps one prisoner *had* been left on the beach. *His* name, *his* battle with Brown & Williamson, went unmentioned. Only two weeks later did Scruggs tell him that he had negotiated a "walk-away" — that B&W would drop its litigation against himself and Williams and the two of them would forgo any claims against the tobacco maker. When Williams expressed reluctance at giving up the personal-injury counterclaim he had filed against B&W, Scruggs told him that he hoped a national tobacco settlement would result in the creation of a fund out of which Williams and other whistle-blowers and antitobacco activists could receive significant payments.

There were other welcome developments. Williams was delighted to learn, for example, that Brown & Williamson claimed its costs in pursuing him, as well as others trying to make use of its documents, totaled $5.8 million. The termination of the litigation with B&W, moreover, meant not only an end to the constant anxiety created by repeated depositions and threats of prosecution, but also an end to the injunction Judge Wine had entered in Kentucky, meaning that for the first time in four years, he could speak publicly about his experiences without fear.

In December 1997, he had an opportunity to do that when he was given an award in Washington, D.C., by a trust established to honor public service. Introduced to the audience as a "hero" and "the first tobacco whistle-blower," he stood on a stage at the Women's National Democratic Club and stiffly accepted a plaque. He then gave a meandering but, in its way, eloquent acceptance speech, mentioning Morton Mintz (the former *Washington Post* reporter, with whom he had explored writing a book), Freon (which he feared was in cigarettes, and would turn into toxic gas when burned), and the documents, which he noted could have been found at various times in his boat, at his friend Nina's, or in his mother's cedar chest.

By 1998, Williams had settled into a life of relative calm in Ocean Springs, though he was still uncertain about what lay ahead. He said he was aware that he would have to pay Scruggs back for all the assistance he had provided, or else face real trouble with the Internal Revenue Service. "My expectation is that somewhere along the line I am going to pay for it . . . or you shall see me trying to play tennis with bad knees in a federal penitentiary," he said.

But he gave no indication of where that money would come from. To Williams's disappointment, it was Wigand's story, not his, that was being made into a movie. While he hoped a national tobacco settlement might include money for him, he was also exploring other options. In the spring of 1998, he sold the sailboat Scruggs had paid for, bought some fishing rods at area pawnshops, and began scouting out powerboats. "I'm going to be a fisherman," he announced, not sounding as though he had even convinced himself.

For the most part, though, Williams appeared untroubled about the future, and seemed to be finding contentment in the prosaic routine of the everyday. He planted banana trees in front of his house, which he tended regularly. He shopped for old furniture at thrift shops, restoring it and selling it back, and he found himself waking up at exactly six o'clock every morning. "I'm like an old lady, I really am," he said, marveling at his existence. "I'm a hausfrau."

In March 1998, Williams was informed that he, Vice President Al Gore, and others had won an award for their tobacco activism from an organization called the Gleitzman Foundation. The award included a payment of $10,000, and there was talk of arranging a ceremony at the White House. That didn't happen, but the honor was bestowed at the elegant Four Seasons hotel in Washington.

"I'm a successful failure now," Williams said.

One of Williams's abiding character traits has been his belief that wealth would soon befall him. He frequently acted as though a "big score" was just around the corner, his second wife Mollie had said. Time and again, reality proved otherwise. Even at the bleakest moments of his battle with Brown & Williamson, he talked of money coming his way from a movie deal, from his personal injury claims against B&W, from a book he would write — from *something*. And in this case, he was right.

Williams had been unhappy about giving up his personal injury claim against B&W, which had first been raised by Fox DeMoisey in his July 1993 letter to Wyatt, Tarrant & Combs announcing that his unnamed client was returning a box of the cigarette maker's documents. And he regarded the possibility of a whistle-blower fund created by a national settlement as too speculative. So in August 1997, Scruggs had agreed in writing to pay Williams $1.8 million, minus any amounts Williams owed him, if payments from a fund didn't materialize. Only then did Williams drop his claims against B&W, which in turn ended its pursuit of both Williams and Scruggs.

In early 1999, Scruggs made good on his word. After deducting amounts for the house he had purchased for Williams, along with certain other items, he paid Williams approximately $1.5 million.

Under the most-favored-nation clause of Mississippi's settlement with the tobacco industry, the industry agreed to adjust the terms of Mississippi's deal if other states received better ones. In May 1998, the industry agreed to settle Minnesota's case for $6.1 billion, just as jurors were about to hear closing arguments after fifteen weeks of trial.

This amount — far more than Minnesota would have received under the proposed national settlement — triggered the deal-sweetening requirement. In July 1998 the cigarette makers agreed to pay the state of Mississippi an additional $550 million. That amount alone was more than half what the state had originally sought when it filed its Medicaid reimbursement suit, and helped bring Mississippi's total recovery to $4.1 billion.

But the tobacco industry also gained ground. It won rulings reducing the scope of other state Medicaid suits, and had Indiana's suit thrown out entirely. In Florida, Brown & Williamson persuaded an appeals court to reverse the $750,000 verdict against the company in the Grady Carter case, in part due to a finding that certain B&W documents — taken by Merrell Williams — had been improperly admitted at trial. A second verdict against B&W was thrown out as well. And, in a huge blow to anti-smoking forces, a federal appeals court overturned a trial-court ruling that had found the Food and Drug Administration had some power to regulate cigarettes. Various Justice Department investigations of the industry, including one into perjury allegations against senior executives, seemed to be winding down, without charges being filed.

There would, however, be no shortage of work for tobacco defense lawyers, especially following the collapse of the national settlement plan. In signing on to represent Philip Morris, Steve Susman got the cigarette giant to pay him a fixed, multimillion-dollar fee for a set number of years, no matter how much, or how little, he worked. When the national and Mississippi settlements were announced in mid-1997, it looked like Susman might be walking away with a windfall, but after the national deal disintegrated and plaintiffs and defendants went back to a war footing, Susman was redeployed to help defend Philip Morris in Oklahoma. "Unfortunately," he joked, "I'm not going to be able to retire to the South Pacific and clip coupons on my no-cut contract."

In November 1998 a plan was announced to settle the remaining thirty-eight state lawsuits against the tobacco industry for $206 billion. But the very fact of the cigarette makers ponying up huge amounts to settle cases, Susman predicted, would inspire a barrage of new litigation. And he was right. All over the country, plaintiffs' lawyers, sensing the industry was vulnerable, filed claims against it.

One Mississippi suit seemed to reprise many elements of tobacco litigation in that state. A Pascagoula-based plaintiffs' lawyer filed suit in rural Jefferson County, on the Louisiana border, on behalf of a black smoker who died of heart disease. The suit was quickly transformed, though, when more than a dozen other plaintiffs joined it. In addition to naming the cigarette companies as defendants, the plaintiffs' lawyers sued asbestos makers, too, claiming that a combination of smoking and asbestos exposure had made the claimants ill. Among the local counsel for the tobacco companies were Jim Upshaw and Joe Colingo.

Meanwhile, Dick Scruggs continued to operate on the national stage as well. As 1998 drew to an end, he was making periodic trips to Washington, trying to convince federal officials to file suit against the tobacco makers on behalf of Medicare, the health care program for the elderly.

If he could make that happen, it would make the state Medicaid litigation look like peanuts.

In purely monetary terms, the state Medicaid cases that began with Mississippi's suit in 1994 were a spectacular success. All told, the tobacco industry agreed to pay the states close to $250 billion over twenty-five years.

But from a broader standpoint of public policy, the states' efforts were far less successful. As esoteric as the Medicaid claims had been, collectively they put enough pressure on the industry so that the debate over smoking and health moved to where it should have been: the legislature. Cigarettes are a legal product. States have allowed and profited from their sale. True, they could be addictive; true, the industry had been deceptive. But using individual court cases to resolve such a complex issue — a legal product that causes grievous harm to millions of people's health when used as intended — makes no sense.

When Congress failed to enact comprehensive legislation on smoking and health in the wake of the proposed tobacco settlement, a chance was lost to achieve meaningful regulation of the cigarette industry and subject it to stringent marketing restrictions. Many took offense that the industry sought protection from litigation in return. But quid pro quos are the stuff of politics. And was this really so much to give up? Are smokers really so deserving of compensation? Juries haven't thought so. Smokers — and potential future smokers — would have been far better off with a policy that was part compromise than with no policy at all.

There is also value to closure. After more than forty years, the tobacco industry and the plaintiffs' bar seem locked in a perpetual struggle, with ever increasing costs. To what end? At best, a stray plaintiff and his lawyer might get lucky in the lawsuit lottery. Even if individual tobacco plaintiffs start to turn the tide, and tobacco makers suffer the fate of the asbestos companies, that seems like a path to disaster — for both sides. With the collapse of national legislation, though, the chance for closure has been lost.

So the cigarette litigation goes on.

A Note on Sources

The vast majority of this book derives from interviews and from court filings and transcripts of trials, depositions, and other proceedings. I enjoyed extensive cooperation from lawyers for both plaintiffs and tobacco companies. But there was one exception: Brown & Williamson declined to comment on any matter for this book. Consistent with its position that the documents taken by Merrell Williams were privileged and confidential, B&W refused to discuss the substance of the documents. The company also declined my requests to interview Merrell Williams's coworkers and Gordon Smith, the principal attorney retained by B&W to pursue Williams in court. In a previously issued statement, the company said: "Documents stolen by a person who is 'out to get the company' should not be portrayed as presenting the whole story. Lifting single phrases or sentences from 30-year-old documents and using that information to distort and misrepresent B&W's position on a number of issues is clearly what is occurring."

Beyond interviews and court records, certain other materials that were of particular help to me are noted below.

PART 1

Indispensable for anyone undertaking a serious exploration of tobacco is Richard Kluger's encyclopedic work *Ashes to Ashes: America's Hundred-Year Cigarette War, the Public Health, and the Unabashed Triumph of Philip Morris* (New York: Alfred A. Knopf, 1996). I turned to Kluger's 807-page book not only for general background on the industry, but also for specifics about the rise of American Tobacco and the history of Pall Mall cigarettes, Nathan Horton's brand. American Tobacco commissioned its own corporate history, which was published in 1954 and titled *"Sold American!"*

For historical information about Holmes County, I turned to an unpublished manuscript authored by J. Daniel Edwards, who teaches at Holmes County Community College. A work in progress, the copy Dan gave me started in the Pleistocene Age and ended just before the Civil War.

PART 2

In recounting Merrell Williams's story I focused far more on his personal plight than on the substance of the documents he took from Brown & Williamson. I nonetheless found *The Cigarette Papers* (Berkeley: University of California Press, 1996) an invaluable resource. Compiled by Stanton A. Glantz of the University of California, San Francisco, and a team of researchers, the book organizes, annotates, and cross-references the B&W documents and offers detailed discussion of their meaning. It was Glantz and his group who put the documents on the Internet at www.library.ucsf.edu/tobacco.

PART 3

I relied on a number of books to learn the history of Pascagoula and its surrounding region. These include *Mississippi Gulf Coast* (Gulfport, Miss.: Gulfport Printing Co., 1939), a publication sponsored by the Federal Writers' Project of the Works Progress Administration; *Pascagoula*, by Jay Higgenbotham (Mobile: Gill Press,1967); and *The Mississippi Gulf Coast* (Northridge, Calif.: Windsor Publications, Inc., 1985), an illustrated history by Charles L. Sullivan.

Paul Brodeur's book *Outrageous Misconduct: The Asbestos Industry on Trial* (New York: Pantheon Books, 1985) offers a compelling chronicle of asbestos litigation, tracing it from its beginnings with a few scattered cases through its transformation into a mass tort.

Jeffrey Wigand's story was first told in detail in the May 1996 issue of *Vanity Fair*, in an article titled "The Man Who Knew Too Much" by Marie Brenner. Two other articles about Wigand that were particularly helpful were "Brown & Williamson Has 500-Page Dossier Attacking Chief Critic," by Suein L. Hwang and Milo Geyelin in the *Wall Street Journal*, February 1, 1996; and "Whistle-Blower's Past Conduct May Give B&W Ammo in a Trial," by R. G. Dunlop in the *Louisville Courier-Journal*, March 28, 1996.

Acknowledgments

Writing a book, I've discovered over the last few years, is no easy task. Yet I'm quite certain that being married to someone who is writing a book may be as difficult, if not more so. I am thus grateful to my wife, Sharon, for her unflagging patience, support, advice, and, perhaps above all, faith. How many other spouses, I wonder, would pick up and move to Mississippi in July? Also along for the ride: my daughters, Rachel and Sophia. They supplied a steady stream of beautiful artwork for my office.

Many of the people mentioned in this book made themselves available for interviews, often many times over, and I tremendously appreciate their generosity with their time. Many more who are not mentioned also granted interviews that provided essential background for the story.

Three law firms — Scruggs, Millette, Bozeman & Dent; the Barrett Law Offices; and Chadbourne & Parke — kindly made their offices available to me for review of public-record files. All of the lawyers and staff at the Scruggs firm were friendly and helpful, but attorney Charles Mikhail deserves special mention. From the time I embarked on this project, he made himself available on a regular basis to bring me up to date on developments in the Mississippi Medicaid case and to direct me to documents in the voluminous case file. As was the situation with many attorneys on both sides of the tobacco wars who labored behind the scenes, his contributions to the litigation are not reflected in this book. A special thanks also to Dick Scruggs's secretary, Charlene Bosarge, who fielded many of my calls and kept me in touch with her ever-roving boss.

I was accorded hospitality in three very different parts of Mississippi: in Pascagoula, from Bruce and Linda Grimes and Robert A. Pritchard; in Holmes County, from Bootsie and Pam Hooker; and in Oxford, from Adrian Aumen.

Scranton's restaurant in Pascagoula became a kind of oasis for me, and at times I felt like a lunchtime regular at the bar, chowing on chicken-fried steak and sipping bottomless glasses of iced tea. Richard Chenoweth, one of the proprietors, was immensely friendly and helpful. And it was at Scranton's that I met Danny Smith, who offered valuable briefings on local politics. Mike Moore's father was also a frequent and amiable lunch companion, a pack of cigarettes always within reach.

Even in an age of electronic research, there are times when there is no substitute for a good librarian. Else Martin, at the Pascagoula Public Library, helped me track down all kinds of material. Lillian Arcuri, of Chadbourne & Parke, was similarly helpful. Dan Goodgame kindly lent me his personal "library" of books about his hometown of Pascagoula and the surrounding Gulf Coast.

Mary Aronson, of Aronson Washington Research in Washington, D.C., was particularly helpful offering contacts in, and insight into, the world of tobacco litigation.

Steven Brill encouraged me to go forward with this project and helped get it launched. My colleague Stephen Adler offered support and was a valued sounding board. Chip Rossetti, my editor at Little, Brown and Company, greeted the manuscript with much-appreciated enthusiasm and did a good deal to make it more readable. Copyeditor Anne Montague buffed and polished with a thoroughness that still leaves me awestruck.

Robert B. Barnett, of Williams & Connolly, is my attorney, and I was happy to have him at my side.

Index